Ontological Semantics

Language, Speech, and Communication
James Pustejovsky, editor

Ontological Semantics

Sergei Nirenburg and Victor Raskin

The MIT Press
Cambridge, Massachusetts
London, England

MIT Press books may be purchased at special quantity discounts for business or sales promotional use. For information, please e-mail special_sales@mitpress.mit.edu or write to Special Sales Department, The MIT Press, 5 Cambridge Center, Cambridge, MA 02142.

This book was set in Times New Roman on 3B2 by Asco Typesetters, Hong Kong.
Printed and bound in the United States of America.

Library of Congress Cataloging-in-Publication Data

Nirenburg, Sergei.
Ontological semantics / Sergei Nirenburg and Victor Raskin.
    p. cm. — (Language, speech, and communication)
Includes bibliographical references and index.
ISBN 0-262-14086-1 (alk. paper)
1. Semantics—Data processing. 2. Discourse analysis—Data processing. 3. Linguistics—Philosophy. 4. Ontology. 5. Semantics (Philosophy) I. Raskin, Victor, 1944– II. Title. III. Series.
P325.5.D38N57   2004
401′.43′0285—dc22   2004042584

10 9 8 7 6 5 4 3 2 1

Contents

Chapter 2

Prolegomena to the Philosophy of Linguistics
33

Chapter 3

**Ontological Semantics and the Study of
Meaning in Linguistics, Philosophy, and
Computational Linguistics   93**

Chapter 9

Acquisition of Static Knowledge Sources for
Ontological Semantics   309

Chapter 10

Preface

Most, if not all, high-end natural language processing (NLP) applications—from the earliest, machine translation, to the latest, question answering and text summarization—stand to benefit from being able to use text meaning. It might be argued that without this ability one cannot expect real breakthroughs in NLP, to bring it to the level of public expectations and broad utility. At the same time, the bulk of work in the field has not, over the years, pertained to treatment of meaning. The main reason given is the complexity of the task of comprehensive meaning analysis. Several generations of NLP workers opted to work on partial tasks (e.g., computational morphology or syntax), building applications that were feasible within the rather limited bounds of currently attainable NLP quality or looking for ways of bypassing the need to treat meaning. (This partly accounts for the many "knowledge-lean," largely corpus-based endeavors that instead of treating meaning head on rely either on a variety of surface-distance measures between input texts and texts that are known to be meaningful or on complex counts of frequency of occurrence of strings in various contexts.)

This book introduces ontological semantics, a comprehensive approach to the treatment of text meaning by computer. Several decades of work in NLP have clearly demonstrated to us the importance of meaning as the crucial element for future high-end NLP applications. We have also been able to appreciate the role of a systematic, theory-based, non–ad hoc approach to meaning. Through most of the past several decades, computational semanticists constituted a pronounced minority in the NLP community. While other branches of computational linguistics often sought to define sound and comprehensive theories, meaning was often handled patchily and non-systematically, using theories that were too coarse grained and partial. Ontological semantics arose from our attempts to buck that trend by propounding theory-based semantic methods. It is the theory that we found missing early on and that we now present as an attempt to systematize our ideas about semantic description as well as representation and manipulation of meaning by computer programs.

Ontological semantics is an integrated complex of theories, methodologies, descriptions, and implementations. In ontological semantics, a *theory* is viewed as a set of statements determining the format of *descriptions* of the phenomena with which the theory deals. A theory is associated with a *methodology* used to obtain the descriptions. *Implementations* are computer systems that use the descriptions to solve specific problems in text processing. Implementations of ontological semantics are combined with other processing systems to produce applications, such as information extraction or machine translation.

The theory of ontological semantics is built as a society of microtheories covering such diverse ground as specific language phenomena, world-knowledge organization, processing heuristics, and issues relating to knowledge representation and implementation-system architecture. Descriptions in ontological semantics include both actual text-meaning representations and such background-knowledge sources as lexical entries, ontological concepts and instances, as well as procedures for manipulating texts and their meanings. Methodologies in ontological semantics are sets of techniques and instructions for acquiring and manipulating knowledge as well as for running specific applications.

Ontological semantics is not a finished product. It is constantly evolving: new implementations are developed in response to needs for enhanced coverage and utility. Some such needs arise from the internal logic of the field; others are due to the requirements of practical applications. In any case, ontological semantics is driven by the necessity to make the meaning-manipulation tasks, such as text analysis, text generation, and reasoning over text-meaning representations, work. As a result, our approach places no premium on using a single method, engine, or formalism in developing the procedures themselves or acquiring the data that support them. Instead, ontological semantics develops a set of heterogeneous methods suited to a particular task and coordinated at the level of knowledge acquisition and runtime system architecture in implementations.

The methodology of ontological semantics has a hybrid character also because it allows for a variable level of automation in all of its processes—both the runtime procedures and the important knowledge-acquisition tasks. Asymptotically, all the processes of ontological semantics will become fully automated. However, to make ontological semantics applicable before it reaches this ideal, human participation must be grudgingly and judiciously built in. In the various extant implementations, the runtime procedures have always been automated, while knowledge acquisition has involved a controlled and channeled human effort. The levels of automation will continue to increase across the board as the approach evolves.

It is arguable that the human level of performance in processing language is a goal that is unattainable by computer programs, either today or, quite possibly, ever. This realization may lead some to reject this goal and focus instead on what are perceived as necessary components of a future NLP system. Often, the focus is further narrowed to methods, formalisms, and tools and excludes broad descriptions of phenomena or procedures. Ontological semantics takes the opposite view: it considers the development of implementations and comprehensive applications the main challenge of NLP. We fully realize that, at any given time, these implementations fall short on quality and coverage. While improving specific methods is important, ontological semantics is more interested in developing all the necessary processing and knowledge modules and combining them in a comprehensive system for a class of real-life NLP applications, at the current stage of their attainability.

We appreciate the attraction in setting and reaching attainable local goals, such as the exploration of a single language phenomenon or the perfection of a processing method or a formalism. We are concerned that such efforts are not at all certain to facilitate any future comprehensive systems. When a potential component of a system is developed in isolation, its integrability, if at all considered by the developers, is assumed. Experience in integrating component microtheories in ontological semantics has demonstrated that it is a major resource drain. It follows that minimizing this effort through coordinated development of microtheories is desirable. In practice, of course, there is always a trade-off between importing a microtheory, which would require an integration step, and developing it in house.

Methodological versatility in ontological semantics helps to avoid the fallacy of trying to apply a method of choice to too many tasks. Such misplaced optimism about the utility of any method often results in increased complexity of implementation and/or lower-quality output. In other words, one has to avoid being burned by the old adage, "If all you have is a hammer, everything looks like a nail." It is a methodological tenet of ontological semantics that every class of phenomena may require a dedicated method. As a result, the approach always addresses options for treatment instead of promulgating the one "correct" way.

Ontological semantics is content oriented. It puts a premium on acquiring all the knowledge required for the left-hand sides of the many heuristic rules that it uses in processing. Heuristics presuppose abductive reasoning—that is, they are defeasible. The reason for choosing abduction is the realistic expectation that text inputs may at any time violate a recorded constraint in the knowledge base.

This book consists of two parts. In part I, ontological semantics is briefly outlined and then positioned vis-à-vis cognitive science and the AI NLP paradigm (chapter 1), the philosophy of science (chapter 2), linguistic semantics and the philosophy of language (chapter 3), computational lexical semantics (chapter 4), and studies in formal ontology (chapter 5). Part II describes the content of ontological semantics. Chapter 6 defines and discusses text-meaning representation as a process and as a structure. Chapter 7 is devoted to the static knowledge sources in ontological semantics—the ontology, the fact repository, the lexicon, and the onomasticon. Chapter 8 sketches the ontological semantic processes involved in text analysis. Chapter 9 deals with acquisition of static knowledge in ontological semantics. Chapter 10 focuses briefly on some important aspects of NLP that were not addressed in the book. The content of the various chapters is highly interrelated, which results in a large number of cross-references.

We believe that the book will be of interest to a variety of scholars and practitioners in our field and adjacent areas. NLP specialists and computational linguists will find here a variety of proposals for computational treatment of specific language phenomena; for the content and format of knowledge resources and their acquisition; and for integration of microtheories into a single implementation system. For AI specialists and cognitive scientists, ontological semantics can be seen as a realization and a practical argument for knowledge-based processing in general, for example, within the model of an intelligent agent; it also provides a detailed instance of a complex and multifaceted knowledge base augmented with browsing, acquisition, and testing tools. Theoretical linguists (especially semanticists) and philosophers of language will benefit from exposure to a number of suggested solutions for natural language meaning representation and processing. Descriptive linguists may find specifications for convenient tools to enhance the efficiency of their work. Philosophers of science may find the discussion of the philosophy of linguistics a useful case study for their deliberations. Cognitive psychologists and psycholinguists may wish to consider whether our model of language processing may have any validity for humans; additionally, our system may be considered as a substrate for psychological and psycholinguistic experimentation in human language processing. Specialists in human factors may be interested in the particulars of the division of labor between humans and computers that ontological semantics proposes for knowledge acquisition.

In the area of linguistic engineering and NLP applications, this book may provide a variety of workers with ideas about the content and structure of static knowledge sources, about the knowledge requirements of various processors and complete applications, about practical descriptions of particular phenomena, about organizing the knowledge-acquisition effort, and about integrating comprehensive systems. We also hope that this book will help practitioners to realize better that treatment of meaning is a sine qua non for attaining a new level of quality in practical applications and that the rather steep price for its inclusion is well worth paying. In addition, the book will hopefully make it clear that the crucial component of success of large applications is content, not formalism.

Throughout the book, we are giving away a strong belief that this is not only about computational semantics but also about semantic theory. We believe that the requirements we imposed on the former must be met by the latter as well. The burden of comprehensive meaning representation has shifted from field linguistics as the primary responsibility of linguistics to natural language processing. While contemporary linguistic semantics, as currently practiced, can afford cyclical single-method infatuations illustrated by a few carefully selected examples, computational semantics must represent the meaning of input text in its entirety to guarantee the quality of results, even if this leads to hybrid, "messy" methodologies integrating multiple microtheories in complex ways. Two major objections to our belief in the equivalence of ontological semantics and semantic theory that can be raised from the "pure linguistics" side are the justification of the human-made ontology at the root of our approach and the role of applications in the justification of our meaning representations. There are two major reasons these objections are unlikely to be made. First, contemporary linguistic theory is not interested much in justification, taking the formalism du jour for granted. Second, it is interested primarily in maximizing the extent to which that formalism may be made to fit selected linguistic material rather than in comprehensive description.

Acknowledgments

We would like to express our gratitude to our colleagues who, over the years, have contributed to the successive implementations and applications of ontological semantics. Allen B. Tucker worked with us on an early conception of knowledge-based machine translation. James H. Reynolds and Irene B. Nirenburg worked on the POPLAR planning application that allowed us for the first time to model intelligent agents and their world model. James Pustejovsky contributed to an early formulation of the microtheory of aspect. Lori Levin collaborated with us on the issue of syntax-driven and ontology-driven semantics. Ira Monarch and Todd Kaufmann were instrumental in building the first acquisition environment for the ontology and an initial formulation of its top levels. Lynn Carlson helped to research the first guidelines of ontological modeling and contributed to the development of several versions of the ontology itself.

Salvatore Attardo and Donalee H. Attardo helped to analyze and catalog contributions of linguistic semantics to computational applications. Manfred Stede provided programming support for this effort. Ralf Brown helped with a variety of tools and conceptual and procedural support for knowledge acquisition and representation; in particular, he formulated an early version of set notation for ontological semantics. Ingrid Meyer and Boyan Onyshkevych, together with Lynn Carlson, formulated an early statement about lexicon structure and content. Christine Defrise contributed to the specification of the format and content of text-meaning representation—notably, she worked on speaker attitudes that eventually became modalities in ontological semantics. Ted Gibson implemented the morphological and syntactic analyzers as parts of the Dionysus implementation of ontological semantics. Eric Nyberg implemented the underlying knowledge-representation language in which the original ontology was formulated, and also contributed, with John Leavitt, to the development of the text-generator module inside Dionysus.

In the Mikrokosmos implementation of ontological semantics, Kavi Mahesh was responsible for the development of the ontology and shared with Steve Beale the work on the semantic analyzer. Steve also worked on the control structure of the implementation as well as on the generation component. Boyan Onyshkevych developed an algorithm for finding the optimum paths between concepts in the ontology, used as the basis of disambiguation in analysis. Evelyne Viegas, Lori Wilson, and Svetlana Sheremetyeva provided management and training support for the knowledge-acquisition effort in the Mikrokosmos and CAMBIO/CREST implementations. Eugene Ludovik and Valery Sibirtsev worked on the version of the semantic analyzer for the CAMBIO/CREST implementation. Spencer B. Koehler was responsible for the acquisition tools in this implementation as well as for managing the actual acquisition of the fact repository and leading the development of the question-answering application in CREST.

We have profited from many discussions, some of them published, of issues in and around ontological semantics with Yorick Wilks, who also read and commented on parts of the manuscript. James Pustejovsky and Graeme Hirst have made useful comments on some of the ideas in the book. Jim Cowie has imparted to us a great deal of his realistic view of NLP in the course of many formal and casual discussions.

Many people have, over the decades, been a source of inspiration and admiration for both or either of us. We have both learned from Igor Mel'čuk's staunch and fearless refusal to conform to the dominant paradigm, as well as from his encyclopedic knowledge of linguistics and ability to mount a large-scale and relentless effort for describing language material. We have always admired Charles Fillmore for having never abandoned an interest in meaning, never sacrificing content for formalism, and never refusing to meet the complexities of semantic description head on. We are also grateful to Allen B. Tucker, who was a great coauthor and enthusiastic supporter in the early days of our joint work in NLP, even before we knew that what we were doing was ontological semantics.

We greatly appreciated Jim McCawley's iconoclastic presence in linguistics and mourn his premature death. We agreed early on that Paul M. Postal's treatment of semantic material in his "Remind" article was the early benchmark for our own descriptive work. Roger Schank, a major representative of the "scruffy" AI tradition of concentrating on the semantic content (no matter how limited the coverage) rather than the formalism, was an important influence. Over the years, we have greatly enjoyed Yorick Wilks's encyclopedic knowledge of philosophy, AI, and linguistics. We have also appreciated his general erudition, so rare in our technocratic times, his energy, his style of polemics, his ever-present wit, and his friendship.

Victor Raskin is forever grateful for the privilege of having worked with Vladimir A. Zvegintzev and Yehoshua Bar Hillel. Sergei Nirenburg would like to thank Victor Lesser for the early encouragement, for the many lessons in how to think about scientific problems, and for warmth and wisdom. Both authors have enjoyed observing many colleagues chasing one fashionable notion after another and admired their enthusiasms, even when we could not share them.

During the preparation of the manuscript we greatly benefited from precise and incisive comments by Yorick Wilks and James Pustejovsky. Marjorie McShane raised significant issues that led to considerable clarifications in the text; she also went over the text with a fine copyediting comb. We appreciated Stephen Helmreich's and Christian F. Hempelmann's comments on the preliminary draft. Katrina E. Triezenberg detected many errors and suggested revisions in the draft used by Victor Raskin to teach an NLP seminar. Both authors are grateful to their students who were exposed to the manuscript early on and responded to it in ways that have led to its subsequent pedagogical improvement. Any remaining errors are entirely our responsibility.

PART I
About Ontological Semantics

In part I of the book, we provide a brief outline of ontological semantics and then proceed to explore its theoretical underpinnings and contexts by positioning it, often polemically, against the pertinent views in adjacent areas that shed light on the nature of this semantic theory.

Chapter 1 offers a brief statement of ontological semantics and places it within the cognitive model of the intelligent agent. It also relates the theory initially to previous work in linguistic and computational semantics as well as to the principal ideas of cognitive science. This comparison will be reprised briefly in chapter 6, the first chapter of part II, devoted to the more detailed presentation of ontological semantics.

Chapter 2 investigates the status of the theory from the point of view of the philosophy of science and compares it to other theories. A special emphasis is placed on the components of the theory—most importantly, its premises and its explicitness about them. This is a complex and poorly explored topic with respect to linguistics. As a result, this chapter may be difficult to read. It can be largely ignored by a less philosophically and (meta)theoretically inclined reader.

Chapter 3 brings into focus several traditions in primarily compositional linguistic semantics—some of them largely forgotten and ignored by contemporary trends in that field—that have informed ontological semantics positively or negatively. This review prominently includes the much-maligned and even more emulated interpretive semantics of Katz and Fodor. It also rejects the formal semantic approach, which has been dominant in semantic theory for about a decade.

Chapter 4 concentrates on the revival of interest in lexical semantics in the late 1980s and early 1990s. The objections to formal semantics continue in the chapter. It also deals with serious issues ontological semantics has with regard to persistent efforts to avoid semantics by motivating meaning distinctions with syntactic ones. The chapter objects to assigning everything that does not corroborate this model outside the purview of semantics—usually, to pragmatics and discourse—thus bypassing the responsibility for complete semantic description.

Chapter 5 places ontological semantics within the discipline of formal ontology. It also relates the approach to the engineering aspect of ontology. The similarities and differences between ontological semantics and other ontological efforts considerably elucidate the ontological nature of our approach.

In the spirit of the principle of the economy of effort and of the remark above on chapter 2, a well-prepared and/or uninterested reader can skip part I, except perhaps for chapter 1, and go straight to part II. Both of us have used the earlier draft in this fashion in our graduate courses and seminars on NLP, where the emphasis is more on practical skills or specific issues rather than on the broad theoretical framework for ontological semantics. It is true, however, that we were there in class in person to decipher a puzzling cross-reference or two or to provide other forms of assistance.

CHAPTER 1
Introduction to Ontological Semantics

This chapter introduces and briefly outlines ontological semantics. After placing the theory in the context of its predecessors in this general part, the chapter goes into the following sections:

• Section 1.1 places the theory in a model of language-communication situation, focusing on the division of labor between two intelligent agents: the discourse producer and the discourse consumer.
• Section 1.2 contains the initial sketch of ontological semantics. This is perhaps the only section that is essential to read before skipping to part II, though sections 1.5 and 1.6 may also turn out to provide some useful preparation for such a reader.
• Section 1.3 mentions briefly the relations of ontological semantics to the non-semantic components of an NLP system. The only other place in the book where this issue is touched on again is section 8.1.
• Section 1.4 addresses the alternative architectures for an NLP system, such as the stratified model, the flat model, and the constraint-satisfaction model, the latter being largely adoped in ontological semantics.
• Section 1.5 characterizes in more detail the functions (but not the actual processing—see chapter 8 for that) of the dynamic sources of ontological semantics, the analyzer and the generator. Of these two, the former gets the most attention in the book (see also the book's conclusion).
• Section 1.6 discusses the function (but not the substance—see chapter 7 for that) of the static sources in ontological semantics: the ontology, the lexicon(s), and their derivatives.
• Section 1.7 explains the role and integration of microtheories in ontological semantics. The microtheories introduce the polymethodological nature of this enterprise and remove it from the realm of the (single) method-driven theories.
• Section 1.8 traces the development of ontological semantics over the last decade and a half and places the various earlier contributions to it both chronologically and in the context of the pertinent applications. This section is largely of interest only to

readers who have kept themselves informed over the years about the activities of the ontologial semantics community.

Ontological semantics is a theory of meaning in natural language and an approach to natural language processing (NLP) that uses a constructed world model, or ontology, as the central resource for extracting and representing the meaning of natural language texts and for reasoning about knowledge derived from texts. This approach also makes it possible to generate natural language texts based on representations of their meaning. The architecture of an archetypal implementation of ontological semantics comprises, at the most coarse-grain level of description,

• A set of static knowledge sources, namely, an *ontology*, a *fact repository*, a *lexicon* connecting an ontology with a natural language, and an *onomasticon* or lexicon of names (one lexicon and one onomasticon are needed for each language)
• *Knowledge-representation languages* for specifying meaning structures, ontologies, and lexicons
• A set of processing modules—at the least, a semantic *analyzer* and a semantic *text generator*

Ontological semantics directly supports such applications as machine translation of natural languages, information extraction, text summarization, question answering, advice giving, collaborative work of networks of human and software agents, and so on. For applications other than machine translation, a reasoning module is added that manipulates meaning representations produced by the analyzer to generate additional meanings that can be recorded in the fact repository and/or serve as inputs to text generation for human consumption.

Any large, practical, multilingual computational linguistic application requires many knowledge and processing modules integrated in a single architecture and control environment. For maximum output quality, such comprehensive systems must have knowledge about speech situations, goal-directed communicative actions, rules of semantic and pragmatic inference over symbolic representations of discourse meanings, and knowledge of syntactic, morphological, and phonological/graphological properties of particular languages. Heuristic methods, extensive descriptive work on building world models, lexicons, and grammars, as well as a sound computational architecture are crucial to the success of this overall paradigm. Ontological semantics is responsible for a large subset of these capabilities.

The above generalized application architecture also includes an "ecological," a morphological, and a syntactic component, both in the analysis and in the generation processes. In applications, such components have usually been developed quite independently of the central ontological semantic component, though the knowledge required for them was often (though not in every implementation) integrated in the overall system lexicons. Thus, for instance, grammar formalisms have remained outside the immediate scope of theoretical work in the ontological semantic model, and indeed several different grammar formalisms have been used to support analysis and generation in the different implementations. Due to this state of affairs, we do not include grammar formalisms and actual rule sets in the core knowledge sources of the model. The interaction between the ontological semantic processing and the rest of the processing takes place in actual implementations through the specification of the content of the input structures to the semantic analyzer and of the output structure of the semantics-based sentence-planner module of the generator.

Our theoretical work in semantics is devoted to developing a general semantic theory that is detailed and formal enough to support natural language processing by computer. Therefore, issues of text-meaning representation, semantic (and pragmatic) processing, the nature of background knowledge required for this processing, and the process of its acquisition are among the central topics of our effort. Ontological semantics shares the commitment to these foundational issues with a number of approaches to processing meaning in artificial intelligence, among them conceptual dependency, preference semantics, procedural semantics, and related approaches (e.g., Schank 1975; Schank and Abelson 1977; Schank and Riesbeck 1981; Wilensky 1983; Wilks 1975a, 1975b, 1977, 1982; Charniak and Wilks 1976; Woods 1975, 1981; Lehnert and Ringle 1982; Waltz 1982; Charniak 1983b; Hirst 1987). Moreover, the influences go beyond purely computational contributions back to cognitive psychology and cognitive science (Miller and Johnson-Laird 1976; Fodor, Beaver, and Garrett 1974; see also Norman 1980). The foundational issues in this research paradigm, in fact, transcend natural language processing. They include the study of other perceptors (e.g., speech, vision) and effectors (e.g., robotic movement, speech synthesis) as well as reasoning (e.g., general problem solving, abductive reasoning, uncertainty, and many other issues). Newell and Simon (1972) provide an influential formulation of the overall paradigm that underlies all the above-mentioned work as well as many contributions that were not mentioned (see also Newell, Shaw, and Simon 1958; Miller, Galanter, and Pribram 1960; Newell 1973; Newell and Simon 1961, 1976; McCarthy and Hayes 1969; McCarthy 1977). This paradigm certainly underlies ontological semantics.

What sets this knowledge-based paradigm apart is the reliance on the glass-box rather than black-box approach to modeling understanding. In other words, these theories do not attempt to account for meaning in terms of fully observable (though, interestingly, not necessarily correctly understood!) phenomena, namely, pairs of inputs and outputs (stimuli and responses; see section 3.4.1) to a language processor, understood as a black box. Instead they aspire to come up with hypotheses about what processes and what knowledge is needed in order to recreate the human ability to process language using computers. This is done by modeling the contents of the black box, necessarily using notions that are not directly observable.

Ontological semantics subscribes to a version of this tenet, the so-called weak AI thesis (see section 2.4.2.2), which avoids the claim that computer programs directly model human semantic capacity. Instead, this hypothesis suggests functional equivalence—that is, that computer programs can attain human-quality results, though not using the exact methods that humans use.

The tenets of ontological semantics overlap with the tenets of semantic theories developed within the generative paradigm in linguistics (Fodor 1977; see also section 3.5). There are also important differences, along at least the following two dimensions:

• The purview of the theory (ontological semantics includes all of the following: lexical and compositional semantics, pragmatics, reasoning)
• The degree to which the theory has been actually both developed and implemented through language description and computer-system construction

A number of differences exist between the mandates of general semantic theory and semantic theory for NLP. In what follows, we suggest a number of points of such difference (this list is an extension of the discussion in Nirenburg and Raskin 1986; see also Raskin 1990—cf. chapter 4).

While it is agreed that both general and NLP-related theories must be formal, the nature of the formalisms can be quite different because different types of reasoning must be supported. A general linguistic theory must ensure a complete and equal grain-size coverage of every phenomenon in the language; an NLP-related theory must be sufficiently flexible and robust to adapt to the purposes of any application. The ultimate criterion of validity for a general linguistic theory is explanatory adequacy; for an NLP-related theory, it is the success of the intended applications. A general linguistic theory can avoid complete descriptions of phenomena once a general principle or method has been established: a small number of clarification examples will suffice for its purposes. In NLP, the entire set of phenomena present in the sublanguages of applications must be covered exhaustively. A general linguistic theory has to be—and, actually, has occasionally been (see, for instance, Raskin 1985a, 1985b)—concerned about the boundary between linguistic and encyclopedic knowledge. This distinction is more spurious in NLP-oriented semantic theories because in order to make semantic (and pragmatic) decisions, a system must have access equally to both types of data (Raskin 2000).

A general linguistic theory can be method driven—that is, seek ways of applying a description technique developed for one phenomenon in the description of additional phenomena (this reflects the predominant view that generalization is the main methodology in building linguistic theories). But an NLP-related theory should be task driven—which means that adequacy and efficiency of description take precedence over generalization (Nirenburg and Raskin 1999).

The research program of ontological semantics is shared to a large degree by the work of Lenat and associates on CYC (e.g., Lenat 1995; Lenat and Guha 1990; see also Mahesh et al. 1996b) and by John Sowa's knowledge-representation efforts (e.g., Sowa 2000). While considerable differences exist in the types of knowledge represented, size and coverage of various knowledge resources, intended applications, the nature of systems implemented on the basis of each approach, and so on, Lenat's and Sowa's work joins ontological semantics in assuming that the task of extracting and formally representing knowledge about the world and language is a necessary condition for attaining truly intelligent computer systems.

1.1 A Model of Language-Communication Situation for Ontological Semantic Theory

Ontological semantics, as a mentalist approach to building NLP-related language-processing theories, is centered around the metaphor of the model of an intelligent agent.[1] An NLP-related theory must account for such properties of intelligent agents as goal- and plan-directed activity, of which language activity is a part—verbal actions, together with perceptual, mental, and physical actions, comprise the effector inventory of an intelligent agent. Such a theory must also take into account the knowledge of the agent's attitudes to the entities in the world model as well as to remembered instances of events and objects in its own episodic memory. Not only are these attitudes often the subject of a discourse, but they influence the form of discourse on other topics.

Building nontrivial natural language processing systems that manipulate meaning is best done using the metaphor of modeling intelligent agents immersed in a language-communication situation. In other words, we prefer to ground our meaning-representation theory on cognitive premises rather than on purely logical ones. In the most basic and simplified terms, we define our model of an intelligent agent as follows. An intelligent agent is a member of a society of intelligent agents. The agent's actions are goal directed. It is capable of perception, internal symbol manipulation, and action. Its actions can be physical, mental, or communicative. The communicative actions are used for communicating with other agents. An agent's perceptual mechanism is a model of the perceptual mechanism of humans. The peculiarities of the perception and action sides of the agent are less central to a discussion of ontolocyical semantics, so we will concentrate on the agent's resident knowledge and the processing environment for the treatment of natural language.

We model the communication situation as follows. It involves at least two intelligent agents—a discourse (text, speech) producer and a discourse consumer. The communication situation also involves the discourse itself—in our case, a text. More precisely (though this is not a crucial distinction from the standpoint of text processing), discourse producer and consumer are roles played by intelligent agents, because each agent can play any of these roles at different times. The message conveyed by a text can be viewed as an action that the discourse consumer perceives as a step in a discourse producer's plan to achieve one of his or her active goals.[2] These plans take into account the knowledge the producer has (or assumes it has) about the target audience. A theory of discourse goals must, therefore, follow the prior introduction of a model of a participant in a language-communication situation.

1.1.1   Relevant Components of an Intelligent Agent's Model

The following components in an agent's model are relevant for its language-processing ability:[3]

· Knowledge about the world, which we find useful to subdivide into:
  – An ontology, which contains knowledge about types of things (objects, processes, properties, intentions) in the world
  – A fact repository, an episodic memory module containing knowledge about instances (tokens) of the above types and about their combinations; a marked recursive subtype of this knowledge is a set of mental models of other agents (see, for instance, Ballim and Wilks 1991, for an analysis of the "artificial believers"), complete with their own components—these models can be markedly different from the "host" model
· Knowledge of natural language(s), including, for each language:
  – Ecological, phonological, morphological, syntactic, and prosodic constraints
  – Semantic-interpretation and semantic-realization rules and constraints, formulated as mappings between lexical units of the language and elements of the world model of the producer
  – Pragmatics and discourse-related rules that map between modes of speech and interagent situations, on the one hand, and syntactic and lexical elements of the meaning-representation language, on the other
· Emotional states that influence the "slant" of discourse generated by an agent (Picard 2000)
· An agenda of active goal and plan instances (the intentional plane of an agent)

1.1.2   Goals and Operation of the Discourse Producer

The discourse-producer goals will be formulated in terms of these different components. Thus, a producer may want to achieve the following types of interagent communicative goals:

1. Modify the discourse consumer's ontology—for example, by giving a definition of a concept

2. Modify the discourse consumer's episodic memory—for example, by stating a fact, describing an object, or relating an event

3. Modify the discourse consumer's model of the producer—for example, by expressing its attitude toward some fact (e.g., *Unfortunately, Peter will come too*)

4. Modify the discourse consumer's attitudes toward facts of the world

5. Modify the discourse consumer's agenda—for example, by threatening, giving an order, or asking a question

6. Modify the discourse consumer's emotional state

A discourse producer can achieve these goals by choosing not only what to say, but also how to say things. Usually, one element of discourse will achieve several goals at the same time. For instance, if the producer has any authority over the hearer, the fact of simply stating its own opinion about a fact (a goal of type 3) may very well affect the hearer's opinions, thus achieving a goal of type 4 (e.g., Wilensky 1983). Goal types are represented in the world model of an agent as postconditions (effects) of complex events (see Carlson and Nirenburg 1990 for the description of the formalism and the motivation behind it; cf. section 7.1.5—see also Moreno Ortiz, Raskin, and Nirenburg 2002).

The producer's processing during generation can be sketched as follows. Given an input stimulus, the producer will activate a goal, choose a rhetorical plan to realize that goal, and generate a text. This is done with the help of its knowledge about the world, about the consumer, about the target language (at both the sentence and the discourse level), and about the relevant pragmatic constraints.

1.1.3 Operation of the Discourse Consumer

The discourse consumer's processing during analysis can be very roughly sketched as follows. Given an input text, the consumer must first attempt to match the lexical units comprising the text, through the mediation of a special lexicon, with elements of the consumer's model of the world. To facilitate this, it will have to analyze syntactic dependencies among these units and determine the boundaries of syntactic constituents. The next step is filtering out unacceptable candidate readings through the use of selectional restrictions, collocations, and special heuristics, stored in the lexicon. The consumer must then also resolve the problems of coreference by finding referents for pronouns, other deictic lexical units, and elliptical constructions. Furthermore, information on text cohesion and producer attitudes has to be determined, as well as, in some applications, the goals and plans that lead the producer to produce the text under analysis.

Many additional processes are involved in interpretation. A semantic theory for natural language processing must also account for their interaction in a computational model—that is, the overall architecture and control of the semantic and pragmatic interpretation process. Control considerations, we believe, must be an integral part of semantic theories for natural language processing, of which ontological semantics is an example. However, many of the current semantic theories, notably those relying on unification as the main processing method, essentially relinquish control over control. A whole dimension of modeling is thus dispensed with, leading to reduction in the expressive power of a theory and extra constraints on building applications. Why not accept unification as one of a number of possible control structures? And, for every processing module, choose a control structure most responsive to the peculiarities of the phenomenon treated? In AI, there is a long tradition of looking for the most appropriate representation of a problem, which will "suggest" the most appropriate algorithm for processing it. It is clear that different representations must be preferred for different problems (see, e.g., Newell and Simon 1972). Adopting a single type of representation and a single control method for all tasks means putting method before phenomena.

1.2 Ontological Semantics: An Initial Sketch

Like any semantic theory for natural language processing, ontological semantics must account for the processes of generating and manipulating text meaning. An accepted general method of doing this is to describe the meanings of words and, separately, specify the rules for combining word meanings into meanings of sentences and, further, texts. Hence the division of semantics into lexical (word) semantics and compositional (sentence) semantics. Semantics for NLP must also address issues connected with the meaning-related activities in both natural language understanding and generation by a computer. While the semantic processing for these two tasks is different in nature—for instance, understanding centrally involves resolution of ambiguity while generation deals with resolution of synonymy for lexical selection—the knowledge bases, knowledge-representation approaches, and the underlying system architecture and control structures for analysis and generation can be, to a realistic degree, shared. This view is a departure from our earlier views (Nirenburg and Raskin 1987a, 1987c), brought about by practical experience in description and implementation of nontoy applications.

In ontological semantics, the meaning representation of a text is derived through

· Establishing the lexical meanings of individual words and phrases comprising the text
· Disambiguating these meanings
· Combining these meanings into a semantic dependency structure covering
  – The propositional semantic content, including causal, temporal, and other relations among individual statements

  – The attitudes of the speaker toward the propositional content
  – The parameters of the speech situation
• Filling any gaps in the structure based on the knowledge instantiated in the structure as well as on ontological knowledge

It is clear from the above description that ontological semantics incorporates information that in some approaches (e.g., Lascarides 1995; Asher and Lascarides 1995) has been delegated to pragmatics.

The final result of the process of text understanding may include some information not overtly present in the source text. For instance, it may include results of reasoning by the consumer, aimed at filling in elements required in the representation but not directly obtainable from the source text. It may also involve reconstructing the agenda of rhetorical goals and plans of the producer active at the time of text production and connecting its elements to chunks of meaning representation.

Early AI-related natural language understanding approaches were criticized for not paying attention to the halting condition on meaning representation (a criticism of the same kind as Weinreich's attack on Katz and Fodor—see section 9.3.5). The criticism was justified to the extent that these approaches did not make a very clear distinction between the information directly present in the text and information retrieved from the understander's background knowledge about the entities mentioned in the text. This criticism is valid when the program must apply all possible inferences to the results of the initial representation of text meaning and not when a clear objective is present, such as resolution of ambiguity relative to a given set of static knowledge sources, beyond which no more processing is required.

It follows that text meaning is, in this view, a combination of

• The information directly conveyed in the NL input
• The (agent-dependent and context-dependent) ellipsis-removing (lacuna-filling) information that makes the input self-sufficient for the computer program to process
• Pointers to any background information that might be brought to bear on the understanding of the current discourse
• Records about the discourse in the discourse participants' fact repository

Additionally, text understanding in this approach includes detecting and representing a text component as an element of a script/plan (in Schank-Abelson-Cullingford-Wilensky's terms—see Schank and Abelson 1977; Cullingford 1981; Wilensky 1983; see also section 7.1.5) or determining which of the producer goals are furthered by the utterance of this text component. We stop the analysis process when, relative to a given ontology, we can find no more producer goals/plans that can be furthered by uttering the sentence. But first we extract the propositional meaning of an utterance using our knowledge about selectional restrictions and collocations among lexical units. If some semantic constraints are violated, we turn on metonymy, metaphor, and other "unexpected" input-treatment means. After the propositional meaning is obtained, we actually proceed to determine the role of this utterance in script/plan/goal processing. In doing so, we extract speech-act information, covert attitude meanings, and eventually irony, lying, and so on. The extant implementations of ontological semantics make no claim about including all these features.

There is a tempting belief among applied computational semanticists that, in a practical application such as MT, the halting condition on representing the meaning of an input text can, in many cases, be less involved than the general one. The reason for this belief is the observation that, when a target-language text is generated from such a limited representation, one can, in many cases, expect the consumer to understand it by completing the understanding process given only partial information. Unfortunately, since, without human involvement, there is no way of knowing whether the complete understanding is, in fact, recoverable by humans, it is, in the general case, impossible to posit a shallower (and hence more attainable) level of understanding. To stretch the point further, humans can indeed correctly guess the meaning of many ungrammatical, fragmentary, and otherwise irregular texts—for example, Charniak's (1983a, 159) example of "lecture, student, confusion, question." This, however, does not mean that an automatic analyzer, without specially designed extensions, will be capable of assigning meanings to such fragments—their semantic complexity is of the same order as that of "regular" text.

1.3   Ontological Semantics and Nonsemantic NLP Processors

Ontological semantics takes care of only a part, albeit a crucial part, of the operation of the major dynamic knowledge sources in NLP: the analyzer and the generator. These processors also rely on syntactic, morphological, and ecological information about a particular language. Syntactic processing establishes the boundaries and nesting of phrases in the text and the dependency structures at the clause and sentence levels by manipulating knowledge about word order and grammatical meanings carried by lexical items. Morphological processing establishes the grammatical meanings carried by individual words, which helps the syntactic processor decide on types of grammatical agreement among the words in the sentence, which, in turn, provides heuristics for determining syntactic dependencies and phrase boundaries. The "ecology" of a language (Donald Walker's term) includes information about punctuation and spelling conventions, representation of proper names, dates, numbers, and so on.

Historically, the integration of all these steps of processing into a single theory and system has been carried out in a variety of ways. Thus, the meaning-text model (Apresyan, Mel'čuk, and Zholkovsky 1969, 1973; Mel'čuk 1974, 1979) dealt with most of these levels of processing and representation, sometimes at a finer-grain size than necessary for ontological semantics. However, that approach did not focus on semantic representation, and its computational applications (e.g., Kittredge, Iordanskaja, and Polguère 1988) did not address semantics at all, concentrating instead on deep and surface syntax and morphology. Conceptual dependency (Schank 1975) did concentrate on semantic representations but neglected to consider syntax or morphology as a separate concern: most of the application programs based on conceptual dependency (and all the early ones) simply incorporated a modicum of treatment of syntax and morphology in a single processor (e.g., Riesbeck 1975; Cullingford 1981). Ontological semantics, while concentrating on meaning, enters into a well-defined relationship with syntactic, morphological, and ecological processing in any application.

The most immediate and important element supporting the relations between ontological semantics and the nonsemantic components of an NLP system is the content of those zones of the ontological semantic lexicon entry that support the process of linking syntactic and semantic dependencies (see section 7.3). Specifically, what is linked is the syntactic dependency and the semantic dependency on clause and phrase heads. This essentially covers all words in a language that take syntactic arguments, which suggests that their meanings are predicates taking semantic arguments. The dynamic knowledge sources use this information to create and/or manipulate a text-meaning representation (TMR). The dynamic knowledge sources, however, also use morphological, syntactic, and other nonsemantic information in their operation.

1.4   Architectures for Comprehensive NLP Applications

The ideal state of affairs in NLP applications (as in all the other complex multi-module software systems) is when each component produces a single, correct result for each element of input. For example, a morphological analyzer can produce a single citation form with a single set of inflectional forms for a given input word. Thus, given the English *lain*, it produces "*lie*; Verb, Intransitive, past participle; 'be prostrate,'" while disambiguating it at the same time from "*lie* 'to make an untrue statement with intent to deceive.'"

Unfortunately, this state of affairs does not always hold. For example, given the Russian *myla* as input, a Russian morphological analyzer will (correctly!) produce three candidate outputs:

1. *mylo* 'soap'; Noun, Neuter, Genitive, Singular
2. *mylo* 'soap'; Noun, Neuter, Nominative, Plural
3. *myt* 'to wash'; Verb, Transitive, Past, Feminine

In context, only one of the multiple outputs will be appropriate. Conversely, the English morphological analyzer will (correctly!) fail to produce a candidate for the

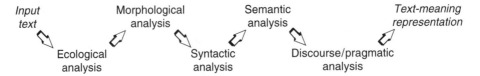

Figure 1.1
Stratified model I: Analysis. A schematic view of a traditional pipelined architecture for the analysis module of a comprehensive NLP system (e.g., an MT system). Results of each processing stage are used as input to the next processing stage in the order of application.

input string *mylo*, because it is not a word in the English language. Or, to use another example, a standard semantic analyzer for English will not be able to interpret the English phrase *kill the project* if the lexicon entry for *kill* (reasonably) lists its meaning as something like "cause not to be alive." Indeed, because projects are not living beings, the combination does not work.

The history of NLP can be viewed as the fight against these two outcomes: underspecification—that is, being unable to cut the number of candidate solutions down to exactly one—and failure to produce even a single candidate solution, due to overconstraining or incompleteness of static knowledge sources. The big problem is that it is difficult, if at all possible, to develop static knowledge sources (lexicons, grammars, and so on) with information that is correct in all contexts that can be attested in running text. Selecting an appropriate computational architecture is one of the methods of dealing with these difficulties as well as of improving the efficiency of the overall process.

1.4.1 The Stratified Model
The most widely used NLP system architecture conforms to the stratified model (see figures 1.1 and 1.2): the task is modularized, and the modules are run on a text one by one, in their entirety, with the cumulative results of the earlier modules serving as inputs to the later modules. This architecture has been a step forward compared to the early architectures, which were not modular in that they heaped all the processing knowledge together rather indiscriminately. (See, for instance, the early MT systems or the early AI NLP systems, such as Margie (Schank 1975).) One of the reasons for introducing the modularity is the difficulty of acquiring static knowledge sources for an "integral" system. Indeed, each of the analysis stages—the original ones of morphology, syntax, and semantics and the later additions of pragmatics, discourse, and, eventually, ecology—was (and still is) a complex problem that is difficult to study even in isolation, let alone taking into account its connections with other language analysis problems.

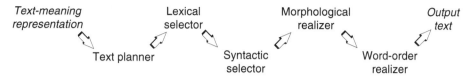

Figure 1.2
Stratified model II: Generation. A schematic view of a traditional pipelined architecture for the generation module of a comprehensive NLP system (e.g., an MT system). Results of each processing stage are used as input to the next processing stage in the order of application.

It is clear that this architecture was designed for processing without specification, overconstraining, or knowledge lacunae. Indeed, it presupposes that each module can successfully complete its processing before the later modules take over. While it was not clear what could be done architecturally to counteract possible overconstraining— or other reasons for a failure to find a solution for an element of input, such as lack of necessary background knowledge—modifications were introduced to the architecture to deal with underspecification.

The most prominent deficiency of the strictly pipelined architecture is the systematic insufficiency of knowledge within a single module for disambiguating among several output candidates. To try to alleviate this problem, the basic architecture can be modified by allowing underspecification of the outputs of individual modules, with the exception of the last one. Underspecification, then, essentially, amounts to postponing decisions of a particular module by allowing it to produce, instead of a single solution, a set of candidate solutions and subsequently using information obtained through the operation of later modules to filter this set (or these sets, if several instances of underspecification occurred). Figure 1.3 illustrates this kind of architecture for the case of text analysis.

1.4.2   The "Flat" Model
The stratified architecture of language processing is, in many ways, constraining. Thus, even in the model with feedback, such as that of figure 1.3, no use is made of the fact that findings of each of the modules can contribute to text-meaning specification directly, not necessarily through the operation of other (later) modules. In addition, the individual results from any module can contribute to determining more than one text-meaning element. Conversely, a particular combination of clues from a variety of sources may make possible the determination of a text-meaning element. None of the above is directly facilitated by the stratificational architecture. Underspecification may be difficult to implement efficiently because, in the simplest case, it necessitates carrying along possibly enormous amounts of intermediate data.

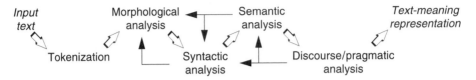

Figure 1.3
Stratified model modified: A schematic view of an enhanced pipelined architecture for the analysis module of a comprehensive NLP system (e.g., an MT system). Thin arrows represent knowledge from later modules that is used to disambiguate results of a prior module.

A "flat" architectural model (see figure 1.4) represents a swing of the pendulum back from pipelining but not back to the lack of modularity. In the flat module, all processing modules operate simultaneously, without waiting for the results of an "earlier" module—for example, the semantic analyzer does not wait until the syntactic analyzer finishes with an input element before starting to work on the latter. Of course, in isolation, the analyzer modules will not be able to complete their processing. However, they will succeed partially. For instance, morphologically uninflected words will be found in the lexicon and the set of their senses instantiated by the semantic processing module irrespective of the results of the syntactic analyzer. If only one sense is recorded for a word in the lexicon, this sense becomes a strong constraint that is used to constrain further the realization choices of other text components.

1.4.3   Toward Constraint-Satisfaction Architectures
One cannot rely on the partial successes of some modules in an unqualified manner. There are many real-world obstacles for a constraint-satisfaction process of this kind. First of all, lexicons can often be incorrect. In particular they may

• Contain fewer senses for a word (or a phrase) than necessary for a task; this state of affairs may cause the compositional semantic process of deriving text-meaning representation to fail because of overconstraining—the process may find no candidates that match the constraints specified in the meanings of TMR components with which they must combine; for example, if in a lexicon only the furniture sense is listed for the word *table*, the process will fail on the input *The two last rows of the table had to be deleted*
• Contain more senses for a word (or a phrase) than sufficient for a task; dictionaries compiled for human use typically contain more senses than should be included in the lexicon of an NLP system; thus, for instance, *Longman's Dictionary of Contemporary English* lists eleven senses of *bank*; should an NLP system use such a dictionary, it will have to be equipped with the means of disambiguating among all these eleven senses, which makes computation quite complex (see section 9.3.5)

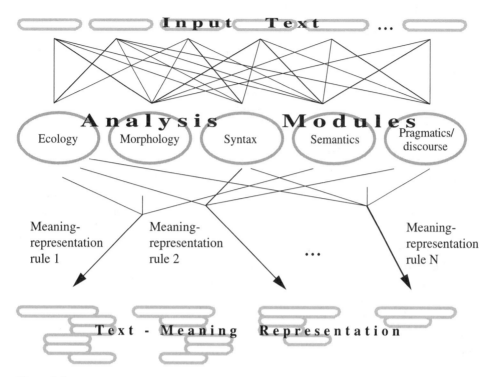

Figure 1.4
In a "flat" model (illustrated here for the case of text analysis), all modules operate and record partial results simultaneously. An intrinsic ordering remains because "later" modules often need results of "prior" modules to produce results or to disambiguate among candidate analyses. However, partial results are still possible even if an earlier module fails on an element of input. The results of the individual module operations provide clues for the left-hand sides of meaning-representation rules. Robustness of the system is further enhanced if the rules are allowed to "fire" even if not all of the terms in their left-hand sides are bound (naturally, this relaxation must be carefully controlled).

• Incorrectly interpret the senses or provide incorrect, that is, too relaxed or too strict, constraints on co-occurrence

While the deficiencies of the lexicon are real and omnipresent in all real-size applications, much more serious difficulties arise from the preponderance in natural language texts, even nonartistic, expository ones, of nonliteral language—metaphors, metonymies, and other tropes. In terms of the basic compositional-semantic processing mode, nonliteral language leads to violations of co-occurrence constraints. Indeed, you do not really crush your opponent in an argument, or have the orchestra play the composer Bach (e.g., Ballim, Wilks, and Barnden 1991; Martin 1992; see also section 8.4.2).

One deficiency of the flat model, as sketched above, is that it does not benefit from the intermediate results of its processing, namely, from the availability of the nascent text-meaning representation. In fact, intermediate results of analysis—that is, elements of the nascent TMR—can provide reliable clues for the analyzer and must be allowed as constraints in the left-hand sides of the text-meaning representation rules. Thus, these rules can draw on the entire set of knowledge sources in comprehensive NLP processing: the lexicons, the ontology, the fact repository, the text-meaning representation, and the results of ecological, morphological, and syntactic processing. Pragmatics and discourse-related issues are folded in the semantic processing in current implementations of ontological semantics. This, however, is not essential from the theoretical point of view: a single theory covering all these issues can be implemented in more than one application module.

The modified flat model can be realized in practice using the so-called blackboard architecture (e.g., Erman et al. 1980; Hayes-Roth 1985), in which a public data structure, a blackboard, is used to store the results of each processing module in the system. This is one way to implement each module's access to the results of every other module (dynamic knowledge source) in the system. The blackboard also contains control and triggering mechanisms to activate certain processes once an item is posted on the blackboard. The actual control in blackboard systems usually uses the agenda mechanism. An agenda is a queue of knowledge-source instantiations (KSIs), each corresponding roughly to a rule—that is, a situation-action pair, where the situation is a combination of constraints. When all its constraints hold, a KSI can "fire" and produce some output to be posted on the blackboard. It is clear that manipulating the positioning of the various KSIs on the agenda (or using multiple-queue agendas) is, in this environment, the best method to improve the control behavior of the system. In fact, a significant amount of scholarship has been devoted to developing intelligent control strategies for blackboard systems, resulting in implementations of metalevel rules and control heuristics.

A different approach to the realization of the modified flat model consists in attempting to represent the entire problem as an interconnected graph of individual choices with constraints imposed on the co-occurrence of local solutions. A method has been developed of avoiding the need for manually constructed control heuristics once the above representation of the problem is achieved (Beale 1997). This method combines the idea of applying rules (KSIs) from any processing module, as soon as all the constraints necessary for their application are established, with the idea of underspecification. The KSIs will then be able to produce partial solutions in the absence of some knowledge elements necessary for producing a single result. As a result, an implicit ordering of KSIs is established automatically through the availability of constraints.

All the control methods specified above rely on two crucial assumptions about the constraints:

• All constraints are binary—that is, they either hold or do not hold.
• In a rule (a KSI), all constraints in the left-hand side must hold before the KSI can fire.

In reality, some constraints are "hard"—that is, inviolable (e.g., the English word *slowest* can only be a superlative adjective, while *uranium* refers exclusively to a chemical element). Some other constraints are "soft" or gradable (e.g., the constraint on the filler of the empty slot in the context *the city of* _____ may well be specified as "name of a city"; however, phrases like *the city of Charlemagne* or *the city of light* are quite acceptable, too—cf. McCawley's (1968) *They named their son something outlandish*).

An extension to the control structure may allow a KSI to fire at a certain stage in the process even if not all of the clauses among its conditions are bound or if one of these constraints only partially satisfies the condition. This requires making the processing architecture more complicated in two (interconnected) ways: first, by introducing a confidence measure for all decisions, and second, by developing procedures for relaxing the constraints based, among other things, on the confidence values of the knowledge used to make decisions.

The relaxation of constraints and the relaxation of constraint applications are evoked when the process detects an instance of overconstraining or an instance of residual underconstraining after all the modules have finished their processing. At this point, the general approach reaches its limit, for a given set of static knowledge sources. This means that finding an appropriate output in such a case can be entrusted to a completely different method, not inherently connected with the spirit of the main approach. In the case of residual lexical ambiguity, for example, many systems resort to selecting an arbitrary—usually the first—sense in the lexicon entry. Alternatively, a word that is more frequent in a corpus may be selected. All such solutions are, in a way, similar to tossing a coin. Such solutions are quite acceptable when a system based on an explanatory theory fails—not necessarily due to theoretical deficiencies but often because of the low quality of some elements in the static knowledge sources of the system. Indeed, more sophisticated corpus-based statistical techniques can be developed and used in these "emergency" cases. We believe that this is the best strategy for tightly coupled "hybridization" of NLP systems—that is, for using knowledge-oriented and corpus-based techniques in a single computational environment. Loosely coupled hybridization involves merging the results of the operation of rule-based and corpus-based systems on the same input. (See Nirenburg et al. 1994 and Frederking and Nirenburg 1994.)

1.5   The Major Dynamic Knowledge Sources in Ontological Semantics

The interplay of semantic and nonsemantic knowledge sources, as suggested in our general approach to NLP, is not, strictly speaking, necessary for the specification of the ontological semantic theory. But we believe that the division of labor and the application architecture we suggest are the most mutually beneficial for each module in an NLP system, because knowledge from a variety of modules must be included in the discovery procedures for the semantic processes. We also believe that it is not appropriate to omit references to syntax, morphology, and ecology while developing a semantic theory for the support of comprehensive NLP applications. It follows that the knowledge sources in our approach transcend purely semantic concerns. The following summarizes the components of the basic dynamic knowledge sources in our model.

1.5.1   The Analyzer
A comprehensive text analyzer consists of

• A tokenizer that treats ecological issues such as all special characters and strings, numbers, symbols, differences in fonts, alphabets, and encodings as well as, if needed, word boundaries (this would be an issue for languages such as Chinese)
• A morphological analyzer that deals with the separation of lexical and grammatical morphemes and establishing the meanings of the latter
• A semantic analyzer that, depending on the concrete NLP application, can contain different submodules, including:
  – A lexical disambiguator that selects the appropriate word sense from the list of senses enumerated in a lexicon entry
  – A semantic dependency builder that constructs the meanings of clauses
  – A discourse-level dependency builder that constructs the meanings of texts
  – A module that manages the background knowledge necessary for the understanding of the content of the text; this module centrally involves processing reference and coreference
  – A module that determines the goals and plans of the speaker, the hearer, and the protagonists of the text
  – A module that tracks the attitudes of the speaker toward the content of the text
  – A module that determines the parameters (indices) of the speech situation—that is, the time, place, identity and properties of the speaker and hearer, and so on
  – A module that determines the style of the text

1.5.2   The Generator

Text generators vary significantly, depending on the application. A major difference is the type of input expected by the generator, which, in turn, determines the kind of generation result possible. If the input to generation is a text-meaning representation, then the most natural generation task would be to construct a text whose meaning is similar to that of the input, in its entirety (e.g., for machine translation) or partially (e.g., for text summarization). If the input to generation is a set of knowledge structures corresponding to the state of a world, the generator is probably incorporated in a reasoning system and may be called on to create a text that analyzes the state of affairs for a human user. One kind of task that the generator may perform is to express the output in the form of the response to a human query. If, for example, the input is in the form of formatted numerical data, the generator is typically called on to present this data as a text (e.g., Kittredge, Polguère, and Goldberg 1986). If the input is a picture, the generator is typically required to describe it (e.g., McDonald and Conklin 1982). Text generators can include the following modules:

• A content-specification module that determines what must be said. The operation of this module, in its most general formulation, results in the specification of meaning of the text to be generated. The content-specification module sometimes includes
  – A communicative-function specification module that decides to include certain information based on the purposes of the communication
  – An interpersonal-function module that determines how much of the input can be assumed to be already known by the hearer
• A text-structure module that organizes the text meaning by organizing the input into sentences and clauses and ordering them
• A lexical selection module that takes into account not only the semantic dependencies in the target language but also idiosyncratic relationships such as collocation
• A syntactic structure selection module
• A morphological realizer for individual words
• The clause- and word-level linearizer

1.5.3   World-Knowledge Maintenance and Reasoning Module

In the framework of ontological semantics, world knowledge is contained in several static knowledge sources: the ontology, the lexicons, and the fact repository (see chapter 7). World knowledge is necessary for lexical and referential disambiguation, including establishing coreference relations and resolving ellipsis as well as for establishing and maintaining connectivity of the discourse and adherence of the text to the text producer's goals and plans.

Different applications use the static knowledge sources differently. While analysis and generation of texts are basic processes used in any application of ontological semantics, some applications require additional processes. In MT, analysis and generation account for most of the system processing because an MT system does not always need to use as much world knowledge as such applications as information extraction (IE) or question answering (QA). This is because the human consumer of MT is expected to fill in any implicit knowledge present in the output text, thus allowing some expressions that are potentially vague and/or ambiguous in the original text to "carry" over to the target text. Thus, while *good book* is potentially ambiguous in that it can mean a book good to read or a well-manufactured book (or any number of other things; see also Raskin and Nirenburg 1998 and Pustejovsky 1995 as well as sections 7.3, 8.4.4, and 9.3.5), the text producer's meaning is not ambiguous in any given instance. And the text consumer, due to the fact that it shares the same basic world knowledge with the producer, can readily recreate the intended meaning. Of course, errors of miscommunication happen, but they are much rarer than successful understanding, as is readily proved by the fact that miscommunication errors are regular subjects of amusing anecdotes. More scientifically (though less amusingly), this finding is sustained by the statistics of error rates in communication gathered by researchers in linguistic error analysis (Fromkin 1973).

In most cases, languages seem to be universally lenient with respect to being able to render vagueness and ambiguity, defined in this sense, either within a language or across languages. For example, in translation, one can in most cases retain deictic (*here*, *now*, *this*, and so on) or referential indices (*he*, *them*, *the same*, and so forth). MT can gloss over these cases unless an indexical mismatch occurs, as for instance, when a source language (say, English) does not have grammatical gender while the target language (say, Hebrew) does, forcing a choice of forms in the translation: the English *them* should be translated into Hebrew as *otam* (masc.) or *otan* (fem.), as required.

To make a decision in a case like the above, one must actually resolve referential ambiguity in the source text. In applications other than MT, this capability is much more necessary, because there is no expectation, for example, in information extraction, that the results of input text processing will be observed and further disambiguated by a human. The background world knowledge is the single most important basis for the disambiguation task. The more knowledge in the fact repository about remembered event and object instances, the higher the chances of the analyzer finding the quantum of information required for disambiguation. The above means that the prototypical ontological semantic system is a learning system. To enhance the quality of future processing, the results of successful text analysis are not only output in accordance with the requirements of a particular application but are also recorded and multiply indexed in the fact repository.

While MT can "go easy" on world knowledge, it still must extract and represent in the TMR every bit of information present in the input text. The situation with IE is different: it does rely on stored world knowledge, not only on the analysis of inputs, to help fill templates, but it does not typically pay a penalty for missing a particular bit of information in the input. This is because there is a realistic expectation that if that bit is important, it will appear in some other part of the input text stream where it would be captured. In other words, the grain size of the TMR varies somewhat depending on the particular application.

1.6   The Static Knowledge Sources

The static knowledge sources of a comprehensive NLP system include the following:

• An ontology, a view of the intelligent agent's world, including knowledge about types of things in the world; the ontology consists of
  – A model of the physical world
  – A model of discourse participants ("self" and others), including knowledge of the participants' goals and static attitudes toward elements of the ontology and toward remembered instances of ontological objects
  – Knowledge about the language-communication situation
• A fact repository containing remembered instances of events and objects; the fact repository can be updated in two ways: either as a result of the operation of a text analyzer, when the facts (event and object instances) mentioned in an input text are recorded, or directly through human acquisition
• A lexicon and an onomasticon for each of the natural languages in the system; the lexicon contains the union of types of information required for analysis and generation;[4] the information in entries for polysemic lexical items includes knowledge supporting lexical disambiguation; the same type of information is used to resolve synonymy in lexical selection during generation; the entries also include information for the use by the syntactic, morphological, and ecological dynamic knowledge sources
• A text-meaning representation formalism
• Knowledge for semantic processing (analysis and generation), including
  – Structural mappings relating syntactic and semantic dependency structures
  – Knowledge for treatment of reference (anaphora, deixis, ellipsis)
  – Knowledge supporting treatment of nonliteral input (including metaphor and metonymy)
  – Text-structure planning rules
  – Knowledge about both representation (in analysis) and realization (in generation) of discourse and pragmatic phenomena, including cohesion, textual relations, producer attitudes, and so on

1.7   The Concept of Microtheories

Decades of research and development in natural language processing have at least taught the practitioners that it is futile to expect that a single comprehensive theory can be developed to account for all the phenomena in the field. A realistic alternative may be to develop a society of *microtheories* responsible for manageable-size chunks of the overall set of phenomena. These components may be circumscribed on the basis of a variety of approaches. There may be microtheories devoted to language in general or particular languages; to parts of speech, syntactic constructions, semantic and pragmatic phenomena, or any other linguistic category; to world knowledge (ontological) phenomena underlying semantic descriptions; and to any of the processes involved in analysis and generation of language by computer.

Examples of microtheories include those of Spanish prepositions, of negation, of passive, of aspect, of speech acts, of reification of properties, of semantic-dependency building, and many others. The working hypothesis here is that it is possible to combine all these, sometimes overlapping, microtheories into a single computational system that accounts for a totality of language phenomena for which it is supposed to serve as a model. The number of microtheories, as described above, can be, of course, very high. In practice, it is necessary to determine which subset of such microtheories is the most appropriate for a particular task. At present, there is no formal mechanism for doing this, and simple common sense is used to keep the number of microtheories and overlaps among them to a possible minimum.

The microtheory approach facilitates the incorporation of fruitful ideas found in linguistics, computational linguistics, cognitive science, AI, philosophy of language, and corpus linguistics. Most linguistic descriptions are, in fact, microtheories, because they deal with fragments of the overall set of language phenomena. The difficulty of combining two linguistic descriptions to form a coordinated single description of the union of the phenomena covered by each individual description is well known and stems from differences in the premises, formats, and purpose. This creates the need to integrate the microtheories by providing a computational architecture that allows the joint operation of all the processing modules based on these microtheories in a particular NLP application.

The integration of microtheories can be carried out in several flat architectural models, for instance, using a blackboard system or a system similar to Hunter-Gatherer (Beale 1997). The nature of the process of adapting a microtheory to the formalism and control conditions of a computational system is illustrated in Pustejovsky and Nirenburg 1988 with the example of the microtheory of aspect and in Raskin and Nirenburg 1998 with the example of the microtheory of adjectives.

From the standpoint of processing architecture, an analysis-related microtheory is thus defined as a set of rules whose right-hand sides are instructions for filling a

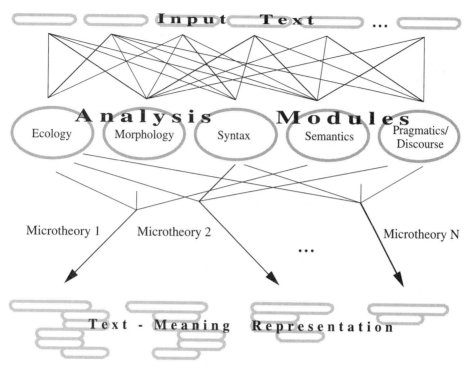

Figure 1.5
When meaning-representation rules are bunched according to a single principle, they become realizations of a microtheory.

particular slot in the TMR representation of a text. Figure 1.5 illustrates an architecture for combining a variety of microtheories. For instance, there might be a rule for each possible value of the PHASE slot in an ASPECT frame in a TMR. The left-hand sides of such rules contain a Boolean formula of a set of conditions for assigning a particular value of PHASE to an input clause derived from a variety of knowledge sources—the nascent TMR, morphology, syntax, semantics, pragmatics, or discourse information. Microtheories supporting generation include rules whose left-hand sides contain a Boolean formula of TMR values and prior lexicalization (and other text planning) decisions and whose right-hand sides include instructions for further lexical selection and other appropriate generation decisions.

1.8   Historical Record of Ontological Semantic Work

The ontological semantics project has been developed for almost two decades. Our understanding of the issues, the metalanguage, and applications have evolved over

Table 1.1
Ontological semantics-related projects

Project name	Content	Dates	Key developers	References
Translator	Knowledge-based MT; original formulation	1984–1986	Sergei Nirenburg, Victor Raskin, Allen B. Tucker	Nirenburg, Raskin, and Tucker 1986
Poplar	Modeling intelligent agents	1983–1986	Sergei Nirenburg, James H. Reynolds, Irene Nirenburg	Nirenburg, Nirenburg, and Reynolds 1985; see also Nirenburg and Lesser 1986
KBMT-89	Medium-scale KBMT, Japanese-English	1987–1989	Sergei Nirenburg, Jaime G. Carbonell, Masaru Tomita, Lori Levin	Nirenburg et al. 1991; Goodman and Nirenburg 1991
Ontos	Ontological modeling and the original acquisition and maintenance toolkit	1988–1990	Sergei Nirenburg, Ira Monarch, Todd Kaufmann, Lynn Carlson	Monarch and Nirenburg 1987, 1988; Carlson and Nirenburg 1990
SMEARR	Extension of Ontos; mapping of linguistic semantics into computational semantics	1988–1991	Victor Raskin, Salvatore Attardo, Donalee H. Attardo, Manfred Stede	Raskin, Attardo, and Attardo 1994a, 1994b
KIWI	Using human expertise to help semantic analysis	1989–1991	Ralf Brown, Sergei Nirenburg	Brown and Nirenburg 1990

Project	Description	Dates	People	References
Dionysus (including DIANA and DIOGENES)	An umbrella project including morphological, syntactic, semantic analysis; text generation and ontological and lexical knowledge acquisition	1989–1992	Sergei Nirenburg, Ted Gibson, Lynn Carlson, Ralf Brown, Eric Nyberg, Christine Defrise, Stephen Beale, Boyan Onyshkevych, Ingrid Meyer	Monarch, Nirenburg, and Mitamura 1989; Nirenburg 1989a, 1989b; Nirenburg, Lesser, and Nyberg 1989; Nirenburg and Nyberg 1989; Defrise and Nirenburg 1990a, 1990b; Nirenburg and Goodman 1990; Onyshkevych and Nirenburg 1991; Nirenburg and Levin 1991; Meyer, Onyshkevych, and Carlson 1990
Pangloss	Another KBMT application, Spanish-English; hybrid system including elements of ontological semantics	1990–1995	Jaime G. Carbonell, Sergei Nirenburg, Yorick Wilks, Eduard Hovy, David Farwell, Stephen Helmreich	Nirenburg 1994; Farwell et al. 1994
Mikrokosmos	Large-scale KBMT; Spanish, English, Japanese; first comprehensive implementation of ontological semantics	1993–1999	Sergei Nirenburg, Victor Raskin, Kavi Mahesh, Stephen Beale, Evelyne Viegas, Boyan Onyshkevych	Beale, Nirenburg, and Mahesh 1995; Mahesh and Nirenburg 1995; Mahesh, Nirenburg, and Beale 1997; Mahesh et al. 1997; Nirenburg, Raskin, and Onyshkevych 1995; Onyshkevych and Nirenburg 1995; Raskin and Nirenburg 1995; Mahesh 1996; Nirenburg et al. 1996; Beale 1997
Savona	A mixed human-computer agent network for generating reports about emerging crises	1997–1998	Sergei Nirenburg, James Cowie, Stephen Beale	Nirenburg 1998b
MINDS	Intelligent information extraction	1998–2000	James Cowie, William Ogden, Sergei Nirenburg, Eugene Ludovik	Ludovik et al. 1999; Cowie et al. 2000a, 2000b; Cowie and Nirenburg 2000

Table 1.1
(continued)

Project name	Content	Dates	Key developers	References
Expedition	Semiautomatic environment for configuring MT systems and language knowledge to support them	1997–2001	Sergei Nirenburg Victor Raskin Marjorie McShane Ron Zacharski James Cowie Rémi Zajac Svetlana Sheremetyeva	Nirenburg 1998a; Nirenburg and Raskin 1998; Oflazer and Nirenburg 1999; Sheremetyeva and Nirenburg 2000a, 2000b; Oflazer, McShane, and Nirenburg 2001
CAMBIO	Mikrokosmos-lite	1999–2001	Sergei Nirenburg Spencer B. Koehler	Nirenburg 2000a
CREST	Question answering	1999–2000	Sergei Nirenburg James Cowie Spencer B. Koehler Eugene Ludovik Victor Raskin	Nirenburg 2000b
MOQA	Question answering	2002–2004	Sergei Nirenburg James Cowie Tanya Korelsky Marjorie McShane Stephen Beale	

this time. Earlier publications may present an outdated view on a number of points of theory and implementation. For the record, table 1.1 shows which NLP projects the various earlier publications on ontological semantics should be attributed to. In this book, we will refer to three implementations of ontological semantics: Dionysus, Mikrokosmos, and CAMBIO/CREST. These implementations represent the major stages in the development of the approach, dating from, roughly, 1992, 1996, and 2000.

Prolegomena to the Philosophy
of Linguistics

Building large and comprehensive computational linguistic applications involves making many theoretical and methodological choices. These choices are made by all language-processing-system developers. In many cases, the developers are, unfortunately, not aware of having made them. This is because the fields of computational linguistics and natural language processing do not tend to dwell on their foundations, or on creating resources and tools that would help researchers and developers to view the space of theoretical and methodological choices available to them and to figure out the corollaries of their theoretical and methodological decisions. This chapter is a step toward generating and analyzing such choice spaces. Issues of this kind typically belong to the philosophy of science, specifically, to the philosophy of a branch of science, hence the title of the chapter. The topic is complex and poorly explored, and the structure of the chapter reflects this complexity:

• In section 2.1, we discuss the practical need for philosophical deliberations in any credible scientific enterprise and, in particular, in our field of (computational) linguistic semantics.
• In section 2.2, we discuss the reasons for pursuing theoretical work in computational linguistics.
• In section 2.3, we propose (surprisingly, for the first time in the philosophy of science) definitions of what we feel are the main components of a scientific theory.
• In section 2.4, we introduce a parametric space for theory building, as applied to computational linguistics. We introduce eleven basic parameters that the philosophy of science can use to reason about properties of a theory. We also discuss the relations between theories and methodologies associated with them.
• In section 2.5, we extend this discussion to include practical applications of theories and their influence on relations between theories and methodologies.
• In section 2.6, we illustrate the impact of choices and decisions concerning one of the eleven parameters—explicitness—for one specific theory: ontological semantics.

• In section 2.7, we comment on the unusual, "postempirical" nature of the approach to philosophy emerging from our studies and compare it to Mao's notorious "blast furnace in every backyard" campaign.

2.1 Reasons for Philosophizing

We introduce the expression "philosophy of linguistics," similar to "philosophy of cognitive science" or "philosophy of artificial intelligence" (cf. Moody 1993, 4), to refer to the study of foundational issues of theory building in linguistics. In our view, such issues underlie and inform various important choices and decisions made in the introduction and development of certain resources (such as lexicons, ontologies, and rules), of certain procedures (such as morphological, syntactic, and semantic analysis and generation), and of certain representations (such as word meaning, sentence structure, sentence meaning, and so on), as well as of the formats for all representations, rules, architectures, and so forth.

Less specifically to linguistics, the impetus for this work is similar to the general reasons for pursuing philosophy of science—to try to understand the assumptions, implications, and other scientific, technological, and societal issues and currents at work in the "object" field. The traditional philosophy of science concentrates on the "hard" sciences, mainly physics and biology. While there are contributions to the philosophy of other fields (such as the above-mentioned view of cognitive science or essays on the philosophy of economics), the science of language has been largely ignored by philosophers.[1]

Our experience in making difficult and often controversial theoretical, methodological, and application-related choices in computational linguistic research made us realize how useful it would be to have a framework within which to make such choices. We felt the need for a basis for our decisions as well as for the alternative choices. Unfortunately, we could find no explicit choice-support framework in any of the several relevant research areas: linguistics, computational linguistics, NLP, artificial intelligence (AI)—of which NLP is a component—or cognitive science.

So we felt we had to venture into analyzing the theory-building process in computational semantics pretty much on our own. The undertaking, we fully recognize, is risky, first because this area is not popular, and second because this undertaking brings us into a field—the philosophy of science—of whose output we have, until now, been only consumers. Still, we see benefits to this exercise, benefits that we will try to describe below. We also hope that attempting to bring our problems to the attention of philosophers of science may underscore the need that disciplines outside the "hard sciences" have for addressing such very basic questions as (1) choosing some particular theoretical constructs over others or none, (2) building a hierarchy of abstract levels of representation (see also Attardo and Raskin 1991 on a solution for that in the philosophy of humor research), (3) optimizing the methodology, and, most importantly, (4) developing adequate justification procedures.

The research for which we first needed to answer the above questions was an application: the knowledge- and meaning-based system of machine translation called Mikrokosmos (see, for instance, Onyshkevych and Nirenburg 1994; Mahesh 1996; Viegas and Raskin 1998; Beale, Nirenburg, and Mahesh 1995; cf. section 1.8). The two highest-risk choices we made were the decision to go for *"deep" meaning analysis* (which the earlier projects in machine translation had used a great deal of hard work and ingenuity to avoid, on grounds of nonfeasibility) and the decision to base our lexicon and sentence representation on a language-independent *ontology* (Mahesh 1996; Mahesh and Nirenburg 1995; Nirenburg, Raskin, and Onyshkevych 1995; see section 7.1), organized as a tangled hierarchy (or lattice) of frames, each of which includes and inherits a set of property slots and their fillers. Together with syntax- and non-syntax-based analysis procedures, the ontology-based lexicon (Onyshkevych and Nirenburg 1994; Viegas and Raskin 1998; Meyer, Onyshkevych, and Carlson 1990; see section 7.3) contributes to the automatic production and manipulation of text-meaning representations (TMRs—see also Carlson and Nirenburg 1990 and chapter 6), which take the status of sentence meanings. Of course, we had to make choices of this kind in earlier implementations of ontological semantics, but it was at this time, with the development of the first large-scale application and the consequent full deployment of ontological semantics, that the need became critical and practically important.

In making the choices while developing the system, we felt that we were consistently following a theory. One sign of this was that the members of the Mikrokosmos team were in agreement about how to treat a variety of phenomena much more often than what could be expected and experienced working on other computational linguistic projects. A tempting hypothesis explaining this state of affairs was that this agreement was based on a shared implied theory. For reasons described in section 2.4.1.3, we feel compelled to try to make that theory explicit.

Returning to the road map of this chapter in more specific terms, we discuss the *need* for theory in section 2.2. Section 2.3 introduces a suggestion about what the *components* of such a theory may be like. Section 2.4 is devoted to developing a set of *parameters* for characterizing a computational linguistic theory and facilitating its comparison with other theories in the field. In section 2.5, we give special consideration to the important issue of the relationship between a *theory and its applications*. Section 2.6 demonstrates, using the example of ontological semantics, the impact of *choosing a certain parameter value* on the way the components of the theory are described. Section 2.7 *summarizes* our findings concerning the relationship between a science and the branch of philosophy devoted to that science.

In what follows, we will assume that the scope of analysis is computational semantics. However, we will feel free to allow ourselves to broaden this scope into

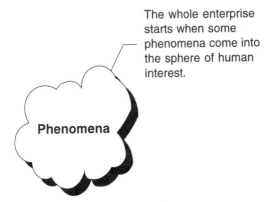

The whole enterprise
starts when some
phenomena come into
the sphere of human
interest.

Phenomena

Figure 2.1
The most generally accepted goal of science is the description of naturally occurring
phenomena.

theoretical linguistics when it can be done with no apparent side effects. The reason
for that is that we would like to relate our work to as many other approaches as
reasonable. Also, we do think that any semantic theory for natural language should
follow these guidelines as well.

2.2   Reasons for Theorizing

In this section, we review several reasons for having explicit theory. They should not
be seen as an exhaustive list.

2.2.1   Introduction: Philosophy, Science, and Engineering

The generally accepted goal of computational linguistics is the development of
computational *descriptions* of natural languages—that is, of algorithms and data for
processing texts in these languages. These computational descriptions are complex
agglomerates, and their acquisition is an expensive and complex undertaking. The
choice of a format of description as well as of the descriptive techniques is of
momentous impact. The format is determined by a *theory* underlying the description. The procedures for acquiring the description constitute a *methodology*. A theory
licenses a class of methodologies appropriate for description in the framework of the
theory. Naturally, it is desirable to select the methodology that facilitates the most
efficient production of descriptions in the theory-determined format. Figures 2.1
through 2.5 illustrate these definitions. The formulation of algorithms, data structures, and knowledge content is a *scientific* enterprise. The optimization of acquisition methodologies and application of the complete description to a practical task is

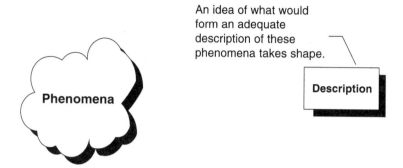

Figure 2.2
It is accepted that, even in the most empirical of theories, there is a step of hypothesis formation that is deductive in nature.

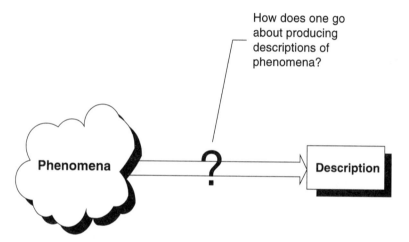

Figure 2.3
The need for methodology becomes clear before the need for theory.

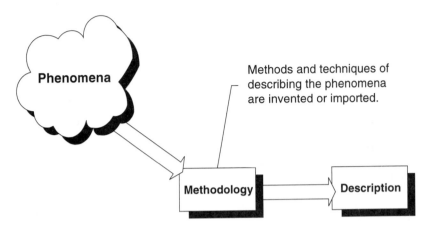

Figure 2.4
Methodologies can be, and often are, imported from other scenarios.

engineering. The formulation of the theory underlying the description must be placed in the realm of the *philosophy* of computational linguistics. The term *philosophy* is used here in the same sense as in "the philosophy of science" but differently than the sense of this term in "the philosophy of language." Indeed, the latter has a natural phenomenon as its subject, whereas the former, similarly to computational linguistics, relates to a branch of human knowledge.

We attempt to explain and clarify these notions. In this section, we concentrate on one small but important facet of our approach, namely, the motivation for caring to develop an overt theory as the basis for computational descriptions of language. The relevant question is, Why is it important to theorize? This is a legitimate question, especially because a large part of the community does not seem to be overly impressed by the need to formulate the principles under which they operate.

2.2.2 Reason 1: Optimization
We can put forward five (well, perhaps four and a half) reasons for overt theorizing. The first reason is that the presence of a theory, we maintain, facilitates the search for the optimum methodology of descriptive language work, constructive engineering-implementation work, formalism development, tool development, and abstract knowledge-system development. If several alternative methodologies are put forward, we must have a means of preferring one over the rest. Selecting methodologies without a theoretical basis is, of course, possible and practiced, often because no reasonable theory is available. This line of action may not lead to unwelcome consequences in a particular application, because pretheoretical commonsense reasoning should not be automatically put down. Nevertheless, there is always a risk that the

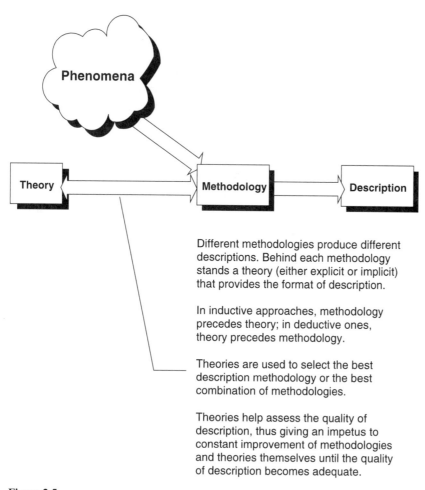

Figure 2.5
Relations between theories and methodologies.

commonsense decisions were made based on partial evidence, which optimizes the choice of method for a partial task and says nothing about the utility of the method outside the immediate task for which it was chosen, whether within the same project or recycled in another project. Besides, the seeming absence of overt theory usually indicates the presence of an implicit, unexamined theory that guides the researcher's actions in an uncontrolled fashion, and this cannot be good.

2.2.3 Reason 2: Challenging Conventional Wisdom
The second reason pertains to what may be called the sociology of our field. (It is likely that every field follows the same pattern, but we will stick to the field we know

best.) We agree with Moody (1993, 2) that "philosophy is the study of foundational issues and questions in whatever discourse (scientific, literary, religious, and so forth) they arise. The foundational issues are hard to define in a way that makes sense across all discourses." We might add that they are equally hard to become aware of and to make explicit in any separately viewed discourse (e.g., scientific) and even within one separate discipline in that discourse (e.g., linguistics).

If a broad community of scholars shares a set of premises, and a large body of results is accumulated and accepted by this community, the need to question or even to study the original premises, statements, and rules from inside the paradigm does not appear to be pressing. This is because a scholar can continue to produce results that are significant within the paradigm as long as there remain phenomena to be described within the subject matter of that paradigm. Such a scholar, then, reasons *within* a theory but not *about* it.

There are many well-known examples of such communities (or paradigms) in twentieth-century linguistics: the American school of structural linguistics, roughly from Bloomfield through Harris; the school of generative grammar (which, in fact, broke into several subparadigms, such as transformational grammar (now extinct, at least in mainstream linguistic theory and practice); government and binding and its descendants; lexical-functional grammar; generalized and head-driven phrase structure grammar; categorial grammar, and so on); systemic grammar; and formal semantics (see also note 17). This "balkanization" of linguistics is taken for granted by any practitioner in the field. It is made manifest by the existence of "partisan" journals, conferences, courses, and even academic programs. It is telling that, in one of the preeminent academic linguistics programs in the United States, the sum total of one course is devoted to linguistics outside the accepted paradigm; it has been informally known for many years as "The Bad Guys."

Of course, this state of affairs makes it more difficult for a newcomer to get a bird's-eye view of our field. It also makes it more difficult for linguists to join forces with representatives of other disciplines for purposes of interdisciplinary research. Consider, as an example, how difficult it is for, say, a psychologist to form a coherent understanding of how linguistics describes meaning. The psychologist will end up with many partisan (and often incompatible) answers to a variety of questions, with no single paradigm proffering answers to all relevant questions.

The above state of affairs exists also in computational linguistics, though the communities here tend to be smaller, and paradigms less stable. For a computational linguist to be heard, he or she must address different paradigms, engaging in debates with people holding alternative points of view. In computational linguistics, such debates occur more or less commonly, mostly for extrascientific sociological reasons. The need for understanding other paradigms and the search for best arguments in a debate may lead to generalizing about the proposed alternative treatments of phenomena, to comparing the approaches, and to evaluating them with respect to a set of features acceptable to all the participants in the debate. We maintain that the grounds for such generalizations, comparisons, and evaluations amount to a philosophy of the field.

Alternatively, a debate among methodological approaches to a linguistic issue can concentrate on judgments about the quality of the descriptions these approaches produce—that is, judging a theory by the results it yields through its applications. Thus, a typical argument between two competing linguistic paradigms may focus on a complex, frequently borderline, example that one approach claims to be able to account for while claiming that the other cannot. Even in this situation, the claim rests on a notion such as descriptive adequacy (Chomsky 1965; see also section 2.3), which is an important element of the underlying linguistic theory. Unfortunately, the notion of descriptive adequacy has never been clearly defined philosophically or empirically, whether as a part of the linguistic theory it must serve or as a separate theoretical entity.

2.2.4 Reason 3: Standardization and Evaluation

The third reason for theorizing is that, without a widely accepted theory, the field will resist any standardization. And standardization is essential for the evaluation of methodologies and integration of descriptions in the field. The unsurprising reason why several well-known standardization initiatives, such as the polytheoretical lexicon initiative of the mid-1980s (see, e.g., Ingria 1987), have not been as successful as one would have wanted (and as many had expected) is that standardization was attempted at the shallow level of formalism. It was not informed by similarities in theoretical statements in the various approaches being standardized.

We also believe that any evaluation of the results of application systems based on a theory should be carried out on the basis of a set of criteria external to the underlying theory. Curiously, this set of criteria in itself constitutes a theory that can be examined, questioned, and debated. Thus, the activity in the area of evaluation of machine translation and other NLP systems and resources, quite intensive in the 1990s (e.g., Ide and Veronis 1998; Arnold, Humphreys, and Sadler 1993; King and Falkedal 1990; O'Connell, O'Mara, and White 1994), could have been viewed as an opportunity to build such a theory.

It seems that questions of theory evaluation and quality judgments about theory start to get asked only after an "initial accumulation" of data and results. A plausible picture or metaphor of the maturation of a field (Bunge 1968) is the interest of its practitioners in issues of choosing high-level unobservable concepts considered necessary for understanding explanatory mechanisms in the field. Rule-based computational linguistics has already matured to this point. Corpus-based computational linguistics may yet reach this point in the future if it has one. The explanatory mechanisms are theoretical in nature, and hence our fourth reason, or half-reason, for theorizing.

2.2.5   Reason 4: Explanation

In most cases, the subject of research is a natural phenomenon requiring an explanation. In the case of linguistics, language is that phenomenon, and it actually fronts for an even more general and mysterious phenomenon or set of phenomena referred to as the mind. A proposed theory may aspire to be explanatory, but it may also choose not to (cf. sections 2.4.2.2 and 2.4.3). But there can be no explanation without theory: in fact, for most users of the term *theory*, it is nearly synonymous with *explanation*.

2.2.6   Reason 5: Reusability

We prefer to view concrete methodologies, tools, or descriptions as instances of a class of methodologies, tools, or descriptions. This will, we hope, help us to recognize a situation where an existing methodology, tool, or description in some sense fits new requirements and can thus be made portable—that is, modified and used—with expectations of a considerable economy of effort. This may happen within or across applications or in the same applications for different languages.

Reusability of technology is a well-known desideratum in engineering. In our NLP work, we have made many practical decisions concerning reusability and portability of methodologies and resources. One of us strongly feels, while the other suspects, that the reason most of our decisions were consistent among themselves was that we have operated on the basis of a shared theory.[2] One of the purposes of writing this book was to lay this theory out and to examine it in comparison with a number of alternatives. As Socrates said, life unexamined is not worth living.

In response to our earlier writings overtly relating descriptions and theory (see, for instance, Nirenburg, Raskin, and Onyshkevych 1995; Nirenburg and Raskin 1996), some colleagues state, off the record, that they cannot afford to spend valuable resources on seeking theoretical generalizations underlying their descriptive work. This position may be justified, we believe, only when the scope of attention is firmly on a single project. Of course, one must strive for a balance between reusing methodologies and tools and developing new ones. We have discussed the issues concerning this balance in some detail in Nirenburg and Raskin 1996.

2.3   Components of a Theory

We posit that a linguistic theory (and a semantic theory or a computational linguistic theory are linguistic theories) has four components. We list them briefly with examples initially taken from one of the best-known linguistic theories, Chomsky's generative grammar. The components of the theory are as follows: the *purview* (e.g., in generative grammar, a language *L* understood as a set of sentences and their theoretical descriptions); the *premises* (e.g., Chomsky's equating grammaticality with the intuitive ability of the native speaker to detect well-formedness of sentences in a natural language; as well as much more basic things, such as accepting the sentence as the sole unit of description or the principle that a sentence must have a unique representation for each syntactic reading it might have); the *body* (e.g., the complete list of rules in the transformational generative grammar of a language); and the *justification* statement(s) (e.g., any statements involving Chomsky's notions of descriptive and explanatory adequacy of a theory). Figures 2.6 and 2.7 illustrate these notions.

2.3.1 Purview

We define the *purview* (or domain) of a theory, a rather straightforward component, as the set of phenomena for which the theory holds itself—and is held—accountable.

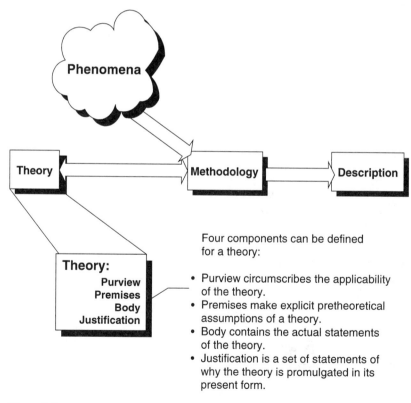

Four components can be defined for a theory:

- Purview circumscribes the applicability of the theory.
- Premises make explicit pretheoretical assumptions of a theory.
- Body contains the actual statements of the theory.
- Justification is a set of statements of why the theory is promulgated in its present form.

Figure 2.6
Components of a theory.

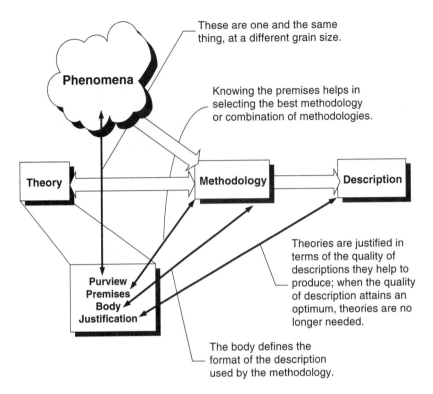

Figure 2.7
Relations among the components of a theory.

For example, one assumes that a semantic theory will cover all meaning-related phenomena in language unless some of them are explicitly excluded. If, however, a statement billed as semantic theory is devoted only to a subset of semantics (as done with grammaticalization of meaning in, for instance, Frawley 1992—cf. Raskin 1994), without explicitly declaring this narrower purview, a misunderstanding between the reader and the author is unavoidable.

In this regard, it seems entirely plausible that some theoretical debates in our field could be rendered unnecessary if only the opponents first clarified the purviews of the theories underlying their positions. In their review of Pustejovsky 1995, Fodor and Lepore (1998) demonstrated that the purview of the theory in which they are interested intersects only marginally with the purview of Pustejovsky's generative lexicon theory. While Pustejovsky was interested in accounting for a wide range of lexical semantic phenomena, his reviewers were content with what has become known in artificial intelligence as "uppercase semantics" (see McDermott 1978; Wilks 1999).[3]

An invocation of the notion of purview can be found in Yngve 1996, where a significant amount of space is devoted to the argument that all of contemporary linguistics suffers from "domain confusion." Yngve takes contemporary linguistics to task for not sharing the purview of the natural sciences (understood as the set of all observable physical objects) and instead operating in the "logical" domain of theoretical constructs, such as utterances, sentences, meanings, and so on rather than strings of sounds, nonlinguistic behaviors accompanying those sounds, and so forth.

In NLP, the purview issue takes a practical turn when a system is designed for a limited sublanguage (Raskin 1971, 1974, 1987a, 1987b, 1990; Kittredge and Lehrberger 1982; Grishman and Kittredge 1986; Kittredge 1987). A typical problem is to determine the exact scope of the language phenomena that the description should cover. The temptation to limit the resources of the system to the sublanguage and not to account for anything outside it is strong because this approach is economical. On the other hand, such a narrow focus interferes with a possibility to port the system to an adjacent or different domain. An overt theoretical position on this issue may help to make the right choice for the situation.

2.3.2 Premises

We understand a *premise* essentially as a belief statement that is taken for granted by the theory and is not addressed in its body. A premise can be a statement like the following: Given a physical system that cannot be directly observed, if a computational system can be designed such that it produces the same outputs for the same inputs as the physical system, then the computational system must have at least some properties shared with the physical system (cf., e.g., Dennett 1979, especially p. 60[4]). This is a formulation of the well-known "black-box" model. Like all premises, this formulation "may be seen as concerning the most fundamental beliefs scientists as a group have regarding the nature of reality, as these beliefs are manifest in their scientific endeavors" (Dilworth 1996, 1). The black-box premise seems to be a version of the influential concept of "supervenience" in the philosophy of science, which, in its psychophysical incarnation, "is the claim that if something has a mental property at a time ... then it has some physical property at that time ..., such that anything with that physical property, at any time ..., also has the mental property" (Zangwill 1996, 68; cf. Kim 1993). In the black-box premise, it is the cognitive, input-output manipulation property that is shared between the computational and the physical systems, and the goal is to determine which of the physical properties of the former—e.g., specific rules—also characterize the latter.

The notion of premise, under various names, has generated a great deal of lively debate in philosophy of science, mostly on the issues of its legitimacy and status vis-à-vis scientific theories. Dilworth (1994, 1996) refers to what we call premises as presuppositions or principles and states that "they cannot have been arrived at through the pursuit of science, but must be, in a definite sense, pre-scientific, or metascientific" (1996, 2). Moody (1993, 2–3) refers to what we call premises as foundational issues, which he defines as presuppositions of scientific statements, such as "there are sets" in mathematics.[5] A crucial point here is that this latter fact should not preclude careful examination of a theory's premises. Many philosophers, however, adhere to the belief (which we consider a non sequitur) that the premises of a theory cannot be rigorously examined specifically because of their metascientific nature (cf. Davidson 1972); for Yngve (1996, 22), no subject-related premises are acceptable in the pursuit of any science.

Premises seem to play the same role as axioms in algebraically defined theories, except that the latter are explicitly stated and thus included in the body of the theory. An axiom is the starting point in truth-preserving derivation of propositions in the body of a theory. A premise participates in such a derivation implicitly. This is why it is rather difficult to explicate the premises of a theory and why theorists often find this task onerous.

Whether they are explicated or implicit, premises play a very important role in scientific work. Just as specifying the purview of a theory establishes the boundaries of the phenomena to be accounted for by that theory, so the premises of a theory determine what questions it should address and what statements would qualify as satisfactory answers to these questions. In this sense, premises can be said to define "the rules of the scientific game." One such important rule is defining what is meant by completion, closure, or success of a theory. Thus, a scientific theory based on the black-box premise is complete, closed, and successful if it succeeds in proving that at least some properties of the computational system are shared by the physical system. In the absence of such a premise, the computational modeling of physical systems would not have a theoretical standing.

The need for overt specification of premises became clear to us when we tried to understand what was funny in the passage from Jaroslav Hašek's (1974, 31) "The Good Soldier Švejk," where a mental-asylum patient is reported to believe that "inside the globe there was another globe much bigger than the outer one." We laughed at the absurdity of the notion because of the unsaid premise that no object can contain a larger one. Trying to prove the falsity of the original statement, we reduced the problem to the linear case of comparing two radii. At this point, we realized that no proof was available for the following statement: "When superimposed, a longer line fully incorporates a shorter line." This statement seems to be taken for granted in elementary geometry. This is an example of a premise. It is possible that any premise could in principle be formalized as an axiom. An axiom is a premise made explicit. And we believe that any theory would profit from making all of its premises into axioms.

2.3.3 Body

The *body* of a theory is a set of its statements, variously referred to as laws, propositions, regularities, theorems, or rules. When still unimplemented, the body of a theory amounts to a statement about the *format* of the descriptions obtainable using this theory. When a theory is implemented, its body is augmented by *descriptions*. In fact, if one assumes the possibility of attaining a closure on the set of descriptions licensed by the theory, at the moment when this closure occurs, the theory loses the need for the format: the body of the theory will simply contain the set of all the descriptions. This, of course, is a strong idealization for a semantic theory, because the set of all utterances that may require meaning representation (that is, description) is, like some fast-food restaurants, always open.

An interesting relation exists between the premises and the body of the theory: that between the ideal and the actual. We agree with Dilworth (1996, 4) that premises (which he terms "principles")

constitute the core rather than the basis of science in that they are not general self-evident truths from which particular empirical truths can be formally deduced, but are rather ideal conceptions of reality which guide scientists' investigations of actual reality. From this perspective, what makes a particular activity scientific, is not that the reality it uncovers meets the ideal, but that its deviation from the ideal is always something to be accounted for.

While the premises of a theory induce an ideal realization in the body, the actual set of propositions contained in the latter, at any given time of practical research, accounts only for a part of the ideal reality and in less depth than the ideal realization expects. Besides being generally true, this distinction has the practical consequence of clarifying the relation between the ideal methodology required by the ideal body and the practical methodologies developed and applied both in theoretical and especially in applicational work (see section 2.5). We will also see, in the account of that work in part II, that, in the process of description, not only our methodologies but also the body of the theory will undergo a change as we improve our guesses concerning the elements of the ideal body.

2.3.4   Justification

The concern for *justification* of theories is relatively recent in the scientific enterprise. For centuries, it was accepted without much second thought that direct observation and experiments provided verification or disproof of scientific hypotheses. It was the logical positivists (see, for instance, Carnap 1936–1937, 1939, 1950; Tarski 1941, 1956; Reichenbach 1938; Popper 1959, 1972; Hempel 1965, 1966; see also Braithwaite 1955; Achinstein 1968), whose program centrally included the impetus to separate science from nonscience, who carefully defined the notion of justification and assigned it a pivotal place in the philosophy of science. In fact, it would be fair to say that the philosophy of science as a field emerged owing to that notion.

Justification is the component of a theory that deals with considerations about the quality of descriptions and about the choices a theory makes in its premises, purview, and body. How is the reliability of our knowledge established? This is a standard question in contemporary scientific practice. According to Blachowicz (1997, 447–448), "All theories of justification which pose this question, must divide the body of knowledge into at least two parts: there is the part that requires justification [that is, our premises, purview, and body—SN&VR] and there is the part that provides it [that is, our justification—SN&VR]."

The process of justifying theories intrinsically involves a connection between the realm of theoretical statements and the directly observable realm of concrete experiences. The critical and highly divisive issue concerning justification is the status of unobservable constructs and, hence, of disciplines outside the traditional natural sciences—that is, fields such as sociology, psychology, economics, or linguistics—where, even in the best case, empirical observation is available only partially and is not always accessible. Besides, serious doubts have gradually emerged about the status of direct observation and its translatability into theoretical statements. An influential opinion from computer science has advocated a broader view of experiment and observation: "Computer science is an empirical discipline. We would have called it an experimental science, but like astronomy, economics, and geology, some of its unique forms of observation and experience do not fit a narrow stereotype of the experimental method. Nonetheless, they are experiments" (Newell and Simon 1976, 35–36).

First, Popper's work (1959, 1972) firmly established the negative rather than positive role of empirical observation. The novelty of the idea that direct observation can only falsify (refute) a hypothesis (a theory) and never verify (confirm) it had a lasting, shocking effect on the scientific community. The matter got more complicated when Quine (1960, 1970) expressed serious doubts concerning the feasibility of the related problem of induction, understood as the ability of the observer to translate direct experience into a set of statements (logical propositions for the positivists) that constitute scientific theories. Once the logical status of observation was withdrawn, it lost its attraction to many philosophers. According to Haack (1997, 8), "A person's experiences can stand in causal relation to his belief-states but not in logical relation to the content of what he believes. Popper, Davidson, Rorty et al. conclude that experience is irrelevant to justification." (See, for instance, Popper 1959, 1972; Davidson 1983, 1984, 1987; Rorty 1979, 1991;[6] cf. Haack 1993.) In other words, direct experience may confirm or disconfirm a person's belief but does nothing to the set of logical propositions describing his or her belief system. Moreover, the modern approach to justification "rejects the idea of a pretheoretical observation vocabulary: rather, it is our scientific theories themselves that tell us, in vocabulary which is inevitably theory-laden, what parts of the world we can observe" (Leeds 1994, 187).

What is, then, the status of theoretical constructs and statements that are unobservable in principle? Orthodox empiricism continues to deny any truth to any such statements (cf. Yngve 1996). Constructive empiricism (e.g., Van Fraassen 1980, 1989) extends a modicum of recognition to the unobservable, maintaining that "we should believe what our best theories tell us about observables—that is, about the observable properties of observable objects—by contrast, we should merely accept what our theories tell us about the in principle unobservable, where accepting a theory amounts to something less than believing it" (Leeds 1994, 187). Realists go one step further: "The hallmark of realism (at least as Dummett understands it) is the idea that there may be truths that are even in principle beyond the reach of all our methods of verification" (Bar-On 1996, 142; cf. Dummett 1976 and especially 1991).

A moderate hybrid view that has been gaining ground combines foundationalism, a mild version of empiricism, with coherentism, a view that places the whole burden of justification on the mutual coherence of the logical propositions constituting a theory. (See Haack 1993, 1997; cf. Bonjour 1997.) According to this view, a scientific theory consists of two kinds of propositions: those that can be verified empirically and those that are unverifiable in principle. The former are justified in the empiricist way, and the latter, on the ground of their internal coherence as well as their coherence with the empirically justified propositions.[7] And all propositions, no matter how they are justified, enjoy equal status with regard to the truth they express.

The dethroning of empirical observation as the privileged method of justification reaches its apogee in the view that the depth and maturation of every science requires the introduction and proliferation of an increasingly elaborate system of unobservable theoretical concepts. This view has even been applied to physics, a traditional playground of the philosophy of science. The extent to which a science is sophisticated and useful is measured in its success to move "from data packages to phenomenological hypotheses, to mechanism hypotheses" (Bunge 1968, 126–127), where the last depend entirely on a complex hierarchy of untestable theoretical concepts. (It can be claimed, then, that linguistics reached this level of sophistication with the explicit postulation of the abstract concept of the phoneme early in the twentieth century, a sound entity that could not be uttered or heard.)

How is justification handled in current efforts in linguistics and natural language processing? There is a single standard justification tool, and it is Popperian in that it is used to falsify theories. Not only is this tool used as negative justification; surprisingly, it also serves as a de facto impetus to improve theories. We will explain what we mean here with an example. In generative grammar, a proposed grammar for a natural language is called descriptively adequate if every string it generates is judged by the native speaker as well formed, and if it generates all such strings and nothing but such strings. A grammar is a set of formal rules. Standard practice to make a contribution in the field is to find evidence (usually, a single counterexample) in language that the application of a rule in a grammar may lead to an ill-formed string. This finding is understood as refutation of the grammar that contains such a rule. The next step, then, is to propose a modification or substitution of the offending rule with another rule (or rules) that avoids this pitfall. An extension of this principle beyond purely grammatical well-formedness as a basis of justification to include presupposition, coherency, and context was tentatively suggested in Raskin (1977b); see also Raskin 1979, 1985c, and section 6.1.

The Popperian justification tool for linguistics leaves much to be desired. First of all, it is best suited to address a single rule (phenomenon) in isolation. This makes the application of the tool a lengthy and impractical procedure for the justification of an entire grammar. Second, according to at least one view in the philosophy of language, "Justification is gradational" (Haack 1997, 7) and must, therefore, allow for quality judgments—that is, for deeming a theory better than another rather than accepting or rejecting an individual theory. In this view, the above tool is not a legitimate justification tool.

Little has been written on the issue of justification in linguistics. It is not surprising, therefore, that in the absence of a realistic set of justification criteria, the largely aesthetic criteria of simplicity, elegance, and parsimony of description were imported into linguistics by Chomsky, apparently from a mixture of logic and the philosophy of science (1957, 53–56; 1965, 37–40), and thereafter widely used to support judgments about grammars. Moreover, once these notions were established in linguistics, they received a narrow interpretation: simplicity is usually measured by the number of rules in a grammar (the fewer rules, the simpler the grammar), while brevity of a rule has been interpreted as the measure of the grammar's elegance (the shorter the rule, the more elegant the theory).[8] Parsimony has been interpreted as resistance to introducing new categories into a grammar.[9]

2.4   Parameters of Linguistic Semantic Theories

In this section, we attempt to sketch the conceptual space within which all linguistic semantic theories can be positioned. This space is composed of diverse parameters. Each theory can be characterized by a particular set of parameter values. This provides each theory with a perspective on a number of choices made in it. This exercise is helpful because, in building theories (as, we should add, in everything else, too), people tend to make many choices unconsciously and are often unaware that these choices exist. Awareness of one's options is a good start toward creating better theories. Creating the choice space for theories in the natural sciences is a job for the philosophy of science. For linguistic theories, it is, therefore, the responsibility of the philosophy of linguistics.

We will list a number of dimensions, parameters, and values for characterizing and comparing semantic theories. The parameters can be grouped somewhat loosely along a variety of dimensions, namely, "related to theory itself," "related to methodology induced by the theory," "related to status as model of human behavior" (e.g., mind, language behavior, and so on), and "related to internal organization" (e.g., microtheories).

2.4.1 Parameters Related to Theory Proper

In this section, we focus on the theoretical parameters of adequacy, effectiveness, explicitness, formality, and ambiguity.

2.4.1.1 Adequacy A theory is adequate if it provides an accurate account of all the phenomena in its purview. Adequacy can be informally gauged through introspection, by thinking, to take an example from linguistics, of additional language phenomena that a particular theory should cover. It can be established rule by rule using the standard linguistic justification tool discussed in section 3.4. There is an additional mechanical test for adequacy in computational linguistics, namely, determining whether a description helps to solve a particular problem, such as figuring out syntactic dependencies inside a noun phrase. As demonstrated by Popper (1959, 1972; see also section 2.3.4), it is much easier to prove that a theory is inadequate than to establish its adequacy.

Our definition of adequacy refers to an ideal case. As mentioned in section 2.3.3, linguistic theories are never quite complete (as a simple example, consider that no dictionary of any language can guarantee that it includes every word in the language). In practice, the parameter of adequacy is applied to theories that have accounted correctly for the phenomena they have covered—that is, for their purviews. One can only hope that the theory will remain adequate as it extends its purview to include new phenomena.

2.4.1.2 Effectiveness We will call a theory *effective* if we can show that there exists, in principle, a methodology for its implementation. We will call a theory *constructive* if a methodology can be proposed that would lead to an implementation of the theory in finite time.[10] Let us first illustrate the above distinction as it pertains not to a linguistic theory but to a readily formalizable theory describing the game of chess. We will discuss this problem in our own terms and not those familiar from game theory. For our purposes here, we will use the game of chess as an objective phenomenon for which theories can be propounded.[11] Theories that can be proposed for chess include the following three competing ones: "White always wins," "Black always wins," or "Neither White nor Black necessarily wins." An early theorem in game theory proves that the first of these theories is, in fact, the correct one, namely, that there is a winning strategy for White. This means several important things: first, that it is possible, in principle, to construct an algorithm for determining which move White must make at every step of the game; second, because the number of possible board positions is finite (though very large), this algorithm is finite, that is, it will halt (there is a rule in chess that says that if a position repeats three times, the game is a draw); third, this algorithm has never been fully developed. Mathematical logic has developed terminology to describe situations of this kind: the first fact above makes the theory that White always wins *decidable* (alternatively, one can say that the problem of chess is *solvable* for White). The third fact says that this theory has not been proven *computable*.

The following is a formal definition of decidability of a theory or of the solvability of a problem in it: "The study of *decidability* involves trying to establish, for a given mathematical *theory* T, or a given problem P, the existence of a decision algorithm AL which will accomplish the following task. Given a sentence A expressed in the language of T, the algorithm AL will determine whether A is true in T—that is, whether $A \in T$. In the case of a problem P, given an instance I of the problem P, the algorithm AL will produce the correct answer for this instance. Depending on the problem P, the answer may be yes or no, an integer, and so on. If such an algorithm does exist, then we will variously say that the *decision problem* of T or P is *solvable*, or that the theory T is *decidable*, or simply that the problem P is solvable. Of AL we will say that it is a decision procedure for T or P" (Rabin 1977, 596; see also Uspenskiy 1960 on the related concepts of decidable and solvable sets).

Establishing the existence of the algorithm and actually computing it are, however, different matters: the mere existence of the algorithm makes the theory *decidable*; the actual demonstration of the algorithm makes it *computable*. There is also the matter of *practical*, as opposed to *theoretical*, decidability (and computability): "Work of Fischer, Meyer, Rabin, and others has ... shown that many theories, even though decidable, are from the practical point of view undecidable because any decision algorithm would require a practically impossible number of computation steps" (Rabin 1977, 599).[12] The above pertains to the second fact about the theory that White always wins: in some cases, the decision algorithm for a theory is infinite— that is, it does not halt. This is not the case for the chess theory in question. However, this may not make this theory practically decidable—or machine tractable— because complexity requirements of the decision algorithm may exceed any available computational resources.[13]

The logical notions of decidability and computability work well for the example of chess but are not applicable, as defined, to linguistic theory, because language is not, strictly speaking, a mathematical system. It is precisely because of the fact that linguistic theories cannot be completely and neatly formalized that we first introduced the concepts of effectiveness and constructiveness to avoid using the more narrowly defined parallel pair of terms *decidability* and *computability*, respectively, outside of their intended mathematical purview. Many of the procedures used in developing linguistic theories are, therefore, difficult to automate fully. For example, in onto-logical semantics, description (namely, the acquisition of static and dynamic knowl-edge sources) is semiautomatic in a well-defined and constraining sense of using human intuition (Mahesh 1996; Viegas and Raskin 1998; see also section 2.5 and chapter 9). The human acquirers are assisted in their work by specially designed training materials. These materials contain guidance of at least two kinds: how to use the tools and how to make decisions. Statements about the latter provide a very good example of the part of the theory that is not formal.

Contemporary linguistic theories aspire to exclude any recourse to human par-ticipation except as a source of typically uncollected judgments about the gram-maticality of sentences. But there is a steep price to pay for this aspiration to full formality, and this statement seems to hold for computational linguistics as well. It is fair to say that, to date, fully formalizable theories have uniformly been of limited purview. Formal semantics is a good example: in it, anything that is not formalizable is, methodologically appropriately, defined out of the purview of the theory (Heim and Kratzer 1998 is a recent example, but see also Frawley 1992; cf. Raskin 1994). For instance, the study of quantification, which lends itself to formalization, has been a central topic in formal semantics, while word-sense definition that resists strict for-malization is delegated to a sister discipline, lexical semantics. The proponents of full formalization inside lexical semantics continue with the purview-constraining prac-tices in order to remain fully formal. In contrast, still other linguistic theories, onto-logical semantics among them, have premises that posit the priority of phenomenon coverage over formalization in cases of conflict; in other words, such theories decline to limit their purview to fit a preferred method.

These not entirely formal[14] theories would benefit the most from a study of the practical consequences of their being constructive, effective but not constructive, or neither effective nor constructive.

Ontological semantics can be presented as a theory producing descriptions of the form $M_S = TMR_S$—that is, the meaning M of a sentence S in a natural language L (e.g., English) is represented by a particular formal text-meaning representation (TMR) expression. In each implementation of ontological semantics, there is an algorithm, the analyzer, for determining the truth of each expression in the above format: it does that by generating, for each sentence, its unique TMR. This estab-lishes the constructiveness of the theory (as well as its effectiveness) post hoc, as it were. We will discuss what, if anything, to do with a theory that is known not to be constructive in section 2.4.2.1.

2.4.1.3 Explicitness Theories overtly committed to accounting in full for all of their components are explicit theories. In section 2.6, we illustrate this parameter with the specific example of ontological semantics. Explicitness has its limits. In a manner akin to justification, discussed above, and all other components and parameters of theories, explicitness is "gradational." Somewhat similarly to the situation with adequacy, explicitness is an ideal notion. A theory that strives to explicate all of its premises, for instance, can never guarantee that it has discovered all of them. But we believe that, both theoretically and practically, one must keep trying to achieve just that; this is basically what this chapter is about.

2.4.1.4 Formality and Formalism A theory can be formal in two senses. Formality may mean completeness, noncontradictoriness, and logically correct argumentation. It may also refer to the use of a mathematical formalism. The two senses are independent—thus, a theory may be formal in both senses, in either sense, or in neither.

Formality in the second sense usually means a direct application of a version of mathematical logic—with its axiomatic definitions, theorems, in short, all its well-established formal derivation machinery—to a particular set of phenomena.[15] The formalism helps establish consistency of the set of statements about the phenomena. It also establishes relations of equivalence, similarity, proximity, and so on among terms or combinations of terms and through this, among the phenomena from the purview of the theory that the logic formalizes. This may result in the imposition of distinctions and relations on the phenomena that are not intuitively clear or meaningful. Wilks (1982, 495) has correctly characterized the attempts to supply semantics for the formalism in order to apply it to NLP, as an "appeal to external authority: the Tarskian semantics of denotations and truth conditions for some suitably augmented version of the predicate calculus (Hayes, 1974; McDermott, 1978)."

A danger of strict adherence to formality in the sense of formalism is the natural desire to remove from theoretical consideration phenomena that do not lend themselves to formalization using the formal language of description. This, in turn, leads to modifications in the purview of a theory and can be considered a natural operation. Indeed, modern science is usually traced back to Galileo and Newton, who made a departure from the then-prevalent philosophical canon in that they restricted the purview of their theories to, very roughly, laws of motion of physical bodies for the former and physical forces for the latter. By doing so, they were able to make what we now accept as scientific statements about their purviews. The crucial issue is the ultimate utility of their theories, even if their purviews were narrower than those of other scholarly endeavors.

Turning back to our own case, we must consider the trade-off in computational linguistics between limiting the purview of a theory and keeping it potentially useful.

Our own attempts to alleviate this tension have found their expression in the concept of microtheories (see section 1.7; also see, for instance, Raskin and Nirenburg 1995). But that, in turn, leads to the ever present issue of integration—that is, how to make these microtheories coexist without contradictions, if this is at all possible.

In an alternative approach, formalism is not the impetus for description but rather plays a supporting role in recording meaningful statements about the phenomena in the purview of the theory. In other words, in this approach, content is primary and formalism secondary. Ontological semantics has been developed on this principle. There is room for formalism in it: TMRs are completely formal, because they are defined syntactically using an explicit grammar, represented in Backus-Naur form (BNF), and semantically by reference to a constructed ontology (see chapter 6). The TMR formalism has been determined by the content of the material that must be described and by the goals of the implementations of ontological semantics. In an important sense, the difference between the two approaches is similar to that between imposing the formalism of mathematical logic on natural language and the short-lived attempts to discover "natural logic," the "inherent" logic underlying natural language (McCawley 1972; Lakoff 1972). While natural logic was never developed or applied, it provided an important impetus for our own work by helping us to understand that formality is independent of a formalism. In this light, we see the structures of ontological semantics as expressing what the natural logic movement could and should have contributed.

Going back to that first sense of formality, we effectively declare it a necessary condition for a theory and do not consider here any theories that do not aspire to be formal in that sense. In practice, this kind of formality means, among other things, that all terms have a single meaning throughout the theory, that there can be no disagreement among the various users about the meaning of a term or a statement, that each phenomenon in the purview is characterized by a term or a statement, and that every inference from a statement conforms to one of the rules (e.g., *modus ponens*) from a well-defined set.

We believe that the best result with regard to formality is achieved by some combination of formalism importation and formalism development. For instance, an imported formalism can be extended and modified to better fit the material. It might be said that this is how a variety of specialized logics (erotetic logic, modal logic, deontic logic, multivalued logic, fuzzy logic, and so on) have come into being. Each of these extended the purview of logic from indicative declarative utterances to questions, modalities, expressions of necessity, and so forth.

The idea of importing a powerful tool, such as a logic, has always been very tempting. However, logical semantics was faulted by Bar Hillel, himself a prominent logician and philosopher, for its primary focus on describing artificial languages. Bar Hillel believed that treatment of meaning can only be based on a system of logic: first, because, for him, only hypotheses formulated as logical theories had any scientific status and, second, because he believed that inference rules necessary, for instance, for machine translation, could only be based on logic. At the same time, he considered such logical systems *unattainable* because, in his opinion, they could not work directly on natural language, using instead one of a number of artificial logical notations. In his words,

The evaluation of arguments presented in a natural language should have been one of the major worries ... of logic since its beginnings. However, ... the actual development of formal logic took a different course. It seems that ... the almost general attitude of all formal logicians was to regard such an evaluation process as a two-stage affair. In the first stage, the original language formulation had to be rephrased, without loss, in a normalized idiom, while in the second stage, these normalized formulations would be put through the grindstone of the formal logic evaluator.... Without substantial progress in the first stage even the incredible progress made by mathematical logic in our time will not help us much in solving our total problem. (Bar Hillel 1970, 202–203)

2.4.1.5 Ambiguity This parameter deals with the following issue: Does the theory license equivalent (synonymous, periphrastic) descriptions of the same objects? On the one hand, it is simpler and therefore more elegant to allow a single description for each phenomenon in the purview, in which case the issue of alternative descriptions and their comparison simply does not arise. However enticing this policy might be, it is difficult to enforce in practice. On the other hand, the same phenomenon may be described in a more or less detailed way, thus leading to alternative descriptions differing in their grain size, which may be advantageous in special circumstances. The presence of alternative descriptions may, in fact, be helpful in an application. For instance, in machine translation, it may be desirable to have alternative descriptions of text meaning, because one of them may be easier for the generator to use in synthesizing the target text. From the point of view of a natural language sentence, the fact that it can be represented as two different TMRs is ambiguity. As far as TMRs are concerned, it is, of course, synonymy, or paraphrase. As we will demonstrate in section 6.6, the extant implementations of ontological semantics have never consciously allowed for TMR synonymy.

2.4.2 Parameters Related to the Methodology Associated with a Theory
Some parameters deal with methodologies. They are briefly reviewed in this section.

2.4.2.1 Methodology and Linguistic Theory Issues related to methodology in linguistic theory have been largely neglected, in part due to Chomsky's (1957, 50–53; 1965, 18–20) belief that no rigorous procedure of theory discovery was possible in principle and that methodological decisions involved in that activity were attained through trial and error and taking into account prior experience. What happens in the implementation of the linguistic theory methodologically apparently depends on its value on the parameter of effectiveness. In constructive theories, the methodological task is to see whether the ideal methodology that "comes with" a theory is executable directly or whether it should be replaced by a more efficient methodology. In linguistics, most constructive theories have relatively small purviews and simple bodies. A simplistic example, for illustration purposes only, would be a theory of feature composition (say, twenty-four features) for the phonemes (say, fifty in number) of a natural language.

Most linguistic theories, however, are nonconstructive and often ineffective—that is, there is no obvious algorithm for their realization in the sense of generating descriptions associated with the theory. Typically, methodological activity in such theories involves the search for a single rule to account for a phenomenon under consideration. After such a rule, say, that for cliticization, is formulated on a limited material, for instance, one natural language, it is applied to a larger set of similar phenomena, for instance, the clitics in other natural languages. Eventually, the rule is modified, improved, and accepted. Inevitably, in every known instance of this method at work, a hard residue of phenomena remains that cannot be accounted for by even the modified and improved rule. More seriously, however, the work on the rule in question never concerns itself with connecting to rules describing adjacent phenomena, thus precluding any comprehensive description of language. This amounts to neoatomicism: one rule at a time instead of the prestructuralist one phenomenon at a time. The expectation in such an approach is that all the other rules in language will fall in somehow with the one being described, an expectation never actually confirmed in an implementation. This is why, in its own implementations, ontological semantics develops microtheories, no matter how limited in purview, which are informed by the need to integrate them for the purpose of achieving a complete description.

In principle, linguistic theories profess to strive to produce complete descriptions of all the data in their purview. In practice, however, corners are cut—not that we are against or above cutting corners (e.g., under the banner of grain size); but they should be the appropriate corners, and they must not be too numerous. When faced with the abovementioned hard residue of data that does not lend itself to processing by the rule system proposed for the phenomenon in question, linguists typically use one of two general strategies. One is to focus on treating this hard residue at the expense of the "ordinary case." (The latter is assumed, gratuitously, to have been described fully.[16]) The other strategy is to discard the hard residue: by either declaring it out of the purview of the theory or by treating the incompleteness of the set of theoretical rules as methodologically acceptable. This latter option results in the ubiquity of etceteras at the end of rule sets or even in lists of values of individual phenomena in many linguistic descriptions.

Our experience has shown that focusing on borderline and exceptional cases often leaves the ordinary case underdescribed. Thus, for instance, in the literature on adjectival semantics, much attention has been paid to the phenomenon of relative adjectives developing a secondary qualitative meaning (e.g., *wooden* (table) > *wooden* (smile)). The number of such shifts in any language is limited. At the same time, as shown in Raskin and Nirenburg 1995, the scalar adjectives, which constitute one of the largest classes of adjectives in any language, are not described in literature much beyond an occasional observation that their meanings seem to involve a scale of sorts.

Describing the ordinary case becomes less important when the preferred model of scientific progress in linguistics stresses incremental improvement by focusing on one rule at a time. Exceptions to rules can, of course, be simply enumerated, with their properties described separately for each case. This way of describing data is known as extensional definition. The complementary way of describing data through rules is known as intensional. Intensional definitions are seen by theoretical linguists as more valuable because they promise to cover several phenomena in one go. In discussing the relations between theories, methodologies, and applications, we will show that the best methodology for a practical application should judiciously combine the intensional and extensional approach, so as to minimize resource expenditure (see section 2.5).

2.4.2.2 Methodology and AI   The somewhat shaky status of methodology in linguistic theory is an example of what can be termed a "subject-specific methodological problem" (Pandit 1991, 167–168). In AI, the other parent of NLP, we find modeling as the only methodological verity in the discipline. Under the "strong AI thesis" (we will use the formulation by the philosopher John Searle (1980, 353; see also Searle 1982a; cf. Searle 1997)), "the appropriately programmed computer really *is* a mind, in the sense that computers given the right programs can be literally said to understand and have other cognitive states," a claim that Searle ascribes to Turing (1950) and that forms the basis of the Turing test. We agree with Moody (1993, 79), that "it is an open question whether strong AI really does represent a commitment of most or many researchers in AI" (see also section 2.4.3).

So instead of modeling the mind itself, under the "weak AI thesis" "the study of the mind can be advanced by developing and studying computer models of various mental processes" (Moody 1993, 79–80). We part company with Moody, however, when he continues that "although weak AI is of considerable methodological interest in cognitive science, it is not of much philosophical interest" (p. 80). The whole point of this chapter is to show how the philosophical, foundational approach to NLP, viewed as a form of weak AI, enhances and enriches its practice.[17]

2.4.2.3 Methodology and the Philosophy of Science The philosophy of science does not have that much to say about the methodology of science. What is of general philosophical interest as far as methodological issues are concerned are the most abstract considerations about directions or goals of scientific research. Dilworth (1994, 50–51, 68–70), for instance, shows how immediately and intricately methodology is connected to and determined by ontology: without understanding how things are in the field of research it is impossible to understand what to do in order to advance the field. At this abstract level, the questions addressed in the philosophy of science are, typically, the essentialist "*'what*-questions' and explanatory-seeking '*why*-questions'" (Pandit 1991, 100), but not the *how*-questions that we will address in section 2.4.2.4 and again in section 2.5.

2.4.2.4 Methodology of Discovery: Heuristics One crucial category of *how*-questions, still of a rather abstract nature, has to do with discovery. In theoretical linguistics, this may be posed as the problem of grammar discovery: given a set of grammatical data—for example, a corpus—one sets out to discover a grammar that fits the data. Chomsky (1957) denies the possibility of achieving this goal formally. AI seems similarly skeptical about automatic discovery, not only of theory but even of heuristics: "The history of Artificial Intelligence shows us that heuristics are difficult to delineate in a clear-cut manner and that the convergence of ideas about their nature is very slow" (Groner, Groner, and Bischof 1983b, 16).

Heuristics have been variously described as "rules of thumb and bits of knowledge, useful (though not guaranteed) for making various selections and evaluations" (Newell 1983, 210), "strategic principles of demonstrated usefulness" (Moody 1993, 105), or in knowledge engineering for expert systems (see, for instance, Mitchie 1979; Forsyth and Rada 1986; Durkin 1994; Stefik 1995; Awad 1996; Wagner 1998), as "the informal judgmental rules that guide [the expert]" (Lenat 1983, 352). Heuristics are tools for the discovery of new knowledge. Over the centuries, they have been considered and presented as important road signs guiding human intelligence.

Heuristics as the art, or science, of discovery (and, therefore, used in the singular) is viewed as originating with Plato or even the Pythagoreans, who preceded him in the sixth century B.C.E. The field eventually concentrated on two major concepts, analysis and synthesis. The method of analysis prescribed the dissection of a problem, recursively, if necessary, into smaller and eventually familiar elements. Synthesis combined familiar elements to form a solution for a new problem. It is not so hard to recognize in these the contemporary top-down and bottom-up, or deductive and inductive, empirical approaches.

Later, heuristics was appropriated by mathematics and turned into a search for algorithms. Descartes (1908; see also Groner, Groner, and Bischof 1983a and

Attardo 1996) finalized this conception as twenty-one major heuristic rules applicable to problems presented algebraically. His more general heuristic recommendations call for a careful study of the problem until clear understanding is achieved; for the use of the senses, memory, and imagination; and for a great deal of practice solving problems that have already been solved by others.

More recently, heuristics has been adopted by the philosophy of science and has become more openly subject-specific than its new parent discipline. There are the heuristics of physics (e.g., Bolzano 1930; Zwicky 1957, 1966; Bunge 1967; Post 1971), psychology (e.g., Mayer and Orth 1901, Bühler 1907, and Müller 1911, all of the Würzburg School, as well as Selz 1935 and, most influentially, Duncker 1935), and, of course, mathematics, where Descartes was revived and Polya's work (1945, 1954, 1962, 1965) became influential if not definitive.

Newell (1983) brought Polya to the attention of the AI community and suggested that AI should model the four major problem-solving steps that Polya postulated— understanding the problem, devising a plan, carrying it out, and examining solutions (see Polya 1945; Newell 1983, 203)—in automatic systems of discovery and learning.[18] The heuristics of other disciplines look very much like Polya's recommendations. They helpfully dissect a potentially complex problem into small steps. They all fall short of explaining specifically, other than with the help of examples, how the dissection should be implemented and how each step is to be performed. It was this aspect of heuristics that led Leibniz (1880) to criticize Descartes and satirize his rules that were too general to be useful: "Sume quod debes et operare ut debes, et habebis quod optas" (Take what you have to take, and work the way you have to, and you will get what you are looking for) (vol. 4, 329; see also Groner, Groner, and Bischof 1983b, 6).

2.4.2.5 Practical Skills and Tools as Part of Methodology While the idea of heuristics has considerable appeal, we have to doubt its practical usefulness on at least two counts. First, our personal problem-solving experience seems to suggest that after the work is done it is not hard to identify, post hoc, some of Polya's steps in the way the solutions were reached.[19] In the process of solving the problems, however, we were not aware of these steps or of following them. Nor, to be fair, were we aware of operating combinatorially Leibniz's "alphabet of human thoughts," the basis of his "generative lexicon" of all known and new ideas (see, for instance, Leibniz 1880, vol. 1, 57, as well as Groner, Groner, and Bischof 1983b, 6–7). Nor did we count a great deal on insights, leading to a sudden and definitively helpful reorganization of a problem (cf. Köhler 1921; Wertheimer 1945).

We do see pedagogical value in Polya's and others' heuristics but we also realize, on the basis of our own experiences as students and teachers, that one cannot learn to do one's trade by heuristics alone. If we look at the few examples of linguistic work on heuristics, we discover, along with attempts to apply general heuristics to the specific field of language (Botha 1981; Pericliev 1990), some useful heuristics for linguistic description (Crombie 1985; Mel'čuk 1988; Raskin and Nirenburg 1995; Viegas and Raskin 1998). However, we fully recognize how much should be learned about the field prior to studying and attempting to apply the heuristics. Similarly, in AI, one should learn programming and algorithm design before attempting to devise heuristics. All these basic skills are part of methodology, though they have often been taken for granted or even considered as pure engineering skills in the philosophical discussions of methodology.

These actual skills are responses to the unpopular *how*-questions that the philosophy of science (or philosophy of language, for that matter, and philosophy in general) never actually asks. We agree with Leibniz's critique of Descartes from this point of view too: heuristics are answers to *what*-questions, but how about *how*?

What does a computational linguist need to know to do his or her work? An indirect answer can be: what they are taught in school. In other words, if what linguists are taught prepares them for plying the trade, then the contents of the linguistics courses are the skills that linguists need. The actual truth is, of course, that linguists end up discarding or at least ignoring a part of what they are taught and supplementing their skills with those acquired on their own.

As we have mentioned, a typical contemporary linguistic enterprise involves a study of how a certain system of grammar fits a phenomenon in a natural language and how the grammar may have to be modified to achieve a better match. This can vary to include a class of phenomena, a set of languages, or sometimes a comparison of two competing grammars. Somewhat simplistically, we can view such a linguistic task as requiring a grammatical paradigm—for instance, lexical-functional grammar—along with all the knowledge necessary for the complete understanding of the paradigm by the linguist. Also necessary are a native speaker of a language (or, alternatively, a representative corpus for the language), as well as algorithms for recognizing language phenomena as members of certain grammatical and lexical categories and of classes described by certain rules established by the paradigm.

In this view, the linguist starts with an empty template, as it were, provided by a grammatical system and finishes when the template is filled out by the material of the language described. Practically, of course, the research always deals with a limited set of phenomena, and then with specific features of that set. This limitation leads to the development of microtheories, in our terminology (see sections 1.7 and 2.4.4).

Similarly, an AI expert needs specific skills that he or she acquires in the process of training in computer science and/or directly in AI. This includes basic programming skills, familiarity with a number of programming languages, and modeling skills, involving the ability to build an architecture for an AI solution to a problem and knowledge of a large library of standard computer routines.

A complete methodology, then, includes both higher-level, at least partially heuristics-based ways of dissecting a new problem and lower-level disciplinary skills, sometimes—and certainly in the case of NLP—from more than one discipline. How does such a complete methodology interact with theory?

2.4.2.6 Disequilibrium between Theory and Methodology Within an established, ideal paradigm, one expects an equilibrium between the theory and methodology. The latter is also expected to determine the kind of descriptions needed to solve the problems and to achieve the goals of the field within that paradigm. Because no active discipline is complete and fully implemented, there is a continuous tug of war, as it were, between the theory of a field and its methodology. As more and more descriptions become necessary, the methodology must develop new tools to implement the expanded goals; as the implementation potential of the methodology grows it may lead to the implementation of new descriptions, and the theory may need to be expanded or modified to accommodate these gains.

In this creative disequilibrium, if the methodology, especially one based on a single method, is allowed to define the purview of a field, we end up with a ubiquitous method-driven approach. Chomskian linguistics is the most prominent example of it in linguistics, actively defining anything it cannot handle out of the field and having to revise the disciplinary boundaries for internal reasons, as its toolbox expands, and for external reasons, when it tries to incorporate the areas previously untouched by it or developed within a rival paradigm. The problem-driven approach, on the other hand, rejects the neatness of a single method on the grounds of principled unattainability. Instead, it must plunge headlong into the scruffiness of a realistic problem-solving situation, which always requires an ever-developing and expanding methodology, leading to inevitably eclectic, hybrid toolboxes.

2.4.2.7 Specific Methodology-Related Parameters Several specific parameters follow from the discussion in sections 2.4.2.1 through 2.4.2.6. The tension between theory building and goal-oriented description of phenomena creates the major parameter in this class, that of *method-driven* ("supply-side") versus *problem-driven* ("demand-side") approaches (see Nirenburg and Raskin 1996, 1999). Other parameters follow more or less obviously from the discussion in this section. If a theory is effective in the sense of section 2.4.1.2, it "comes" with a methodology but the methodology may be not *machine tractable*. Whether it is or not, constitutes another methodology-related parameter, this one limited to effective theories. A theory may come packaged with a set of clear subject-specific heuristics, and if it does, this is a value of yet another parameter, *heuristics availability*. A similarly formulated parameter concerns the availability of a clear set of *skills/tools* associated with the purview of the theory.

2.4.3 Parameters Related to the Status of Theory as Model of Human Behavior

A formal or computational theory may or may not make a claim that it is a model of a natural process. The best-known claim of this sort is the "strong AI hypothesis" (see also section 2.4.2.2) which sees AI "as relevant to psychology, insofar as [it takes] a computational approach to psychological phenomena. The essence of the computational viewpoint is that at least some, and perhaps all, aspects of the mind can be fruitfully described for theoretical purposes by using computational concepts" (Boden 1981, 71–72). Whether a theory makes *strong-hypothesis* claims constitutes a parameter.

This issue is actually an instance of the central question of the philosophy of science, namely, the status of theoretical categories and constructs with regard to reality, which we already touched on in the discussion of justification in section 2.3.4. While going over the extensive discussions of this issue in philosophical literature, we could not help wondering why we could not strongly identify our own theory of ontological semantics with any one of the rival positions. The most appealing position seems to be the least extreme one. A version of realism, it assumes a coexistence within the same theory of categories and constructs that exist in reality, on the one hand, and those that are products of the mind, on the other hand, as long as the statements about both kinds are coherent with each other.

We finally realized that the reason for our lack of strong identification, as well as for a halfhearted commitment to one of the positions, is that ontological semantics does not aspire to the status of a strong hypothesis. In other words, it does not claim any psychological reality. It does not claim that humans store word senses, concepts, or sentential meaning in the format developed in ontological semantics for the lexicon, ontology, or TMRs, respectively. Nor does this claim extend to equating in any way the processes of human understanding or production of sentences with the mechanisms for analysis and synthesis of texts in ontological semantics. We do not think that this takes away from the status of ontological semantics in the realm of science. It is, however, a potentially serious objection to our belief that ontological semantics is also a semantic theory of natural language.

2.4.4 Parameters Related to the Internal Organization of a Theory

When dealing with a purview of considerable size, the pure theorist may be driven away from the natural desire to put forward a single comprehensive theory by the sheer complexity of the task. The alternative strategy is to break the purview up into chunks, develop separate theories for each of them, and then to integrate them. This has been common practice in linguistics as well as in other disciplines, though the integration task received relatively little attention. Ontological semantics has undergone such chunking, too. In it, we call the components of the theory microtheories (see section 1.7). The microtheories can be circumscribed on the basis of a variety of approaches. There are microtheories devoted to language in general or particular languages; to different lexical categories, syntactic constructions, semantic and pragmatic phenomena, or any other linguistic category; to world-knowledge ("ontological") phenomena underlying semantic descriptions; and to any of the processes involved in analysis and generation of texts by computer.

2.4.5 Parameter Values and Some Theories

We believe that it would be useful to characterize and compare computational linguistic theories in terms of the parameters suggested above. Because we are not writing a handbook on the field, we will not discuss every known approach. That could have led to misunderstanding due to incompleteness of information, and—most seriously, as we indicated in section 2.4.1.3—the lack of theoretical explicitness of many approaches.[20] Besides, the parameters we suggested are not binary: rather, their multiple values seem to reflect a pretty complex "modal logic." An admittedly incomplete survey of the field of linguistic and computational semantics (see also Nirenburg and Raskin 1996) has yielded the parameter values listed as row headings in table 2.1. The columns of the table correspond to the tests for determining what value of a given parameter is assigned in a theory. To determine what value a parameter is to be assigned in theory X we should go, for each such candidate parameter, through the following test. The test consists of seven steps inquiring if

· The theory overtly addresses the parameter
· The theory develops it
· Addressing the parameter falls within the purview of the theory
· The parameter is possible in the theory
· The parameter is necessary for it
· The parameter is at all compatible with the theory
· The status of the parameter in the theory is at all determinable

For each parameter, the outcome of this test is a seven-element set of answers that together determine the value of this parameter. Each combination of answers is assigned a name. For example, the set "yes, yes, yes, yes, yes/no, yes, yes" is called DD—that is, this parameter is considered "declared and developed" in the theory. The names are used only as mnemonic devices. The interpretation of the actual labels is not important. What counts is the differences in the answer sets. The yes/no answer means that this test is not relevant for a given parameter value. Each named set of answers forms a row in table 2.1.

In almost direct contradiction to the bold statement in note 20, we proceed to illustrate in table 2.2, somewhat irresponsibly and as nonjudgmentally as possible, how the parameters introduced in this section apply to four sample theories, Bloom-

Table 2.1
Types of values for a parameter

	Declared by theory?	Developed in theory?	Within purview of theory?	Possible in theory?	Necessary for theory?	Compatible with theory?	Determinable in theory?
Declared, developed (DD)	yes	yes	yes	yes	yes/no	yes	yes
Declared, part-developed (DP)	yes	partially	yes	yes	yes/no	yes	yes
Declared, possible (DO)	yes	no	yes	yes	yes/no	yes	yes
Declared, nonpurview (DU)	yes	no	no	yes	no	yes/no	yes
Declared, purview (DR)	yes	no	yes	no	no	yes	yes
Impossible (IM)	yes/no	no	no	no	no	no	yes
Undeclared, possible, unnecessary (UU)	no	no	yes/no	yes	no	yes	yes
Undeclared, necessary (UN)	no	no	yes	yes	yes	yes	yes
Undeclared, part-developed (UP)	no	partially	yes	yes	yes/no	yes	yes
Indeterminable (IN)	yes/no	yes/no	yes/no	yes/no	yes/no	yes/no	no

Table 2.2
Illustration of parameter values and sample theories

Parameter\theory	Ad	Ef	Ex	Fy	Fm	Am	Md	Mt	Ha	Sh	Mi
Descriptive linguistics	UN	UN	IM	DD	UU	IN	DD	IM	IM	IM	UU
Standard theory	DP	DD	DP	DD	DD	UN	DD	IM	IM	DO	UU
Generative lexicon	UN	UN	UN	DD	DP	IN	DD	IN	IN	UU	UU
Ontological semantics	DP	DD	DD	DD	UU	DP	IM	DD	DP	UU	DP

field's (1933) descriptive (structuralist) linguistics, Chomsky's (1965) standard theory, Pustejovsky's (1995) generative lexicon, and ontological semantics. In doing so, we ignore yet another complication in assigning parameters to theories: that judgments about parameter values are often impossible to make with respect to an entire theory. Parameter values may refer only to some component of a theory and be undefined or difficult to interpret for other components.

What makes the parameterization of a theory complex is that the status of a theory with regard to each parameter may vary. The tests, in addition, are not necessarily independent of each other. Besides, the same parameter value named in the first column may correspond to several combinations of results of the parameter tests. Thus, because of all those yes/no values in the last row, the value of a parameter in a theory may be "Undeterminable (IN)" for 2^6 combinations of test-result situations of the parameter assigned that value in a theory.

The eleven parameters in table 2.2 are the ones listed and described in section 2.4.1.4, namely, adequacy (Ad), effectiveness (Ef), explicitness (Ex), formality (Fy), formalism (Fm), ambiguity (Am), method-drivenness (as opposed to problem-drivenness) (Md), machine tractability (Mt), heuristics availability (Ha), strong hypothesis (as in strong AI) (Sh), and internal organization as microtheories (Mi).

Table 2.2 claims then, for instance, that the generative lexicon theory does not address such parameters as adequacy, efficiency, and explicitness; it declares and develops formality and method-drivenness; it addresses and partially develops its formalism; it does not address its status with regard to the strong hypothesis and internal organization, the two unnecessary but possible parameters in this theory; and there is no information to help to determine its take on the theoretical parameters of ambiguity, machine tractability, and the availability of heuristics.

Ontological semantics, by contrast, addresses and develops effectiveness, explicitness, formality, and machine tractability; it addresses and partially develops adequacy, ambiguity, and availability of heuristics; it does not address such possible but unnecessary parameters as formalism and strong hypothesis, while method-drivenness is excluded.

In section 2.6, a more responsible and detailed illustration of the values of just one parameter, explicitness, will be presented using the material of ontological semantics—the one theory we can vouch for with some confidence.

2.5 Relations among Theory, Methodology, and Applications

In the sections above, we have discussed theories, their components, and their relations to methodology and description. In this section, we venture into the connections of theories with their applications.

2.5.1 Theories and Applications

Theories can be pursued for the sake of pure knowledge. Some theories can also be used in applications—in other words, they are applicable (or applied) theories. Applications are tasks whose main purpose is different from acquiring knowledge about the world of phenomena. Rather, applications usually have to do with tasks directed at creating new tools or other artifacts. We have preached (Nirenburg and Raskin 1987a, 1987c; Raskin 1987a, 1987b) and practiced (Raskin and Nirenburg 1995, 1996a, 1996b; Nirenburg and Raskin 1996, 1999) selective incorporation of components of linguistic theory into applied theories for natural language processing applications. Linguistic theories may contain categories, constructs and descriptions useful for concrete applications in full or at least in part. At the very least, reference to the sum of linguistic knowledge may help NLP practitioners avoid reinventing various wheels. The relations among theories, applications, and methodologies are summarized in figures 2.8 through 2.11. The findings hold not only for linguistic theories but for theories in general. There are, however, significant differences between applications and theoretical descriptions.

2.5.1.1 Difference 1: Goals   The first difference is in the goals of these pursuits. A theoretical linguistic description aims at modeling human-language competence. Developing, say, a grammar of Tagalog qualifies as this kind of pursuit. By contrast, developing a learner's grammar or a textbook of Tagalog would be typical applications. The practical grammar or a textbook may include material from the theoretical grammar for the task of teaching Tagalog as a foreign language. This utilitarian applicational task is different from the descriptive theoretical task. An application is a system (often, a computational system) developed to perform a specific constructive task, not to explain a slice of reality. As such, it is also an engineering notion.

From the methodological point of view, the work on theoretical descriptions does not have to be completed before work on applications based on them can start. The learner's grammar may be shorter and cruder than a theoretical grammar and still succeed in its application. In practice, an application may precede a theoretical

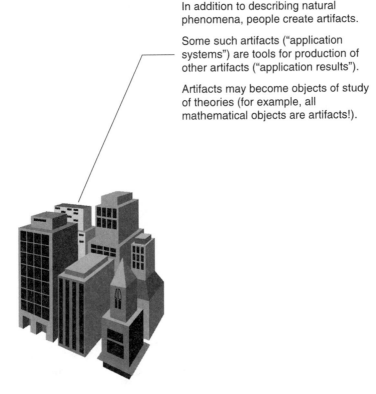

In addition to describing natural
phenomena, people create artifacts.

Some such artifacts ("application
systems") are tools for production of
other artifacts ("application results").

Artifacts may become objects of study
of theories (for example, all
mathematical objects are artifacts!).

Figure 2.8
Applications and some of their characteristics.

description and even provide an impetus for it. In fact, the history of research and
development in machine translation (an application field) and theoretical computational linguistics is a prime example of exactly this state of affairs, where necessity (as
understood then) was the mother of invention (of computational linguistic theories).

2.5.1.2 Difference 2: Attitude toward Resources The second difference between
theories and applications is in their relation to the issue of resource availability. A
theory is free of resource considerations and implies unlimited resources (expense,
time, space, anything). In fact, implementing a linguistic theory can very well be
considered an infinite task. Indeed, linguists have worked for several centuries
describing various language issues but still have not come up with a complete and
exhaustive description of any language or dialect, down to every detail of reasonable granularity. There are always things remaining to be concretized or researched.
Complete description remains, however, a declared goal of science. Infinite pursuit of

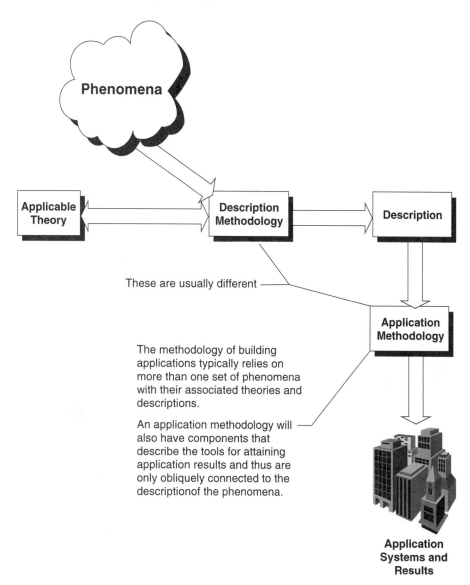

Figure 2.9
Some properties of application methodology.

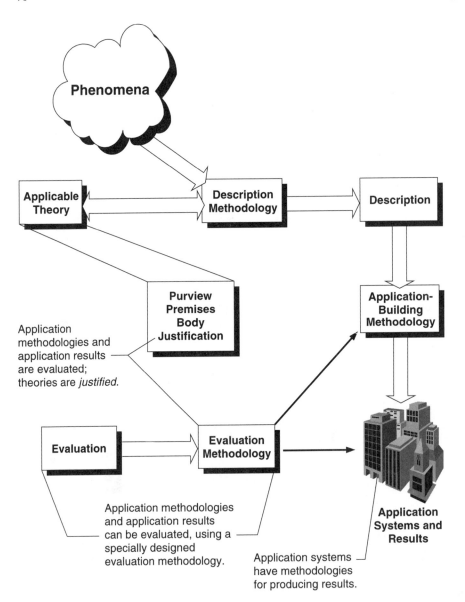

Figure 2.10
More types of methodologies: evaluation methodology and methodology of running applications, as opposed to the methodology of building applications.

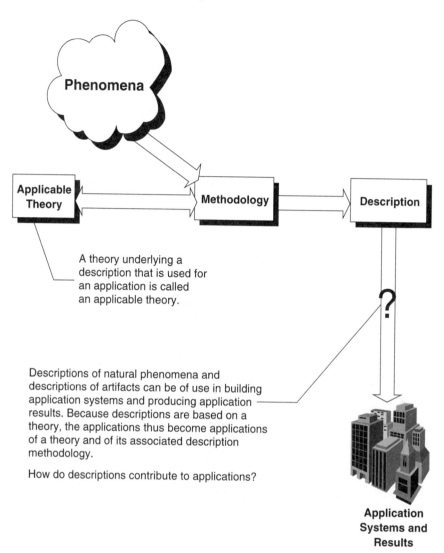

Phenomena

Applicable Theory

Methodology

Description

A theory underlying a description that is used for an application is called an applicable theory.

Descriptions of natural phenomena and descriptions of artifacts can be of use in building application systems and producing application results. Because descriptions are based on a theory, the applications thus become applications of a theory and of its associated description methodology.

How do descriptions contribute to applications?

Application Systems and Results

Figure 2.11
Introducing a different type of methodology.

a complete theory seems to be a right guaranteed by a Ph.D. diploma, just as pursuit of happiness is an inalienable right guaranteed by the U.S. Constitution.

In contrast to this, any high-quality application in linguistics requires a complete[21] description of the sublanguage necessary for attaining this application's purpose (e.g., a Russian-English MT system for texts in the field of atomic energy). By introducing resource-driven constraints, an application turns itself into a finite problem. A corresponding change in the methodology of research must ensue: concrete application-oriented methodologies crucially depend on resource considerations. Thus, in a computational application, the machine tractability of a description, totally absent in theoretical linguistics (see note 13), becomes crucial. The above implies that methodologies for theoretical descriptions are usually different from application-oriented methodologies.

2.5.1.3   Difference 3: Evaluation   Yet another difference is that theories must be *justified* in the sense described above, while applications must be *evaluated* by comparing their results with human performance on the same task or, alternatively, with results produced by other applications. This means, for instance, that a particular learner's grammar of Tagalog can be evaluated as being better than another, say, by comparing examination grades of two groups of people who used the different grammars in their studies. No comparable measure can be put forward for a theoretical description.

2.5.2   Blame Assignment
An interesting aspect of evaluation is the difficult problem of "blame assignment": when the system works less than perfectly, it becomes desirable to pinpoint which component or components of the system is to blame for the substandard performance. Knowing how to assign blame is one of the most important diagnostic tools in system debugging. Because this task is very hard, the real reasons certain complex computational applications actually work or do not work are difficult to establish. As a result, many claims concerning the basis of a particular application in a particular theory cannot be readily proved. It is this state of affairs that led Wilks (1992, 279) to formulate (only partially in jest) the following "principle": "There is no theory of language structure so ill-founded that it cannot be the basis for some successful MT." To extend this principle, even a theory that is seriously flawed, a theory that is not consistent or justifiable, and that is infeasible and ineffective, can still contribute positively to an application.

The situation is further complicated by the fact that applications are rarely based exclusively on a single linguistic theory that was initially used as its basis. The modifications made in the process of building an application may, as we mentioned before, significantly change the nature of the theory components and parameters.

Elements of other theories may find their way into an implementation. And finally, the developers may make important decisions that are not based on any overtly stated theory at all.[22]

2.5.3   Methodologies for Applications
Methodologies for applications differ from methodologies associated with theories.

2.5.3.1   "Purity" of Methodology   An important methodological distinction between theories and applications has to do with the debate between method-oriented and problem-oriented approaches to scientific research (cf. section 2.4.2.7 as well as Nirenburg and Raskin 1999 and Lehnert 1994). While it is tenable to pursue both approaches in working on a theory, applications, simply by their nature, instill the primacy of problem-orientedness. Every "pure" method is limited in its applicability, and in the general case, its purview may not completely cover the needs of an application. Fidelity to empirical evidence and simplicity and consistency of logical formulation are usually taken as the most general desiderata of scientific method, fidelity to the evidence taking precedence in cases of conflict (cf. Caws 1967, 339). An extension of these desiderata into the realm of application may result in the following methodological principle: Satisfaction of the needs of the task and simplicity and consistency of the mechanism for its attainment are the most general desiderata of applied scientific work, with the satisfaction of the needs of the task taking precedence in cases of conflict.

2.5.3.2   Solutions Are a Must, Even for Unsolvable Problems   In many cases, application tasks in NLP do not have proven methods that lead to their successful implementation. Arguably, some applications include tasks that are not solvable in principle. A well-known example of reasoning along these lines is Quine's (1960) demonstration of the impossibility of translation between natural languages. Quine introduces a situation in which a linguist and an informant work on the latter's native language when a rabbit runs in front of them. The informant points to the rabbit and says *gavagai*. Quine's contention is that there is no way for the linguist to know that this locution should be translated into English as "rabbit" or "inalienable rabbit part" or "rabbitting." For a translation theorist, the acceptance of Quine's view may mean giving up on a theory. A machine-translation application will not be affected by this contention in any way. Quine and the linguistic theorist do not face the practical need to build a translation system; an MT application does. It must produce a translation—that is, find a working method—even in the absence of theoretical input.

A reasonable interpretation of Quine's claim is that no translation is possible without some loss of meaning. The truth of this tenet is something that every practical translator already knows from experience, and a number of devices have been used by human and even some machine translators to deal with this eventuality. Ample criticism has been leveled at Quine for this claim from a variety of quarters (Katz 1978, 209—see also Katz 1972/1974, 18–24; Frege 1963, 1; Tarski 1956, 19–21; Searle 1969, 19–21; Nirenburg and Goodman 1990; cf. section 9.3.6). A recent proposal in the philosophy of science can be used to reject Quine's claim on purely philosophical grounds. It states that "what makes a particular activity scientific is not that the reality it uncovers meets the ideal, but that its deviation from the ideal is always something to be accounted for" (Dilworth 1996, 4). In other words, unattainability of a theoretical ideal means not that the theory should be given up but that it should be supplemented by statements explaining the deviations of reality from the ideal. If this is true of theoretical pursuits, it is a fortiori so for applications.

2.5.4 Aspects of Interactions among Theories, Applications, and Methodologies
Theories, applications, and methodologies interact in interesting ways.

2.5.4.1 Explicit Theory Building How do theory, methodology, and applications actually interact? One way of thinking about this is to observe the way computational linguists carry out their work in constructing theories, methodologies, and applications. This is a difficult task because, in writing about their work, people understandably prefer to concentrate on results, not on the process of their own thinking.[23] Katz and Fodor (1963) provide one memorable example of building a theory by overtly stating the reasoning about how to carve out the purview of the theory to exclude the meaning of the sentence in context.[24] But they are in a pronounced minority. One reason for that, both in linguistics and in other disciplines, is a pretty standard division of labor between philosophers and scientists. The former are concerned about the foundational aspects of the disciplines and do not do primary research; the latter build and modify theories and do not deal with foundational issues.[25]

2.5.4.2 Partial Interactions When one analyzes the influence of theory on methodology and applications, it quickly becomes clear that often it is not an entire theory but only some of its components that have a direct impact on a methodology or an application. Some methods—for example, the well-established ones of field linguistics (see, for instance, Samarin 1967; Bouquiaux and Thomas 1992; Payne 1997)—rely essentially on some premises of a theory (e.g., "the informant's response to questions of the prescribed type is ultimate") but not really on any universally accepted body. Different field linguists will have different approaches to, for instance, syntax or morphology, which would be reflected in differences in the questions to the informant but not necessarily in differences among the discovered phenomena.

2.5.4.3 Theoretical Premises Pertaining to Applications   One premise of computational linguistic theory pertaining directly to the methodology of application building is that whenever successful and efficient *automatic* methods can be developed for a task, they are preferred over those involving humans. Another premise, which is probably quite universal among the sciences, is that if a *single method* can do the task, it is preferable to a combination of methods because combining methods can usually be done only at the cost of modifying them in some way to make them co-exist. This premise is in opposition to yet another one: that recognizing theoretical overlaps between a new task and a previously accomplished one can save resources because some methods can be *reused*.

Yet another premise states that the need to create a *successful application* is more basic than the desire to do it using a single, automatic, logically consistent, and economical method. This tenet forces application builders to use a mixture of different techniques when a single technique does not deliver. But, additionally, when gaps remain, for which no adequate method can be developed, this tenet may lead application builders to using nonautomatic methods as a way of guaranteeing success of an application. In practice, at the commercial end of the spectrum of comprehensive computational linguistic applications, a combination of human and automatic methods is a rule rather than an exception, as is witnessed in many systems of human-aided machine translation, "workstations" for a variety of human analysts, and so on.

Finally, there is the *resource* premise: applications must be built within the available resources of time and human effort and can only be considered successful if producing results in these applications is also cost-effective in terms of resource expenditure. This premise is quite central for all applications, while in purely theoretical work it is of marginal importance. This is where it becomes clear that the theory underlying an application may vary from a theory underlying regular academic research motivated only by the desire to discover how things are.

2.5.4.4 Constraints on Automation   It is often resource-related concerns that bring human resources into an otherwise automatic system. Why specifically may human help within a system be necessary? Given an input, a computational linguistic application engine would produce application results algorithmically. That is, at each of a finite number of steps in the process, the system will know what to do and what to do next. If these decisions are made with less than complete certainty, the process becomes heuristic (see also section 2.4.2.4). Heuristics are by definition defeasible. Moreover, in text processing, some inputs will always be unexpected—that is, such that solutions for some phenomena contained in them have not been thought through beforehand. This means that predetermined heuristics are bound to fail, in some cases. If this state of affairs is judged unacceptable, then two options present themselves to the application builders: to use an expandable set of dynamically modifiable heuristics to suit an unexpected situation (as most AI programs would like to but typically are still unable to do) or to resort to a human "oracle."

2.5.4.5   Real-Life Interactions   Irrespective of whether applications drive theories or theories license applications, it is fair to suppose that all research work starts with the specification of a task (of course, a task might be to investigate the properties of an application or a tool). The next thing may be to search for a methodology to carry this task out. This imported methodology may be general or specific, depending on the task and on the availability of a method developed for a different task but looking promising for the one at hand. A converse strategy is to start with developing an application methodology and then look for an application for it. An optional interim step here may be building a theory prior to looking for applications, but normally, the theory emerges immediately as the format of descriptions/results produced by the methodology.

2.5.5   Examples of Interactions among Theories, Applications, and Methodologies
Of course, this discussion may be regarded as somewhat too general and as belaboring the obvious, even if one goes into further detail on the types of theories, methodologies, and applications that can interact in various ways. However, several examples can help to clarify the issues.

2.5.5.1   Statistics-Based Machine Translation   Let us start, briefly, with statistics-based machine translation. The name of this area of computational linguistic study is a convenient combination of the name of an application with the name of a method. The best developed effort in this area is the MT system Candide, developed at IBM Yorktown Heights Research Center (Brown et al. 1990).

It is not clear whether the impetus for its development was the desire to use a particular set of methods—already well established in speech processing by the time work on Candide started—for a new application, MT, or whether the methods were selected after the task was posited. The important point is that from the outset, Candide imported a method into a new domain. The statistical methods used in Candide (the trigram modeling of language, the source-target alignment algorithms, the Bayesian inference mechanism, and so on) were complemented by a specially developed theory. The theory was of text translation, not of language as a whole, and it essentially provided methodological guidelines for Candide. It stated, roughly, that the probability of a target language string T being a translation of a source language string S is proportional to the product of the probability that T is a legal string in the target language and the probability that S is a translation of T. In such a formulation, these statements belong to the body of the theory, premised on a statement that probability (and frequency of strings in a text) affect its translation.

The task has been methodologically subdivided into two, corresponding to establishing the probabilities on the right-hand side of the theoretical equation. For each of these subtasks, a complete methodology was constructed. It relied, among other things, on the availability of a very large bilingual corpus. In fact, had such a corpus not been available, it should have been constructed for the statistical translation methodology to work. And this would have drawn additional resources, in this case, possibly rendering the entire methodology inapplicable. As it happened, the methodology initially selected by Candide did not succeed in producing results of acceptable quality, due to the complexity of estimating the various probabilities used in the system and the rather low accuracy of the statistical models of the target language and of the translation process. To improve the quality of the output, the Candide project modified its methodology by incorporating versions of morphological and syntactic analysis and some other computational linguistic methods into the process. As a result, the quality of Candide output came closer to, though never quite equaled, that of the best rule-based MT systems. The hybridization of the approach has never been given any theoretical status. Simply put, in addition to the statistical theory of MT, Candide now (consciously or not) employed the theory underlying the morphological and syntactic analyzers and their respective lexicons. The application-building methodology has been modified in order to better satisfy the needs of an application. Had the Candide effort continued beyond 1995, it might have changed its methodology even further, in hopes of satisfying these needs.

2.5.5.2 Quick Ramp-Up Machine Translation Developer System As another example, let us briefly consider the case of the project Expedition, under development at NMSU CRL from 1997 to 2001. The project's stated objective is to build an environment (that is, a tool, or an implemented methodology) that will allow fast development, by a small team with no trained linguist on it, of moderate-level machine translation capabilities from any language into English. As a resource-saving measure, the system is encouraged to make use of any available tool and/or resource that may help in this task. As specified, this application is a metatool, a system to help build systems.

Once the objectives of the application have been stated, several methodologies could be suggested for it. These methodologies roughly fall into two broad classes—the essentially corpus-based and the essentially knowledge-based[26] ones. The reasoning favoring the corpus-based approach is as follows. Because the identity of the source language is not known beforehand, and preparing for all possible source languages is well beyond any available resources, the easiest thing to do for a new source language is to collect a corpus of texts in it and apply to it the statistical tools that are becoming increasingly standard in the field of computational linguistics: text segmentors for languages that do not use breaks between words, part-of-speech taggers, grammar-induction algorithms, word-sense disambiguation algorithms, and so on. If a sizable parallel corpus of the source language and English can be obtained, then a statistics-based machine-translation engine could be imported and used in the project. However, the corpus-based work, when carried out with purity of method, is usually not devoted to complete applications, while when it is (as in the case of Candide), it requires a large dose of "conventional" language descriptions and system components.

The reasoning favoring the knowledge-based approach is as follows. Because the target language in the application is fixed, a considerable amount of work can be prepackaged: the target application can be supplied with the English text generator and the English side of the lexical and structural transfer rules for any target language. Additionally, both the algorithms and grammar and lexicon writing formats for the source language can be largely fixed beforehand. What remains is facilitating the acquisition of knowledge about the source language, its lexical stock, its grammar, and its lexical and grammatical correspondences to English. This is not an inconsiderable task. The variety of means of realization for lexical and grammatical meanings in natural languages is notoriously broad. For many languages, published grammars and machine-readable monolingual and bilingual dictionaries exist, but their use in computational applications, as practice in computational linguistics has shown (see, for instance, Amsler 1984; Boguraev 1986; Evens 1988; Wilks et al. 1990; Guo 1995), requires special resource expenditure, not incomparable to that for building an NLP system.

Creating the knowledge for natural language processing applications has occupied computational linguists for several generations, and has proved to be quite an expensive undertaking, even when the knowledge acquirers are well trained in the formats and methods of description and equipped with the best corpus-analysis and interface tools. Considering that the users of the knowledge-elicitation tool will not be trained linguists and also taking into account that the time allotted for developing the underlying application (the machine-translation system) is limited, the "traditional" approach to knowledge acquisition (notably, with the acquirer initiating all activity) has never been a viable option. The best methodological solution, under the circumstances, is to develop an interactive system that guides the acquirer through the acquisition steps—in fact, an automatic system for language knowledge elicitation of the field-linguistics type. The difficulties associated with this methodology centrally include its novelty (no linguistic knowledge-acquisition environment of this kind has ever been attempted) and the practical impossibility of anticipating every phenomenon in every possible source language.

The field of computational linguistics as a whole has, for the past five years or so, devoted a significant amount of effort to finding ways to mix corpus- and rule-based methods, in the spirit of the central methodological principle for building applications discussed above.[27] The Expedition project is no exception. However, based on the expected availability of resources (the project's main thrust is toward processing the less described, "low-density" languages) and on the generality of the task, the "classical" computational linguistic methodology was selected as the backbone of the project. A separate study has been launched into how to "import" any existing components for processing a source language into the Expedition system.

Because no trained linguists will participate in the acquisition of knowledge about the source language, it was decided that, for pedagogical reasons, the work would proceed in two stages: first, the acquisition (elicitation) of a computationally relevant description of the language; then the development of rules for processing inputs in that language, using processing modules that would be resident in the system. In both tasks, the system will hold much of the control initiative in the process. In order to do so, the elicitation system (in Expedition, it is called *Boas*, honoring Franz Boas (1858–1942), the founder of American descriptive linguistics, as well as a prominent anthropologist) must know what knowledge must be elicited. For our purposes in this chapter, a discussion of the first of the two tasks will suffice. (For a more detailed discussion of Boas, see Nirenburg 1998a; Nirenburg and Raskin 1998; McShane et al. 2002.)

The great variety of categories and expressive means in natural languages (as illustrated, for instance, by the complexity of tools and handbooks for field linguistics) is a major obstacle for Boas. A priori, the creation of a complete inventory of language features does not seem to be a realistic task. The goal of carrying this task through to a concrete, systematic, and applicable level of description is not attained—and not always attempted or even posited as an objective—by the workers in the areas of linguistic universals and universal language parameters (see, for instance, Greenberg 1978; Chomsky 1981; Berwick and Weinberg 1984; Webelhuth 1992; Dorr 1993; Dorr et al. 1995; Kemenade and Vincent 1997). Methodologically, therefore, three choices exist for Boas: a data-driven method, a top-down, parameter-driven method, and some combination of these methods. As it happens, the last option is taken, just as in the case of the choice of corpus- or rule-based methodology for Expedition.

The data-driven, bottom-up strategy works in Boas, for example, for the acquisition of the source-language lexicon, where a standard set of English word senses is given to the acquirer for translation into the source language.[28] The top-down, parameter-oriented strategy works in elicitation of the morphological and syntactic categories of the language, together with their values and means of realization. Sometimes these two strategies clash. For example, if closed-class lexical items, such as prepositions, are extracted in the lexicon, it is desirable (in fact, essential) for the purposes of further processing not only to establish their translations into English (or, in accordance with the Boas methodology, their source-language translations, based on English) but also their semantics, in terms of what relation they realize (e.g., directional, temporal, possession, and so on). This is needed for disambiguating prepositions in translation (a notoriously difficult problem in standard syntax-oriented approaches to translation). In languages where the category of grammatical case is present, prepositions often "realize" the value of case jointly with case endings. For instance, in Russian, *s*+Genitive realizes a spatial relation of downward direction, with the emphasis on the origin of motion, as in "He jumped off the table"; *s*+Accusative realizes the comparative meaning: "It was as large as a house"; while *s*+Instrumental realizes the relation of "being together with": "John and/together with Bill went to the movies" (see, for example, Nirenburg 1980 for further discussion).

Under the given methodological division, however, Boas will acquire knowledge about case in the top-down, parameter-oriented way and information about prepositions in the bottom-up, data-driven way. For Russian, for instance, this knowledge will include the fact that the language features the parameter of case, that this parameter has six values, and that these values are realized through inflectional morphology by suffixation, with the major inflectional paradigms listed. To reconcile the two approaches in this case, the lexical acquisition of prepositions for languages with grammatical case will have to include a question about what case form(s) a given preposition can introduce.

Note that, throughout this discussion, a particular theory of language was assumed, because most of the categories, values, realizations, and forms used in the descriptions have been introduced in a theory, while work on Boas has essentially systematized and coordinated these theoretical concepts, adding new concepts mostly when needed for completeness of description. This is why, for example, the lists of potential values for the theoretical parameters adopted in Boas (such as case, number, syntactic agreement, and others) are usually longer than those found in grammar books for individual languages and even general grammar books: the needs of the application necessitate extensions. Thus, for instance, the set of potential values of case in Boas includes more members than the list of sample cases in Blake 1994, even if one does not count name proliferation in different case systems for essentially the same cases.[29]

For the purposes of this chapter, a central point of the above discussion is the analysis of the reasoning of the application builders. After some general methodological decisions were made, existing theories of language knowledge processing were consulted, namely, the theories underlying the methodology of field linguistics and those underlying the study of universals. Their utility and applicability to the task at hand were assessed and, as it happened, certain modifications were suggested in view of the peculiarities of the application. Of course, it was possible to "reinvent" these approaches to language description. However, the reliance on prior knowledge both saved time and gave the approaches used in the work on Boas a theoretical point of reference. Unfortunately, the actual descriptions produced by the above linguistic theories are of only oblique use in the application under discussion.

Boas itself is a nice example, on which one can see how theory, methodology, description, and application interact. The parameters for language description developed for Boas belong to the *body* of the theory underlying it. The general application-oriented methodological decisions (discussed above in terms of availability and nature of resources), together with the various specially developed front-end and back-end tools and procedures, constitute the *methodology* of Boas. The knowledge elicited from the user by Boas is the *description*. The resulting system is an *application*. Overt reasoning about methodology and theories helped in the formulation of Boas and Expedition. One can realistically expect that such reasoning will help other computational linguistic projects, too.

2.6   Using the Parameters

In this section, we discuss, by way of selective illustration, how the philosophical approach proposed here has been used to characterize and analyze ontological semantics. We concentrate on a single parameter: explicitness. Additionally, because of the four constituent parts (purview, premises, justification, and body) of a theory, the body is, by nature, the most explicit (indeed, it is the only constituent described in most computational linguistic contributions), we will concentrate here on the other three constituents. A detailed statement about the body of ontological semantics is the subject of part II of this book. Details about its various implementations have been published and are cited throughout the book. To summarize, the analysis part of ontological semantic implementations interprets input sentences in a source language as meaning-rich text-meaning representations (TMRs), written in a metalanguage whose terms are based on an independent ontology. Word meanings are anchored in the ontology. The procedure of analysis relies on the results of ecological, morphological, and syntactic analysis and disambiguates and amalgamates the meanings of lexical items in the input into a TMR "formula." The generation module takes the TMR, possibly augmented through reasoning over the ontology and the fact repository, as input and produces natural language text for human consumption.

The main purpose of the discussion that follows is to articulate what it takes to go from relying on a covert, uncognized theory underlying any linguistic research, however application-oriented by design, to an inspectable, overt statement of the theoretical underpinnings of such an activity. This discussion is motivated and licensed by the conclusions about the benefits of using theory from section 2.2.

2.6.1 Purview

The purview of ontological semantics is meaning in natural language. Meaning in ontological semantics can be static or dynamic. The former resides in lexical units (morphemes, words, or phrasals) and is made explicit through their connections to ontological concepts. Dynamic meaning resides in representations of textual meaning (that is, meaning of clauses, sentences, paragraphs, and larger text units), produced and manipulated by the processing components of the theory. The theory, in effect, consists of a specification of how, for a given text, (static, context-independent) meanings of its elements (words, phrases, bound morphemes, word order, and so on) are combined into a (dynamic, context-dependent) text-meaning representation, and vice versa. This is achieved with the help of static knowledge resources and processing components. The theory recognizes four types of static resources:

- An *ontology*, a language-independent compendium of information about the concepts underlying elements of natural language
- A *fact repository* (FR), a language-independent repository of remembered instances of ontological concepts
- A *lexicon*, containing information, expressed in terms of ontological concepts, about lexical items, both words and phrasals
- An *onomasticon*, containing names and their acronyms

The knowledge supporting the ecological, morphological, and syntactic processing of texts is "external" to ontological semantics. Much of the knowledge necessary for carrying out these three types of processing resides outside the static resources of ontological semantics—in morphological and syntactic grammars and ecological rule sets. However, some of this information actually finds its way into the ontological semantic lexicon—for example, to support linking.

The analyzer and the generator of text are the main text-processing components. The reasoning module is the main application-oriented engine that manipulates TMRs. The term *dynamic*, therefore, relates simply to the fact that there are no static repositories of contextual knowledge, and the processing modules are responsible for deriving meaning in context. A broader sense of dynamicity is that it serves the compositional property of language, having to do with combining meanings of text elements into the meaning of an entire text.

In the above view, the purview of ontological semantics includes that of formal semantics, which covers, in our terms, much of the grammatical meaning and parts of text-meaning representation and adds the purview of lexical semantics. While the purview of ontological semantics is broader than that of formal semantics or lexical semantics, it is by no means unlimited. It does not, for instance, include, in the specification of the meaning of objects, any knowledge that is used by perception models for recognizing these objects in the real world.

2.6.2 Premises

In this section, we discuss several premises of ontological semantics and, whenever possible and to the best of our understanding, compare them with related premises of other theories. The premises we mention certainly do not form a complete set. Ontological semantics shares some premises with other scientific theories and many premises with other theories of language.

2.6.2.1 Premise 1: Meaning Should Be Studied and Represented

At the risk of sounding trivial or tautological, we will posit the first premise of ontological semantics as: "Meaning should be studied and represented." This follows directly from the purview of our theory. We share the first part of the premise, that meaning should be studied, with all semanticists and philosophers of language and with knowledge-based strains in AI NLP, but not with the linguists and computational linguists who constrain their interest to syntax or other areas.

We assume that meaning can and should be represented. We share this premise with most schools of thought in linguistics, AI, and philosophy. Notable exceptions include late Wittgenstein and the ordinary language philosophy (Wittgenstein 1953, I.10ff, especially 40 and 43; Ryle 1949, 1953; Grice 1957; Austin 1961a—see also Caton 1963; Chapell 1964) as well as some contributions within connectionism (see, for instance, Brooks 1991; Clark 1994), whose initial antirepresentationalism has been in retreat since Fodor and Pylyshyn's (1988) challenge (e.g., Horgan and Tienson 1989, 1994; Pollack 1990; Berg 1992). Note that issues of the nature and the format of representation, such as levels of formality and/or machine tractability, belong in the body of the theory (see note 13 and section 2.4.1.4) and are, therefore, not discussed here.

2.6.2.2 Premise 2: The Need for Ontology

Ontological semantics does not have a strong stance concerning connections of meanings to the outside world (denotation, or extension relations). It certainly does not share the implicit verificationist premise of formal semanticists that the ability to determine the truth value of a statement expressed by a sentence equals the ability to understand the meaning of the sentence. One result of this difference is our lack of enthusiasm for truth values as semantic tools, at least for natural language, and especially as the exclusive tool of anchoring linguistic meanings in reality.

Unlike Wittgenstein or Wilks (e.g., 1972, 1982, 1992; Nirenburg and Wilks 1997), we still recognize as a premise of ontological semantics the existence of an (intensional) ontological signification level that defines not only the format but also the vocabulary (the metalanguage) of meaning description. While this level is distinct from denotation (it is not directly a part of the outside world), it is also distinct from language itself.

In ontological semantics, the English expressions *Morning star* and *Evening star* will both be mapped into an instance of the ontological concept PLANET, namely, VENUS, which is stored in the fact repository, while the corresponding English word *Venus* is listed in the English onomasticon (see section 2.6.1). The fact-repository entry VENUS, in turn, is an instance of the ontological concept PLANET. It is this latter type of general concept that is the ultimate source of meaning for most individual open-class lexical units in ontological semantics.

Computational ontology, in its constructive, operational form as a knowledge base residing in computer memory, is not completely detached from the outside world, so that a variation of the familiar word-meaning-thing triangle (Ogden and Richards 1923; Stern 1931; Ullman 1951; Zvegintzev 1957) is still applicable here. The relation of the ontology to the outside world is imputed by the role ontological semantics assigns to human knowledge of the language and of the world—namely, to interpret elements of the outside world and encode their properties in an ontology. As a corollary, the image of the outside world in ontological semantics includes entities that do not "exist" in the narrow sense of existence used in formal semantics; in this, we agree with Hirst (1991), where he follows Meinong (1904) and Parsons (1980).

For ontological semantics in action, the above triangular relation typically takes the form of sentence-meaning-event, where meaning is a statement in the text-meaning representation (TMR) language and EVENT is an ontological concept. But ontological semantics is not completely solipsistic. The connection between the outside world (the realm of extension) and ontological semantics (the realm of intension) is carried out through the mediation of the human acquirer of the static knowledge sources.[30] This can be illustrated by the following example. The ontology contains a complex event MERGER, with two companies as its participants and a detailed list of component events, some of which are contingent on other components. In ontological semantics, this is a mental model of this complex event, specifically, a model of "how things can be in the world." Ontological semantics in operation uses such mental models to generate concrete mental models about specific mergers—that is, "what actually happened" or even "what could happen" or "what did not happen."

These latter models are not necessarily fleeting (even though a particular application of ontological semantics may not need such models once they are generated and used). In ontological semantics, they can be recorded as "remembered instances" in the knowledge base and used in subsequent NLP processing. Thus, for MERGER, remembered instances will include a description of the merger of Exxon and Mobil or of Chrysler and Daimler-Benz. The remembered instances are intensional because they add a set of agentive, spatiotemporal, and other "indices" to a complex event from the ontology.

We share with formal semanticists the concern for relating meaning to the outside world (cf. Lewis's 1972 concern about "Markerese"), but we use a different tool for making this relation operational, namely, an ontology instead of truth values (see, for instance, Nirenburg, Raskin, and Onyshkevych 1995). We basically accept the premises of mental-model theorists (e.g., Johnson-Laird 1983; Fauconnier 1985) that such models are necessary for semantic description, in particular, for accommodating entities that do not exist in the material sense. However, we take their concerns one step forward in that we actually construct the mental models in the ontology and the knowledge base of remembered instances.

We agree with the role Wittgenstein and Wilks assign to the real world—that is, the lack of its direct involvement in the specification of meaning. We diverge from them in our preference for a metalanguage that is distinct from natural language in the definitions of its lexical and syntactic units. Our position is explained by our desire to make meaning representation machine-tractable—that is, capable of being processed by computers. This desideratum does not obtain in the Wittgenstein/Wilks theoretical approach, whose motto, "meaning is other words," seems, at least for practical purposes, to lead to a circularity, simply because natural language is notoriously difficult to process by computer, and this latter task is, in fact, the overall purpose and the starting point of the work in the field. Note that, in his practical work, Wilks, a founder of computational semantics, does not, in fact, assume such a strong stance and does successfully use non–natural language semantic representations (e.g., Wilks and Fass 1992a).

This deserves, in fact, some further comment, underscoring the difference between Wilks, the application builder, and Wittgenstein (and possibly Wilks again), the theorist(s). The later Wittgenstein claim that "meaning is use" (see above) was non-representational: he and his followers made it clear that there could not exist an x, such that x is the meaning of some linguistic expression y. Wilks does say, throughout his work, that meaning is other words and thus sounds perfectly Wittgensteinian. In Wilks 1999, however, he finally clarifies an important point: for him, "other words" mean a complex representation of meaning—not a simple one-term-like entity of "uppercase" semantics. If this is the case, then not only is he Wittgensteinian, but so is Pustejovsky (1995)—and us—but Wittgenstein is not! Moreover, being ontology oriented, which Wilks (1999) stops just barely short of, is then super-Wittgensteinian, because ontological semantics leads to even more intricate representations of meaning.

2.6.2.3 Premise 3: Machine Tractability We are interested in machine-tractable representations of meaning (cf. note 13) because of another premise, namely, that meaning can be manipulated by computer programs. We share this premise with many computational linguists and AI scholars but with few theoretical linguists or philosophers of language. For ontological semantics, machine tractability goes hand in hand with the earlier premise of meaning representability. There are, however, some approaches that subscribe to the premise of machine tractability but not to the premise of meaning representability—for example, the word-sense disambiguation effort in corpus-oriented computational linguistics (e.g., Resnik and Yarowsky 1997; Yarowsky 1992, 1995; Cowie, Guthrie, and Guthrie 1992; Wilks, Slator, and Guthrie 1996; Wilks and Stevenson 1997; see, however, Kilgariff 1993, 1997a, 1997b, and Wilks 1997).

2.6.2.4 Premise 4: Qualified Compositionality Another important theoretical premise in the field is compositionality of meaning. It essentially states that the meaning of a whole is fully determined by the meanings of its parts and is usually applied to sentences as wholes and words as parts. Ontological semantics accepts this premise, but in a qualified way. The actual related premise in ontological semantics is as follows: while sentence meaning is indeed largely determined by the meanings of words in the sentence, there are components of sentence meanings that cannot be traced back to an individual word, and there are word meanings that do not individually contribute to sentence meaning. A trivial example of noncompositionality is the abundance of phrasal lexical units in any language. The main tradition in the philosophy of language (formal semantics) has, since Frege (1892), accepted complete compositionality as the central theoretical tenet. A variety of researchers have criticized this hypothesis as too strong for natural language (e.g., Wilks 1982). We concur with this criticism.

2.6.3 Justification

The justification component of ontological semantics is responsible for answering questions about why we do things the way we do. We see it as a process of reviewing the alternatives for a decision and making explicit the reasons for the choice of a particular purview, of premises, and of the specific statements in the body.

While descriptive adequacy is a legitimate objective, and simplicity, elegance, and parsimony are generally accepted desiderata in any kind of scientific research, they are not defined specifically or constructively enough to be directly portable to ontological semantics. In any case, we are not sure to what extent the "Popperian justification tool" used in theoretical linguistics (see section 2.3.4) is sufficient for ontological semantics or for the field of NLP in general. In fact, all debates in the NLP community about ways of building better NLP systems contribute to the justification of the (usually hidden) theories underlying the various methods and proposals—even when they are directly motivated by evaluations of applications.

Still, what is descriptive adequacy in ontological semantics? Surely, we want to describe our data as accurately as possible. To that end, it is customary in NLP to divide all the data into a training component and a test component, on which the description, carried out using the training component, is verified.

In principle, every statement in ontological semantics may be addressed from the point of view of justification. Thus, for example, in the Mikrokosmos implementation of ontological semantics, a choice had to be made between including information about lexical-rule content and applicability in the lexicon or keeping it in a separate static knowledge source and using it at runtime (Viegas et al. 1996). The decision was made in favor of the former option because it was found experimentally that the existence of exceptions to lexical-rule applicability, which led some researchers to the study of a special device, "blocking," to prevent incorrect application (see Ostler and Atkins 1991; Briscoe, Copestake, and Lascarides 1995), made it preferable to mark each pertinent lexical entry explicitly as to whether a rule is applicable to it. Reasons for justifying a choice may include generality of coverage, economy of effort, expectation of better results, compatibility with other modules of the system and the theory, and even availability of tools and resources, including availability of trained personnel.

The above example justifies a statement from the body of ontological semantics. We discover, however, that it is much more important and difficult to justify the purview and the premises of a theory than its body. Moreover, we maintain that the same premises can be combined with different bodies in the theory and still lead to the same results. The rule of thumb seems to be as follows: look how other NLP groups carry out a task, compare it with the way you go about it, and find the essential differences. As we already mentioned, sociologically speaking, this job is the hardest within a large and homogeneous research community in which the examination of the theoretical underpinnings of the common activity may not be a condition of success. In what follows, an attempt is made to justify each of the stated premises of ontological semantics in turn.

2.6.3.1 Why Should Meaning Be Studied and Represented? We believe that meaning is needed, in the final analysis, to improve the output quality of NLP applications, in that it allows for better determination and disambiguation of structural, lexical, and compositional properties of texts in a single language and across languages, and thus for better choices of target-language elements in translation, or better fillers for information-extraction templates, or better choices of components of texts for summarization. Knowledge of meaning presents grounds for preference among competing hypotheses at all levels of description, which can be seen especially clearly in a system where evidence in the left-hand side of rules can be of mixed—semantic, syntactic, and so on—provenance.

Reticence on the part of NLP workers toward meaning description is not uncommon and is based on the perception that the semantic work is not well defined, or too complex, or too costly. Our practical experience seems to have demonstrated that it is possible to define this work in relatively simple terms, and that it can be split into a small number of well-defined tasks. (To be sure, a comprehensive treatment of a number of "hard-residue" phenomena, such as metaphor, may still remain unsolved in an implementation, which is standard fare in all semantic-analysis systems.) For the level of coverage attained, the resource expenditure appears quite modest.

The above arguments are designed primarily for a debate with non-semantic-based rule-governed approaches (see, e.g., the brief descriptions in chapters 10, 11, and 13–15 of Hutchins and Somers 1992). Now, from the standpoint of corpus-based NLP, the work of semantics can be done by establishing meaning relations without explaining them directly, for example, on pairs of source- and target-language elements in MT. The task of integrating a set of target elements generated on the basis of a source-language text through these uninterpreted correspondences into a coherent and meaningful target sentence becomes a separate task under this approach. It is also addressed in a purely statistics-based way by "smoothing" it, using comparisons with a target-language model in the statistical sense (Brown and Frederking 1995).

2.6.3.2 Why Is Ontology Needed? It is practically and technologically impossible to operate with elements of the outside world as the realm of meaning for natural language elements. Therefore, if one wants to retain the capability of representing and manipulating meaning, a tangible set of meaning elements must be found to substitute for the entities in the outside world. The ontology in ontological semantics is the next best thing to being able to refer to the outside world directly. It is a model of that world actually constructed so that it reflects, to the best of the researcher's ability, the outside world (including beliefs, nonexisting entities, and so on). Moreover, the ontology records this knowledge not in a formal, "scientific" way but rather in a commonsense way, which, we believe, is exactly what is reflected in natural language meanings.

There are computational approaches to meaning that do not involve an overt ontological level. We believe (and argue for it, for instance, in Nirenburg and Raskin 1996—cf. chapter 4 below) that the description of meaning is more overt and complete when the metalanguage used for this task is independently and comprehensively defined.

2.6.3.3 Why Should Meaning Be Machine Tractable? This premise is rather straightforward because it is dictated by the nature of the description and applications of the theory. These descriptions and applications should be formulated so that they can be incorporated as data, heuristics, or algorithms in computer programs. Machine tractability is not implied by the formality of a theory. For example, it is widely understood now, though not for a long time, that a meticulous and rigorous logical formalism of Montague grammars is not machine tractable (see note 13) because, for one thing, it was never developed with a computer application in mind and thus lacked the necessary procedurality.

A pattern of discrepancy between theoretical and machine-tractable formalisms extends beyond semantics. Thus, attempts to develop a syntactic parser directly on the basis of early transformational syntax failed. This eventuality could be predicted if the term *generative* in *generative grammar* were understood in its intended mathematical—rather than procedural—sense (see Newell and Simon 1972).

2.6.3.4 Why Should Meaning Be Treated as Both Compositional and Noncompositional?

This premise is not shared by two groups of researchers. Some philosophers of language declare their opposition to the notion of compositionality of meaning (e.g., Searle 1982b, who dismissed the phenomenon as pure "combinatorics"[31]). This position also seems to follow from Wittgenstein's antirepresentationalist stance. Conversely, formal semanticists and most philosophers of language rely entirely on compositionality for producing meaning representations. As indicated above, we hold ourselves accountable both for compositional and noncompositional aspects of text meaning, such as phrasals, deixis, and pragmatic meaning, and it is the existence of both of these aspects that justifies this premise.

2.7 "Postempirical" Philosophy of Linguistics

In this chapter, we have argued for the need for theory as well as for the philosophy of the field underlying and determining the process of theory building. We have discussed the components of a linguistic theory and argued that distinguishing them makes the task of theory building more manageable and precise. We introduced and discussed several important parameters of theories. We then extended the discussion of the philosophical matter of theory building into applications. We finished by partially demonstrating how and why one sample parameter, albeit a crucially important one, works on a particular theory.

The experience of working on ontological semantic implementations has been critical for this effort. First, the complexity forced us to make many choices. Second, the necessity to make the choices in a consistent and principled way has become evident. We are in the business of creating descriptions; we were developing methodologies for producing those descriptions; the format of the descriptions and, therefore, the nature of the methodologies, we had concluded (see sections 2.4.2 and 2.5), were determined by a theory. We needed to make this theory explicit, and we needed a basis for preferring one theory over the others at numerous junctures. All of the above has led us to develop a somewhat uncommon, "postempirical" philosophy, and we would like to comment on this briefly.

The canonical relationship between theory and practice in science is that a theory precedes an experiment (see, for instance, Hegel 1983; Kapitsa 1980). More accurately, a theoretical hypothesis is formed in the mind of the scholar and an experiment is conducted to confirm the hypothesis (or rather to fail to falsify it this time around, as Popper would have it—see section 3.4). This kind of theory is, of course, preempirical, and the approach is deductive.

In reality, we know, the scientist may indeed start with the deductive theory-to-practice move but then come back to revise the theory after the appropriate experiments in the reverse practice-to-theory move, and that move is inductive.[32] The resulting approach is hybrid deductive-inductive, which alternates the theory-to-practice and practice-to-theory moves and leads to the theory-to-practice-to-theory-to-practice-to-theory-to-etc. string, which is interrupted when the scientist completes setting up all the general rules of the body of a theory. This is, apparently, the content of what we called postempirical philosophy: surely, some metatheoretical premises—and, we have progressively come to believe, even broader and less strict presuppositions of a general cultural, social, and historical nature—informed us before we started developing ontological semantics. But it was the process of its implementation that clarified and modified those premises and led to the specification of the theory underlying the implementation activity.

When the general rules of the body of a theory are represented as, basically, universally quantified logical propositions, such a theory falls within the twentieth-century analytical tradition in philosophy. Note that ontological semantics adopts the analytical paradigm—the only one recognized by linguistics, computational linguistics, and AI—uncritically. Contrary to our principles of making explicit choices on a principled basis, we never questioned the analytical paradigm and never compared it to its major competitor in contemporary philosophy, namely, phenomenology.[33]

The above iterative deductive-inductive sequence shows that a theory can emerge postempirically, and commonly they do, at least in part. What is much less common, we believe—and we made quite an effort to find a precedent for the position we propound here—is postempirical philosophy of science. In fact, there is an ongoing conflict between the philosophers of science and scientists—or, more accurately, the active process of the two parties ignoring each other rather than engaging in explicit mutual criticism. As Moody explains, "The dynamics of this collaboration are not always completely friendly. Certain philosophical conclusions may be unwelcome or even unacceptable to the scientist, who may insist that she is the only one qualified to have an opinion. This is especially likely when philosophers pass harsh judgment upon some research program and its alleged findings" (1993, 5; cf. note 25 above).

And this brings us to what we consider the most important result of this exercise in the philosophy of linguistics. Whether we have achieved what we set out to achieve in this chapter, there are two uncommon perspectives that we have displayed here by virtue of the postempirical nature of our philosophy of science, as exemplified by our philosophy of linguistics. First, this philosophical proposal is offered by two practicing scientists, and the proposal emerged from practice, which effectively bridges the philosopher-scientist gap. Second, the practice demanded specific recommendations for significant (and tough) choices in theory building, thus pushing the philosophy of science back to the essential "big" issues it once aspired to address.

It is almost routine in contemporary philosophy itself to lament the predominance of highly sophisticated, and often outright virtuoso, discussions of intricate technical details in a single approach over consistent pursuits of major research questions. Our work seems to indicate that there are—or should be—hungry consumers in academic disciplines, whose work needs answers to these big questions, and these answers are expected to come from the philosophy of science. Should it be a centralized effort for the discipline, or should every scientist do the appropriate philosophy-of-science work personally as he or she proceeds? We have had to take the latter route, that of self-sufficiency. We cannot help wondering whether we have done it right, or whether it was more like the Maoist attempt of the 1960s to increase the Chinese national steel-production output by making every family manufacture a little steel every day after dinner in their pocket-size backyard blast furnace.

Ontological Semantics and the Study of Meaning in Linguistics, Philosophy, and Computational Linguistics

This chapter contains a very brief historical survey of the study of meaning in linguistics and philosophy (see Raskin 1983 and 1986 for a more detailed discussion). Its purpose is limited to placing ontological semantics in the realm of linguistic and philosophical semantics. As a semantic theory, ontological semantics is based on a certain number of traditions. They have influenced its premises, positively or negatively, as well as providing some elements of its body and suggesting methods of justification (see section 2.3). Ontological semantics has a broader purview than most of these traditions. Most importantly, ontological semantics is ready for practical applications the way most semantic theories were not designed to accommodate. While this chapter builds up to sentential, compositional semantics in theoretical linguistics, chapter 4 focuses mostly on lexical semantics in computational linguistics. Both chapters, however, have to veer off occasionally in the direction of the other kind for the sake of coherence, and so some of the material here addresses word meaning inasmuch as it leads to sentence meaning.

The chapter is structured in the following way:

• Section 3.1 starts off the buildup with a very brief sketch of the roots of linguistic semantics.

• Section 3.2 follows semantics into its first attempt to become a science by formulating rules of historical meaning change. The notion of rule in contemporary semantics, including ontological semantics, differs from those rules primarily by incoporating the formalism of mathematical logic.

• Section 3.3 brings up the important notion of reference, traditionally missing from linguistic semantics but occasionally showing up as "denotation" or "extension." The notion of instance in ontological semantics is illuminated by this brief review.

• Section 3.4 introduces the main notion of contemporary semantics, meaning representation—that is, the introduction of an apparatus for describing meaning other than by synonyms or paraphrases.

• Section 3.5 brings the discussion to sentential, compositional meaning, first as addressed by formal semantics early on (and revived massively in the 1990s) and then by the first-ever linguistic semantic theory, Katz and Fodor's interpretive semantics. The universally accepted division of semantics into lexical and compositional, abided by ontological semantics as well, was first formally introduced in that much-maligned approach.
• Section 3.6 addresses a few key ideas informing ontological semantics that come from a variety of other late twentieth-century approaches. The most interesting one among those ideas is the division of the information in each sentence into given and new: in ontological semantics, it is captured through the mechanism of instantiation and coreference.
• Section 3.7 summarizes the ideas on compositional semantics, the main challenge of linguistic semantics, including, of course, ontological semantics, from the computational perspective.

Readers familiar with contemporary semantic theory and its evolution as well as with computational semantics may choose to skip this chapter and thus may miss a number of opportunities to disagree with us.

3.1 Prehistory of Semantics

Before the study of meaning emerged as a separate linguistic discipline in the late nineteenth century, a number of disjointed ideas about meaning had accumulated over the millennia. For instance, Plato's "Kratylos" dialogue is devoted essentially to a discussion about whether words are natural and necessary expressions of notions underlying them or merely arbitrary and conventional signs for these notions, which might be equally well expressed by any other collection of sounds. The closely related problem of sound symbolism has recurred with every new generation of semanticists. In modern times, de Saussure's (1916), Jakobson's (1965), and Benveniste's (1939) debate on the arbitrariness of the linguistic sign has addressed the same issue. The currently active area of word-sense disambiguation can be traced back at least to Democritus, who commented on the existence of polysemy and synonymy (1717; cf. Lurfle 1970). Modern work on diachronic changes in word meaning was anticipated by Proclus (1987, 1989). Aristotle (1968) contributed to the definition of what we would now call the distinction between open- and closed-class lexical items, as well as providing a taxonomy of parts of speech and another for metaphors (or tropes).

An ancient Indian (see, for instance, Zvegintzev 1964) school of linguistic thought was preoccupied with the question of whether the word possesses a meaning in isolation or acquires it only in a sentence. This argument was taken up by Gardiner (1951) and Grice (1957). Practical work with meaning can be traced back to the

Middle Ages and the trailblazing lexicographic and thesaurus-building work by Arab scholars (see, for example, Zvegintzev 1958).

3.2 Diachrony of Word Meaning

In 1883, the French classical philologist Michel Bréal (1832–1915) published an article (Bréal, 1964, 7–8) containing the following passage:

The study where we invite the reader to follow us is of such a new kind that it has not even yet been given a name. Indeed, it is on the body and the form of words that most linguists have exercised their acumen: the laws governing changes in meaning, the choice of new expressions, the birth and death of idioms, have been left in the dark or have only been casually indicated. Since this study, no less than phonetics and morphology, deserves to have a name, we shall call it *Semantics*.

(As Bréal indicates in the footnote to the term, it comes from the Greek verb σημαινω *semaino* "to signify")—that is, "the science of meaning."[1]

Semantics was thus originally established as a historical discipline. This was not surprising in the post-Darwin era, when the historical approach was dominant in science. What Bréal, Hermann Paul (1886), and Arsène Darmesteter (1887) initiated, and what was later continued by Wundt (1921), Meillet (1922), Wellander (1973), and Sperber (1958), was the following: studying changes of meaning, exploring their causes, classifying them according to logical, psychological, and/or other criteria, and, if possible, formulating the general "laws" and tendencies underlying such changes. The examples in table 3.1 illustrate the types of phenomena discussed by Bréal and his colleagues.

Bréal (1997) was also the first to introduce what we would now call lexical rules ("laws," in his terminology). Thus, he talks about the diachronic law of specialization (lexicalization or degrammaticalization, in current terminology), according to which words undergo change from synthetic to analytic expression of grammatical meaning—for example, Latin: *fortior* > French: *plus fort*. Bréal's law of differentiation says that synonyms tend to differentiate their meaning diachronically: thus, the Swiss French *paîle* changed its neutral meaning of "room" for that of "garret," after the French *chambre* had ousted it. The law of irradiation (analogy, in modern terms) deals with cases when an element of a word assumes some component of the word's meaning and then brings this meaning over to other words in which it occurs. For example, the Latin suffix *-sco* acquired its inchoative ("beginning") meaning in such words as *adolesco*, "to grow to maturity," and later irradiated that meaning into *maturesco*, "to ripen," or *marcesco*, "to begin to droop." (In a contemporary American English example, *-gate* acquired the meaning of "scandal" in *Watergate* and contributed this meaning to many other names of scandals, like *Koreagate* or *Monicagate*.)

Table 3.1
Examples of meaning change

Type of change	Language	Word	Old meaning	New meaning
Restriction	Latin	*felix*	female of any animal	cat
	Latin	*fenum*	produce	hay
	Greek	κτηματα	possessions	cattle
	German	*Mut(h)*	soul, intelligence	courage
	English	*meat*	food	meat
Expansion	French	*gain*	harvest	produce, result
	French	*temps*	temperature	weather
	French	*briller*	beryl	shine
	English	*dog*	dachshund	dog
Metaphor	Latin	*putare*	count	think
	Latin	*aestimare*	weigh the money	evaluate
	English	*bead*	prayer	bead
Concretion	Latin	*vestis*	the act of dressing	vest, jacket
	Latin	*fructus*	enjoyment	fruit
	Latin	*mansio*	stopping	mansion
	English	*make love*	court	have sex
Abstraction	Latin	*Caesar*	Caesar	caesar, emperor
	English	*Bismarck*	Bismarck	great statesman

3.3 Meaning and Reference

The next major question that interested semanticists was the relation between word meaning and the real world (that is, the entities to which words referred). The distinction between meaning and reference was introduced in logic by Frege (1892).[2] To illustrate the difference between meaning and reference, Frege used the following example: the expressions *Morning Star* and *Evening Star* have a different meaning (stars appearing in the morning and evening, respectively) but refer to the same entity in the world, the planet Venus.

The distinction was introduced into linguistic semantics by Ogden and Richards (1923), who presented it as the triangle (see figure 3.1). According to Ogden and Richards, the thought of reference "symbolizes" the symbol and "refers" to the referent. The relationship between the symbol and the referent is thus indirect ("imputed").

By postulating the disconnect between the word (symbol) and the thing it refers to (referent)—a revolutionary idea at the time—Ogden and Richards attempted to explain the misuse and abuse of language. For instance, language is often used to refer to things that do not, in fact, exist. As prescriptive linguists, they believed that, if only people used words right, many real-world problems would disappear. In

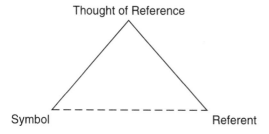

Figure 3.1
Ogden and Richards's original word-meaning triangle. A language symbol (a word) does not directly connect with its referent in the world. This connection is indirect, through a mental representation of the element of the world.

this, they anticipated the concerns of the general semanticists, such as Korzybski (see section 3.6), whose best-known book was, in fact, titled *Language and Sanity* (1933), as well as Hayakawa (1975). Ogden and Richards thus proceeded from the assumption that speakers can avoid "abusing" language—that is, that language can and should be made, in some sense, logical. Carnap (1937) was, independently, sympathetic to this concern and tried to develop principles for constructing fully logical artificial languages for human consumption. Wittgenstein (1953, 19[e]) would make a famous observation that "philosophical problems arise when language *goes on holiday*" that resonates with the original thinking of Ogden and Richards.[3]

3.4 The Quest for Meaning Representation I: From Ogden and Richards to Bar Hillel

While Ogden and Richards identified the symbols with words and the referents with things in the world, they made no claim about the nature of the thought of reference (that is, meaning). Stern (1931) placed the latter in the domain of "mental content" situated in the mind of the speaker. In this, he anticipated work on mental models (e.g., Miller and Johnson-Laird 1976), mental spaces (Fauconnier 1985), and artificial believers (e.g., Ballim and Wilks 1991). Over the years, there have been several types of reactions to the task of meaning representation, and various researchers have opted for quite different solutions.

3.4.1 Option 1: Refusing to Study Meaning
Stern postulated the nature of meaning but said nothing about how to explore it. Of course, it is not at all clear how to go about this task of describing something that is not as directly observable as words or real-world objects. In the behaviorist tradition, ascendant in the United States roughly between 1920 and 1960, the study of

unobservable objects became unacceptable (see a pertinent discussion in section 2.3.4). That is why Bloomfield (1933) declared that meaning is but a linguistic substitute for the basic stimulus-response analysis of human behavior. In his classic example, he described the behavior of a human being, Jill. When she is hungry (stimulus) and sees an apple (another stimulus), she picks it up and eats it (response). But stimuli and responses need not be real-life states of affairs and actions. They can be substituted for by language expressions. Thus, in the situation above, Jill may substitute a linguistic response for her action by informing Jack that she is hungry or that she wants the apple. This message becomes Jack's linguistic stimulus, and he responds with a real-life action. Thus, Bloomfield does not reject the concept of meaning altogether. However, it is defined in such a way that the only methodology for discovering and describing, for instance, the meaning of a particular word, is by observing any common features of the situations in which this word is uttered (cf. Dillon 1977).

Without any definition of the features or any methods or tools for recording these features, this program is patently vacuous, and Bloomfield himself considered the task of providing such definitions and methods infeasible. As a result, he did the only logical thing: he declared that semantics should not be a part of the linguistic enterprise. This decision influenced the progress of the study of meaning in linguistics for decades to come. Indeed, until Katz and Fodor 1963, meaning was marginalized in linguistics proper, though studied in applied fields, such as anthropology, which contributed to the genesis of componential analysis of word meaning (see section 3.4.3), or machine translation, which has maintained a steady interest in (lexical) semantics. Thus, a pioneer of machine translation stated: "MT is concerned primarily with *meaning*, an aspect of language that has often been treated as a poor relation by linguists and referred to psychologists and philosophers. *The first concern of MT must always be the highest possible degree of source-target semantic agreement and intelligibility*. The MT linguist, therefore, must study the languages that are to be mechanically correlated in the light of source-target semantics" (Reifler 1955, 138).

3.4.2   Option 2: Semantic Fields, or Avoiding Metalanguage

Before componential analysis emerged as a first concrete approach to describing word meaning, Trier (1931), Weisgerber (1951), and others distinguished and analyzed "semantic fields"—that is, groups of words whose meanings are closely interrelated. A simple topological metaphor allowed the authors to position the words with "contiguous" meanings next to each other, like pieces of a puzzle. The original semantic fields defined contiguity on a mixture of intuitive factors including, among others, both the paradigmatic (synonymy, hyperonymy, antonymy, and so on) and the syntagmatic (what we today would call thematic or case-role) relations among word meanings. Characteristically, none of these relations were either formally defined or represented in the semantic fields: in other words, the semantic-field approach explored semantics without an overt metalanguage. In this sense, semantic fields anticipated a direction of work in corpus linguistics in the 1990s, where paradigmatic relations among word meanings are established (but once again, with neither word meanings nor semantic relations overtly defined or represented) by automatically matching the contexts in which they are attested in text corpora. It is not surprising that the same corpus linguists have widely used thesauri (originating in modern times with Roget 1852)—practical lexicographic encodings of the intuitive notion of semantic fields that, in fact, predated the work on semantic fields by almost a century.

Hjelmslev (1958) compared semantic fields across different languages. This gave him the idea about determining the minimal differentiating elements (*semes*, in Hjelmslev's terminology) of meaning that would allow one to describe word meaning in any language. Not only do the semes provide a bridge to componential analysis, they also anticipate modern work in ontology. The notion of semantic fields was given an empirical corroboration when Luria (e.g., Vinogradova and Luria 1961) showed through a series of experiments that human conditional reflexes dealing with associations among words are based on the speaker's subconscious awareness of structured semantic fields.

3.4.3 Option 3: Componential Analysis, or the Dawn of Metalanguage

The anthropologists Kroeber (1952), Goodenough (1956), and Lounsbury (1956) suggested a set of semantic features (components) to describe terms of kinship in a variety of cultures. Using an appropriate combination of these features, one can compose the meaning of any kinship term. Thus, the meaning of *father* is the combination of three feature-value pairs: {GENERATION: −1; SEX: male; CLOSENESS-OF-RELATIONSHIP: direct}. If the approach could be extended beyond closed nomenclatures to cover the general lexicon, this would effectively amount to the introduction of a parsimonious metalanguage for describing word meaning, because relatively few features could be used in combinations to describe the hundreds of thousands of word meanings, presumably in any language. Leaving aside for the time being the unsolved (and even unstated) issue of the nature of the names for the component features (are they words of English or elements of a different, artificial, language?), the componential-analysis hypothesis promised exciting applications in practical lexicography, language training, and computer processing of language.

It was shown later by Katz and Fodor (1963) that the general lexicon could be represented using a limited number of semantic features only if one agreed to an incomplete analysis of word meaning. They called the "residue" of the word meaning after componential analysis the *semantic distinguisher* and did not analyze that concept any further. Thus, one of the senses of the English word *bachelor* was represented by the set of componential features (*semantic markers* to Katz and Fodor) of

(Human) (Adult) (Male) and the semantic distinguisher [Who has never married]. This meaning is, for Katz and Fodor, a combination of the meaning of *man*, derived fully componentially, and an unanalyzed residue. Katz and Fodor realized, of course, that each such residue could be declared another marker. However, this would have led to unconstrained proliferation of the markers, which would defeat the basic idea of componential analysis: describing many in terms of few.

3.4.4   Option 4: Logic, or Importing a Metalanguage

Greenberg (1949) introduced first-order predicate calculus as the metalanguage for componential analysis. As a result, various features (components) were assigned different logical status. Some were predicates; others, arguments; still others, functors. Thus, if xPy is defined as "x is a parent of y," f is defined as "female," $u \neq v$ and $x \neq y$, then $(\exists u)\,(\exists v)\,[uPx\ \&\ uPy\ \&\ vPx\ \&\ vPy\ \&\ x = f]$ means "x is a sister of y." Greenberg demonstrated that his system was, indeed, capable of expressing any kind of kinship relationship. It was not important for him that his formulas could be expressed in a number of ways in natural language, not always using strictly synonymous phrases. For example, the formula above can be expressed as "y has a sister," "y is a brother or sister of x," or even "u and v have at least two children, and one of them is a girl." If a relationship—for instance, equivalence—is posited for two formulas, the result is a true or false statement. Also, formulas usually have entailments—for instance, that u and v in the formula above are not of the same sex. The categories of truth and entailment, while peripheral for an empiricist like Greenberg, are central to any approach to semantics based on logic.

While Greenberg used mechanisms of logic to analyze word meaning, the main thrust of the logical tradition in the study of language had been to apply its central notion, the proposition, to the study of the sentence. Extending the Ogden and Richards triangle to sentence level from word level, we obtain the relationships shown in figure 3.2. The logicians renamed the labels of the nodes in this triangle with terms defined inside their system (see figure 3.3). The main difference between

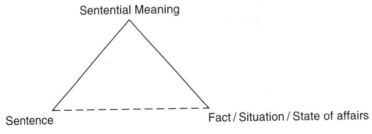

Figure 3.2
Ogden and Richards's triangle extended to sentence level from word level.

the logical triangle in figure 3.3 and the one in figure 3.2 is that, in the former, none of the elements relates directly to natural language. A proposition is the result of a translation of a sentence into the metalanguage of logic. Its extension (also referred to as *denotation*) is formally defined as the truth value of the proposition, realized as either "true" or "false." The intension of a proposition is defined as a function from the set of propositional indices, such as the speaker, the hearer, the time and location of the utterance, and a "possible world" in which it is uttered, to the proposition's extension (see, e.g., Lewis 1972). While these definitions are very natural from the point of view of logic, we will argue later that, outside of it, they are not necessarily so.

Bar Hillel (1970, 202–203) characterized the overall program of exploring language using the tool of formal logic as follows:

It seems that ... the almost general attitude of all formal logicians was to regard [semantic analysis of natural language] as a two-stage affair. In the first stage, the original language formulation had to be rephrased, without loss, in a normalized idiom, while in the second stage, these normalized formulations would be put through the grindstone of the formal logic evaluator.... Without substantial progress in the first stage even the incredible progress made by mathematical logic in our time will not help us much in solving our total problem.

The first stage may have been motivated by the desire—shared by such very different scholars as Ogden and Richards, on the one hand, and Carnap, on the other—to make natural language more logical and thus to avoid obfuscation through polysemy, use of metaphor, and other phenomena that make semantic analysis difficult. Another related goal was to cleanse language of references to nonexistent entities that make analysis through logic impossible. Indeed, had this goal been achieved, Russell (1905; see also Frege 1952a) would not have had to devote so much thought to the issue of the truth value of the proposition contained in the utterance *The present king of France is bald* (see note 10).

The implementation of the first of Bar Hillel's two stages of the logic program for semantics would have enabled the second stage to express a complete analysis of

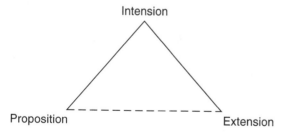

Figure 3.3
The meaning triangle at the sentence level, using logicians' terms.

the meaning of natural language utterances in logical terms. The development of the second stage proved much more attainable (provided one assumed the success of the first stage). Given this assumption, the second stage was able to concentrate on such purely technical issues in logic as the calculation of truth values of complex propositions, given the truth values of their components; truth preservation in entailments; or the assignment of appropriate extensions to entities other than objects and propositions (for instance, events or attributes).

Bar Hillel's charge concerning the first stage of the program of logic vis-à-vis language could, in fact, be mitigated if one took into account the attempts by logicians to account at least for the syntactic properties of natural language sentences. Ajdukiewicz's (1935) work that eventually led to the development of categorial grammar (Bar Hillel 1953) was the first attempt to describe phrase and sentence structure formally. The grammar introduces two basic notions—the sentence (S) and the noun (N)—and presents the syntactic value of the sentence as the product of its constituents. Thus, a one-place predicate, such as *sleep* in *George sleeps*, obtains the value of S/N, which means that it is the element that, when a noun is added to it, produces a sentence ($N \times S/N = S$). Similar formulas were built for other types of predicates, for modifiers, determiners, and other lexical categories. This work was the first example of the logical method applied to a purely linguistic concern, falling outside the program of logic proper. Indeed, it deals, though admittedly not very well, with the syntax of natural language, which is much more complex than the formal syntax of a logical system.

Ajdukiewicz's work seems also to have first introduced into linguistics and logic the idea of a process through which one can compose a characterization of a complex entity out of the characterizations of its constituents. After Ajdukiewicz, Bar Hillel and Chomsky, among others, applied this method to the syntax of natural language without necessarily preserving the original formalism. Later, Katz and Fodor in linguistic semantics and Montague within the logic camp extended this method to deriving the meaning of a sentence from the meanings of its constituents. Work on compositional syntax led to ideas about the compositional derivation of sentence meaning from meanings of phrases, and the latter from meanings of words.

3.5 The Quest for Meaning Representation II: Contemporary Approaches

The quest has continued across a number of newer approaches.

3.5.1 Formal Semantics

Semantic compositionality (see, for instance, Partee 1984a) deals with the contribution of sentence constituents to the truth value of a proposition expressed by a sentence. The basic process of calculating truth values resembles syntactic analysis in categorial grammar, with sentence constituents being assigned labels in which the syntactic category S is replaced by the truth value t. Thus, in Heim and Kratzer 1998, the extension of a simple proposition like *George snores*, denoted as [[George snores]], is defined as a function of [[snores]] called with the argument [[George]], or [[George snores]] = [[snores]] ([[George]]). If the proposition *George snores* is true (which it is if George, in fact, snores), the formula becomes t = [[snores]] ([[George]]). More generally, for one-place predicates like snore, t = [[predicate]] ([[argument]]). Conflating logical terms with lexical categories, as is customary in formal semantics, we can write t = [[V]] ([[PrN]]), where V stands for verb and PrN, for proper noun.

It is precisely this operation of assigning appropriate extensions to the components of a proposition that is described as "a principle of compositionality, which states that the meaning of a complex expression is determined by the meaning of its constituents and the manner in which they are combined" (Ladusaw 1988, 91). Let us see how this program for formal semantics handles the following four central issues on its agenda: "1. What is the formal characterization of the objects which serve as semantic representations? 2. How do these objects support the equivalence and consequence relations which are its descriptive goal? 3. How are expressions associated with their semantic representations? 4. What are semantic representations? Are they considered to be basically mental objects or real-world objects?" (p. 92).

The formal characterization of semantic representations refers to the metalanguage of double brackets for representing extensions. By contributing correctly to the calculation of the truth value of the propositions, these representations clearly support such truth value-based relations as equivalence, consequence (entailment), and all the others. The expressions are associated with their semantic representations by the act of assignment. Whether semantic representations are mental or real-world objects does not directly influence the compositional process, though this issue is the object of active research and debate (with, e.g., Fodor and Lepore 1998 and Fauconnier 1985 arguing for the mentalist position and, e.g., Barwise and Perry 1983 contributing to the opposing view).

Thus, on their own terms, formal semanticists can declare that their program indeed responds to the four questions they consider central to the semantic enterprise. As a result, the bulk of the research focuses on the refinement of the logical formalism and extension assignments, and on extending the range of linguistic examples that can illustrate the appropriateness of the logical formalism. Over the years, formal semantics has concentrated on studying the meaning of the syntactic classes of nouns and verbs, thematic roles, space (including deixis), aspect, tense, time, modality, negation, and selected types of modification, with the greatest amount of effort devoted to the issue of quantification. Practically any book or article on formal semantics has been devoted to a subset of this inventory (see Montague 1974; Dowty 1979; Dowty, Wall, and Peters 1981; Partee 1973b, 1976; Hornstein 1984; Bach 1984;

Chierchia and McConnell-Ginet 1990; Frawley 1992; Cann 1993; Chierchia 1995; Heim and Kratzer 1998).

As mentioned, the truth value of a proposition establishes a direct relation between the sentence containing the proposition and the state of affairs in the world—that is, between language and the extralinguistic reality that language "is about" (Ladusaw 1988, 91; Chierchia and McConnell-Ginet 1990, 11). This tenet is so basic and essential to the formal semantics program that the truth values assume the dominant role in it: only issues that lend themselves to truth-conditional treatment are added to the inventory of formal semantics tasks. As a result, many issues escape the attention of formal semanticists—in other words, are declared to be outside the purview of this approach. Among the important issues that cannot be treated using truth values are conversion of natural language sentences into logical propositions[4] (cf. Bar Hillel's comment on the subject discussed in section 3.4.4); representation of lexical meanings for most open-class lexical items,[5] which would enable a substantive representation for the meaning of a sentence; as well as the resolution of most kinds of semantic ambiguity, notably every ambiguity not stemming from a syntactic distinction.

The insistence on using truth values as extensions for propositions leads to assigning the same extension to all true propositions, and thus effectively equating, counterintuitively, all sentences expressing such propositions. The formal semanticists perceived both this difficulty and the need for overcoming it: "If sentences denote their truth values, then there must be something more to sentence meaning than denotation, for we don't want to say that any two sentences with the same truth value have the same meaning" (Chierchia and McConnell-Ginet 1990, 57). So, the category of intension was introduced to capture the differences in meaning among propositions with the same extension. If one uses the standard definition of intension (see section 3.4.4), such differences can only be represented through different values of the intensional indices. Since the values of the speaker, the hearer, and the time and place of the utterance are, in and of themselves, insufficient to capture realistic semantic differences, the set of all objects mentioned in the propositions is added as another index (see, e.g., Lewis 1972). This addition preempts the necessity to explain the semantic difference between two sentences pronounced in rapid succession by the same speaker in the same place and intended for the same hearer simply by the minuscule difference in the value of the time index. For example, if Jim says to David in Las Cruces, New Mexico, on September 15, 1999 at 14:23:17, *The new computer is still in the box*, and, at 14:23:19, *Evelyne is still in Singapore*, the index values {computer, box} and {Evelyne, Singapore}, respectively, distinguish the propositions underlying these utterances much more substantively than the two-second difference in the value of the time index.

The sentence *The new computer is still in the box* shares all the index values with such other sentences as *The computer is in the new box*, *The old computer is in the box*,

The box is behind the new computer, The new computer resembles a box, and many others. These sentences obviously differ in meaning, but the intensional analysis with the help of the indices, as defined above, fails to account for these differences. The only method to rectify this state of affairs within intensional analysis is to introduce new indices—for instance, a predicate index, an index for each attribute of each predicate and object, and so on. In other words, for an adequate account of all semantic differences among sentences, the framework will need an index for every possible meaning-carrying linguistic entity that might occur in the sentence. When this is achieved, it will appear that the original indices of speaker, hearer, time, and place prove to contribute little, if anything, to the representation and disambiguation of sentence meaning.[6]

While this method of extending the intensional analysis of meaning is plausible, it has not been pursued by formal semantics.[7] This is not because formal semanticists did not recognize the problem. Kamp (1984, 1) formulated it as follows:

Two conceptions of meaning have dominated formal semantics of natural language. The first of these sees meaning principally as that which determines conditions of truth. This notion, whose advocates are found mostly among philosophers and logicians, has inspired the disciplines of truth-theoretic and model-theoretic semantics. According to the second conception, meaning is, first and foremost, that which a language user grasps when he understands the words he hears or reads. The second conception is implicit in many studies by computer scientists (especially those involved with artificial intelligence), psychologists and linguists— studies which have been concerned to articulate the structure of the representations which speakers construct in response to verbal input.

Kamp adhered to both of these conceptions of meaning. His discourse representation theory (DRT) proposed to combine the two approaches, specifically, by adding to the agenda of formal semantics a treatment of coreference and anaphora. He suggested that, in the mind of the speaker, there exists a representation that keeps tabs on all the arguments of all predicates and that helps to recognize deictic antecedents and referents of all definite descriptions. This proposal amounts to adding another index to intensional semantics, which is definitely useful. However, the same discourse representation structure will still represent sentences with different meanings. In other words, even after Kamp's enhancements, formal semantics will still assign the same sets of index values to sentences with different meanings.

Barwise and Perry (1983) took a completely different road to obviating the difficulties stemming, in the source, from the foundational tenet of reliance on truth values. They declared that the extension of a proposition is not a truth value but rather a complex entity they called the *situation*. This extension was rich enough to allow for semantically different sentences to have different extensions, which made the account much more intuitive and closer to what "a language user grasps" about meaning, thus bridging the gap mentioned by Kamp. Their approach ran into two kinds of difficulties. First, there are no tools to describe actual situations within the repertoire of formal semantics, including neither a methodology nor a tradition of large-scale descriptive work, and Barwise and Perry did not attempt to borrow that expertise from elsewhere—for example, field linguistics. Second, they came under attack from fellow logicians and philosophers of language for using a category, situation, which was dangerously close to the category of fact, which, in turn, had long been known to philosophers as practically impossible to define and manipulate properly (Austin 1962; cf. 1961a, 1961b).[8]

3.5.2 Semantic vs. Syntactic Compositionality

Sentences are syntactically compositional because they consist of clauses, which, in turn, consist of phrases, which, in turn, consist of other phrases and words. In other words, saying that sentences are syntactically compositional is tantamount to saying that they have syntactic structure. Sentence meaning is compositional because, to a large extent, it depends on a combination of the meanings of sentence constituents, which implies the concept of semantic structure. That both syntactic structure and semantic structure are compositional does not imply that the two structures are in any sense isomorphic or congruent: in other words, it does not follow that the syntactic and semantic constituents are the same.

Formal semanticists are aware of the possible distinctions between the shape of the syntactic and semantic structures. Thus "in theory, the semantically relevant structure of a complex expression like a sentence may bear little or no relation to the syntactic structure assigned to it on other linguistic grounds (on the basis, for example, of grammaticality judgments and intuitions about syntactic constituency)" (Chierchia and McConnell-Ginet 1990, 91).

Having observed a parallelism between the (morphological) lexicon and phrase structure rules in syntax, on the one hand, and the (semantic) lexicon and compositional rules in semantics, on the other, Ladusaw observes that "the distinction between lexical and compositional in semantics is not necessarily the same as between lexical and phrasal in syntax. Polymorphemic words may have completely compositional meanings and apparently phrasal constituents may have idiomatic meanings. See Dowty (1978) and Hoeksma (1984) for a discussion of the relationship between compositionality and the lexical/syntactic distinction."

We basically agree with this observation, though we believe that it does not go far enough in stating the inherent discrepancies between syntactic and semantic compositionality. First, experience in multilingual descriptive work clearly shows that word boundaries and, therefore, the demarcation lines between morphology and syntax, are blurred and unimportant for grammatical description (see, e.g., Kornfilt 1997 on Turkish agglutination or Dura 1998 on Swedish compounding). Second, even a nonpolymorphemic word may have a compositional meaning, as Postal (1971) showed on the example of the English *remind*, which he analyzed as STRIKE + SIMILAR. Raskin and Nirenburg 1995 identifies many cases of syntactic modification (such as adjective-noun constructions) in which no semantic modification occurs. Thus, *occasional pizza* actually means that somebody eats pizza occasionally, and *good film* means that somebody watches the film and likes it.

Unfortunately, as formal semanticists readily admit, the reality of research in the field with regard to the relationship between syntactic and semantic compositionality is different: "In practice, many linguists assume that semantics is fed fairly directly by syntax and that surface syntactic constituents will generally be units for purposes of semantic composition. And even more linguists would expect the units of semantic composition to be units at some level of syntactic structure, though perhaps at a more abstract level than the surface" (Chierchia and McConnell-Ginet 1990, 91). We could not have said this better ourselves (cf, e.g., Nirenburg and Raskin 1996; see also chapter 4).

3.5.3 Compositionality in Linguistic Semantics
Similarly to formal semanticists, Katz and Fodor (1963) believe that semantic compositionality is determined by syntactic compositionality. Their semantic theory, the first linguistic theory of sentence meaning, was conceived as a component of a comprehensive theory of language competence that had at its center a syntactic component, specifically, the transformational generative grammar. The comprehensive theory implied an order of application of the constituent theories, with the output of the syntactic component serving as the input for the semantic component.

Having realized that Chomsky's syntax was a model of the speakers' grammatical competence, more specifically, their ability to judge word strings as well-formed or not well-formed sentences of a language, Katz and Fodor extended the same approach to semantics. Only instead of well-formedness (or grammaticality), they were interested in the speakers' judgments of meaningfulness. They defined semantic competence as a set of four abilities:

- Determining the number of meanings for each sentence
- Determining the content of each meaning
- Detecting semantic anomalies in sentences
- Perceiving paraphrase relations among sentences

Their semantic theory consists of two components: the dictionary and the compositional projection (or amalgamation) rules. In the dictionary, each entry contains a combination of lexical-category information, such as common noun, with a small number of general semantic features (see section 3.4.3). Starting at the terminal level of the phrase structure represented as a binary tree, the projection rules take pairs of lexical entries that were the children of the same node and amalgamate their semantic markers. A special rule is devised for each type of syntactic phrase. The procedure continues until the semantics of the root node of the tree, S, is established. For example, the head-modifier projection rule essentially concatenates the semantic features in the entries for the head and the modifier. A more complex verb-object rule inserts the entry for the object NP into the slot for object in the verb's entry. A special slot in the entries for nominal modifiers and verbs lists selectional restrictions (represented as Boolean combinations of semantic features) that constrain the modifier's capacity to combine with particular heads and the verb's capacity to combine with certain verbal subjects and objects, respectively. Projection rules fire only if selectional restrictions are satisfied. Otherwise, the sentence is pronounced anomalous.

Katz and Fodor's was the first theory that combined lexical and compositional semantics. They were also the first to address explicitly the purview of their enterprise and deliberately to constrain it. While semantic competence, as the authors defined it, obviously includes the speaker's capacity to understand each sentence in context, Katz and Fodor saw no way of accommodating this capability within a formal theory. Instead, they declared the sentence meaning "in isolation" to be the only viable goal of their, and any other, theory. Without the disambiguating role of the context, this results in a counterintuitive treatment of virtually any sentence as ambiguous. In other words, they did not have a procedure for determining which of the potential meanings of a sentence was appropriate in a text. They could claim, however, that this latter task was not one of the four aspects of semantic competence that their theory was set up to model. While this claim was correct, it led to a serious discrepancy between the goal of their theory and the actual semantic competence of the speakers. This amounted to trading a real and necessary but seemingly unattainable goal for a well-defined and specially designed objective that seemed attainable. In this respect, there is no theoretical difference between Katz and Fodor's substitution and the decision to study truth values in lieu of meaning on the part of formal semanticists, except that Katz and Fodor were aware of the substitution and open about it. It matters also, of course, that their theory produced a list of possible meanings out of which the desired one could be selected.

The appearance of Katz and Fodor's article, followed by Katz and Postal 1964, had the effect of energizing research on compositional semantics within linguistics. Many leading linguists commented on this theory, often criticizing quite severely its various tenets, with the curious exception of the above meaning-in-isolation flaw. Thus, Weinreich (1966) perceptively accused Katz and his coauthors of having no criteria for limiting the polysemy in their dictionary entries. Lakoff (1971) convinc-

ingly showed that in order for the proposed semantic theory to work, the overall
"architecture" of the linguistic theory needed to be changed. Staal (1967) and Bar
Hillel (1967) observed that the proposed theory could not accommodate such important semantic relations as the conversives—for example, *buy/sell*. Nonetheless, no
critic of Katz and his coauthors (see, however, Raskin 1986) attacked their four-part
agenda (even though the issue of paraphrases was manifestly ignored in the theory[9]),
and gauging any subsequent semantic proposals against the background of Katz and
Fodor's theory was common practice for a period of time.

Remarkably, Katz and Fodor achieved their compositional semantic goals without feeling any need for truth values, which is, of course, directly opposite to the
formal semantics approach. Another related difference is Katz and Fodor's emphasis, often exaggerated by their critics, on disambiguation, while formal semantics has
no interest and no tools for dealing with the problem. The definitive response to Katz
and Fodor's theory from formal semanticists was formulated by Lewis (1972), who
pointed out the failure of their semantic features, markers, and distinguishers (which,
for him, were just words in "Markerese"), as failing to relate language to the extralinguistic reality. It was as an alternative to Katz and Fodor's theory that Lewis formulated the first cohesive proposal of intensional semantics.

As we discuss in sections 2.6.2.2 and 4.3.2, the position of ontological semantics
is different from both Katz and Fodor's and Lewis's. We only partially agree with
Jackendoff (1983, x) that "the standard notions of truth and reference play no significant role in natural language semantics."[10] First, we maintain that reference
is relevant for the study of coreference and anaphora (both of which, in ontological
semantics, are subsumed by the phenomenon of reference) relations in text. Second,
while we agree that truth plays no role in the speaker's processing of meaning, we
are also aware of the need to "anchor" language in extralinguistic reality. Formal
semanticists use truth values for this purpose. We believe that this task requires a
tool with much more content, and that an ontology can and should serve as such a
tool. On the other hand, we find the "Markerese" accusation spurious: there is
no legitimate way to confuse semantic markers with words of English. We deflect
a similar criticism concerning the use of English labels for ontological concepts by
explicitly setting up these labels as language-independent entities with their own
content and by training the personnel working with these labels to distinguish between elements of the ontology and elements of language.

3.6   A Trio of Freestanding Semantic Ideas from Outside Major Schools

Ontological semantics contains elements that reverberate against a few interesting
semantic ideas that have been proposed outside of the major semantic approaches
and that have never been fully incorporated by those approaches.

The intuition that each utterance carries a reference to information already known to the hearer as well as information new to the hearer was first formulated as the basis of the so-called functional perspective on the sentence by the founders of the Prague Linguistic Circle (Mathesius 1947). It has been a recurring issue in semantics and pragmatics ever since, under different terminological systems (see, for instance, Kuno 1972; Chafe 1976; Clark and Haviland 1977; Prince 1979, 1981). The distinction, while definitely useful, cannot provide a comprehensive representation of sentential meaning—it can only contribute as an add-on to a full-fledged semantic system. Before generative grammar, however, this phenomenon was studied essentially in isolation. In generative grammar, the distinction, introduced as presupposition and focus (Chomsky 1971), was supposed to be added to the semantic component, but the idea was never implemented. More recently, work has been done on incorporating the topic-focus dichotomy into formal syntax and semantics (e.g., Krifka 1991; Rooth 1992; Birner and Ward 1998; Hajičová, Partee, and Sgall 1998) and into the study of prosody and intonation (e.g., Féry 1992; Hajičová 1998). In computational linguistics, information about focus and presupposition was used primarily (e.g., McKeown 1985), though not exclusively (e.g., Grosz 1977), in natural language generation, and was implemented through a set of special clues. Ontological semantics accommodates the distinction between old and new information using the mechanism of the saliency modality parameter (supported by the mechanisms of instantiation and coreference). The microtheory of saliency includes several clues for establishing the appropriate values (see section 8.5.3).

Humboldt (1971) and Whorf (1953) introduced the intriguing idea that different languages impose different worldviews on their speakers. Humboldt spoke of the magic circle drawn by the language around the speaker, a metaphor characteristic of Romanticism in science, art, and culture that was the dominant contemporary worldview, at least in Germany. Whorf, on the other hand, amassed empirical data on such crucial, for him, differences among languages as the circular notion of time in Hopi as opposed to the linear notion of time in what Whorf referred to as "Standard Average European." Whorf's claims of this nature depended primarily on the availability of single-word expressions for certain ideas: the unavailability of such an expression for a certain idea was interpreted by him as the absence of this idea in the world of the speaker of that language. Taking this claim absurdly far, one arrives at the conclusion that an Uzbek, whose language reportedly has only three words for color, can distinguish fewer colors than the speakers of languages with a larger color taxonomy. Whorf's own and subsequent research failed to produce any justification for the prime nature of the single-word claim (see chapter 5, note 9). Like most other approaches, ontological semantics subscribes to the principle of effability (see section 9.3.6), which directly contradicts the Whorf hypothesis. Moreover, ontological semantics is based on an ontology that is language independent and thus assumes the conceptual coherence of all natural languages. The lexicon for every language inside ontological semantics uses the same ontology to specify meanings, and, because it must cover all the meanings in the ontology, some of the entry heads in the lexicon will, for a particular language, end up phrasal.

Among Alfred Korzybski's (1933) many bizarre ideas about semantics, completely marginalized by the field, there was a persistent theme of instantiating a mention of every object. He claimed that no mention of, say, a table could be made without its unique numbered label, no mention of a person, without an exact date in the life of this person about which the statement is made. This idea is a precursor to instantiation in ontological semantics, a basic mechanism for meaning analysis.

3.7 Compositionality in Computational Semantics

When Katz and Fodor described semantic processes, they had in mind mathematical processes of derivation. With the advent of computational processing of language, a natural consequence was algorithmic theories of language processing, often with the idea of using their results as the bases of some computational applications, such as machine translation or text understanding. The goals of computational semantics have been, by and large, compatible with those of linguistic semantics—that is, representing the meaning of the sentence in a manner equivalent to human understanding (as aspired to by linguistic semanticists) or as close to human understanding as possible, or at least complete, coherent, and consistent enough to support computational applications of language processing (as computational semanticists would have it).

There are, however, two significant differences between the goals of computational semantics and those of linguistic semantics. First, computational semantics does not claim that its rules are contained in the mind of the native speaker; in other words, the strong-AI claim (see section 2.4.3) is not on its agenda. Second, it requires comprehensive coverage of language material instead of limiting itself to illustrative examples of select phenomena (see section 4.4). It is not surprising, in view of the above, that Wilks and Fass (1992a, 1182; see also the longer version in Wilks and Fass 1992b; cf. the earlier work in Wilks 1971, 1972, 1975a) state that "to have a meaning is to have one from among a set of possible meanings" and posit as the central goal of a computational semantic theory "the process of choosing or preferring among those," which is why Wilks's theory is called *preference semantics*. While the second goal is missing from Katz and Fodor's theory and from linguistic theory in general, there is also a significant difference between treating meaning as a set of possible meanings, as they do, and realizing that actually meaning is always only one element from this set. This lack of interest in disambiguation was acceptable in a theory that explicitly and deliberately concerned itself mostly with potential meaning rather than with calculating the meaning of a particular sentence in a particular text. The latter goal is, of course, the overall goal of computational semantics.

Wilks and Fass (1992a, 1183) see preference semantics as "a theory of language in which the meaning of a text is represented by a complex semantic structure that is built up out of components; this compositionality is a typical feature of semantic theories. The principal difference between [preference semantics] and other semantic theories is in the explicit and computational treatment of ambiguous, metaphorical and nonstandard language use." The components of the theory include up to 100 semantic primitives including case roles, types of action, types of entities, and types of qualifiers; word senses expressed in terms of the primitives; a hierarchy of templates corresponding to phrases, clauses, and sentences; inference rules used for resolving anaphora; and some text-level structures. Preferences are essentially procedures for applying heuristics to selection restrictions and other constraint-satisfaction statements, as well as for selecting the outcome (that is, a semantic representation) with the greatest semantic "density" and "specificity" (p. 1188). There is no expectation in the approach that all preferences will somehow "work," and provisions are made for such eventualities, so that some meaning representation is always guaranteed to exist. In other words, this approach is based on a realistic premise that the computer program will have to deal with an incomplete and imprecise set of resources such as lexicons and grammars.

Preference semantics is a comprehensive approach to meaning in natural language not only because it combines lexical semantics with compositional semantics, but also because it aspires to a full meaning representation of each sentence. Other approaches in computational semantics were—deliberately or otherwise—less general and concentrated on particular issues. Thus, Schank's (e.g., 1975, Schank and Riesbeck 1981; Lehnert 1978; Wilensky 1983) school of computational semantics, conceptual dependency, used a different and more constrained set of semantic primitives to represent the meaning of both words and sentences. But it eventually concentrated on story understanding based on the idea of a progressively more abstract hierarchy of text-level knowledge structures—scripts, plans, goals, memory organization packets, and so on. Hirst (1987), following Charniak (e.g., 1983b), further developed the mechanism to calculate preferences, and each computational semantic project (e.g., among many, Hobbs and Rosenschein 1977; Sowa 1984) propounded a different representation formalism for both text meaning and lexical semantics.

Over the years of work in linguistic and then computational semantics, the early aspirations for parsimony of primitive elements for describing lexical meaning have gradually given way to the more realistic position, first stated by Hayes (1979), that in computational semantics (and, for that matter, in all of artificial intelligence) a much more realistic hope is to keep the ratio of description primitives, a', to entities under description, a, as small as possible: $a'/a \ll 1$. Experience shows that if the number of primitives is kept small, descriptions tend to become complex combinations of the primitives that are hard to interpret and use. Given the additional fact that such primitives are rarely explicitly described, let alone formally defined, there is a strong pressure to stretch the range of each primitive, resulting in vagueness of primitive meaning. This issue strikes us as being of primary importance. While many approaches use primitives (whether overtly or implicitly), very few expend sufficient energy on their explicit characterization, which is essential for reliability of knowledge acquisition and meaning representation. We see ontologies as the loci for precisely such characterizations.

Much valuable experience, both positive and negative, has been accumulated in formal, linguistic, and computational semantics. Ontological semantics aspires to take advantage of the results available in the field. We see the principal differences between ontological semantics and other semantic theories as follows:

• First, besides introducing ontology as a locus for establishing a rich set of primitives, we see ontological semantics also as the best means of supporting multilingual NLP applications because ontological information is—by definition and by practice of acquisition—language independent.

• Second, ontological semantics is a comprehensive theory integrating lexical semantics with compositional semantics and moving into pragmatics.

• Third, ontological semantics is designed to adjust semantic-description depth to the needs of an application (see section 2.5.4).

• Fourth, ontological semantics has an emphasis on full-coverage description of text at a predetermined level of granularity because a computational procedure has no tolerance for what has become a staple in the mainstream linguistic literature. We are referring to assumed similarities of descriptions of many phenomena with those few that were actually illustrated, careless extrapolations to adjacent phenomena, and those ubiquitous etceteras in vitally important lists.

CHAPTER 4

Choices for Lexical Semantics

In this chapter, we discuss the positions taken by ontological semantics on certain issues and preferences in lexical semantics. We fashion some of the chapter as a dialogue with Pustejovsky 1995, agreeing with it on some issues and disagreeing on others. (The fact that the latter type of comment may seem more prominent in the chapter should not overshadow the fact that we count Pustejovsky as a representationalist, antiformalist ally in important computational semantic debates. It is a sign of a true scientist that he has allowed us to use his book as a kind of a foil and did not attempt to forestall our criticism in his editorial comments.)

The chapter focuses on four central issues raised in the lexical semantics of the late 1980s to early 1990s, as follows:

• Section 4.1 deals with the notion of the "generative" lexicon as opposed to the "enumerative" lexicon. The former is presumed to be capable of accommodating "novel" meanings, while the latter can only reflect the fixed, corpus-attested senses of the lexical entries. The section removes the opposition as largely imputed, claiming that any good lexicon, including, of course, the ontological semantic ones, cannot help being generative.

• Section 4.2 discusses the complicated issue of the relationship between semantics and syntax, both the myth and reality of it. At stake is the premise that lexical semantic distinctions must mirror some syntactic distinctions and that, therefore, one can capture the former through the latter. We reject this rather common premise and explain why.

• Section 4.3 is this chapter's necessary venture into compositional semantics as an exploration of one particular issue: what kind of sentential-meaning component is presumed by the generative lexicon approach. We take exception to expecting too little from compositional semantics, namely, only what formal semantics can do, and to relegating too much work in accounting for meaning to the "wastebasket" of pragmatics.

• Section 4.4 puts forward the comprehensively descriptive nature of NLP. As opposed to the current disciplinary practices in "pure" linguistics, full-coverage computational work requires a full representation of every element of the processed text. Focusing specifically on the uncommon, unusual, borderline, or controversial phenomena and assuming the common cases as a given will simply not do.

The chapter complements, in a sense, chapter 3 and, together with it, completes the task of relating ontological semantics to other pertinent linguistic semantic approaches and issues.

4.1 Generativity

A popular idea in lexical semantics has been to make the lexicon "generative." The reasons for this are both theoretical—to extend the idea of generativity from grammar to the lexicon—and practical: looking for ways of saving effort in acquisition of lexicons through the use of automatic devices. Pustejovsky (1991, 1995) introduces the generative lexicon (GL) in opposition to the lexicons in which all the senses are independent and simply enumerated. In this section, we attempt to demonstrate that, while GL may indeed be superior to an enumerative lexicon based exclusively on corpus-attested usages, it has no special advantages over a well-compiled broad-coverage enumerative lexicon suitable for realistic applications. In particular, the claimed ability of GL to account for the so-called novel word senses is matched by good-quality enumerative lexicons. The difference between generative and enumerative lexicons is, then, reduced to a preference for using lexical knowledge at runtime or at lexicon-acquisition time. The generativity of a lexicon turns out to be synonymous with (striving for) high quality of a lexicon, and GL may have been a popular but by no means the only way to achieve this goal.

4.1.1 Generative Lexicon: Main Idea

There are several theoretical and descriptive avenues that the quest for automating lexical acquisition can explore:

• Using paradigmatic lexical relations of a lexeme, such as synonymy, antonymy, hyperonymy, and hyponymy to specify the lexical meaning of another lexeme; in other words, if a lexical entry is acquired, it should serve also as a largely prefilled template for the entries of words that stand in the above lexical relations to the original item

• Using a broader set of paradigmatic relations for the above task, such as the one between an organization and its leader (e.g., *company: commander, department: head, chair, manager*)

• Using syntagmatic lexical relations for the above task—for instance, those between an object and typical actions involving it (e.g., *key: unlock, lock*)

The paradigmatic and syntagmatic relations among word meanings have been explored and implemented in dictionaries of various sizes and for various languages by the members of the meaning-text school of thought since the mid-1960s (Zholkovsky, Leont'eva, and Martem'yanov 1961; Apresyan, Mel'čuk, and Zholkovsky 1969, 1973; Mel'čuk 1974, 1979). These scholars extended the list of paradigmatic relations well beyond the familiar synonymy, antonymy, and hypo-/hyperonymy. They included more specific semantic relations, such as, for instance, *Oper*, a relation between an object and a typical action performed with it as an instrument: *Oper(key) = lock, unlock*. Givón (1967) and McCawley (1968, 130–132) came up with similar ideas independently, even if they did not implement them in any actual descriptions.

The emphasis in the above work was on describing meanings of words in terms of those of other words. In the late 1980s and mostly early 1990s, the group of scholars in the Aquilex project[1] focused their attention on regular polysemy and explored how to apply paradigmatic and syntagmatic relations to the task of formulating meanings of word senses in terms of other senses of the same lexeme. They proposed to do it with the help of lexical rules that mapped lexicon entries for new senses to those of the existing senses. Each rule corresponded to a specific relation between senses, such as the well-known "grinding" rule that explained the noncount (*I like rabbit*) use of nouns typically denoting animals by the semantic shift to the meat of that animal (see section 4.4). The idea of regular polysemy ascends to some ideas of Apresyan (1974), where the term was actually introduced. Pustejovsky's work can be seen as a part and an extension of the Aquilex effort on systematic polysemy. His idea of generativity in the lexicon was, therefore, that

- Senses of a polysemous lexical item can be related in a systematic way, with types of such relations recurring across various lexical items.
- By identifying these relations, it is possible to list fewer senses in a lexical entry and to derive all the other senses with the help of (lexical) rules based on these relations.

Our own experience in lexical semantics and particularly in large-scale lexical acquisition since the mid-1980s[2] also confirms that it is much more productive to derive as many entries as possible from others according to as many lexical rules as can be found: clearly, it is common sense that acquiring a whole new entry by a ready-made formula is a lot faster. The problem is that tuning the rules to avoid overgeneration is a very difficult empirical task that resists automation, the "blocking" and "antiblocking" proposals (see Briscoe, Copestake, and Lascarides 1995; see also section 4.4) notwithstanding. In the Mikrokosmos implementation of ontological semantics, a set of lexical rules was developed and used to automatically augment the size of an ontological semantic lexicon for Spanish from about 7,000 manually acquired entries to about 38,000 entries (Viegas et al. 1996b; see also section 9.3.3). As in the case of other lexical-rule proposals, these included incorrect entries resulting from over-generation by rules that were too powerful. Subsequent manual filtering reduced the overall number by almost 50 percent.

4.1.2   Generative vs. Enumerative?

Some claims made about the generative lexicon do not seem essential for its enter-prise. In this and the next subsection, we critically examine them, in the spirit of freeing a good idea of unnecessary ballast.

The generative lexicon is motivated, in part, by the shortcomings of the entity it is juxtaposed with, the enumerative lexicon. The enumerative lexicon is criticized for:

• Just listing the senses for each lexical item without establishing any relations among them
• The arbitrariness of (or, at least, a lack of a consistent criterion for) sense selection and coverage
• Failing to cover the complete range of usages for a lexical item
• Inability to cover novel, unattested senses

Enumerative lexicons that display the above features are certainly real enough (most human-oriented dictionaries conform to the description to some extent), and there are quite a few of them around. However, there may be good enumerative lexicons that cannot serve as foils for the generative lexicon. Enumerative lexicons could, in fact, be acquired using a well-thought-out and carefully planned procedure based on a sound and efficient methodology, underlain, in turn, by a theory. There is no rea-son whatsoever to believe that such an enumerative lexicon will be unable to cover exactly the same senses as the generative lexicon, with the relations among these senses as clearly marked.

In ontological semantics, the acquisition methodology allows for the application of lexical rules and other means of automating lexical acquisition both at the time when the lexicon is acquired (acquisition time) and when it is used (runtime). In the gener-ative lexicon, only the latter option is presupposed. Whether, in a computational application, lexical rules are triggered at acquisition or runtime may have computa-tional significance, but their generative capacity (e.g., in the sense of Chomsky 1965, 60, i.e., their output) is not affected by that, one way or another (see Viegas et al. 1996).

4.1.3   Generative Lexicon and Novel Senses

In a modern enumerative approach, such as that used in ontological semantics, text corpora are routinely used as sources of heuristics for establishing both the bound-aries of a word sense and the number of different word senses inside a lexeme. However, unlike in the generative lexicon, an ontological semantic lexicon will include senses obtained by other means, including lexical rules. All the applicable lexical rules are applied to all eligible lexical entries, thus creating entries for all the derived senses, many of them not attested in the corpora.

Assuming the potential equivalence of the content of the generative lexicon, on the one hand, and a high-quality enumerative lexicon, on the other, the claimed ability of the generative lexicon to generate novel, creative senses of lexical items needs to be examined more closely. What does this claim mean? What counts as a novel sense? Theoretically, it is a sense that has not been previously attested to and that is a new, original usage. This, of course, is something that occurs rather rarely (*pace* Wilks 1997, who quotes Greene 1989 as claiming that such usages account for 20 percent of a corpus; we suspect, however, that Greene was using a dictionary with too many senses—cf. section 9.3.5). Practically, it is a sense that does not occur in a corpus or in the lexicon based on this corpus. Neither the generative lexicon nor a good enumerative lexicon will—or should—list all the senses overtly. Many of those senses may be derived through the application of lexical rules. But even if not listed, such derived senses are present in the lexicon virtually, as it were, because they are fully determined by the preexisting domain of a preexisting lexical rule.

Does the claim of novelty mean that senses are novel and creative if they are not recorded in some given enumerative lexicon? If so, then the object chosen for comparison is low quality (unless it was built based exclusively on a given corpus of texts) and therefore not the most appropriate one, because one should assume a similar quality of the lexicons under comparison. While the literature is not quite explicit on this point, several contributions (e.g., Johnston, Boguraev, and Pustejovsky 1995; Copestake 1995) seem to indicate the implicit existence of a given inferior lexicon or a nonrepresentative corpus against which the comparison is made.

The other line of reasoning for justifying the claim of novelty involves the phenomena of type shifting and type coercion. A creative usage is one arising from a rule that would overcome a sortal or other incongruity to avoid having to reject an input sentence as ill-formed. But there are rules that make type shifting and type coercion work. They are all preexisting—not post hoc—rules, and, therefore, like other lexical rules, fully determine, or enumerate (see below), their output in advance.[3]

The above both clarifies the notion of a novel, creative sense as used in the generative lexicon approach and raises serious doubts about its validity. One wonders whether the phenomenon is, really, simply the incompleteness of the corpus and the lexicon relative to which these senses are claimed to be novel. The claim of novelty is then reduced to a statement that it is better to have a high-quality corpus or lexicon than a lower-quality one, and, obviously, nobody will argue with that! A truly novel and creative usage will not have a ready-made generative device for which it is a possible output, and this is precisely what will make this sense novel and creative.

Such a usage will present a problem for a generative lexicon, just as it will for an enumerative one or, as a matter of fact, for a human trying to treat creative usage as metaphorical, allusive, ironic, or humorous at text-processing time. The crucial issue here is understanding that no lexicon will cover all the possible senses that words can assume in real usage. Ontological semantics views the analysis of such "novel" senses as a special case of treating unattested input (see section 8.4.3).

4.1.4   Permeative Usage?

Another claimed advantage of the generative lexicon is that it "remembers" all the lexical rules that relate its senses. We submit, however, that, after all these rules have worked, the computational applications using the lexicon would have no use for them or any memory—or, to use a loaded term, trace—of them whatsoever. In other words, the decidability of the fully deployed set of all listed and derived senses is of no computational consequence.

Pustejovsky (1995, 47–50) comes up with the notion of permeability of word senses to support his claim that a lexical rule has a "memory." Comparing *John baked the potatoes* and *Mary baked a cake*, he wants both the change-of-state sense of *bake* in the former example and the creation sense in the latter to be present, to overlap, to permeate each other. The desire to see both of these meanings present is linked, of course, to the implicit premise that these two meanings of *bake* should not both be listed in the lexicon but rather that one of them should be derived from the other. The argument, then, runs as follows: See these two distinct senses? Well, they are both present in each of the examples above, thus permeating the other. Therefore, they should not be listed as two distinct senses. Or, putting it more schematically: See these two senses? Now you don't!

Our position on this issue is simple. Yes, there are perhaps two distinct senses—if one can justify the distinction (see section 9.3.5 for a detailed discussion of methods to justify the introduction of a separate sense in a lexeme). No, they do not, in our estimation, both appear in the same normal (not deliberately ambiguous) usage. Yes, we do think that the two senses of *bake* may be listed as distinct, with their semantics dependent on the semantic properties of their themes. Yes, they can also be derived from each other, but what for and at what price?

We also think the permeative analysis of the data is open to debate, because it appears to jeopardize what seems to us to be the most basic principle of language as practiced by its speakers, namely, that each felicitous speech act is unambiguous. It is known that native speakers, while adept at understanding the meaning of natural language text, find it very hard to detect ambiguity.[4] It stands to reason that it would be equally difficult for them to register permeation, and we submit that they actually do not, and that the permeating senses are an artifact of the generative lexicon approach. This, we guess, is a cognitive argument against permeation.

Encouraging permeative usage amounts to introducing something very similar to deliberate ambiguity, a kind of "sense-and-a-half" situation, into semantic theory, both at the word-meaning level as permeability and at the sentence-meaning level as co-compositionality (see also sections 3.3, 3.4, and 3.7). It seems especially redundant when an alternative analysis is possible. One of the senses of *cake* should and would indicate that it often is a result of baking—there are, however, cold, uncooked dishes that are referred to as cakes as well. No sense of *potato* would indicate that—instead, *potato*, unlike *cake*, would be identified as a possible theme of *cook*, and *cook* will have *bake* and many other verbs as its hyponyms. This analysis takes good care of disambiguating the two senses of *bake* via the meaning of their respective themes, if a need for such disambiguation arises. In fact, it still needs to be demonstrated that it is necessary or, for that matter, possible, to disambiguate between these two senses for any practical or theoretical purpose, other than to support the claim of permeability of senses in the generative lexicon approach. And, circularly, this claim is subordinate to the imperative, implicit in the generative lexicon approach, to reduce the number of senses in a lexicon entry to a preferable minimum of one.

4.1.5   Generative vs. Enumerative "Yardage"

To summarize, some central claims associated with the generative lexicon seem to compare it with low-quality or badly acquired enumerative lexicons and to disregard the fact that any reasonable acquisition procedure for an enumerative lexicon will subsume, and has subsumed in practice, the generative devices of the generative lexicon.

When all is said and done, it appears that the difference between the generative lexicon and the high-quality enumerative lexicon is only in some relatively unimportant numbers. The former aspires to minimize the number of listed senses for each entry, reducing it ideally to one. The latter has no such ambitions, and the minimization of the number of listed entries in it is affected by the practical consideration of the minimization of the acquisition effort, as mentioned in section 4.1.1.

To reach the same generative capacity from a smaller range of listed senses, the generative lexicon will have to discover, or postulate, more lexical rules. Our practical experience shows that this effort may exceed, in many cases, the effort involved in listing more senses, even if each such sense must be created from scratch.

A final note on generativity in the lexicon: in an otherwise pretty confused argument against Pustejovsky's treatment of *bake* and his efforts to reduce the two meanings to one (see section 4.1.4), Fodor and Lepore (1998) manage to demonstrate that any gain from that reduction will be counterbalanced by the need to deal both with the process of attaining this goal and with the consequences of such treatment of polysemy.[5] We cannot help agreeing with their conclusion, albeit achieved from questionable premises, that "the total yardage gained would appear to be negligible or nil" (p. 7).

4.2   Syntax vs. Semantics

The principal choice for lexical semantics with respect to its relations with syntax is whether to assume that each syntactic distinction suggests a semantic difference. Similarly to the situation in compositional semantics (see section 3.5.2), a theoretical proposal in lexical semantics may occasionally claim not to assume a complete isomorphism between the two, but in practice, most lexical semanticists accept this simplifying assumption.

GL's position on this issue, shared by many lexical semanticists, is expressed variously as the dependence of semantics on "basic lexical categories" (Pustejovsky 1995, 1), on "syntactic patterns" and "grammatical alternations" (p. 8), as the search for "semantic discriminants leading to the distinct behavior of the transitive verbs" in the examples (p. 10), or as an "approach [that] would allow variation in complement selection to be represented as distinct senses" (p. 35). The apparently thorough and constant dependence of lexical semantics on syntax comes through most clearly in the analyses of examples.

Thus, introducing a variation of Chomsky's (1957) famous examples of *John is eager to please* and *John is easy to please* and analyzing them in terms of *tough*-movement and the availability or nonavailability of alternating constructions, Pustejovsky (1995, 21–22) makes it clear that these different syntactic behaviors essentially constitute the semantic difference between adjectives like *eager* and adjectives like *easy*. We have demonstrated elsewhere (e.g., Raskin and Nirenburg 1995) that much more semantics is involved in the analysis of differences between these two adjectives and that these differences are not at all syntax dependent. *Easy* is a typical scalar, whose value is a range on the ease-difficulty scale and that modifies events; *eager* is a modality-derived (namely, the volitive modality typically expressed by wantlike verbs—see also section 8.5.3) adjective modifying the agent of the event. This semantic analysis does explain the different syntactic behaviors of these adjectives but not the other way around.

One interesting offshoot of the earlier syntax-versus-semantics debates has been growing interest in "grammatical semantics," the subset of the semantics of natural languages that deals with the meaning of closed-class lexical items, such as quantifiers (see, for instance, Frawley 1992—cf. Raskin 1994) or the semantic import of syntactic taxonomies (e.g., B. Levin 1993; cf. the discussion in Nirenburg and L. Levin 1992). This is a perfectly legitimate enterprise as long as one keeps in mind that semantics does not end there.

Wilks (1996) presents another example of an intelligent division of labor between syntax and semantics. He shows that up to 92 percent of homography recorded in the *Longman Dictionary of Contemporary English* (LDOCE) (1987) can be disambiguated based exclusively on the knowledge of the part-of-speech marker of a homograph. Homography is, of course, a form of polysemy, and it is useful to know that the labor-intensive semantic methods are not necessary to process all of its cases. Thus, semantics can focus on the residual polysemy where syntax does not help. In a system not relying on LDOCE, a comparable result may be achieved if word senses are arranged in a hierarchy, with homography at the top levels, and if disambiguation is required only down to some nonterminal node in that hierarchy.

It is also very important to understand that, ideally, grammatical semantics should not assume that each syntactic distinction is reflected in a semantic distinction. Instead, it should look at grammaticalized semantic distinctions—that is, at semantic phenomena that have overt morphological or syntactic realizations. Consequently, work in grammatical semantics should not consist of detecting semantic distinctions for classes of lexical items with different values on a given syntactic feature (see, for instance, Briscoe, Copestake, and Lascarides 1995; Copestake 1995; or Briscoe and Copestake 1996).

The dependence on syntax in lexical semantics may lead to artificially constrained and misleading analyses. Thus, the analysis of the sense of *fast* in *fast motorway* (see, for instance, Lascarides 1995, 75) as a new and creative sense of the adjective as opposed, say, to its sense in *fast runner*, ignores the important difference between syntactic and semantic modification. It is predicated on the implicit conviction that the use of the adjective with a different noun subcategory—which constitutes, since Chomsky 1965, a different syntactic environment for the adjective—automatically creates a different sense for *fast*. As shown in Raskin and Nirenburg 1995, however, many adjectives do not modify semantically the nouns they modify syntactically, and this phenomenon covers many more examples than the well-known *occasional pizza* or *relentless miles*. Separating syntactic and semantic modification in the case of *fast* shows that it is, in fact, a modifier for an event. Its surface realization can be, at least in English, syntactically attached to the realizations of several semantic roles of, for instance, *run* or *drive*, namely, AGENT in *fast runner*, INSTRUMENT in *fast car*, and LOCATION (or PATH) in *fast motorway*. Throughout these examples, *fast* is used in exactly the same sense, and letting syntax drive semantics distorts the latter seriously. We maintain that it is incorrect and unnecessary either to postulate a new sense of *fast* in this case or to relegate it to the "dustbin of pragmatics," which amounts in practice to justifying a failure to treat this phenomenon at all. In section 8.4.4, we show how ontological semantics proposes to treat this phenomenon as a standard case of semantic ellipsis.

Distinguishing word senses on the basis of differences in syntactic behavior does not seem to be a very promising practice (cf. the Dorr, Garman, and Weinberg 1994–1995 attempt to develop B. Levin's approach into doing precisely this). This is true also because such an endeavor can only be based on the implicit assumption of isomorphism between the set of syntactic constructions and the set of lexical meanings. But it seems obvious that there are more lexical meanings than syntactic distinctions, orders of magnitude more. That means that syntactic distinctions can at best define classes of lexical meanings, and indeed that is precisely what the earlier incursions from syntax into semantics achieved: rather coarse-grained taxonomies of meanings in terms of a rather small set of features.

4.3   Lexical Semantics and Sentential Meaning

Semantics as a whole can be said to be the study of lexical and sentential meaning. When the work of lexical semantics is finished, the question arises of how word meanings are combined into the meaning of a sentence. In many lexical semantic approaches, including GL, it is assumed that deriving sentential meaning is the task of formal semantics (see section 3.5.1). The other choice would be developing a dedicated theory for this purpose. An orthogonal choice is whether simply to acknowledge the need for treating sentential meaning as the continuation of work in lexical semantics or to actively develop the means of doing so. In what follows, we will discuss these choices. We will not reiterate our discussion of sentential semantics in section 3.5: what we are interested in here is how (and, actually, whether) the proposer of a lexical semantic approach addresses its integration with an approach to sentential semantics.

We should mention, without developing it further—because we consider it unsustainable and because no realistic semantic theory has been put forth on this basis—a possible extreme point of view that denies the existence of lexical semantics by claiming that words only acquire meanings in sentences (cf. Grice 1957, which takes this claim further into nonrepresentationalism by denying that sentences have meanings before acquiring them in actual utterances; see also sections 2.6.2.2, 2.6.3.4, and note 33 in chapter 2). What is at issue is the tension between the meaning of text and word meaning. The compositional approach assumes the latter as a given, but one has to be mindful of the fact that word meaning is, for many linguists, only a definitional construct for semantic theory, "an artifact of theory and training" (Wilks 1996). Throughout the millennia, there have been views in linguistic and philosophical thought that only sentences are real and basic, and that words acquire their meanings only in sentences (see, for instance, Gardiner 1951, who traces this tradition back to the earliest Indian thinkers; Firth 1957, Zvegintzev 1968, and Raskin 1971 treat word meaning as a function of the usage of a word with other words in sentences but without denying the existence of word meaning; Grice 1975).

4.3.1   Formal Semantics for Sentential Meaning

In spite of Pustejovsky's (1995, 1) initial and fully justified rejection of formal semantics as a basis for achieving the GL goals with respect to sentential meaning, all

that he found in contemporary linguistic semantics for dealing with sentential meaning was the analysis of quantifiers and other closed-class phenomena. Formal semantics essentially claims a monopoly on compositionality and, within its limited
purview, extends itself into lexical semantics.[6]

This creates a problem for the GL approach: there is no ready-made semantic
theory it can use for the task of sentential-meaning representation of the sufficiently
fine granularity that NLP requires. This situation is familiar to all lexical semanticists. In GL, Pustejovsky tries to enhance the concept of compositionality as an alternative to standard formal semantics. In the GL approach, compositionality ends
up as a part of lexical semantics proper, while formal semantics takes over in the
realm of sentential meaning.

As we argued in section 3.5.1, however, formal semantics is not necessarily the best
candidate for the theory of sentential meaning. It is a direct application of mathematical logic to natural language. All the central concepts in logic are taken from
outside natural language, and the fit between these concepts and the language phenomena is not natural. Formal semantics thus follows a method-driven approach,
exploring all the language phenomena to which it is applicable and of necessity
ignoring the rest. An alternative to such an approach is a problem-driven approach,
an investigation of all relevant language phenomena, with methods and formalisms
derived for the express purpose of such an investigation (see Nirenburg and Raskin
1999).

4.3.2 Ontological Semantics for Sentential Meaning

Problem-driven approaches to semantics include conceptual dependency (e.g., Schank
1975), preference semantics (Wilks 1975a), and our own ontological semantics. In
ontological semantics, to recapitulate briefly, sentential meaning is defined as an
expression, text-meaning representation (TMR), obtained through the application
of the sets of rules for syntactic analysis of the source text, for linking syntactic
dependencies into ontological dependencies, and for establishing the meaning of
source-text lexical units. The crucial element of this theory is a formal world model,
or ontology, which also underlies the lexicon and is thus the basis of the lexical semantic component. The ontology is, then, the metalanguage for ontological lexical
semantics and the foundation of its integration with ontological sentential semantics.

We are not ready to go as far as claiming that lexical semantics and sentential semantics must always have the same metalanguage, but we do claim that each must
have a metalanguage. We know that not all approaches introduce such a metalanguage explicitly (see sections 2.4.1.3 and 2.4.5, especially table 2.2). In lexical semantics, this means, quite simply, that every theory must make a choice concerning
the conceptual status of its metalanguage. The introduction of an explicit ontology
is one way to make this choice. Other choices also exist, as exemplified by the GL

approach, in which "nonlinguistic conceptual organizing principles" (Pustejovsky 1995, 6) are considered useful, though they remain undeveloped.

We believe that the notational elements that are treated as theory in GL can be legitimately considered elements of semantic theory only if they are anchored in a well-designed model of the world, or an ontology. Without an ontology, the status of these notions becomes uncertain, which may license an osmosis- or emulation-based usage of them: a new feature and certainly a new value for a feature can always be expected to be produced if needed, the ad hoc way. A good example of this state of affairs is the basic concept of "qualia" in GL.

The qualia structure in GL consists of a prescribed set of four roles with an open-ended set of values. The enterprise carries an unintended resemblance to the type of work fashionable in AI NLP in the late 1960s and 1970s: proposing sets of properties (notably, semantic cases or case roles) for characterizing the semantic-dependency behavior of argument-taking lexical units (see, e.g., Bruce 1975). That tradition also involved proposals for systems of semantic atoms—or primitives—used for describing actual meanings of lexical units. This latter issue is outside the sphere of interest of GL, though not, in our opinion, of lexical semantic theory.

The definitions of the four qualia roles are in terms of meaning and share all the difficulties of circumscribing the meaning of case roles. Assignment of values to roles is not discussed by Pustejovsky in any detail, and some of the assignments are problematic. An example is the value "narrative" for the constitutive role (which is defined as "the relation between an object and its constitutive parts" (1995, 76)) for the lexicon entry of *novel* (p. 78). The usage of "telic" has been made quite plastic as well (pp. 99–100), by introducing "direct" and "purpose" telicity, without specifying a rule about how to understand whether a particular value is direct or purpose.

One would expect to have all elements such as the four qualia specified explicitly with regard to their scope, and this is, in fact, what theories are for. What is the conceptual space from which the qualia and other notational elements of the approach emerge? Why does GL miss an opportunity to define that space explicitly in such a way that the necessity and sufficiency of the notational concepts introduced become clear —including, of course, an opportunity to falsify its conclusions on the basis of its own explicitly stated rules?[7] An explicit ontology would have done all of the above for GL.

To be fair, some suggestions have been made for generalizing meaning descriptions in GL using the concept of lexical conceptual paradigms (e.g., Pustejovsky and Boguraev 1993; Pustejovsky and Anick 1988; Pustejovsky, Bergler, and Anick 1993). These paradigms "encode basic lexical knowledge that is not associated with individual entries but with sets of entries or concepts" (Bergler 1994–1995, 169). Such "metalexical" paradigms combine with linking information through an associated syntactic schema to supply each lexical entry with information necessary for semantic processing. While it is possible to view this simply as a convenience device that allows the lexicographer to specify a set of constraints for a group of lexical entries at once (as was, for instance, done in the KBMT-89 project (Nirenburg et al. 1991)), this approach can be seen as a step toward incorporating an ontology.

Bergler 1994–1995 extends the amount of these "metalexical" structures recognized by the generative lexicon to include many elements that are required for actual text understanding. Thus, it presents a set of properties she calls a "style sheet," whose genesis can be traced to the "pragmatic factors" of PAULINE (Hovy 1988). It stops short, however, of incorporating a full-fledged ontology and instead introduces nine features, in terms of which she describes reporting verbs in English. A similar approach to semantic analysis with a set number of disjoint semantic features playing the role of the underlying meaning model was used in the Panglyzer analyzer (see, for instance, Nirenburg 1994).

There is a great deal of apprehension and, we think, miscomprehension about the nature of ontology in the literature, and we addressed some of these and related issues in section 2.6.2.2 and in chapter 5, as well as in Nirenburg, Raskin, and Onyshkevych 1995. One recurring trend in the writings of scholars from the AI tradition is toward erasing the boundaries between ontologies and taxonomies of natural language concepts. This can be found in Hirst 1995, which acknowledges the insights of Kay 1971. Both papers treat ontology as the lexicon of a natural (though invented) language, and Hirst objects to it, basically, along the lines of the redundancy and awkwardness of treating one natural language in terms of another. Similarly, Wilks, Slator, and Guthrie (1996, 59) see ontological efforts as adding another natural language (see also Johnston, Boguraev, and Pustejovsky 1995, 72), albeit artificially concocted, to the existing ones, while somehow claiming its priority.

By contrast, in ontological semantics, an ontology for NLP purposes is seen not at all as a natural language but rather as a language-neutral "body of knowledge about the world (or a domain) that a) is a repository of primitive symbols used in meaning representation; b) organizes these symbols in a tangled subsumption hierarchy; and c) further interconnects these symbols using a rich system of semantic and discourse-pragmatic relations defined among the concepts" (Mahesh and Nirenburg 1995, 1; see also section 7.1). The names of concepts in the ontology may look like English words or phrases, but their semantics is quite different and is defined in terms of explicitly stated interrelationships among these concepts. The function of the ontology is to supply "world knowledge to lexical, syntactic, and semantic processes" (Mahesh and Nirenburg 1995, 1), and, in fact, we use exactly the same ontology for supporting multilingual machine translation.

An ontology like that comes at a considerable cost. It demands a deep commitment in time, effort, and intellectual engagement, and requires a dedicated methodology based on a theoretical foundation (see chapter 5). The rewards, however, are also huge: a powerful base of "primitives," with a rich content and connectivity made available for specifying the semantics of lexical entries, contributing to their consistency and nonarbitrariness.[8]

4.3.3   Lexical Semantics and Pragmatics

In much of lexical and formal semantics, three major postsyntactic modules are often distinguished, though not at all often developed: lexical semantics, compositional semantics, and pragmatics. Pragmatics is variously characterized as "commonsense knowledge," "world knowledge," or, even more vaguely, context. It is perceived as complex, and, alternatively, not worth doing or not possible to do, at least for now (see, for instance, Pustejovsky 1995, 4; Copestake 1995). Occasionally, brief incursions into this terra incognita are undertaken in the framework of syntax-driven lexical semantics (see, for instance, Asher and Lascarides 1995; Lascarides 1995) in order to account for difficulties in specific lexical descriptions. Pragmatic information is, then, added to corresponding lexical entries to explain the contextual meanings of words. Curiously, pragmatics is, in this view, related to lexical semantics but not to sentential semantics.

An important point for us in understanding this position is that scholars firmly committed to formality (and formalism; see section 2.4.1.4) felt compelled to venture into an area admittedly much less formalizable, because without this, it would not have been possible to account for certain lexical semantic phenomena. The next logical step, then, would be to come up with a comprehensive theory and methodology for combining all kinds of pertinent information with lexical meaning and characteristics of the process of deriving sentential meaning. We believe that continued reliance on truth-conditional formal semantics as a theory of sentential meaning would make such an enterprise even more difficult than it actually is.

Ontological semantics does not see any reason even to distinguish pragmatics in the above sense from deriving and representing meaning in context—after all, any kind of language- or world-related information may, and does, provide clues for semantic analysis. The sentential semantics in our approach is designed to accommodate both types of information. As Wilks and Fass (1992a, 1183) put it, "Knowledge of language and the world are not separable,[9] just as they are not separable into databases called, respectively, dictionaries and encyclopedias" (see also Nirenburg 1986). Practically, world knowledge, commonsense knowledge, or contextual knowledge, is recorded in the language-independent static knowledge sources of ontological semantics—the ontology and the fact repository. The main question that an ontological semanticist faces with respect to that type of knowledge is not whether it should be recorded, but rather how this is done best.

4.4   Description Coverage

In principle, any theory prefers to seek general and elegant solutions to an entire set
of phenomena in its purview. In practice, lexical semantics has to choose whether to
account only for those phenomena that lend themselves to generalization or to hold
itself responsible for describing the entire set of phenomena required by a domain or
an application.

GL shares with theoretical linguistics the practice of high selectivity with regard
to its material. This makes such works great fun to read: interesting phenomena are
selected; borderline cases are examined. The tacit assumption is that the ordinary
cases are easy to account for, and so they are not dealt with. As we mentioned elsewhere (Raskin, Attardo, and Attardo 1994a, 1994b; Raskin and Nirenburg 1995),
in the whole of transformational and posttransformational semantic theory, only a
handful of examples have ever actually been described, with no emphasis on coverage. Lexical semantics is largely vulnerable on the same count.

Large-scale applications, on the other hand, require the description of every lexical
semantic phenomenon (and a finer-grained description than what can be provided by
a handful of features, often conveniently borrowed from syntax). The task is to develop a theory for such applications underlying a principled methodology for complete descriptive coverage of the material. The implementation of any such project
would clearly demonstrate that the proverbial common case is not so common: there
are many nontrivial decisions and choices to make, often involving large classes of
data.

Good theorists carry out descriptive work in full expectation that a close scrutiny
of data will lead to often-significant modifications of their a priori notions. The task
of complete coverage forces such modifications on preempirical theories. Thus, the
need to describe the semantics of scalars forced the development of the previously
underexplored phenomenon of scale—for example, *big* (scale: SIZE), *good* (scale:
QUALITY), or *beautiful* (scale: APPEARANCE) in the study of the semantics of adjectives
(Raskin and Nirenburg 1995, 1998).

There are many reasons to attempt to write language descriptions in the most
general manner—the more generally applicable the rules, the fewer rules need to be
written; the smaller the set of rules (of a given complexity), the more elegant the
solution, and so on. In the area of the lexicon, for example, the ideal of generalizability and productivity is to devise simple entries that, when used as data by a set
of syntactic- and semantic-analysis operations, regularly yield predictable results in a
compositional manner. To be maximally general, much of the information in lexical
entries should be inherited, based on class membership, or should be predictable
from general principles.

However, experience with NLP applications shows that the pursuit of generalization for its own sake promises only limited success. In a multitude of routine cases, it becomes difficult to use general rules because they tend to overgenerate. The enterprise of building a language description maximizing the role of generalizations is neatly encapsulated by Sparck Jones (1991, 137): "We may have a formalism with axioms, rules of inference, and so forth which is quite kosher as far as the manifest criteria for logics go, but which is a logic only in the letter, not the spirit. This is because, to do its job, it has to absorb the *ad hoc* miscellaneity that makes language only approximately systematic."

This state of affairs, all too familiar to anybody who has attempted even a medium-scale description of an actual language beyond the stages of morphology and syntax, leads to the necessity of directly representing, usually in the lexicon, information about how to process small classes of phenomena that could not be covered by general rules. An important goal for developers of NLP systems is thus to find the correct balance between what can be processed on general principles and what is idiosyncratic in language, what we can calculate and what we must know literally, what is compositional and what is conventional. In other words, the decision as to what to put into a set of general rules and what to store in a static knowledge base such as the lexicon becomes a crucial early decision in designing computational linguistic theories and applications. Thus, the question is: to generalize or not to generalize?

The firmly negative answer ("never generalize") is not common in NLP applications these days. After all, some generalizations are very easy to make and exceptions to some rules do not faze too many people: morphology rules are a good example.[10] A skeptical position on generalization—that is, "generalize only when it is beneficial"—is usually taken by developers of large-scale applications, having to deal with deadlines and deliverables. Only rules with respectable-sized scopes are typically worth pursuing according to this position (see Viegas et al. 1996b). The "nasty" question here is: Are you ready then to substitute "a bag of tricks" for the actual rules of language? Of course, the jury is still out on the issue of whether language can be fully explained or modeled—at least, until we learn what actually goes on in the mind of the native speaker—with anything that is not, at least to some extent, a bag of tricks.

Rules and generalizations can not only be expensive but also in need of corrective work due to overgeneralization, and this has been a legitimate recent concern (see, for instance, Copestake 1995; Briscoe, Copestake, and Lascarides 1995). Indeed, a rule for forming the plurals of English nouns, though certainly justified in that its domain (scope) is vast, will produce, if not corrected, forms like *gooses* and *childs*. For this particular rule, providing a "stop list" of (around 200) irregular forms is relatively cheap and therefore acceptable on the grounds of overall economy. The rule for forming mass nouns determining the meat (or fur) of an animal from count nouns denoting animals (as in *He doesn't like camel*), discussed in Copestake and Briscoe 1992 as the "grinding" rule, is an altogether different story. The delineation of the domain of the rule is rather difficult (e.g., one has to deal with its applicability to *shrimp* but not to *mussel*; possibly to *ox* but certainly not to *heifer*; and, if one generalizes to nonanimal food, its applicability to *cabbage* but not *carrot*). Some mechanisms were suggested for dealing with the issue, such as, for instance, the device of "blocking" (see Briscoe, Copestake, and Lascarides 1995), which prevents the application of a rule to a noun for which there is already a specific word in the language (e.g., *beef* for *cow*). Blocking can only work, of course, if the general lexicon is sufficiently complete, and even then a special connection between the appropriate senses of *cow* and *beef* must be overtly made, manually.

Other corrective measures may become necessary as well, such as constraints on the rules, counterrules, and so on. They need to be discovered. At a certain point, the specification of the domains of the rules loses its semantic validity, and complaints to this effect have been made within the approach itself (see, for example, Briscoe and Copestake 1996 about such deficiencies in Pinker 1989 and B. Levin 1993; see also Pustejovsky 1995, 10, about B. Levin's 1993 classes).

A semantic lexicon that stresses generalization faces, therefore, the problem of having to deal with rules whose scope becomes progressively smaller—that is, the modified rules become applicable to fewer and fewer lexical units as the fight against overgeneration (carried out by means of blocking and other means) is gradually won. At some point, it becomes methodologically unwise to continue to formulate rules for the creation of just a handful of new senses. It becomes easier to define these senses extensionally, simply by enumerating the elements in the domain of the rule and writing the corresponding lexical entries overtly.

Even if it were not the case that the need to treat exceptions reduced the scope of the rules postulated to do that, the overall size of the original scope of a rule, such as the grinding rule (see also Atkins 1991; Briscoe and Copestake 1991; Ostler and Atkins 1991), should cause a considerable amount of apprehension. It is quite possible that the size of its domain is commensurate with the size of the set of nouns denoting animals or plants to which this rule is not applicable. That should raise a methodological question about the utility of this rule. Is it largely used as an example of what is possible or does it really bring about savings in the descriptive effort? Unless one claims and demonstrates the latter, one runs a serious risk of ending up where the early enthusiasts of componential analysis found themselves, after long years of perfecting their tool on the semantic field of kinship terms (see, for instance, Goodenough 1956; Greenberg 1949; Kroeber 1952; Lounsbury 1956). The scholarship neglected the fact that this semantic field was unique in being an ideal fit for the method (n binary features describing 2^n meanings). Other semantic fields, however, quickly ran the technique into the ground through the runaway proliferation of semantic features needed to be postulated for covering those fields adequately (see also section 3.4.3). We have found no explicit claims in all the excellent articles on grinding and the blocking of grinding about extensibility of the approach to other rules or rule classes. In other words, the concern for maximum generalization within one narrow class of words is not coupled with a concern for developing a methodology of discovering other lexical rules.

We believe that the postulation and use of any small rule, without an explicit concern for its generalizability and portability, is not only bad methodology but also bad theory because a theory should not be littered with generalizations whose applicability is narrow. The greater the number of rules and the smaller their domains, the less manageable—and elegant—the theory becomes. Even more importantly, the smaller the scope and the size of a semantic class, the less likely it is that a formal syntactic criterion (test) can be found for delineating such a class, and the use of such a criterion for each rule seems to be a requirement in the generative lexicon paradigm. This means that other criteria must be introduced, those not based on surface syntax observations. These criteria are, then, semantic in nature (unless they are observations of frequency of occurrence in corpora). We suspect that if the enterprise of delineating classes of scopes for rules were taken in a consistent manner, the result would be the creation of an ontology. Because there are no syntactic reasons for determining these classes, new criteria will have to be derived—specifically, the criteria used to justify ontological decisions in our approach.

This conclusion is further reinforced by the fact that the small classes set up in the battle against overgeneralization are extremely unlikely to be independently justifiable elsewhere within the approach. This situation goes against the principle of independent justification that has guided linguistic theory since Chomsky 1965, where the still-reigning and, we believe, valid paradigm for the introduction of new categories, rules, and notational devices into a theory was introduced. Now, failure to justify a class independently opens it to the charge of ad hoc-ness, which is indefensible within the paradigm. The only imaginable way out lies, again, in an independently motivated ontology. The next chapter places our notion of such an independently motivated ontology in the context of other ontological approaches.

CHAPTER 5

Formal Ontology and the Needs
of Ontological Semantics

In this chapter, we briefly discuss the philosophical and formal approaches to ontology as they relate to the needs of ontological semantics. We try to position ontological semantics within the field of formal ontology, though we do not attempt to catalog all the existing ontology development projects. A comprehensive survey is difficult to accomplish, largely because few ontologies are accessible for comparison, either in their entirety or in terms of their architecture and acquisition.

In this chapter we attempt to do four things:

• In section 5.1, we place ontology in the context of the philosophical discipline of metaphysics. Metaphysics deals with the most basic categories, and it is a scary thought—in the spirit of Nils Bohr's principle of complementarity, with the tool influencing the object under observation—that a different category choice may change one's entire picture of the world. We will see that some claims associated with metaphysics pertain to our concerns but many do not, and we discuss briefly to what extent that should concern us.

• In section 5.2, we address a number of formal issues in ontology, as developed in the field and as they pertain to our needs. This is the area in which most ontologists work—both academically, studying the mathematical properties of ontologies, and as engineers, constructing actual ontologies and methodologies for their interchange. Characteristically, this work—including the recent Semantic Web initiative—is not about natural language, so again, not all the findings in formal ontology cross into ontological semantics.

• In section 5.3, we discuss the important distinction between ontology and natural language, primarily in relation to the phenomenon of ambiguity. In this and the next section, the differences between the ontology in ontological semantics and other ontologies are discussed in detail.

• In section 5.4, we push this discussion to the point of offering a wish list from ontological semantics to be considered as an extended agenda of formal ontology, so that the findings of the latter can be of more use to the former.

5.1 Ontology and Metaphysics

Guarino (1998a, 4) suggests a distinction between "Ontology" and "ontology." The former is an academic discipline within philosophy, and for it we will use a more appropriate name, *metaphysics*—a term many scholars have hesitated to use since the positivists "made it into a term of abuse [accusing it of] isolating statements about mental life from any possibility of verification or falsification in the public world" (Kenny 1989, ix). We would like to restore the term to its legitimate domain. Like Kenny and other authors of recent works reinstating metaphysics (see, for instance, Jubien 1997; Loux 1998), we must avoid "the confusion that can be generated by bad metaphysics" and crave "the clarity which is impossible without good metaphysics" (Kenny 1989, ix).

Metaphysics is a traditional philosophical discipline, perhaps the most ancient one, since it can be traced back at least to Aristotle. It "attempt[s] to provide an account of being qua being" (Loux 1998, x). In accounting for being, metaphysics delineates the "categories of being" (p. x). These categories form the basic philosophical concepts, and those, in turn,

underlie all genuine scientific inquiry because science cannot even begin in the absence of philosophical assumptions and presuppositions. These assumptions are generally not stated explicitly and so may not even be noticed by practicing scientists or students of science. But they are there.

As an example, physics presupposes the following three things: (1) that there exists a physical reality independent of our mental states; (2) that the interactions of the stuff constituting this reality conform to certain general laws; and (3) that we are capable of grasping physical laws and obtaining evidence that favors or disfavors specific proposed laws.... The first two are metaphysical in nature while the third is epistemological.... They are not at all self-evidently true.... They are not themselves part of the subject matter of physics.   (Jubien 1997, 3–4)

Now, the list of basic categories proposed by metaphysics, the "'official' philosophical inventory of things that are ... is usually called an ontology" (Loux 1998, 15; cf. also Bergman 1992; Grossman 1992; Chisholm 1996). This is, of course, Guarino's lowercase ontology; it is the sense also in which our ontology, that of ontological semantics, exists.

The philosophical discipline of metaphysics faces a number of difficult, empirically unsolvable issues. The central one is the existence of properties on which philosophers have always been divided into two basic camps (by now, with innumerable gradations), namely, the realists and the naturalists/nominalists. The realists recognize the existence of two types of entities, individuals, which exist in time and space, and properties of individuals, which are abstract and, as such, atemporal and aspatial. The naturalists recognize the existence of just individuals.

Both camps have serious problems. The realists have to cope with two different kinds of existence, including the unobservable and directly unverifiable existence of abstract properties. Free of that concern, the naturalists have a hard time explaining away the similarity of two individuals in terms of purely physical existence. Over the centuries, the battle has seen many ingenious proposals on both sides, but the issue will not and possibly cannot go away.

How does this serious problem affect an ontology? What impact does it have on ontological semantics? Had it sided with the naturalists, it would not have had any properties in the ontology, but of course it does. Furthermore, the ontology in ontological semantics includes abstract and nonexistent entities alongside physical entities. In fact, a very large branch of this ontology, in all its implementations, is devoted to mental objects; another is devoted to mental processes. A close comparison of the ontological node for a typical mental entity and a typical physical entity will show that the fillers of the pertinent properties do reflect the distinction—for example, a mental process will manipulate mental objects and a physical, only physical ones.

What ontological semantics aims to reflect is the use of concepts by humans as they see them, introspectively and speculatively; and people do talk about properties, fictional entities (unicorns or Sherlock Holmes), and abstract entities as existing. For us, however, the decision to include the abstract and fictional entities in the ontology is not motivated by the fact that these entities can be referred to in a natural language. Rather, we believe that languages can refer to them precisely because people have these concepts in their universe.

Constructing an ontology should not be viewed as a task for metaphysics. Instead, because it is a problem of representing knowledge, it belongs in epistemology. That is, the object of study here is human knowledge about entities, not entities themselves. Inasmuch as humans know about unicorns as well as, say, goats, the respective concepts in the ontology have the same status. It is not, therefore, important for a constructed ontology that unicorns do not "exist" and goats do. The main criterion for inclusion is a consensus among the members of the community using the ontology (and generating and understanding documents to be processed with the help of the ontology) concerning the properties of a concept. The basic conclusion of this line of thought is that epistemology (and, therefore, any constructed ontology) is neutral with respect to the major metaphysical issue of existence.[1]

There is another claim routinely made about metaphysics that strikes us as importantly incorrect, even if it is made by those who, like ourselves, recognize the importance of metaphysics. "Metaphysics," Loux (1998, x) states, "is the most general of all disciplines; its aim is to identify the nature and structure of all that there is." But is it really? On the one hand, the very top levels of an ontology should contain the most basic—and general—categories that no particular area of research will claim as their own. Bateman refers to these levels as the *Upper Model* (see Bateman 1990, 1993; Hovy and Nirenburg 1992 reserves the term *ontology* for the top levels only, and uses *domain model* for the lower levels). On the other hand, metaphysics is not responsible for the nature and structure of, say, microbiological entities: microbiology, a part of biology, is. So, like all other disciplines, metaphysics has its specific and fairly limited domain: it is that of the universally shared basic categories.

The choice of categories for use by a science, while definitely influenced by metaphysics, whose categories are usually involved, is guided by the philosophy of that science and not by metaphysics per se. It is also quite realistic to think, even if a particular example may be hard to come by, that a specific discipline may stumble on an important general property and claim a place for it among the basic properties of metaphysics. Practically, it means that designing ontology is not a simple matter of putting the metaphysical categories on top and letting specific disciplines and domains add descendants.

5.2   Formal Ontology

Formal ontology is still a developing discipline, and a discipline clearly distinct from ontological semantics in its perspective, so we will not presume here to review or to analyze it in its entirety nor to anticipate or to prescribe the directions of its development. Instead, we will review briefly some of the more pertinent aspects of formal ontology, those bearing theoretically and practically on ontological semantics.

5.2.1   Formal Basis of Ontology

While metaphysics is an ancient discipline and ontology has been commented on by every major philosopher of modernity, most influentially perhaps by Kant and Hegel, Husserl (1900–1901) is usually credited with founding formal ontology. He saw the field as parallel to formal logic: "Formal logic deals with the interconnections of truths ... [while] formal ontology deals with the interconnections of things, with objects and properties, parts and wholes, relations and collectives" (Smith 1998, 19).

Formal ontology is seen as being founded on the mathematical disciplines of mereology, which studies the relations between parts and wholes, the theory of dependence, and topology. There is a body of work studying these disciplines, their relations to ontologies, and issues concerning their applications to ontology (see, for instance, Simons 1987; Bochman 1990; Smith 1996, 1997, 1998; Varzi 1994, 1996, 1998[2]). Other scholars have developed formal devices within mereo(topo)logy to accommodate elements of ontology like space and time (Muller 1998), particular kinds of artifacts (Reicher 1998), deontic phenomena (Johannesson and Wohed 1998), and inheritance models (Schäfer 1998), among others. Complex ontological entities, such as patterns (Johansson 1998; Johannesson and Wohed 1998), stand out in this respect (cf. our own complex events in Carlson and Nirenburg 1990; section 7.1.5 below; Moreno Ortiz, Raskin, and Nirenburg 2002). To all of this, one must add the study of inheritance (see, for instance, Horty, Thomason, and Touretzky 1990).

More substantively, Guarino (1995, 5–6) sees "formal ontology ... as the theory of a priori distinctions: among the entities of the world (physical objects, events, regions, quantities of matter ...); among the meta-level categories used to model the world (concepts, properties, qualities, states, roles, parts ...)." The two distinctions have—or should have—a different, hierarchical status in any formal theory: the higher-level distinctions are metaphysical, and the lower-level distinctions should be formulated in terms of those metaphysical distinctions or, at the very least, should be strongly determined by them.

The semantic aspect of formal ontology is, of course, a serious problem, as it is with any formal theory. In the matter of ontological definition, according to Guarino (1997, 298), "The ultimate definition should make clear that it includes a structure, not just the taxonomy, that all the relations are given in terms of their meaning, and that there is a logical language that corresponds to the ontology, so that 'an ontology is an explicit, partial account of the intended models of a logical language.'"

In this regard, Guarino finds Gruber's (1993, 199) much quoted view of an ontology as an explicit specification of a conceptualization to be extensional and shallow because a conceptualization can be—and has been—easily confused with a state of affairs. Guarino wants to add intension to it—that is, to assign meaning to the relationship (see Guarino 1997 as well as 1998a, 5; cf. section 3.5.1). He is not entirely clear about the practical steps for doing that but we believe his objective is on target. Nor is it entirely clear whether, for him, intensions are supposed to capture uninstantiated events while he sees extensions as instantiations. Distinguishing between uninstantiated and instantiated events is important, but the intension-extension dichotomy may be an imperfect tool for doing this. We believe that conceptualization and instantiation belong to different stages in ontological work: the former takes place during ontology acquisition while the latter is associated with ontology use. A recurring state of affairs deserves to be conceptualized, and an appropriate concept should be added to the ontology. In the process of using an ontology, it is usually the instance of a concept that is created and manipulated. Guarino may also be mistaken about the extensionality of Gruber's definition.[3] It seems that the distinction was immaterial for Gruber's own, largely engineering, design-oriented focus on ontology (see section 5.2.2).

Guarino's insistence on complete semantic interpretability of formal ontological statements is most laudable. In fact, he addresses a very sensitive point when he sympathetically quotes a remark by Woods (1975, 40–41) that philosophers have generally stopped short of trying to actually specify the truth conditions of the basic atomic propositions, dealing mainly with the specification of the meaning of complex expressions in terms of the meanings of elementary ones. Researchers in artificial intelligence are faced with the need to specify the semantics of elementary propositions as well as complex ones.

Formal ontological statements in ontological semantics are, of course, TMR propositions (see chapter 6), and they are fully semantic in nature.

5.2.2   Ontology as Engineering

While ontology has the crucially important philosophical aspect discussed above, Guarino (1998a, 4) is essentially correct in observing that

in its most prevalent use in AI, an ontology refers to an *engineering artifact*, constituted by a specific *vocabulary* used to describe a certain reality, plus a set of explicit assumptions regarding the *intended meaning* of the vocabulary words.[4] This set of assumptions has usually the form of a first-order logical theory, where vocabulary words appear as unary or binary predicate names, respectively called concepts and relations. In the simplest case, an ontology describes a hierarchy of concepts related by subsumption relationships; in more sophisticated cases, suitable axioms are added in order to express other relationships between concepts and to constrain their intended interpretation.

Gruber (1995, 909), unnecessarily, takes the same idea away from philosophy and metaphysics, while coming up with useful engineering criteria for ontology design:

Formal ontologies are *designed*. When we choose how to represent something in an ontology, we are making design decisions. To guide and evaluate our designs, we need objective criteria that are founded on the purpose of the resulting artifact, rather than based on *a priori* notions of naturalness or Truth. Here we propose a preliminary set of design criteria for ontologies whose purpose is knowledge sharing and interoperation among programs based on a shared conceptualization.

1. *Clarity*. An ontology should effectively communicate the intended meaning of defined terms. Definitions should be *objective*.... Wherever possible, a complete definition (a predicate defined by necessary and sufficient conditions) is preferred over a partial definition (defined by only necessary or sufficient conditions).
2. *Coherence*. An ontology should be coherent: that is, it should sanction inferences that are consistent with the definitions.... If a sentence that can be inferred from the axioms contradicts a definition or example given informally, then the ontology is incoherent.
3. *Extendibility* [sic].... One should be able to define new terms for special uses based on the existing vocabulary, in a way that does not require the revision of the existing definitions.
4. *Minimal encoding bias*.... Encoding bias should be minimized [to allow for various encoding options].
5. *Minimal ontological commitment*.... An ontology should make as few claims as possible about the world being modeled, allowing the parties committed to the ontology freedom to specialize and instantiate the ontology as needed.

The degree of commitment to an ontology in an information system may vary from zero to vague awareness to ontology-drivenness. "In some cases," Guarino (1998a, 3) writes, "the term 'ontology' is just a fancy name denoting the result of familiar activities like conceptual analysis and domain modeling, carried out by means of standard methodologies." Ontology really comes into its own when its "own methodological and architectural peculiarities" (p. 3) come into play. In this case, the ontology becomes an integral component of the information system, "cooperating at run time towards the 'higher' overall goal" (p. 11). While definitely "ontology driven," ontological semantics can, we believe, claim an even higher status: it is actually ontology based, or ontology centered.

5.2.3   Ontology Interchange

Another important issue in formal ontology that we will touch on briefly here is the movement to share and reuse ontologies. In fact, this is what Gruber's criterion 5 above includes. There are two nontrivial issues with ontology interchange. One of them is the dichotomy, well known in descriptive and computational linguistics, between a specific domain and a multidomain situation. The other involves the difficulties associated with merging different ontologies.

When designing an ontology for a domain (or describing a sublanguage of natural language; see section 9.3.6 as well as Raskin 1990), one can take full advantage of its limited nature and achieve a higher accuracy of description. This comes, however, at a price: the more domain specific the description the less portable it is outside of the domain. Furthermore, some scholars claim that no domain knowledge is or can be independent of a particular task for which it is developed and a particular method employed—this approach is, of course, well known in physics. According to Bylander and Chandrasekaran (1988, 66), ontology design cannot be free of the so-called interaction problem: "Representing knowledge for the purpose of solving some problem is strongly affected by the nature of the problem and the inference strategy to be applied to the problem." Ignoring the long-standing debate on the issue in post-Bohr physics, Guarino (1997, 293) mounts his own defense, coupled with a reasonable plea:

I will defend here the thesis of the independence of domain knowledge. This thesis should not be intended in a rigid sense, since it is clear that—more or less—ontological commitments always reflect particular points of view (for instance, the same physical phenomenon may be described in different ways by an engineer, by a physicist or by a chemist); rather, what I would like to stress is the fact that reusability across multiple tasks or methods *can and should be systematically pursued.*[5]

The ontological community has devoted considerable effort to pursuing this goal systematically. In a widely shared opinion, Gruber (1993, 200; cf. Nirenburg, Raskin, and Onyshkevych 1995) stated correctly that knowledge-based systems and services are expensive to build, test, and maintain. A software engineering methodology based on formal specifications of shared resources, reusable components, and standard services is needed. We believe that specifications of shared vocabulary can play an important role in such a methodology.

The second nontrivial issue in ontology interchange is developing formal tools for making the importation and interchange of ontologies possible. Gruber (1993) proceeded to define such a formal tool, Ontolingua, the best-known system for translating ontologies among notations. Ontolingua uses KIF, the Knowledge Interchange Format, designed by Genesereth and Fikes (1992):

KIF is intended as a language for the publication and communication of knowledge. It is intended to make the *epistemological-level* (McCarthy & Hayes 1969) content clear to the reader, but not to support automatic reasoning in that form. It is very expressive, designed to accommodate the state of the art in knowledge representation. But it is not an implemented representation system.   (Gruber 1993, 205)

All of this is quite appropriate for translating ontologies because the same can be said of ontologies themselves. Designing ontologies for portability means that

explicit specifications of . . . ontologies are essential for the development and use of intelligent systems as well as for the interoperation of heterogeneous systems.
   Ontology construction is difficult and time consuming. This large development cost is a major barrier to the building of large scale intelligent systems and to widespread knowledge-level interactions of computer-based agents. Since many conceptualizations are intended [or can be found] to be useful for a wide variety of tasks, an important means of removing this barrier is to encode ontologies in a reusable form so that large portions of an ontology for a given application can be assembled from existing ontologies in ontology repositories. (Farquhar et al. 1995, 1; cf. Farquhar, Fikes, and Rice 1996, 1997)

To this effect, the Fikes group has actually implemented a website for ontology importation and integration (http://www-ksl-svc.stanford.edu:5915). In fact, a number of prototype ontology-merging environments have been developed and reported in the literature. Thus, Chimaera (McGuinness 2000) and PROMPT (Fridman Noy and Musen 2000) allow users to generate integrated ontologies that contain concepts from several ontologies. ONION (Mitra, Wiederhold, and Kersten 2000) resorts to the so-called articulation rules that define similarities and differences among ontologies. FCA-Merge (Stumme and Madche 2001), GLUE (Madhavan et al. 2002), and AnchorPROMPT—an extension of PROMPT—provide sets of pairs of related concepts with a value of certainty associated with each pair.
   The nature of merging differs among the systems. For example, Chimaera deals only with concept hierarchies and does not relate to properties or instances, while PROMPT takes into account properties and their fillers. Some merging approaches rely centrally on the existence of instances (e.g., GLUE), while FCA-Merge addi-

tionally requires that the ontologies that are merged share a certain number of instances. The nature of interaction between the merging system and the user also varies greatly—while in some systems the users are called on to compare text files, in others (e.g., ONION or PROMPT) a graphical interface is supplied. In practice, all of the above systems have been tested on relatively small ontologies that do not deal with language understanding. Thus, for instance, PROMPT was evaluated on two ontologies describing academic departments. When it comes to merging larger-scale and deeper ontologies, recommendations become more vague. For example, Hovy (1998) suggested several generic empirical heuristics for merging ontologies (one of which was the ontology from the Mikrokosmos implementation of ontological semantics) that were based on such entirely generic commonsense heuristics as comparing names and natural language definitions of concepts in several ontologies, as well as distance between concepts in an ontological hierarchy.

Our own experience in augmenting and modifying existing ontologies shows that, while often simpler than acquiring ontologies from scratch, it is still a labor-intensive effort that can be facilitated in many ways, of which the specification of a reusable format may not even be the most important. The development of dedicated semiautomatic ontology-acquisition methodologies and tools is, in our estimation, much more useful, specifically because it concentrates on content, not format.

5.2.4 The Semantic Web

The emergence of the World Wide Web (WWW) in the 1990s has provided a new impetus for work in the area of ontology interchange, while at the same time opening a new arena for the application of semantics. Indeed, though in the past, the main practical reasons for working on understanding language and the world have centered on "traditional" applications, such as machine translation, information retrieval, or text summarization, now new vistas have opened and new challenges have appeared due to the spectacular increases in the availability of information and relative ease of access to it. The downside of this explosion has been the increased difficulty involved in searching and otherwise manipulating the huge amounts of data. It does not take a rocket scientist to realize that this problem could be ameliorated by making the content of the Web searchable, at least partially, on the basis of its semantic content, not simply on the basis of matching strings and metasyntactic tags. But once one starts thinking about using semantics in the context of the Web, the line of thought quickly transcends the issues of search and extends into the exciting possibilities of supporting collaborative work in teams and—even more appealing—teams that include both human and artificial (robotic, software) agents. This latter goal is, in fact, in some sense a return to the original vision of AI people and science fiction writers alike—that of a society in which machines "lived" and worked alongside people.

This realization and its urgency have revived interest in computational semantics outside the field proper. Exciting new visions have been outlined, and a Semantic Web community has come into being, recruiting among the usual WWW enthusiasts, AI people, and designers of programming and knowledge-representation languages as well as formal semanticists (who have adopted the designation of ontologists).

The new field started out, very reasonably, by delineating its goals and—especially importantly—design desiderata. The latter centrally included:

• *Generality.* Berners-Lee (1998a, 1) describes this as follows: "When looking at a possible formulation of a universal Web of semantic assertions, the principle of minimalist design requires that it be based on a common model of great generality. Only when the common model is general can any prospective application be mapped onto the model."

• *Simplicity and low cost.* According to Hendler (2001, 30), "A crucial aspect of creating the semantic web is to make it possible for a number of different users to create machine-readable content without being logic experts. In fact, ideally, most of the users shouldn't even need to know that web semantics exists. Lowering the cost of mark-up isn't enough—for many users it needs to be free. That is, semantic mark-up should be a by-product of normal computer use. Much like current web content, a small number of tool creators and web ontology designers will have to know the details, but most users will not even know ontologies exist."

The proposals just outlined were critically examined. The consensus could be summarized as follows:

• "Traditional" artificial intelligence has not led to the development of realistic-scale practical applications ("The concept of machine-understandable documents does not imply some magical artificial intelligence which allows machines to comprehend human mumblings. It only indicates a machine's ability to solve a well-defined problem by performing well-defined operations on existing well-defined data. Instead of asking machines to understand people's language, it involves asking people to make the extra effort" (Berners-Lee 1998c, 1)).

• The knowledge-representation area, while generating useful ideas, has failed to translate them into a coherent, large-scale action ("Knowledge representation is a field which currently seems to have the reputation of being initially interesting, but which did not seem to shake the world to the extent that some of its proponents hoped" (p. 2)).

• Prior work on world modeling and reconciliation among different formal models can be useful but still does not measure up to the standards of the emerging Semantic Web ("Other concerns at this point are raised about the relationship to Knowledge representation systems: has this not been tried before with projects such as KIF and

Cyc? The answer is yes, it has, more or less, and such systems have been developed a long way. They should feed the semantic Web with design experience and the Semantic Web may provide a source of data for reasoning engines developed in similar projects. Many KR systems had a problem merging or interrelating two separate knowledge bases, as the model was that any concept had one and only one place in a tree of knowledge. They therefore did not scale, or pass the test of independent invention. The RDF world, by contrast, is designed for this in mind, and the retrospective documentation of relationships between originally independent concepts" (p. 2)).

• First-order predicate calculus (FOPC) and higher-order logic, the traditional reasoning techniques, should be criticized (a) for expressing things that are at the same time undecidable and not effectively computable, (b) for being rigid (in the sense of not tolerating inconsistency), and (c) for failing to have made a historical impact (p. 3).

Recommendations for the organization of the Semantic Web include the following components (Berners-Lee 1998b, 9):

1. XML provides a basic format for structured documents, with no particular semantics.
2. The basic assertion model provides the concepts of assertion (property) and quotation.... This allows an entity-relationship-like model to be made for the data, giving it the semantics of assertions [through] propositional logic....
3. The schema language provides data typing and allows document structure to be constrained to allow predictable computable processing. XML schema's data types are used.
4. The Ontology layer ... provides more powerful schema concepts, such as inverse, transitivity, and so on. Uniqueness and/or unambiguousness of properties, when know[n], allow a system to spot different identifiers which in fact are talking about the same thing.
5. A conversion language allows the expression of inference rules allowing information in one schema to be inferred from a document in another. This is part of rules layer.
6. An evolution rules language allows inference rules to be given which allow a machine with a certain algorithm to convert documents from one RDF [resource description framework] schema into another....
7. The logical layer turns a limited declarative language into a Turing-complete logical language, with inference and functions. This is powerful enough to be able to define all the rest, and allow any two ... applications to be connected together.... One can see this language as being a universal language to unify all data systems just as HTML was a language to unify all human documentation systems.
8. A proof language ... allows one agent to send to another an assertion, together with the inference path to that assertion from assumptions acceptable to the receiver.

The above program is far from being complete at the time of this writing (and will, quite likely, remain so for some time). However, it is possible to project the capabilities of any environment based on the above goals, preferences, and components. The advantages of the Semantic Web over the existing mark-up approaches, such as

HTML and unenhanced XML, are clear: it makes it possible to go beyond direct typesetting and layout commands to establishing labels that can be given useful semantics. For example, if a character string is marked by the tag "title," the semantics of the latter can be defined as a procedure to typeset it in a certain way (e.g., with capitalization, using a relatively large font, centering it on the line, boldfacing it, and so on). This capability has already been used in moving from HTML to XML, to allow freedom of style while retaining the role of a character string on a Web page.

Thus, while for a human user there is no particular advantage to this enhancement—because titles would be displayed in the same way whether encoded in HMTL or XML—the computer will be able now to refer to a character string as the title of a page. The semantics necessary for this is establishing a relation "title" between two strings—the title of a page, and the page itself. An open-ended inventory of such relations, encoded in RDF (or a descendant of that formalism), constitutes the semantics of the Semantic Web. To appreciate the contribution of the Semantic Web to understanding WWW material, it is important to realize that this semantics establishes a relation between uninterpreted character strings, and the creators of the Semantic Web have made it clear on multiple occasions that interpreting these character strings automatically is not within the purview of the Semantic Web (cf. Berners-Lee's words, quoted above, about "human mumblings").

The implication seems to be that the suggested level of semantic description is sufficient because interpreting such character strings and, more broadly, tagging the Web content for the Semantic Web, will be done by people. In other words, it is expected that Web authoring will include making the Web pages into the "semantic documents." This means that human Web authors will spend more time creating each page. This is clearly understood by Semantic Web developers, and they raise the issue of incentives for Web authors to become Semantic Web taggers. For example, Katz and Lin (2002) prudently point out that people will not spend extra time marking up their data unless they perceive a value for their efforts. But suppose (against logical expectations) that the incentive issue has been successfully solved. Is the road to the Semantic Web now free of content-related obstacles? The answer is in the affirmative if the Web authors who have been newly entrusted with Semantic Web tagging

• Can determine all the material that needs to be tagged
• Are familiar with the tag inventory and understand what the tags mean
• Can determine the appropriate tag or tags for each element that must be tagged
• Can perform consistently over time and with other taggers

These abilities obviously require training that further adds to the overall cost of producing Semantic Web–tagged material. This training involves internalizing the

meaning of tags and constraints on their use as well as a mastery of the appropriate
formalism (such as RDF). The tags are defined with the help of universal resource
identifiers (URIs) that are essentially pointers to Web pages containing tag descriptions. Thus, a URI for the tag "title" (http://dublincore.org/2002/08/13/dces#title) is
as follows (the description of the tag "title" is boldfaced; those of all the other tags
are just indexed in the example below):

```
<?xml version="1.0" ?>
<!DOCTYPE rdf:RDF (View Source for full doctype...)>
- <rdf:RDF xmlns:rdf="http://www.w3.org/1999/02/22-rdf-
syntax-ns#" xmlns:rdfs="http://www.w3.org/2000/01/rdf-
schema#" xmlns:dc="http://purl.org/dc/elements/1.1/"
xmlns:dcterms="http://purl.org/dc/terms/">
- <rdf:Property rdf:about="http://purl.org/dc/elements/1.1/title">
<rdfs:label xml:lang="en-US">Title</rdfs:label>
<rdfs:comment xml:lang="en-US">A name given to the resource.
</rdfs:comment>
<dc:description xml:lang="en-US">Typically, a Title will be a name
by which the resource is formally known.</dc:description>
<rdfs:isDefinedBy rdf:resource="http://purl.org/dc/elements/
1.1/" />
<dcterms:issued>1999-07-02</dcterms:issued> </rdf:Property>
<rdf:Property rdf:about="http://purl.org/dc/elements/1.1/
contributor"> </rdf:Property>
<rdf:Property rdf:about="http://purl.org/dc/elements/1.1/creator">
</rdf:Property>
<rdf:Property rdf:about="http://purl.org/dc/elements/1.1/
publisher"> </rdf:Property>
<rdf:Property rdf:about="http://purl.org/dc/elements/1.1/subject">
</rdf:Property>
<rdf:Property rdf:about="http://purl.org/dc/elements/1.1/
description"> </rdf:Property>
<rdf:Property rdf:about="http://purl.org/dc/elements/1.1/date">
</rdf:Property>
<rdf:Property rdf:about="http://purl.org/dc/elements/1.1/type">
</rdf:Property>
<rdf:Property rdf:about="http://purl.org/dc/elements/1.1/format">
</rdf:Property>
<rdf:Property rdf:about="http://purl.org/dc/elements/1.1/
identifier"> </rdf:Property>
```

```
<rdf:Property rdf:about="http://purl.org/dc/elements/1.1/
language"> </rdf:Property>
<rdf:Property rdf:about="http://purl.org/dc/elements/1.1/
relation"> </rdf:Property>
<rdf:Property rdf:about="http://purl.org/dc/elements/1.1/source">
</rdf:Property>
<rdf:Property rdf:about="http://purl.org/dc/elements/1.1/
coverage"> </rdf:Property>
<rdf:Property rdf:about="http://purl.org/dc/elements/1.1/rights">
</rdf:Property>
</rdf:RDF>
```

The prospective tagger must first find this page, locate the tag in question (it will, of course, be easier using a browser/editor), understand the semantics of the fillers of the "comment" and "description" properties, and then learn to assign the tag "title" to the appropriate elements of any Web page that he or she is writing. The ultimate success of this operation will depend on whether the title of each text is easily identifiable and also whether the annotator understands what other options there are for formally referring to the resource—that is, how to interpret "typically" in the example above. Thus, we were not sure what we would mark as the title for the *Scientific American* (www.sciam.com) page containing Berners-Lee, Hendler, and Lassila 2001; a Web author thinking in terms of "headline" may have trouble deciding whether it is the same as "title." In short, it seems that human tagging for the Semantic Web is costly and not necessarily reliable. Hendler's desideratum of low-cost or no-cost tagging seems, after all, to be attainable only through automation.

If we move to the issue of automatic tagging for content, a different set of problems arises. While there may be hope that people will understand and be able to use uninterpreted character strings in the Semantic Web property definitions efficiently, a full-fledged NLP effort is necessary to automate the process. This, in turn, means that it might be impossible to follow the widely proclaimed tenet of the Semantic Web movement that "the Semantic Web will enable machines to COMPREHEND semantic documents and data, not human speech and writings" (Berners-Lee, Hendler, and Lassiter 2001). In other words, to sustain the vision of the Semantic Web, two distinct though interconnected prerequisites are necessary: being able to translate between natural language texts and their semantic representations, and manipulating the latter for the purposes of inference that underlies the operation of truly intelligent software agents. The Semantic Web community has consciously concentrated on the latter. It seems to us that the former is unavoidable, and ontological semantics can help the Semantic Web community bridge this gap.

There is a strong methodological similarity between the situation faced by the Semantic Web and the environment in which mathematical logic began to flourish over sixty years ago with regard to natural language meaning. At that time, a distinction was already made between translating natural language into a logical (or semantic) format and manipulating the latter according to formal rules of inference. The early mathematical logicians simply abandoned the former task and concentrated on the latter (cf. Bar Hillel's criticism in section 2.4.1.4). Within the Semantic Web movement, the exclusion of the "scruffy" language processing has been a conscious decision, though it is questionable whether it could be sustained in practice.

In fact, there is a growing realization in the NLP community (e.g., Lenci, Calzolari, and Zampolli 2002; Narayanan et al. 2002) that its work and the Semantic Web effort should and will be closely coordinated. We share the opinion of Lenci et al. (2002) that "semantic content processing lies at the heart of the Semantic Web enterprise and requires to squarely address the complexity of natural language. Existing experience in language resource development proves that such a challenge can be tackled only ... by establishing a highly advanced environment for the representation and acquisition of lexical information."

5.3   Ontology and Natural Language

In the preceding two sections, we discussed well-explored areas of philosophical and formal ontology, primarily as they pertain to ontological semantics. In this section, we are venturing into the difficult and underexplored part of formal ontology, namely, the relations between ontology and natural language.

5.3.1   A Basic Distinction between Ontology and Natural Language

Guarino (1998b; see also Guarino and Welty 2002) criticizes several existing ontologies, including the one in the Mikrokosmos implementation of ontological semantics, for allowing ambiguity in certain ontological nodes. An example is the treatment of the node WINDOW as both an artifact and a place, thus effectively postulating what, from Guarino's point of view, is a nonexisting concept that subsumes the properties of both. Similarly, he objects to a link from the COMMUNICATION-EVENT node to both SOCIAL-EVENT and MENTAL-EVENT as parents.

This criticism can be appropriate only if ambiguity in ontological concepts is not allowed in any form. In that case, the distinction between natural language and ontology is simple and clear-cut: words can be ambiguous; concepts cannot.[6] To accommodate the absence-of-ambiguity principle, an ontology should have different nodes in different places for the concepts WINDOW-ARTIFACT and WINDOW-PLACE, or for MENTAL-COMMUNICATION-EVENT and SOCIAL-COMMUNICATION-EVENT, even if it chooses to use the same English word in their labels.

If ambiguity so clearly demarcates words from concepts, it is rather surprising that Guarino (1998a, 3) considers linguistics a participant in the development of an ontology: "On the methodological side, the main peculiarity is the adoption of a *highly interdisciplinary approach*, where philosophy and linguistics play a fundamental role in analyzing the structure of a given reality at a high level of generality and in formulating a clear and vigorous vocabulary." In what sense, does—or can—linguistics contribute to this enterprise? Bateman (1993, 83) provides a reasonably clear explanation: "Ontology construction [should be based] on an understanding of natural language." Hovy and Nirenburg (1992) are more cautious and circumspect: the knowledge we obtain from our understanding of a particular natural language should be integrated with and into a language-neutral ontology, presumably by combining the material from different languages. It should be stressed, however, that both of the above opinions relate more to the ability of people to perceive and manipulate knowledge through language than to the formal discipline of linguistics and its legitimate purview.

Moreover, the use of the term *vocabulary* in the initial quote above licenses mixing ontological nomenclature with units of the dictionary of a natural language, thus further contributing to the unjustified fusion of the metalanguage of ontological description with natural language. As we have argued elsewhere (see Nirenburg, Raskin, and Onyshkevych 1995; Nirenburg and Raskin 1996, 18–20; sections 2.6.2.2 and 4.3.2), some scholars persist in this natural language fallacy positively, as it were, by insisting on using natural language words instead of ontological concepts to represent natural language meanings, and others persist in it negatively by trying to expose an ontology as camouflaged natural language. The former has a long history, if not a legitimate place in natural language semantics; the latter is rather easily refuted by indicating that ontological concepts have no ambiguity.

The confusion has a deep philosophical origin, going back at least fifty years, namely, to the so-called linguistic turn in philosophy (cf. note 1 in chapter 2), involving the move away from world phenomena or even their representations in human concepts[7] to the analysis of the meaning of propositions about these phenomena or concepts. Kenny (1989, viii) gives this move a fair assessment:

In the last half-century many people have described themselves as adherents of, and many people have described themselves as enemies of, linguistic philosophy. Neither adherence nor opposition is a very useful stance unless one makes clear what one means by calling a particular style of philosophy "linguistic."

"Philosophy is linguistic" may mean at least six different things. (1) The study of language is a useful philosophical tool. (2) It is the only philosophical tool. (3) Language is the only subject-matter of philosophy. (4) Necessary things are established by linguistic convention. (5) Man is fundamentally a language-using animal. (6) Everyday language has a status of privilege over technical and formal systems. These six propositions are independent of each other. (1) has been accepted in practice by every philosopher since Plato. Concerning the other five, philosophers have been and are divided, including philosophy within the analytic tradition. In my opinion, (1) and (5) are true, and the other four false.

In our opinion, (5) does not contribute to the issue at hand, and the rest are false. Language is no more or less a tool of philosophy than it is for any other human endeavor. Studying language takes away from philosophy like studying the screwdriver takes away from driving in a screw. We are actually with Chisholm (1996, 8), when he writes:

Aristotle says that in discussing the categories, he is concerned in part with our ordinary language. And he says this often enough to provide encouragement to those contemporary philosophers who believe that the statements of metaphysicians, to the extent that they are not completely empty, tell us something about our language. One of our principal concerns, however, is that of finding the *ontological presuppositions* of statements about language.

Where some readers of this book may expect to find discussions of language, they will find discussions of thinking and intentionality instead.

We would like to take it a little further still by claiming that Chisholm's ontological presuppositions are ontological content or ontological meaning, which is separate from natural language meaning.

5.3.2   The Real Distinction between Ontology and Natural Language

In this section, we question the premise that ambiguity is what distinguishes natural language and ontology. In particular, we will explore whether an ontology really must be unambiguous and whether this ideal is at all attainable. Next, we will argue that the real distinction is that languages emerge and are used by people, while ontologies are constructed for computers.

Is the objection of formal ontology to having a single concept WINDOW with the properties of both opening and artifact justified? The objection is predicated on the premise that there must be no ambiguity in ontology. What does this premise mean in reality? In a formal logical system, no two concepts can have the same name, and, conversely, no single concept can be referred to by more than one name. Obviously, no such blatant violation of formality can be expected in any practical ontology. So, what was, then, criticized by Guarino in the Mikrokosmos decision to use a single concept for WINDOW? It was precisely the decision to declare WINDOW a single concept carrying no ambiguity.

Why would one prefer to split WINDOW into two different concepts? The claim that the English word *window* has two distinct senses would have no bearing on this ontological decision because it should not be expected that there will be a one-to-one relationship between the space of word senses in a natural language (or, more accurately, the union of all word senses in all natural languages) and that of ontological concepts. On the contrary, it seems more important that there is apparently no natural language in the world in which the word for WINDOW does not realize both the opening and the artifact senses of the word. This semantic universal is probably the strongest evidence we may have that people seem to conflate the two concepts.

This phenomenon (known variously as regular polysemy, vagueness, underspecification, sense permeability, and so on) is pervasive: *book* (or *newspaper* or even *poem*) in all languages refers both to a physical object and its informational content; *say* (or *smile* or *wink*) to a physical phenomenon and to conveying a message; *bank* (or *school* or *shop*) to an organization and a building housing it, and so on. Will formal ontology require that each of the concepts corresponding to these word senses be duplicated in the manner suggested?

In the same vein, should there be different concepts for *eat* corresponding to eating with a spoon, with a fork, with chopsticks, or with one's fingers? After all, each of the above are distinct processes.[8] Would it matter if in some language there were, in fact, different words for some of these processes? In general, languages do not use isomorphic sets of lexeme names. This has given rise to the widespread study of cross-language mismatches and translation divergences (see, for instance, Viegas et al. 1999, 190–195), as in the well-known example of English *wall* versus Italian *muro* ("outside wall") and *parete* ("inside wall").

If an ontology is constructed according to Bateman—that is, based on an understanding of a natural language—and that language happens to be Italian, then the ontology will have two separate concepts for the inside and outside wall. Using such an ontology in NLP and defining lexical senses in ontological terms as it is done, for instance, in the Mikrokosmos implementation of ontological semantics, the two Italian words will be directly mapped into these concepts. Using the same ontology to support the acquisition of the English lexicon, the entry for *wall* will have a connection to two ontological concepts, and this is the definition of *polysemy* in ontological semantics. In other words, *wall* would have one sense more than if the ontology contained just one concept for WALL. It might be counterintuitive for an English speaker to consider that *wall* has two senses corresponding to the inside and the outside walls.

If, on the other hand, the ontology construction is based on English, there will be a single concept for *wall* in it. From the point of view of the Italian speaker, this concept would be seen as a nonterminal node in the ontological hierarchy, which would have the concepts for *muro* and *parete* as its children. This concept could be made a terminal node, thus becoming a conflation of the putative child concepts, very similarly to what Guarino sees happening in the case of using a single concept for WINDOW that conflates the notions of opening and artifact. There must be a reason to include or not to include the children in the ontology. We have just seen that decisions based on Italian and English are incompatible, which means that Bateman's principle of "basing ontology construction on an understanding of natural language" is not feasible.

We can think of a practical, descriptive reason for not splitting the concept of WALL. Let us assume that Italian is the only language that makes the above distinction. An ontology with two separate concepts will add a sense to the entries of the word for *wall* in all the other languages, which will result in many extra senses in the universal lexicon. If, on the other hand, the concept is not split, the only price to pay is to add a disambiguation constraint to the lexical entries for *muro* and *parete*.

A criterion for deciding when to stop splitting ontological concepts and, more generally, how to demarcate them, deserves to be one of the cornerstones of formal ontology. It seems to have to do with Gruber's (1995, 909; see also section 5.2.2) general ontology-design criterion of "minimal ontological commitment," and it needs further elaboration, along with other topics in formal ontology (see section 5.4). In linguistic semantics, it is hard to establish a similar principle for limiting the polysemy of a lexical item, and typically, monolingual dictionaries prefer to multiply the senses, the number of which can be radically reduced without loss both for theoretical and practical purposes (see Nirenburg, Raskin, and Onyshkevych 1995; Raskin and Nirenburg 1998, 192–199; section 9.3.5). In multilingual dictionaries, an important motivation for distinguishing word senses in one language is the presence in another language of different words for realizing these senses. In an early contribution to universal lexical semantics, Hjelmslev (1958) proposed to format multilingual lexical-semantic descriptions as shown in table 5.1. In the table, the French column features two sets of synonyms—*arbre/bois₁* and *bois₂/forêt* and one polysemous word, *bois*. Here and below, the subscripts refer to the upper parts of a word's rectangular space as 1 and the lower parts as 2, with the parts divided by the continuation of a divider from another language. The Danish column features two polysemous words, each with two senses and one set of synonyms, *troe₂/skov₁*. The German column features three single-sense words (at least for the senses illustrated in the table).

Table 5.1
Crosslingual semantic divergences

French	German	Danish
arbre ("tree")	*Baum*	*troe*
bois 1. "wood" material 2. "wood" part of landscape	*Holz*	
forêt ("forest")	*Wald*	*skov*

What Hjelmslev implied here is a method of crosslinguistic lexical-semantic analysis. Dolgopol'skiy (1962) implemented this method using material from twenty-eight languages. This method is based on a geometric metaphor: should one choose to extend all horizontal lines across the entire table, the resulting rows will correspond to what Hjelmslev called *values*—that is, relative, differential meanings. One would think that, in ontological terms, these values would correspond to the most detailed, atomistic conceptual representations, excluding any possibility of concept ambiguity or conflation. In reality, some of these extensions will be hard to interpret. Thus, the extension to the left of the line between *troe* and *skov* would split the concept of wood as material into two unmotivated concepts.

As any dictionary of French, German, or Danish will demonstrate, the words in the table realize three distinct senses—those of plant, material, and landscape feature. It is an accident that these three senses correspond to the German words. One should expect that, in other cases of crosslinguistic description, it will be another language that will turn out to be nonpolysemous.[9] And yet in other cases, no language may be found to provide nonpolysemous coverage of the senses involved. The most appropriate ontology for representing the senses of the words in the table should contain three concepts corresponding to the German word senses. As will be discussed in the next section, we see it as a task for formal ontology to explore why this is so and what criteria can be discovered for making such decisions. We have a very strong intuition that these three concepts must be represented in the ontology to the exclusion of all alternatives. Such a decision strikes us as "natural" and obvious. As we have mentioned elsewhere (Nirenburg, Raskin, and Onyshkevych 1995), this feeling is shared by all the members of our research team, which makes such decisions reproducible. It is not entirely clear to us what this certainty is based on, and we believe it is the task of formal and philosophical ontology to address this issue.

Ambiguity is pervasive in language and must be addressed. We have seen that it cannot be expunged from any specific implementation of ontology, because there are no purely conceptual limits on grain size. Moreover, an effort to split ontological concepts into the ever-smaller unambiguous units leads to a sharp increase in polysemy and, therefore, makes the task of disambiguation so much more difficult. As we will argue in the next section, no ontology exists in a vacuum. It interacts with other resources, such as knowledge-representation languages, lexicons, analyzers, generators, general-reasoning modules, and so on. It is safe to assume that the overall amount of ambiguity to be addressed in any application is fairly constant at a given grain size. The differences among the various approaches to the treatment of ambiguity may be articulated as differences in the distribution across the above resources of the knowledge necessary for resolving the ambiguity. So, if an ontology is made less ambiguous, it only means that the ambiguity will have to be treated increasingly elsewhere.

The confusion about ambiguity creeps into the important issue of the distinction between ontology and natural language in yet another way. Wilks (Wilks, Slator, and Guthrie 1996, 59; Nirenburg and Wilks 1997; see also section 2.6.2.2 and references there) has eloquently argued that the very fact of using English words as labels for ontological concepts smuggles natural language ambiguity into ontology, and thus there is no basic difference between the representation language of ontology and a natural language:

YW: The first feature of language that should concern us in this discussion is as follows: can predicates of a representational language avoid ending up ambiguous as to sense? The negative answer to this question would make RLs NL-like. It will also mean that understanding a representation involves knowing what sense a symbol is being used in. If NLs are necessarily extensible as to sense—and words get new senses all the time—then can RLs that use NL symbols avoid this fate? (Nirenburg and Wilks 1997, 4—from Wilks's contribution to the dialog-format article)

What Wilks seems to ignore here is that the meanings of the ontological labels are constructed—in the sense of being formally defined for use by the computer. The computer perceives these labels straightforwardly; no comparison or reference is made to any words of any natural language with which these labels can be homographous. Wilks is right that a human reading such a label is likely to slip into an alternative sense of the homographous word not intended by the creator of the label. However, the computer has no capability of doing so.

It appears then that the crucial distinction between ontology and natural language does not lie exactly in the nonambiguity of the one and ambiguity of the other. This distinction is in the constructed and overtly defined nature of ontological concepts and labels on which no human background knowledge can operate unintentionally to introduce any ambiguity, as opposed to pervasive uncontrolled ambiguity in natural language. The entire enterprise of natural language processing is about designing knowledge structures for the computer to use. We have not yet achieved that goal, so we cannot suspect that a computer would be able to confuse an ontological concept or its label with its homographous, and possibly polysemous, lexeme of a natural language.

Guarino's criticism concerning ambiguity in ontological concepts (see section 5.3.1) does not apply to ontological semantics because, in our approach, we allow multiple inheritance of properties in an ontological concept from two or more different ancestors. Thus, BOOK will inherit the properties of both ARTIFACT and MENTAL-OBJECT, but with traceable attribution of properties to the appropriate ancestor. In other words, our approach is, in fact, a notational variant of Guarino's desideratum, with the added benefit of facilitating the expected connections between the two senses of the word that help to analyze such inputs as *Don't pack this book. It is boring.* The selectional restrictions on *pack* stipulate that the object that is packed should be physical (we will describe the process of semantic analysis in detail in chapter 8). In the second sentence, however, the subject of *boring* cannot be a physical object, because it is reasonable to assume that only content can be boring. So, when the analyzer proceeds to look for the antecedent of *it*, it will seek a descendant of MENTAL-OBJECT and will fail. This is clearly not a desired outcome. The device of the multiple inheritance for BOOK will remedy this situation. To summarize, while we agree with Guarino that there are two distinct senses for BOOK, we choose a notation that can accommodate both this need and the requirement to reflect the connection between the two senses that is actively present in every human agent's knowledge of the world. Failure to represent this kind of connection, in our opinion, defeats the practical ontological enterprise of representing that knowledge adequately.

5.4   A Wish List for Formal Ontology from Ontological Semantics

Practical ontology building expects assistance from formal and philosophical ontology. In this section, we compile a wish list of issues that practical ontology builders would want to see tackled and solved in a principled way. The issues relate to

· The status of ontology vis-à-vis other knowledge resources in an application
· The choice of what concepts to acquire
· The choice of what content to assign to each concept
· The evaluation of the quality of an ontology using both the glass-box and black-box evaluation paradigms

In practical applications, ontologies seldom, if ever, are used as the only knowledge resources. In the representative application of knowledge-based MT, for example, the ontology is used

· To supply the language for explaining lexical meanings, which are recorded in the lexicons of particular languages
· To provide the contentful building blocks of a text-meaning representation language
· To provide the heuristic knowledge for the dynamic knowledge resources such as semantic analyzers and generators

Formal ontology must help ontology builders constrain the relationships between ontological concepts, structures that represent text meaning and lexicon entries. In particular, an account must be available of the difference between ontological concepts as entity types, and text-meaning elements (and the semantic components of lexicon entries) as entity instances. What we believe it means for formal ontology is the necessity to define the status, beyond knowledge-representation format, of ontological instances. The latter come in several kinds, the most important for our discussion here being the following: instances of ontological concepts used for defining lexical meaning in lexicon entries, and facts—that is, representations that result from the compositional combination of meanings of individual words and/or phrases in the input into the meaning specification of a text.

A crucial concern for an ontology builder is the decision on what concepts to introduce and how to represent each of them. A good ontology will have good coverage and be reasonably homogeneous.[10] While coverage is determined by the domain and the nature of the application, formal ontology can help to decide how to organize the concepts that must be included in the ontology—for instance, how to organize the most economical concept hierarchy and how to define the nonterminal nodes in it. Formal ontology will be much more useful in practice if it agrees not only to put forward desired properties of ontologies but also to offer criteria for the processes of ontology construction and judgments about sufficient depth and breadth of coverage. In other words, we are suggesting that formal ontology, as a theory, must be supplemented by a methodology (see sections 2.4.2 and 2.5).

As we have just mentioned, formal ontology effectively concentrates on evaluating the quality of ontologies. In fact, even in that endeavor, we would benefit from a broadening of the scope of such evaluations. At present, formal ontology is concerned with the inherent properties of ontologies, considered independently of any concrete application. This is done by examining the content of the ontologies in search of potential contradictions, ambiguities, and omissions. This type of evaluation is often called glass-box evaluation, because the internal workings of a resource are transparent to the investigator. Practical ontologists would benefit from extending the purview of the evaluation into a glass-box evaluation of an ontology under construction. Equally important is its extention into a black-box evaluation of both existing and nascent ontologies, when the ontology itself is opaque to the investigator and the quality of the system is judged by the quality of output of an application based on the ontology (see also figure 2.11). In fact, Mahesh et al. (1996b) is a good example of such an evaluation: it had to develop the principles and criteria on the fly. It would have been better to take them off the formal ontology shelf.

This chapter largely concludes the enterprise of contextualizing ontological semantics among other relevant approaches. Part II contains a detailed description of the main components of the theory.

PART II
Ontological Semantics as Such

In part II of the book, we discuss the static and dynamic knowledge sources in ontological semantics. We start with an extended example of representing meaning of a natural language text. Next, we describe the static knowledge sources of ontological semantics, after which we present a sketch of ontological semantic processing. Figure II.1 illustrates the interactions among the data, the processors, and the static knowledge sources in ontological semantics.

Ontological semantic applications include machine translation, information extraction (IE), question answering (QA), general human-computer dialog systems, text summarization, and specialized applications combining some or all of the above with additional functionality (e.g., advice-giving systems). Of course, such applications are attempted without ontological semantics, or, for that matter, without any treatment of meaning at all. If, however, these applications are based on ontological semantics, then any kind of input to the system (an input text for MT, a query for a question-answering system, a text stream for information extraction, and so on) first undergoes several stages of analysis (tokenization, morphological, syntactic, semantic, and so forth; see chapter 8 for details). If successful, these stages in the end generate the meaning of a text: "text meaning representation" or TMR. The TMR serves as input to specialized processing relevant for a particular application. For example, in MT, the TMR needs to be translated into a natural language different from the one in which the input was supplied. The program that carries this task out is usually called the text generator. In IE, TMRs are used by the special rules as sources of fillers of IE template slots. In question answering, the TMR presents the proximate meaning of the user's query. The QA processor must first understand exactly what the user wants the system to do, then find the necessary information either in the background world knowledge sources (most often, the fact repository, but sometimes the ontology or the lexicons), and then generate a well-formed answer.

The static knowledge sources include the language-dependent ones—the rules for text tokenization, detecting proper names and acronyms, and other preprocessing tasks (we call these tasks "ecological"), for morphological, syntactic, and ontological semantic analysis. The information for the latter three types of analysis resides largely in the lexicons of the system, though special rules (e.g., syntactic grammars) are separate from lexicons. In the current state of ontological semantics, onomasticons—repositories of proper names—are separated from regular lexicons. The language-independent static knowledge sources are the ontology and the fact repository (FR). The ontology contains information about how things can be in the world, while the FR contains actual facts—that is, events that took place or objects that existed, exist, or have been reported to exist. In other words, the ontology contains concept types, whereas the FR contains remembered concept instances. Onomasticons contain information about words and phrases in natural language that name remembered concept instances. These concept instance names are also recorded as property fillers in

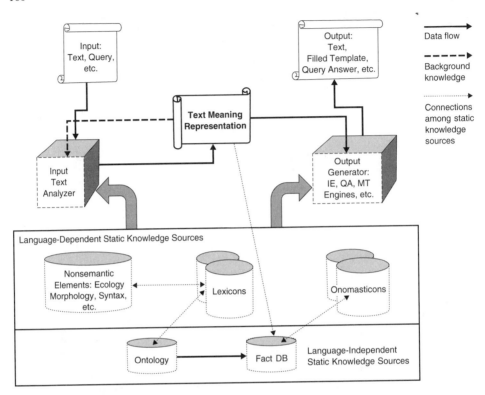

Figure II.1
The data, the processors, and the static knowledge sources in ontological semantics. All ontological semantic applications include analysis of input text as a crucial component. The production of a semantic text meaning representation (TMR) is the result of the analysis process.
The analysis modules and output generators use all the available static knowledge sources.
TMRs are selectively stored in FR for future reference, support of various applications, and
treatment of reference.

FR frames. Note that the FR also contains other, unnamed, concept instances. More
detailed descriptions of all the static knowledge sources are given in chapter 7.

In most applications of ontological semantics, a side effect of the system's operation is selective augmentation of the FR with the elements of TMRs produced during
the input analysis stage. This way, this information remains available for future use.
In this sense we can say that ontological semantic applications involve learning: the
more they operate, the more world knowledge they record and the better-quality
results they may expect.

CHAPTER 6
Meaning Representation in
Ontological Semantics

6.1 Meaning Proper and the Rest

Consider the following text as input to an ontological-semantic processor:

(1) Dresser Industries said it expects that major capital expenditure for expansion
of U.S. manufacturing capacity will reduce imports from Japan.

In "computerese"—that is, in the form in which we expect a semantic analyzer to be
able to process and represent the above text—the text will be glossed, for example, as
follows:

(2) A spokesperson for the company called Dresser Industries made this statement:
Dresser Industries expects that imports into the U.S. from Japan will decrease
through large capital investment for the purpose of expanding the manufacturing
potential in the U.S.; the expenditure precedes expansion, which precedes reduction,
and all of them take place after the statement.

In a somewhat more formal fashion, the meaning of (1) glossed in (2) can be seen to
include the following meaning components:

(3) (i) That *Dresser Industries* is a phrase, moreover, a set phrase, a proper name
   (ii) That it is the name of a company
   (iii) That this name is used in the original text metonymically—the company
   name, in fact, stands for its unnamed spokesperson(s)
   (iv) That the spokesperson made a statement (that is, not a question or a
   command)
   (v) That the company (once again, metonymically) has a certain belief, namely,
   an expectation
   (vi) That the scope of the expectation is the reduction of imports into the
   United States from Japan
   (vii) That the reduction of imports is expected to take place through capital
   investment

(viii) That the purpose of the investment is to increase the capacity for manufacturing in the United States

(ix) That *United States* refers to a nation, the United States of America, and *Japan* refers to another nation, Japan

(x) That the object of manufacturing, left unnamed in the original text, is most likely goods

(xi) That the decrease occurs in the amount of goods that the United States imports from Japan

(xii) That the time at which reduction of imports occurs follows the time of investment, which, in turn, precedes the expansion of manufacturing capacity

(xiii) That the time at which the statement was made precedes the time of investment

(xiv) That what is expanded is not necessarily the actual manufacturing output but the potential for it

The set of expressions in (3) can be viewed as the meaning of (1). In fact, this is the level at which text meaning is defined in the Mikrokosmos implementation of ontological semantics. However, it is important to understand that there may be alternative formulations of what constitutes the meaning of (1) or, for that matter, of any text. So, it seems appropriate at this point to discuss the general issue of how exactly to define text meaning. It might come as a surprise that this is not such an easy question! One attempt at making the idea of meaning better defined is the introduction of the notion of literal meaning (cf., e.g., Hausser 1999, 20). Thus, we could have declared that what we represent in our approach is the literal meaning of texts. However, this decision meets with difficulties because the notion of literal meaning may not be defined sufficiently precisely. For instance, (3) can be construed as the literal meaning of (1). However, under a different interpretation, deciding to resolve the organization-for-employee metonymy in (3.iii) and (3.v) may be construed as going beyond literal meaning. The expressions in (3) can be seen as the literal meaning of (1) if one agrees that *Dresser Industries*, being a company, cannot actually be the agent of saying. If this constraint is lifted, by allowing organizations to be agents of speech acts, then the literal meaning will not require the resolution of metonymy. In other words, this kind of literal meaning will be represented by eliminating (3.iii) and (3.v) from (3). In fact, if this approach is adopted throughout, the concept of metonymy will be summarily dispensed with (Mahesh, Beale, and Nirenburg 1996; section 8.4.2). Because the concept of literal meaning can be understood in a variety of ways, we found it unhelpful for defining which kinds of information belong in text meaning and which remain outside it, while still possibly playing a role (of background knowledge used for inference making in reasoning applications) in text processing in a variety of applications.

We have just considered the possibility of representing the meaning of (1) using less information than shown in (3). It is equally possible to view an expanded version of (3) as the meaning of (1). One example of such expansion would add the statements in (4) to the list (3):

(4) (i) That the company Dresser Industries exists
(ii) That Dresser Industries has an opinion on the subject of reducing imports from Japan
(iii) That the most probable source of investment that would lead to the expansion of the U.S. manufacturing capacity is either Dresser Industries itself or a joint venture of which it is a part
(iv) That the goal of reducing imports is a desirable one

Statement (4.i) is known as a(n existential) presupposition for (1). Statement (4.ii) is an entailment of (1). Should they be considered integral parts of the meaning of (1)? Information in (4.iii) and (4.iv) is inferred from (1) on the basis of general knowledge about the world. For example, (4.iii) relies on the belief that unless otherwise indicated, it is highly probable that Dresser Industries also plans to participate in the expansion of the U.S. manufacturing capacity. It is noteworthy that, unlike for (4.i) and (4.ii), (4.iii) and (4.iv) are not expected to be always true.

Let us explore what this actually means in a little more detail. One way of approaching the task of determining the exact meaning of a text is by using the negation test, a typical linguistic tool for justifying an element of description by showing that its exclusion leads to some sort of deviance, such as a contradiction (see, e.g., Raskin 1985c). Indeed, the negation of any element of (3) contradicts some component of the meaning of (1). We may take this as an indication that each element of (3) is a necessary part of the meaning of (1). But is it correct to say that *any* statement whose negation contradicts (1) is a necessary part of the meaning of (1)? Let us consider a few more cases.

It is easy to see why (5.i) and (5.ii) are contradictory. Each consists of (1) and the negation of one of the component clauses of (1). Obviously, the contradiction results from the fact that the negated component is an integral part of the meaning of (1).

(5) (i) Dresser Industries *said* it expects that major capital expenditure for expansion of U.S. manufacturing capacity will reduce imports from Japan, *and* Dresser Industries *did not say* that it expects that major capital expenditure for expansion of U.S. manufacturing capacity will reduce imports from Japan.
(ii) Dresser Industries said it *expects* that major capital expenditure for expansion of U.S. manufacturing capacity will reduce imports from Japan, *and* Dresser Industries said it *does not expect* that major capital expenditure for expansion of U.S. manufacturing capacity will reduce imports from Japan.

Similarly, contradictory statements will result from adding the negations of (4.i) and (4.ii) to (1), to yield (6.i) and (6.ii):

(6) (i) Dresser Industries said it expects that major capital expenditure for expansion of U.S. manufacturing capacity will reduce imports from Japan, and Dresser Industries does not exist.

(ii) Dresser Industries said it expects that major capital expenditure for expansion of U.S. manufacturing capacity will reduce imports from Japan, and Dresser Industries has no opinion on the subject of reducing imports from Japan.

The source of contradictions in (6) is different, however, from the source of contradictions in (5). The statements added in (6) do not negate anything directly stated in (1). They negate a presupposition and an entailment of (1), respectively: if it is not presupposed that Dresser Industries exists, (1) makes no sense; if it does not follow from (1) that Dresser Industries has an opinion on the subject of imports from Japan, (1) does not make sense, either. As we can see, the negation tool fails to distinguish between the actual elements of the meaning of (1), on the one hand, and the presuppositions and entailments of (1), on the other. This outcome gives us two alternatives—either to include presuppositions and entailments in the meaning of (1) (or, by extension, of any statement) or to ignore the results of the negation test in this case.

This distinction turns out to be problematic for people as well. Thus, delayed-recall experiments (Chafe 1977) show something that trial lawyers have always known about witness testimony, namely, that people never recall exactly what was said—only the gist of it—and that they routinely confuse the presuppositions and entailments of a statement with what the statement actually asserts. The distinction may, however, be quite important in those NLP applications where it is important to distinguish between what is conveyed by the text directly and what is present only by implication. For example, at the text generation step of machine translation what must be translated are the statements actually made and not what they presuppose or entail, because readers will presumably be able to recreate all the implications that were present but not overtly stated in the original text.

The negation tool does, however, work well for (4.iii) and (4.iv). Adding their negations to (1) yields (7.i) and (7.ii), which are somewhat odd but not contradictory:

(7) (i) Dresser Industries said it expects that major capital expenditure for expansion of U.S. manufacturing capacity will reduce imports from Japan, and it is not the case that Dresser Industries or a joint venture of which it is a part are the most probable source of investment in the U.S. manufacturing capacity.

(ii) Dresser Industries said it expects that major capital expenditure for expansion of U.S. manufacturing capacity will reduce imports from Japan, and the goal of reducing imports is not a desirable one.

We conclude that the reason for the absence of contradictions in (7) is that (4.iii) and (4.iv) do not negate any elements of the meaning of (1). In general, we assume that if adding the negation of a statement to another statement is not contradictory, then the former statement does not constitute a part of the meaning of the latter statement. One can also say then that there are no contradictions in (7) because (4.iii) and (4.iv) are possible but not necessary entailments from (1).

Many more such possible statements can be inferred from (1) based on the general knowledge about companies and how publicity works—for instance,

(8) (i) That Dresser Industries has a headquarters
 (ii) That it has employees
 (iii) That it manufactures particular products and/or offers particular services
 (iv) That the addressee of the statement by the spokesperson of Dresser Industries was the general public
 (v) That the statement has probably been made through the mass media, and so on

Even more inferences can be made from (1) based on the general understanding of goals that organizations and people typically pursue, as well as the plans they follow to attain those goals:

(9) (i) That there is a benefit for Dresser Industries in expanding the U.S. manufacturing capacity
 (ii) That capital investment is a plan toward attaining the goal of expanding manufacturing capacity
 (iii) That this goal can play the role of a step in a plan to attain the goal of reducing imports
 (iv) That Dresser Industries knows about using mass media as a plan for attaining a variety of goals

All the inferences in statements (7) through (9) are not "legal" (cf. Charniak and McDermott 1985, 21) deductions but rather abductive, defeasible, negatable inferences. For this reason, none of them are included in the specification of the meaning of (1). The distinction between meaning proper, on the one hand, and presuppositions, entailments, and inferences, on the other, may not be as important for NLP applications whose results are not intended for direct human consumption—for example, for text data mining aiming at automatic population of databases. People, however, are capable of generating presuppositions, entailments, and inferences on the fly from a brief message. Indeed, brevity is at a premium in human professional and business communication. Text meaning or even condensed text meaning are thus the central objects of manipulation in such common applications as machine translation and text summarization, respectively.

For computers, brevity of the kind to which we are referring has little real physical sense in these days of inexpensive storage devices and fast indexing and search algorithms. What is difficult for computer systems is precisely making reliable and relevant inferences. Therefore, spelling out as many inferences as possible from a text and recording them explicitly in a well-indexed manner for future retrieval is essential for supporting a variety of computational applications.

It is important for a computational semantic theory to provide the means of supporting both these precepts—of brevity and of explicitness. A representation of text meaning should be as brief as possible, if it is to be the source for generating a text for human consumption. The knowledge about both the building blocks of the meaning representation and the types of inferences possible from a particular text meaning should be stored in an accessible fashion. These kinds of knowledge are interchangeable with the change of inputs—what was a part of text meaning for one source text may end up being a source of inference for another. Any computational semantic application must support this capability of dynamically assigning some of the resident knowledge to direct meaning representations and reserving the rest for possible inferences. In ontological semantics, these goals are achieved through the interrelationship among text meaning representations (TMRs), the lexicons, and the ontology.

6.2   TMR in Ontological Semantics

The meaning of natural language texts is represented in ontological semantics as a result of a compositional process that relies on the meanings of words, of bound morphemes, of syntactic structures, and of word, phrase, and clause order in the input text. The meanings of words reside in the lexicon and the onomasticon (the lexicon of names). The bound morphemes (e.g., markers of Plural for nouns) are processed during morphological analysis and get their meanings recorded in special rules, possibly added to classes of lexical entries. Information about dependency among lexical elements and phrases, derived in syntax, helps to establish relationships of semantic dependency. Word and phrase order in some languages play a similar role.

It is clear then that the knowledge necessary for ontological semantic analysis of text should include not only the lexical material for the language of the text but also the results of the morphological and syntactic analysis of the input text. Let us follow the process of creating an ontological semantic TMR using the example in (1), repeated here as (10):

(10) Dresser Industries said it expects that major capital expenditure for expansion of U.S. manufacturing capacity will reduce imports from Japan.

Table 6.1
Results of morphological analysis

Root	Part of speech	Features
Dresser Industries	Phrase proper	Number: singular
say	Verb	Tense: past
it	Pronoun	Number: singular; person: third
expect	Verb	Tense: present; number: singular; person: third
that	Binder	
major	Adjective	
capital	Noun	Number: singular
expenditure	Noun	Number: singular
for	Preposition	
expansion	Noun	Number: singular
of	Preposition	
U.S.	Acronym	Number: singular
manufacturing	Verb	Form: gerund
capacity	Noun	Number: singular
reduce	Verb	Tense: future (*will* marks this in the text)
import	Noun	Number: plural
from	Preposition	
Japan	Noun proper	

English is a morphologically impoverished language, but morphological analysis of (10) will still yield some nontrivial results (see table 6.1).[1] Results of syntactic analysis of (10) can be represented in the following structure (which is modeled on the f-structure of LFG (e.g., L. S. Levin 1991)):

```
(11)
root      say
cat       verb
tense     past
subject
          root      dresser industries
          cat       phrase-proper
comp
          root      expect
          cat       verb
          tense     present
          subject
                    root      it
                    cat       pronoun
```

```
object
        root    reduce
        cat     verb
        tense   future
        subject
                root        expenditure
                cat         noun
                modifier root   capital
                        cat     noun
                        modifier root   major
                                cat     adjective
                oblique root    for
                        cat     preposition
                        object root     expansion
                                cat     noun
                                oblique root    of
                                        cat     preposition
                                        object root capacity
                                                cat noun
                                                modifier root       manufacturing
                                                        cat         verb
                                                        modifier root U.S.
                                                                cat phrase-proper

        object  root    imports
                cat     noun
        oblique root    from
                cat         preposition
                object root     japan
                        cat     noun-proper
```

We will now use the results of the morphological and syntactic analysis presented above in building a TMR for (10). TMRs are written in a formal language with its own syntax, specified in section 6.4. For pedagogical reasons, at many points in our presentation here, we will use a somewhat simplified version of that language and will build the TMR for (10) step by step, not necessarily in the order that any actual analyzer will follow.

The first step in ontological semantic analysis is finding meanings for heads of clauses in the syntactic representation of input. In our example, these are *say*, *expect*, and *reduce*. As we will see, they all will be treated differently in TMR construction. In addition, the TMR will end up containing more event instances ("proposition heads"; see section 8.2.1) than there are verbs in the original text. This is because ontological semantics is "transcategorial" in that meanings are not conditioned by part-of-speech tags. Specifically, in (1) the nouns *expenditure* and *expansion* occupying the syntactic positions corresponding typically to heads of noun phrases, are mapped into instances of event-type concepts in the TMR.

In (12), we present the syntactic structure (SYN-STRUC) and semantic structure (SEM-STRUC) components of the entry for *say* in the ontological semantic lexicon of

English. The meaning of *say* instantiates the ontological concept INFORM. The representation of this concept, shown in (13), contains a number of properties ("slots"), with a specification of what type of object can be a legal value ("filler") for each property.

```
(12)
say-v1
      syn-struc
            1    root    say    ; as in Spencer said a word
                 cat     v
                 subj    root    $var1
                         cat     n
                 obj     root    $var2
                         cat     n
            2    root    say    ; as in Spencer said that it rained
                 cat     v
                 subj    root    $var1
                         cat     n
                 comp    root    $var2
      sem-struc
            1 2  INFORM                ; both syn-strucs have the same
                         AGENT ^$var1  ; semantic structure; '^' is read
                                       ; as 'the meaning of'; the
                         THEME ^$var2  ; variables provide mappings
                                       ; between syntactic and semantic
                                       ; structures; ontological concepts
                                       ; are in SMALL CAPS
```

```
(13)
INFORM
      DEFINITION      "the event of asserting something to
                      provide information to another person or
                      set of persons"
      IS-A            ASSERTIVE-ACT
      AGENT           HUMAN
      THEME           EVENT
      INSTRUMENT      COMMUNICATION-DEVICE
      BENEFICIARY     HUMAN
```

So far, then, the nascent TMR for (1) has the form:

(14)
INFORM-1
         AGENT value   _____
         THEME value   _____

The arbitrary but unique numbers appended to the names of concepts during ontological semantic processing identify instances of concepts. The numbers themselves
are also used for establishing coreference relations among the same instances. At the
next step of semantic analysis, the process seeks to establish whether fillers are available in the input for these properties. If the fillers are not available directly, there are
special procedures for trying to establish them. If these recovery procedures fail to
identify the filler but it is known that some filler must exist in principle, the special
filler UNKNOWN is used.

   The AGENT slot in (14) cannot be filled directly from the text. The reason for that
is as follows. The procedure for determining the filler attempts to use the syntax-to-
semantics mapping in the lexicon entry for *say*, to establish the filler for the particular slots. The lexicon entry for *say* essentially states that the meaning, ^$var1, of the
syntactic subject of *say*, $var1, should be the filler of the AGENT slot of INFORM. Before
inserting a filler, the system checks whether it matches the ontological constraint for
AGENT of INFORM and discovers that the match occurs on the RELAXABLE-TO facet
of the AGENT slot, because *Dresser Industries* is an organization. Note that the
ontological status of DRESSER INDUSTRIES is that of a (named) instance of the concept CORPORATION (see section 7.2 for a discussion of instances and remembered
instances).

   The TMR at this point looks as illustrated in (15).

(15)
INFORM-1
         AGENT value   Dresser Industries
         THEME value   _____

The theme slot in (14) requires a more complex treatment.[2] The complement of *say*
in the syntactic representation (11) is a statement of expectation. According to a
general rule, the direct object of the syntactic clause should be considered as the
prime candidate for producing the filler for THEME. Expectation, however, is considered in ontological semantics to be a modality and is, therefore, represented in
TMR as a property of the proposition that represents the meaning of the clause that
modifies it syntactically. Before assigning properties, such as this modality, we will
first finish representing the basic meanings that these properties characterize. Therefore, a different candidate for filling the theme property must be found. The next
candidate is the clause headed by *reduce*. Consulting the lexicon and the ontology
and using the standard rules of matching selectional restrictions yields (16):

```
(16)
INFORM-1
      AGENT value   Dresser Industries
      THEME value   DECREASE-1
DECREASE-1
      AGENT value   unknown
```

Continuing along this path, we fill the case roles THEME and INSTRUMENT in (16), as well as their own properties and the properties of their properties, all the way down, as shown in (17):

```
(17)
INFORM-1
      AGENT          value   Dresser Industries
      THEME          value   DECREASE-1
DECREASE-1
      AGENT          value   unknown
      THEME          value   IMPORT-1
      INSTRUMENT     value   expend-1
IMPORT-1
      AGENT          value   unknown
      THEME          value   unknown
      SOURCE         value   Japan
      DESTINATION    value   USA
EXPEND-1
      AGENT          value   unknown
      THEME          value   MONEY-1
                             AMOUNT   value  >0.7
      PURPOSE        value   INCREASE-1
INCREASE-1
      AGENT          value   unknown
      THEME          value   MANUFACTURE-1.THEME
MANUFACTURE-1
      AGENT          value   unknown
      THEME          value   unknown
      LOCATION       value   USA
```

Some elements of (17) are not self-evident and require an explanation. First, the value of the property AMOUNT of the concept MONEY (which is the meaning of *capital* in the input) is rendered as a region on an abstract scale between 0 and 1, with the value corresponding to the meaning of the word *major*. The same value would be assigned to other words denoting a large quantity, such as *large*, *great*, *much*, *many*, and so on. The meanings of words like *enormous*, *huge*, or *gigantic* would be assigned a higher value, say, >0.9. The THEME of INCREASE is constrained to SCALAR-OBJECT-ATTRIBUTE and its ontological descendants, of which AMOUNT is one. The filler of the THEME of INCREASE-1 turns out to be the property AMOUNT itself (not a value of this property!) referenced as the THEME of manufacture-1, rendered in the familiar dot notation.

Now that we have finished building the main "who did what to whom" semantic dependency structure, let us add those features that are in ontological semantics factored out into specific parameterized properties, such as speech act, modality, time, or coreference. The top proposition in (18) reflects the speech-act information that in the text (1) is not expressed explicitly, namely, the speech act of publishing (1) in whatever medium. The speech act introduces an instance of the ontological concept AUTHOR-EVENT (see also section 6.5).

```
(18)
AUTHOR-EVENT-1
      AGENT    value   unknown
      THEME    value   inform-1
      time
               time-begin          >INFORM-1.time-end
               time-end            unknown

INFORM-1
      AGENT    value   Dresser Industries
      THEME    value   DECREASE-1
      time
               time-begin          unknown
               time-end            <DECREASE-1.time-begin
                                   <IMPORT-1.time-begin
                                   <REDUCE-1.time-begin
                                   <EXPEND-1.time-begin
                                   <INCREASE-1.time-begin
DECREASE-1
      AGENT         value      unknown
      THEME         value      IMPORT-1
      INSTRUMENT    value      EXPEND-1
      time
               time-begin          >INFORM-1.time-end
                                   >EXPEND-1.time-begin
                                   >IMPORT-1.time-begin
               time-end            <IMPORT-1.time-begin
IMPORT-1
      AGENT         value      unknown
      THEME         value      unknown
```

```
        SOURCE         value        Japan
        DESTINATION    value        USA
        time
               time-begin          >INFORM-1.time-end
                                    <EXPEND-1.time-begin
               time-end            unknown
EXPEND-1
        AGENT          value           unknown
        THEME          value           MONEY-1
                                          AMOUNT   value   >0.7
        PURPOSE        value           INCREASE-1
        time
               time-begin          >INFORM-1.time-end
               time-end            <INCREASE-1.time-begin
INCREASE-1
        AGENT          value        unknown
        THEME          value        MANUFACTURE-1.THEME
        time
               time-begin          >INFORM-1.time-end
                                    <MANUFACTURE-1.time-begin
               time-end            unknown
MANUFACTURE-1
        AGENT          value        unknown
        THEME          value        unknown
        LOCATION       value        USA
        time
               time-begin          >INFORM-1.time-end
               time-end            unknown
MODALITY-1
        modality-type               potential     ; this is the meaning of
                                                  ; expects in (1)
        modality-value              1             ; this is the maximum value
                                                  ; of potential
        modality-scope              DECREASE-1
        modality-attributed-to      Dresser Industries
MODALITY-2
        modality-type               potential     ; this is the meaning of
                                                  ; capacity in 1
        modality-value              1
        modality-scope              MANUFACTURE-1
co-reference-1
        INCREASE-1.AGENT MANUFACTURE-1.AGENT
co-reference-2
        IMPORT-1.THEME MANUFACTURE-1.THEME
```

The time property values in each proposition, all relative since there is no absolute
reference to time in the input sentence, establish a partial temporal order of the

various events in (1)—for example, that the time of the statement by Dresser Industries precedes the time of reporting. The expected events may only take place after the statement is made. It is not clear, however, how the time of reporting relates to the times of the expected events because some of them may have already taken place between the time of the statement and the time of reporting.

Inserting the value UNKNOWN into appropriate slots in the TMR actually undersells the system's capabilities. In reality, while the exact filler might indeed not be known, the system knows many constraints on this filler. These constraints come from the ontological specification of the concept in which the property that gets the UNKNOWN filler is defined. If included in the TMR, the constraints turn it into what we define as extended TMR (see section 6.7). Thus, the AGENT of IMPORT-1 is constrained to U.S. import companies. The AGENT of EXPEND-1 is constrained to people and organizations that are investors. The AGENT of INCREASE-1 and MANUFACTURE-1 is constrained to manufacturing corporations. The THEME of IMPORT-1 and MANUFACTURE-1 is constrained to GOODS (the idea being that if you manufacture some goods, you do not have to import them). The facts that *Dresser Industries* is a company while *Japan* and *USA* are countries are stored in the onomasticon.

6.3 Ontological Concepts and Nonontological Parameters in TMR

The above example was presented to introduce the main elements of a TMR in ontological semantics. A careful reader will have established by now that our approach to representing text meaning uses two basic means: instantiation of ontological concepts and instantiation of semantic parameters unconnected to the ontology. The former (see (17)) creates abstract, unindexed[3] propositions that correspond to any of a number of possible TMR instantiations. These instantiations (see the material in (18) not present in (17)) are obtained by supplementing the basic ontological statement with concrete contextual values of parameters such as aspect, style, coreference, and others.

One strong motivation for this division is size economy in the ontology. Indeed, one could avoid introducing the parameter of, say, aspect—opting instead for introducing the ontological attribute ASPECT whose DOMAIN is EVENT and whose RANGE is the literal set of aspectual values. The result would be either different concepts for different aspectual senses of each verb—for example, the concepts READ, HAVE-READ, BE-READING, and HAVE-BEEN-READING instead of a single concept READ or the introduction of the ontological property ASPECT for each EVENT concept. The former decision would mean at least quadrupling the number of EVENT-type concepts just in order to avoid introducing this one parameter. An objection to the latter decision is that aspect—as well as modality, time, and other proposition-level parameters—is defined for concept instances, not ontological concepts themselves.

The boundary between ontological and parametric specification of meaning is not fixed in ontological semantics. Different specific implementations are possible. In the Mikrokosmos implementation of ontological semantics, the boundary between the parametric and ontological components of text meaning is realized as formulated in the Backus Naur Form (BNF) specification in the next section.

6.4   The Nature and Format of TMR

In this section, we introduce the format of the TMR. As it is presented, this format does not exactly correspond to those in any of the implementations of ontological semantics. We present a composite version that we believe to be easiest to describe. The TMR format in actual implementations can and will be somewhat different in details—for instance, simplifying or even omitting elements tangential to a particular application. The BNF below specifies the syntax of the TMR. The semantics of this formalism is determined by the purpose for which the BNF constructs are introduced. Therefore, the convenient place for describing the semantics of the TMR is in the sections devoted to the process of deriving TMRs from texts (see chapter 8).

In the BNF, "{ }" are used for grouping; "[ ]" means optional (i.e., 0 or 1); "+" means 1 or more; and "*" means 0 or more.

Informally, the TMR consists of a set of propositions connected through text-level discourse relations. Parameters at this top level of TMR specification include modality, style, coreference, and TMR time (see section 8.6).

```
TMR ::=
     PROPOSITION+
     DISCOURSE-RELATION*
     MODALITY*
     STYLE
     REFERENCE*
     TMR-TIME
```

A proposition is a unit of semantic representation corresponding to a single predication in text (in Mikrokosmos, all TMRs have been produced as a result of analysis of a natural language text). Syntactically, single predications are typically realized as clauses. At the level of proposition, aspect, modality, and time of proposition, the overall TMR time and style are parameterized.

```
PROPOSITION ::=
proposition
     head:          concept-instance
     ASPECT
     PROPOSITION-TIME
     STYLE
```

The terms in small caps are nonterminal symbols; those in boldface are reserved words; the terms in italics are terminal symbols in the TMR. The main carrier of semantic information is the head of a proposition. Finding the head and filling its properties with appropriate material in the input constitute the two main processes in ontological semantic analysis—instantiation and matching of selectional restrictions (see section 8.2.2).

```
ASPECT ::=
aspect
    aspect-scope: concept-instance
    phase:         begin | continue | end | begin-continue-end
    iteration:     integer | multiple
```

The symbols "concept-instance," "integer," "boolean," and "real-number" (see below) are interpreted in a standard fashion (see section 7.1 for an explanation of the notion of instantiation) and are not formally described in this BNF (see section 8.5.1 for an explanation of the interpretation of aspect in ontological semantics).

```
TMR-TIME ::= set
                    element-type    proposition-time
                    cardinality     >= 1
```

TMR-time is defined as a set of all the values of times of propositions in the TMR. This effectively imposes a partial ordering on the propositions. It can be derived automatically from the values of proposition-time.

```
PROPOSITION-TIME ::=
time
    time-begin: TIME-EXPR*
    time-end:   TIME-EXPR*
```

Time expressions refer to point times; durations are calculated from the beginnings and ends of time periods:

```
TIME-EXPR ::= << | < | > | >> | >= | <= | = | != {ABSOLUTE-
      TIME | RELATIVE-TIME}
ABSOLUTE-TIME ::= {+/-}YYYYMMDDHHMMSSFFFF [ [+/-] real-number
      temporal-unit]
```

The above says that times of propositions are given in terms of the times of their beginnings and ends and can be expressed through a reference to an absolute time, represented as year-month-day-hour-minute-second-fraction-of-second (negative values refer to times before common era) or to a time point that is a certain time period before or after the above reference point.

```
RELATIVE-TIME ::= CONCEPT-INSTANCE.TIME [ [+/-] real-number
    temporal-unit]
```

Alternatively, time-begin and time-end can be filled with relative times—that is, a reference to the time of another concept instance, such as an event, again possibly modified by the addition (*a week after graduation*) or subtraction (*six years before he died*) of a time period (see section 8.5.2 for a detailed discussion of proposition time).

```
STYLE ::=
style
      formality:      (0,1)
      politeness:     (0,1)
      respect:        (0,1)
      force:          (0,1)
      simplicity:     (0,1)
      color:          (0,1)
      directness:     (0,1)
```

Definitions of the above properties are given in section 8.6.4.

```
DISCOURSE-RELATION ::=
      relation-type:     ontosubtree (discourse-relation)
      domain:            proposition+
      range:             proposition+
```

"ontosubtree" is a function that returns all the descendants of the ontological concept that is its argument, including the argument itself. In the above specification, the function returns all the discourse relations defined in the ontology.

```
MODALITY ::=
modality
      modality-type:            MODALITY-TYPE
      modality-value:           (0,1)
      modality-scope:           concept-instance*
      modality-attributed-to:   concept-instance*
```

The value (0,1) refers to the abstract scale of values or intervals running between zero and unity. This and other types of property fillers (for example, the literal values of the modality-type property; see below) are discussed in greater detail in section 7.1.

```
MODALITY-TYPE ::= epistemic | deontic | volitive | potential |
                  epiteuctic | evaluative | saliency
```

The semantics of the above labels is described in section 8.5.3.

```
REFERENCE ::= SET
              element-type (coreference concept-instance
              concept-instance+)
              cardinality > 1
```

The above is a way of recording coreference information as a set of coreference chains in the input text (see section 8.6.1 for a discussion).

```
SET ::=
set
      element-type:    concept | concept-instance
      cardinality:     [ < | > | >= | <= | <> ] integer
      complete:        boolean
      excluding:       [ concept | concept-instance ]*
      elements:        concept-instance*
      subset-of:       SET
```

The set construct, as used in ontological semantics, is rather complex. The motivation for including all the above properties is the ease of formalizing a variety of kinds of references in natural language texts to groups of objects, events, or properties. "Element-type," "cardinality," and "subset-of" are self-explanatory. The property "complete" records whether the set lists all the elements that it can in principle have. In other words, the set of all college students will have the Boolean value "true" in its "complete" slot. This mechanism is the way of representing universal quantification. The value of the English word *some* (which can be understood as an existential quantifier) is represented by the Boolean value "false" in the "complete" slot. The "excluding" property allows one to define a set using set difference, for instance, to represent the meaning of such texts as *Everybody but Bill and Peter agreed*. The "elements" property is used for listing the elements of the set directly.

The above definitions determine the range of what can be represented in TMRs, and the task of the ontological semantic enterprise is to generate a legal TMR structure for any input text in any language and, conversely, to generate text in a natural language given its TMR specification. The same TMR representation can also capture any content, not necessarily expressed in natural language. It can, for example, be used for recording the interim and final results of reasoning by intelligent agents. We fully expect that, as the actual coverage in the ontology and the lexicons increases and as the quality of semantic analysis grows, the TMR format will be extended to accommodate these improvements. Such an extension, we believe, will largely involve movement toward a finer grain size of semantic description, which the existing formalism should readily allow. At the present stage of development, the TMR, together with the static (ontology, lexicons) and dynamic (analyzer) knowledge sources that are used in generating and manipulating it, already provides very substantial coverage for a broad variety of semantic phenomena. In a compact way, it represents practically attainable solutions for most issues that have concerned the computational linguistics and NLP community for over forty years.

Thus, TMR results, in part, from the process of disambiguation undertaken by the various modules of the analyzer (ecological, morphological, syntactic, semantic, and so on; see sections 8.1 through 8.4). In dealing with this issue, we incorporate and extend the ideas about semantic selectional restrictions introduced by Katz and Fodor (1963; cf. section 3.5.3; also see McCawley 1968). Of course, Katz and Fodor were content only to illustrate their approach using the example of one simple sentence. They also adopted the then-prevalent presupposition of the existence of a static and complete division of all the words into word senses on the basis of a limited set of semantic primitives. In contrast, ontological semantics implemented broad-coverage semantic analysis on the basis of static and dynamic selectional restrictions on the meanings of various components of ontological events, as realized in the language by constraints on the co-occurrence of lexical units. Selectional restrictions in ontological semantics are not based on markers taken from a flat-list inventory, as envisaged by Katz and Fodor and as further developed by Fodor (e.g., 1994; see also Fodor and Lepore 1998) in the equally atomistic "language of thought." Rather, their values are full-blown ontological concepts, with properties modifiable to facilitate the expression of even the finer differences of meaning. They are stored in ontological and lexical definitions of both events and objects and even allow for selectional restrictions in a nonhierarchical manner—that is, mutual restrictions on the co-occurrence of, say, two or more different case role fillers for one event (see section 8.3.1). This latter capability in ontological semantics was in part inspired by Wilks's (1975a, 1975b, 1977) preference semantics.

Some recent research activity in word-sense disambiguation has been carried out within the SENSEVAL movement (e.g., Kilgariff and Rosenzweig 2000). Unlike most of the SENSEVAL participants, we concentrate on comprehensive disambiguation of all lexical units in the text rather than scoring the disambiguation results on assigning occurrences of a few words in the text to one of several senses delimited in the training corpus. Moreover, ontological semantics views word-sense disambiguation as just one of several components of the compositional semantic process aimed at producing meaning representation. We should overtly note that our attitude toward SENSEVAL is predicated strictly on the coverage issue and not on the preference of most SENSEVAL participants for nonrepresentational methods based essentially on calculating uninterpreted "distances" between word occurrences in texts. In fact, there is a place for such methods among the various engines of ontological semantics. SENSEVAL has proved that small sets of words can be disambiguated with high accuracy and often using unsupervised methods, in the style of Yarowsky 1995. We agree with Wilks (1998) that blanket disambiguation, his "all-word paradigm . . . is the real task and there is no evidence that the small scale will scale up to the large because much of sense disambiguation is mutual between the words of the text which cannot be used by the small set approach."

The principle of practical effability in ontological semantics (see section 9.3.6), implemented by reducing the number of senses in a lexicon entry (see section 9.3.5) and making them more "inclusive," is in the tradition of earlier research on using machine-readable dictionaries (MRDs) in NLP (e.g., Amsler 1984; Ahlswede et al. 1985; Boguraev et al. 1989; Calzolari 1989; Zernik 1991; Guo 1995; Wilks, Slator, and Guthrie 1996). The premises of the MRD research paradigm were adopted by the Aquilex project (see note 1 in chapter 4) and its successors and found one of their logical conclusions in the one-sense-per-entry imperative of Pustejovsky 1995.

In ontological semantics, MRDs play a marginal role in lexical acquisition. Instead, ontological semantics shares with FrameNet (e.g., Fillmore, Wooters, and Baker 2001) the preference for acquiring lexical entries from scratch and using human semantic competence and advanced acquisition environments. Where ontological semantics diverges from FrameNet is in its emphasis on comprehensive coverage and immediate support of practical applications, which necessitates limitations on the grain size of lexical description counterbalanced by a much more developed language-independent ontology.

Ontological semantics concentrates on the task of extracting, representing, and manipulating meaning and contends that any and all knowledge sources—morphology, syntax, and so on (see chapter 8)—should be used to help a system attain that goal. This stance is different from that of the conceptual-dependency paradigm (e.g., Schank 1975), which strived to perform semantic analysis in a "pure" form, without declared reliance on syntactic analysis. In practice, syntax has naturally found its way into every one of the conceptual-dependency analyzers. This has happened much the way rule-based processing later found its way into the statistics-based MT system Candide (Brown et al. 1990), the authors' claims of a totally new processing paradigm notwithstanding (cf. Wilks 1994). At the same time, ontological semantics cannot subscribe to the understandable but unrealistic hope of Dorr (1993, 1994), Levin (1993), and others (see section 4.2) that semantic distinctions can be fruitfully determined on the exclusive basis of syntactic distinctions.

While the above-mentioned group is overoptimistic about the use of Jackendoff's (1983) lexical-conceptual structures (LCSs) and Levin's observations about verb diathesis, at least they are dealing squarely with the lexical and compositional semantics of open-class lexical items. A large group of semanticists moves even further away from what ontological semantics claims is the crux of the semantic analysis matter and concentrates exclusively on a subset of lexical and compositional semantic problems having to do largely with quantification, scoping, and other overtly grammaticalized phenomena that lend themselves to interpretation in terms of formal logic (see section 3.5.1). Ontological semantics opts for a different approach to such phenomena. Instead of seeking to build declarative logics to explain them, it has formulated meaning procedures, whenever possible attached to lexicon entries for the so-called closed-class items (pronouns, conjuctions, quantifiers, and so on), to affect TMRs directly, without the mediation of the ontology, as is the case with most open-class words (and, curiously, most prepositions, which are technically a type of closed-class item). In fact, the meaning procedures in ontological semantics may be direct descendants of the proposals of procedural semantics (Winograd 1972; Woods 1981; see also Wilks 1982).

At its present stage of development, ontological semantics contains sketches of a variety of microtheories (see section 1.7) that describe a variety of types of phenomena in language that require semantic treatment. Most of these microtheories have been subjects of studies by our predecessors. Ontological semantics aims at incorporating as much of the usable content in prior work as possible and then extending the microtheories further to achieve increasingly better coverage of phenomena and higher quality of results produced by ontological semantic engines. Work on the microtheories is ongoing, and any new results will be included in future implementations of ontological semantics.

Thus, following and expanding the general ideas in early AI work on scripts, plans, and goals in natural language processing (e.g., Charniak 1972; Schank and Abelson 1977; Wilensky 1983; also see section 1.1), ontological semantics develops the microtheory of complex events (see section 7.1.5) to reach the suprasentential, text level of description. Another text-level microtheory, that of discourse relations (see section 8.6.3), is informed by the prior work in both the formal semantics tradition (e.g., Kamp 1984) and NLP (e.g., Grosz and Sidner 1986).

The ontological semantic microtheory of aspect has been informed by the work of Vendler (1967) and others (see section 8.5.1). The microtheory of modality (see section 8.5.3) is informed by work in such diverse areas as semantics of belief (e.g., Partee 1973a), belief ascription (e.g., Ballim and Wilks 1991), saliency (e.g., Tversky and Kahnemann 1973), thematic structure (see references in section 3.6), attitudes (Anscombre and Ducrot 1983), and modal logic (e.g., Hughes and Cresswell 1968). The basic microtheory of semantic dependency building, in its component dealing with treatment of deviations from expectations, has been influenced by the vast collection of work on treatment of tropes (mostly, metaphor and metonymy; e.g., Lakoff and Johnson 1980; Fass 1991). Ontological semantics does not, at this time, formulate a stand-alone microtheory of spatial relations (see Lemon 1996 and references therein on semantics in spatial logics; cf. Nirenburg and Raskin 1987 for an early ontological semantic perspective). Instead, it incorporates the relevant knowledge into the lexical meanings of prepositions and spatial adjectives and adverbs. With respect to representation of time, the corresponding microtheory in ontological semantics (see sections 8.5.2 and 8.6.2) is informed by the work on temporal logics (e.g., Allen 1984).

The microtheory of reference in ontological semantics (see section 8.6.1; cf. McShane and Nirenburg 2002), an expanding area of research at the time of this writing (McShane, forthcoming), has been unable, unlike the other microtheories, to profit significantly from earlier efforts in this field. The primary reason for this is that, in the absence of the underlying ontology, one has to struggle hard for a handle that can be used in identifying the points of reference. In general, since reference is a semantic phenomenon, it is unfairly disadvantageous to try to deal with it without explicitly formulated semantic underpinnings, and this has been the weakness of such otherwise interesting work as Baldwin 1997, Kehler and Shieber 1997, or Harabagiu and Maiorano 1999.

This is a good place to note that ontological semantics differs in principle from the approach espoused by Moldovan, Harabagiu, and their associates (e.g., Mihalcea and Moldovan 1999) in our insistence on acquiring and using as much knowledge as possible to bring to bear on computational linguistic processes. In contrast, the Moldovan group investigates what they term "knowledge-lean" methods that manifest themselves, for instance, in ingenious and inventive attempts to mine meaning from WordNet (see, e.g., Harabagiu and Moldovan 1998; Moldovan et al. 2000). Within the rapidly growing field of formal ontologies, ontological semantics occupies the place closest to the needs and goals of natural language processing, and this may be its main substantive difference from other modern knowledge-based approaches, such as CYC (Lenat 1995) or conceptual graphs and their content (e.g., Sowa 1984, 2000).

To summarize, ontological semantics is informed by and captures a vast body of knowledge about natural language meaning made available by relevant research in NLP. As a result, ontological semantics is naturally inclusive and oriented toward an integrative approach to the treatment of meaning, and prefers to study the phenomena in vivo and in toto rather than concerning itself with abstract reasoning about individual issues. Architecturally, ontological semantics is a society of ever-evolving microtheories that come together and are fixed at various times for the purposes of creating a practical application. Such an attitude promotes community-level collaboration as our modus operandi. We are always ready to jettison a particular microtheory in favor of a better one. The price to pay—the need to write format conversions among formalisms and reinterpret the semantics of metalanguage—is very often entirely reasonable from the standpoint of the end benefit.

6.5   Further Examples of TMR Specification

In this section, we will discuss some of the standard ways of treating a few less obvious cases of meaning representation using the TMR format.

If an input text contains a modifier-modified pair, then the meaning of the modifier is expected to be expressed as the value of a property of the modified (see Raskin and Nirenburg 1996a on the microtheory of adjectival meaning as a proposal for modification treatment in ontological semantics). This property is, in fact, part of the meaning of the modifier whose other component is the appropriate value of this property. Thus, if COLOR is listed in the ontology as a characteristic property of the concept CAR (either directly or through inheritance—in this example, from PHYSICAL-OBJECT), *a blue car* will be represented as

```
CAR-5
      INSTANCE-OF    value    CAR
      COLOR          value    blue
```

If a modifier does not express a property defined for the ontological concept corresponding to its head, then it may be represented in one of a number of available ways, including the following:

• As a modality value—for instance, the meaning of *favorite* in *your favorite Dunkin' Donuts shop* is expressed through an evaluative modality scoping over the head of the phrase
• As a separate clause, semantically connected to the meaning of the governing clause through coreference of property fillers
• As a relation among other TMR elements

On a more general note with respect to reference, consider the sentence *The Iliad was written not by Homer but by another man with the same name.*[4] We will not discuss the processing of the ellipsis in this sentence (see section 8.4.4 for a discussion of treating this phenomenon). After the ellipsis is processed, the sentence will look as follows: The *Iliad was not written by Homer, the Iliad was written by a different man whose name was Homer*. The meanings of the first mention of *Homer* and *Iliad* are instantiated from the concepts HUMAN and BOOK, respectively. Like Japan and USA in (18), they will be referred to by name in the TMR. The second mention of *Homer* will be represented "on general principles"—that is, using a numbered instance of HUMAN, with all the properties attested in the text overtly listed. There are two event instances referred to in the sentence, both of them instances of AUTHOR-EVENT:

```
AUTHOR-EVENT-1
       AGENT value   Homer
       THEME value   Iliad

modality-1                       ;a method of representing negation
       modality-scope            AUTHOR-EVENT-1
       modality-type             epistemic
       modality-value            0
```

```
AUTHOR-EVENT-2
     AGENT value   HUMAN-2
                          HAS-NAME value Homer
     THEME value   Iliad
co-reference-3
     Homer HUMAN-2
modality-2
     modality-scope      co-reference-3
     modality-type       epistemic
     modality-value      0
```

Another example of a special representation strategy is questions and commands. In fact, to deal with this issue, we must first better understand how we are treating assertions. All our examples so far have been assertions, though we have not characterized them as such, because there was nothing with which to compare them. In linguistic and philosophical theory, assertions, questions, and commands are types of illocutionary acts, or less formally, speech acts (Austin 1962; Searle 1969, 1975). This brings up the general issue of how to treat speech acts in TMRs.

Our solution is to present every proposition as the theme of a communication event whose agent is the author (speaker) of the text that we are analyzing. Sometimes, such a communication event is overtly stated in the text—for example, *I promise to perform well on the exams*. Most of the time, however, such an event is implied—for instance, *I will perform well on the exams*, which can be uttered in exactly the same circumstances as the former example and have the same meaning.[5] Note that we included the implicit communication event with the reporter as the author in the detailed example (18).

Similarly, for questions and commands, the implicit communication event must also be represented in order to characterize the speech act correctly. We represent questions using values of the ontological concept REQUEST-INFORMATION, with its theme filled by the element about which the question is asked. If the latter is the value of a property of a concept instance, this is a special question about the filler of this property. For example, the question *Who won the match?* is represented as

```
WIN-32
     THEME value   SPORTS-MATCH-2
REQUEST-INFORMATION-13
     THEME value   WIN-32.AGENT
```

If an entire proposition fills the THEME property of REQUEST-INFORMATION, this is a general yes/no question. For example, *Did Arsenal win the match?* will be represented as

```
WIN-33
      AGENT value   Arsenal
      THEME value   SPORTS-MATCH-3

REQUEST-INFORMATION-13
      THEME value   WIN-33
```

The meaning of the sentence *Was it Arsenal who won the match?* will be represented as

```
WIN-34
      AGENT value   Arsenal
      THEME value   SPORTS-MATCH-3

REQUEST-INFORMATION-13
      THEME value   WIN-33

modality-11
         modality-type      salience
         modality-scope     WIN-32.THEME
         modality-value     1
```

Commands are treated in a similar fashion, except that the ontological concept used for the—often implicit—communication event is REQUEST-ACTION, whose theme is always an EVENT.

Speech-act theory deals with an unspecified large number of illocutionary acts, such as promises, threats, apologies, greetings, and so on. Some such acts are explicit—that is, the text contains a specific reference to the appropriate communication event—but most are not. To complicate matters further, one type of speech act, whether explicit or implicit, may stand for another type. Thus, in *Can you pass the salt?* what on the surface seems to be a direct speech act, a question, is, in fact, an indirect speech act of request.

Because speech-act theory has never been intended or used for text processing, neither Austin nor Searle was interested in the boundaries of meaning specification and the differences between meaning proper and inferences. Thus, a significant distinction was ignored. This state of affairs has practical consequences, too. As we have discussed in section 6.1, in NLP it is important to know when to stop meaning analysis.

Therefore, it is important to understand that such speech acts as assertions, questions, and commands (and very likely nothing else) are part of the meaning of a text, while others are typically inferred, unless they are overtly stated in the text (e.g., *I regret to inform you that the hotel is fully booked*). As with all inferences, there is no guarantee that the system will have all the knowledge necessary for computing such inferences. As a result, the analysis may have to halt before all possible inferences have been made. As was mentioned in section 6.1 (see also section 6.7), very few such inferences are needed for the application of machine translation.

6.6 Synonymy and Paraphrases

The issue we are discussing in this section is whether ontological semantics can generate two different TMRs for the same input and whether different inputs with the same meaning are represented by the same TMR. The former phenomenon is synonymy, the latter, paraphrase in natural language. What we are interested in here is whether these phenomena are carried over into the TMR.

In an ontological semantic analysis system, for a given state of static knowledge resources, a given definition of the TMR format, and a given analysis procedure, a given input will always yield the same TMR statement. The above means that there is no synonymy of TMRs. There is a one-to-one relationship between a textual input and a TMR statement. Sentence- or text-level synonymy in natural language—that is, paraphrase—will not, therefore, necessarily lead to generating a single TMR for each sentence from a set of paraphrases, unless those paraphrases are purely syntactic, as, for instance, in active-, passive-, and middle-voice variations.

The sentences *Michael Johnson won the 400 m, Michael Johnson got the gold medal in the 400 m, Michael Johnson finished first in the 400 m,* and even *Michael Johnson left all his rivals behind at the finish line in the 400 m in Sydney,* as well as many others, may refer to the same event without being, strictly speaking, paraphrases. The analysis system will assign different TMRs to these inputs. This is because the analysis procedure is in some sense "literal minded" and simply follows the rules of instantiating and combining the elementary meanings from the lexicon, the ontology, and the fact repository (FR). In defense of this literal-mindedness, do not let us forget that all the above examples do, in fact, have, strictly speaking, different meanings and deal with different facts. It is another matter that these facts are closely connected and, if they indeed all refer to the finals of the 400 m run at the 2000 Sydney Olympics, characterize different aspects of the same event. In terms of formal semantics, any one of these coreferring sentences conjoined with the negation of any other yields a contradictory statement. This means that an inferential relationship holds between any two of such sentences (cf. (9) above).

Is it important to know that all these (and possibly other) examples refer to the same event? It might be that for the application of MT this is not that important. However, in information-extraction and question-answering systems, it is essential to understand that all the examples above provide the same information. So, if the question was *Who won the men's 400 m in Sydney?* any of the above examples can provide the answer. Also, if we turn these examples into questions, all of them can be input into a QA system with the same intent. The desire to recognize that the set of questions *Did Michael Johnson win the 400? Who got the gold in the men's 400?* and others corefer makes it necessary, unlike in MT, to find a way of connecting them. To accommodate such a goal in these applications, additional provisions should be furnished in the static knowledge sources. Complex events in the ontology (section 7.1.5) and the fact repository (section 7.2) fit the bill. The sentences in the example above would instantiate different components of the same instance of the complex event SPORTS-RESULT in the ontology. For a QA system to be able to provide an answer to questions based on these sentences, the FR must contain this instance of SPORTS-RESULT with its properties filled.

6.7 Basic and Extended TMRs

The input text provides initial information to be recorded in the TMR by an ontological semantic analysis system. The input sentence *John sold the blue car* results in a TMR fragment with instances of BUY, HUMAN, and CAR. The latter's COLOR property is filled with the value "blue." The instances of HUMAN and CAR fill the properties SOURCE and THEME, respectively, in the instance of BUY. The important thing to realize here is that in addition to having established the above property values triggered by direct processing of the input, the system knows much more about the ontological concept instances used in this TMR—for example, that BUY has an AGENT property, among many others. While the values of the properties that have not been overtly stated in the text do not become part of the specification of an instance, they can still be retrieved from the ontology, by traversing the INSTANCE-OF relation from the instance to its corresponding concept. Thus, the system can abductively infer that the car was sold to another person from the fact that AGENT of BUY has a SEM constraint HUMAN, even though the input does not overtly mention this. In principle, this conclusion can be overridden by textual evidence.

If the blue car has been already mentioned in the text (which is likely because of the definite article in the input), then the corresponding instance of car is already available. If the instance was created by processing the input *John owned a blue Buick and a red Ford*, then the TMR already contains an instance of a car whose COLOR property is "blue" and whose MAKE property is filled by BUICK. The MAKE property in the ontological concept for CAR has CAR-MANUFACTURER as its filler. The constraint from the text is more specific. Therefore, if coreference can be established, the quality of processing will be enhanced if the more specific constraint is used.

Now, in addition to other parts of the TMR, there is another source of such constraints, the fact repository (see section 7.2), where information about remembered instances of ontological concepts is stored. So, if for some reason it is important to remember John's Buick, then any information from any text already processed by a system or entered by a human acquirer (from the point of view of the FR itself, the

method of acquisition is immaterial) can provide the most specific set of constraints
for a concept instance in the TMR. Again, successful coreference resolution is a precondition. Thus, the FR may contain information about John's Buick that its model
is Regal or that its model year is 1998.

The overall picture of the TMR is, then, as follows. It contains frames triggered by
the input sentence, where some of the property fillers come from the currently processed input, some others from other parts of the TMR, still others from FR, and the
rest from the ontology. The overridability status of the fillers of different provenance
is not the same—the constraints from the input take overall precedence, followed by
constraints from the same TMR, constraints from the FR (also called Fact DB), and
constraints from the ontology, in this order.

The basic TMR contains only the first two levels of constraints—those from the
current input and from other parts of the TMR. Information from the FR and the
ontology that was not overtly mentioned in the text should not be, if at all possible,

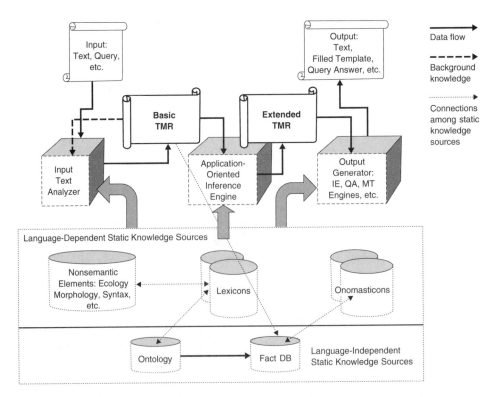

Figure 6.1
The data, the processors, and the static knowledge sources in ontological semantics II: With
extended TMRs and the inference engine included.

used in generating text in a target language for the application of MT. Some other applications, such as IE and QA, generally cannot avoid using the inferred information (see the examples in section 6.6). The TMR that contains information from outside input texts is the *extended TMR*. The inferred information is listed using the DEFAULT, SEM, and RELAXABLE-TO facets (see section 7.1.1 for the definition), while the *basic TMR* information is stored using the VALUE facet of the corresponding property. Figure 6.1 is a modified version of figure II.1 to which extended TMRs, the procedures that produce it and connections with other dynamic and static knowledge sources have been added.

The Static Knowledge Sources: Ontology, Fact Repository, and Lexicons

In ontological semantics, static knowledge sources include the ontology, the fact repository, and, for each of the languages used in an application, a lexicon that includes an onomasticon—that is, a lexicon of names (see figure 7.1). The ontology provides a metalanguage for describing the meaning of lexical units of a language as well as for the specification of meaning encoded in TMRs. To accomplish this, the ontology contains the definitions of concepts that are understood as corresponding to classes of things and events in the world. Formatwise, the ontology is a collection of frames, or named collections of property-value pairs. The fact repository contains a list of remembered instances of ontological concepts. In other words, if the ontology has the concept for CITY, the FR may contain entries for London, Paris, or Rome; if the ontology has the concept for SPORTS-EVENT, the FR will have an entry for the Sydney Olympics.

The ontological semantic lexicon does not just contain semantic information. However, when it comes to semantics, it specifies what concept, concepts, property, or properties of concepts defined in the ontology must be instantiated in the TMR to account for the meaning of a particular lexical unit of input. Lexical units that refer to proper names are listed in the onomasticon. The entries in the onomasticon directly point to elements of the FR. Onomasticon entries are indexed by name (the way these words and phrases appear in the text), while in the corresponding entry of the FR the instances are named by appending a unique number to the name of their corresponding concept.

The notion of instantiation is central to ontological semantics. Instances of ontological concepts are produced during the analysis of natural language texts and manipulated during their synthesis. They are also used alongside concepts in a variety of inference-making processes that derive conclusions based on the analysis of input but are not overtly specified in the text. The FR simply makes the information in TMRs produced within various applications permanently available for further processing, as needed.

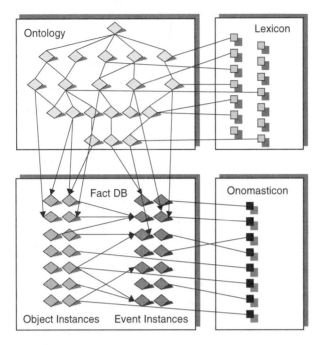

Figure 7.1
A schematic view of the interactions among the major ontological semantic knowledge sources—the ontology, the fact repository, the lexicon, and the onomasticon.

Figure 7.1 illustrates the relationships among static knowledge sources. The modules in the left-hand column contain world knowledge, those in the right-hand column, elements of natural language. The modules in the top row refer to general entities, referring to any instance of a word or a concept; the modules in the bottom row specify instances of concepts and their names that point to the named-concept instances.

7.1 The Ontology

We have already introduced a format, the TMR, for representing text meaning in ontological semantics (see chapter 6). It is time now to concentrate on the provenance of the most essential building blocks of the TMR, specifically, the meanings of most open-class lexical items that constitute the starting point for the compositional semantic process that, if successful, leads to a basic TMR (the compositional semantic processing is described in detail in chapter 8). In ontological semantics, such lexical meanings are represented as expressions in a special metalanguage whose vocabulary labels representations of events, objects, and their properties and whose syntax is specially designed to facilitate expressing complex lexical meanings. The representations of the meaning of individual events, objects, and their properties are organized in a structure called an ontology.

The difference between the language of the TMR and the language of the ontology largely parallels the distinction between the description languages (those that do not contain predication, in linguistic terms) and assertion languages (which contain predication) in AI knowledge-representation systems such as NIKL (Kaczmarek, Bates, and Robins 1986) or KRYPTON (Brachman, Fikes, and Levesque 1983). The most important difference between ontological semantics and knowledge representation in AI is the former's accent on broad practical coverage of semantic phenomena and the latter's accent on the theoretical completeness and noncontradictoriness of the formal representation system.

To build large and useful natural language processing systems one has to go beyond formalism and actually commit oneself to a detailed version of a "constructed reality" (Jackendoff 1983). Interpreting the meanings of textual units is really feasible only in the presence of a detailed world model whose elements are triggered (either directly or indirectly, individually or in combinations) by the appearance in the input text of various textual units whose lexicon entries contain pointers to certain ontological concepts.

World-model elements should be interconnected through a set of properties, which will enable the world modeler to build descriptions of complex objects and processes in a compositional fashion, using as few basic primitive concepts as possible. At the same time, having the complete description of a world as its main objective, an ontological semanticist will not have the motivation or inclination to spend time searching for the smallest set of basic concepts that could be combined to provide a complete description of the world. Parsimony is desirable and justified only if the completeness and clarity of the description are not jeopardized. Indeed, parsimony often stands in a trade-off relation with the simplicity of knowledge formulation and ease of its manipulation. In other words, in practical approaches, it may be well worth one's while to allow larger sets of primitives in exchange for being able to represent meaning using simpler and more transparent expressions. It is clear from the above that we believe that, as in software engineering, where programs must be readily understandable by both computers and people, ontological (and other static) knowledge in an ontological semantic system must be readily comprehensible to people who acquire and inspect it as well as to computer programs that are supposed to manipulate it.

In ontological semantics, the real primitives are properties—attributes of concepts and relations among concepts. These properties are not just uninterpreted labels. They are functions from their domains (sets of ontological elements whose semantics they help describe) into value sets. The latter can thus also be considered primitive elements in the ontology. All other concepts are named sets of property-value pairs that refer to complex objects that are described using combinations of the primitives. What this means is that ontological semantics features a relatively small set of primitive concepts, but at the same time has a rather rich inventory of elements available for representing and manipulating lexical meaning.

An ontological model must define a large set of generally applicable categories for world description. Among the types of such categories are:

• Perceptual and commonsense categories necessary for an intelligent agent to interact with, manipulate, and refer to states of the outside world
• Categories for encoding interagent knowledge, which includes one's own as well as other agents' intentions, plans, actions, and beliefs
• Categories that help describe metaknowledge (i.e., knowledge about knowledge and its manipulation, including rules of behavior and heuristics for constraining search spaces in various processor components)
• Means of encoding categories generated through the application of the above inference knowledge in the contents of an agent's world model

The choice of categories is not a straightforward task, as anyone who has tried realistic-scale world description knows all too well. Here are some examples of the issues encountered in such an undertaking:

• Which of the set of attributes pertinent to a certain concept should be singled out as "concept forming" and thus have named nodes in the ontology corresponding to them, and which others should be accessible only through the concept of which they are properties? As an example, consider whether one should further subdivide the class VEHICLE into WATER-VEHICLE, LAND-VEHICLE, AIR-VEHICLE; or, rather, into ENGINE-VEHICLE, ANIMAL-PROPELLED-VEHICLE, GRAVITY-PROPELLED-VEHICLE; or, perhaps, into CARGO-VEHICLE, PASSENGER-VEHICLE, TOY-VEHICLE, MIXED-CARGO-AND-PASSENGER-VEHICLE? Or maybe it is preferable to have a large number of small classes, such as WATER-PASSENGER-ANIMAL-PROPELLED-VEHICLE, of which, for instance, ROWBOAT will be a member?
• Which entities should be considered objects and which ones relations? Should we interpret a cable connecting a computer and a terminal as a relation (just kidding)? Or should we rather define it as a PHYSICAL-OBJECT and then specify its typical role in the static episode or "scene" involving the above three objects? Should one differentiate between RELATIONS (links between ontological concepts) and ATTRIBUTES (mappings from ontological concepts into symbolic or numerical value sets)? Or rather define ATTRIBUTES as one-place RELATIONS? Is it a good idea to introduce the ontological category of attribute-value set with its members being primitive unstructured meanings (such as the various scalars and other, unordered, sets of properties)? Or

is it better to define them as full-fledged ontological concepts, even though a vast majority of relations defined in the ontology would not be applicable to them (such a list will include case relations, meronymy, ownership, causals, and so on)? As an example of a decision on how to define an attribute, consider the representation of colors. Should we represent colors symbolically, as, say, red, blue, and so forth, or should we define them through their spectrum wavelengths, position on the white-black scale, and brightness (cf. Schubert, Papalaskaris, and Taugher 1983)?

• How should we treat sets of values? Should we represent *The Julliard Quartet* as one concept or a set of four? What about *The Pittsburgh Penguins*? What is an acceptable way of representing complex causal chains? How does one represent a concept corresponding to the English phrase *toy gun*? Is it a gun? Or a toy? Or none of the above? Or is it perhaps the influence of natural language and a peculiar choice of meaning realization on the part of the producer that pose this problem—maybe we do not need to represent this concept at all?

In most of the individual cases such as the above, there is considerable leeway in making representation decisions. Additionally, there is always some leeway in topological organization of the tangled hierarchy, which most often is not crucially important. In other words, many versions of an ontological world model, while radically different on the surface, may be, in fact, essentially the same ontology, with different assignment of importance values among the properties of a concept. For example, physical objects may first be classified by color and then by size, shape, or texture. However, unless there are good heuristics about priorities among such cross-classifying properties, there will be $n!$ different topologies for the ontological hierarchy for n properties at each level. There is no reason to waste time arguing for or against a particular ordering, though various considerations of convenience in description may arise.

Sometimes such choices go beyond ontology proper. In section 8.5, we discuss the various possibilities of distributing the meaning components between propositional and parameterized representations in TMRs. These differences influence the way ontological hierarchies are structured. In some other cases, some components of lexical meaning representation are relegated to the lexicon instead of being specified directly in the ontology. For example, the ontology of Dahlgren, McDowell, and Stabler 1989 uses the individual/group distinction (e.g., *wolf/pack*) very high in the hierarchy as one of the basic ontological dichotomies, while the ontology used in each of the implementations of ontological semantics relegates this distinction to a set representation in the TMR (and, consequently, a similar representation in the semantics zone of lexicon entries for words denoting groups).

It is important to realize that the differences in the topology of the ontological hierarchy and in the distribution of knowledge among the ontology, TMR parameters and the lexicon are relatively unimportant. What is much more crucial is the focus on coverage and on finding the most appropriate grain size of semantic description relative to the needs of an application (see section 9.3.6).

7.1.1   The Format of Mikrokosmos Ontology

In this section, we formally introduce the syntax and semantics of the ontology—the former by using a BNF, while the latter more informally, by commenting on the semantics of the notation elements and illustrating the various ontological representation decisions. We introduce the semantics of the ontology incrementally, with the semantics of new features appearing after they are introduced syntactically. In the BNF, once again, "{ }" are used for grouping; "[ ]" means optional (i.e., 0 or 1); "+" means 1 or more; and "*" means 0 or more.

```
ONTOLOGY ::= CONCEPT+
```

An ontology is organized as a set of concepts, each of which is a named collection of properties with their values at least partially specified. For example, the ontological concept PAY can be represented, in a simplified manner, as follows:

```
PAY
        DEFINITION    "to compensate somebody for goods or services
                      rendered"
        AGENT         HUMAN
        THEME         COMMODITY
        PATIENT       HUMAN
```

Remember that in the above ontological definition, PAY, HUMAN, COMMODITY, AGENT, THEME, DEFINITION, and PATIENT are not English words, as might be construed, but rather names of ontological concepts that must be given only the semantics assigned to them in their ontological definitions. DEFINITION, AGENT, THEME, and PATIENT are the properties that have values (or fillers) assigned to them at this stage in the specification of the concept PAY. In terms of the underlying representation language for the ontology, concepts are frames and properties are slots in these frames. This is, of course, the standard interpretation of concepts and properties in all frame-based representation schemata (e.g., Minsky 1975; Bobrow and Winograd 1977; Schank and Abelson 1977). An important notational convention is that each concept in the filler position represents all the concepts in the subtree of the ontology of which it is the root. This means, for example, that if the concept of PAY is used to represent the meaning of the sentence *John paid Bill ten dollars*, *John* and *Bill* will match HUMAN (because they will be understood as instances of people), while *ten dollars* will match COMMODITY. The above representation is in an important sense a shorthand. We will present a more varied and detailed picture of the actual constraints (values, fillers) for concepts as we continue this presentation.

```
CONCEPT ::= ROOT | OBJECT-OR-EVENT | PROPERTY
```

Concepts come in three different syntactic formats, corresponding to semantic and topological differences in the organization of the ontology. First of all, ontological concepts are not simply an unconnected set. They are organized in an inheritance hierarchy (we will see how in a short while). This device is common in knowledge representation in AI because it facilitates economies of search, storage, and access to ontological concepts. Semantically, the first difference among the concepts is that of "freestanding" versus "bound" concepts. The former represent OBJECT and EVENT types that are instantiated in a TMR. The latter represent PROPERTY types that categorize the OBJECTs and the EVENTs and are not normally individually instantiated but rather become slots in instantiated OBJECTs and EVENTs.[1]

```
ROOT ::= ALL DEF-SLOT TIME-STAMP-SLOT SUBCLASSES-SLOT
```

The root is a unique concept in the ontology. It does not inherit properties from anywhere, because it is the top node in the inheritance hierarchy. It has the two special slots (properties)—DEF-SLOT and TIME-STAMP-SLOT—that are used for administrative purposes of human access and control and do not typically figure in the processing by an application program, and another special slot that lists all the concepts that are its immediate SUBCLASSES. The above slots belong to the very small ONTOLOGY-SLOT subtree of the property branch of the ontology. They are clearly "service" properties that do not carry much semantic content and are needed to support navigation in the ontology as well as to facilitate its acquisition and inspection. TIME-STAMP-SLOT is used for version control and quality control of the ontology, and we will not list it in the examples for the sake of saving space. In the extant implementations of ontological semantics, the root concept is called ALL (see figure 7.2, where the TIME-STAMP property is routinely omitted for readability).

```
OBJECT-OR-EVENT ::= CONCEPT-NAME DEF-SLOT TIME-STAMP-SLOT
        IS-A-SLOT [SUBCLASSES-SLOT] [INSTANCES-SLOT] OTHER-SLOT*
```

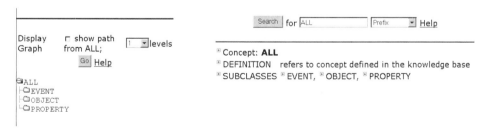

Figure 7.2
ALL, the top concept in the Mikrokosmos ontology.

A few content-related remarks are in order before continuing the formal characterization of the ontology. Ontological events and objects are the main tools for representing the essential elements of the world model, denoting what can happen in the world and to what or whom. Properties are auxiliary in the sense that they are used to distinguish formally among different events and among different objects. In an early implementation of ontological semantics we introduced the concept of STATE alongside OBJECT and EVENT. However, it became clear that states neatly subdivide between properties and events. States can be expressed as properties because, in ontological semantics, properties are timed. This allows one to represent the fact that a state occurs for a duration of time and not indefinitely. States can be expressed as events in our approach because it includes parameterization in general and parameterization of aspectual meanings in particular. Thus, while *know* is intuitively a state, in ontological semantics it is treated as the same basic event as that describing the meaning of *learn* (see section 7.1.5).

OBJECTS and EVENTS have names, definitions, and time stamps. They are descendants of some other OBJECT or EVENT, respectively, as indicated by the IS-A slot; some of them have SUBCLASSES, and some have (remembered) instances stored in the FR (see section 7.2). Finally, they possess unique value sets for particular properties that differentiate them from other concepts. The latter information, introduced under OTHER-SLOT, is stored as fillers of the RELATION and ATTRIBUTE properties (see below).

```
PROPERTY ::= RELATION | ATTRIBUTE | ONTOLOGY-SLOT
```

Properties are the ontology's conceptual primitives. As an example, in the Mikrokosmos implementation of ontological semantics, there are about 300 such properties that help to define about 6,000 concepts. Properties appear in the ontology in two guises, as defined types of concepts in the property branch and as slots in the definitions of objects and events. We will first explain how the latter are used and then will describe the properties as concepts.

```
OTHER-SLOT ::= RELATION-SLOT | ATTRIBUTE-SLOT
RELATION-SLOT ::= RELATION-NAME FACET CONCEPT-NAME+
ATTRIBUTE-SLOT ::= ATTRIBUTE-NAME FACET {number | literal}+
FACET ::= value | sem | default | relaxable-to | not |
     default-measure | inv | time-range | info-source
```

A slot is the basic mechanism for representing relationships between concepts. In fact, the slot is the fundamental metaontological predicate, based on which the entire ontology can be described axiomatically (see section 7.1.6). Several kinds of fillers that properties can have are described by introducing the device of facet in the representation language in order to handle the different types of constraints. All properties (slots) have all permissible facets defined for them (though not necessarily filled in every case), except as mentioned for the special slots below. In the latest implementation of ontological semantics, permissible facets are as follows (the facets TIME-RANGE and INFO-SOURCE will be discussed in section 7.2, the section on the FR):

VALUE: The filler of this facet is an actual value; it may be the instance of a concept, a literal symbol, a number, or another concept (in the case of the ontology slots, see below). Most of the constraints in TMR are realized as fillers of the VALUE facet. In the ontology, in addition to ontology slots, the VALUE facet is used to carry factual truths—for example, that a Gregorian year has exactly twelve months:

```
YEAR
      ...
      NO-OF-MONTHS value   12
      ...
```

SEM: The filler of a SEM facet is either another concept or a literal, a number, or a scalar range (see below). In any case, this kind of filler serves as a selectional restriction on the filler of the slot. It is through these selectional restrictions that concepts in the ontology are related (or linked) to other concepts in the ontology (in addition to taxonomic links). The constraints realized through the SEM facet are abductive—that is, it is expected that they might be violated in certain cases. The more appropriate description of the ontological concept PAY will be as follows:

```
PAY
      DEFINITION     value   "to compensate somebody for goods or
                             services rendered"
      AGENT          sem     HUMAN
      THEME          sem     COMMODITY
      PATIENT        sem     HUMAN
```

Indeed, the AGENT or PATIENT of paying may be not a HUMAN but, for example, an ORGANIZATION; the THEME of paying may be an EVENT, as in *John repaid Bill's hospitality by giving a lecture in his class*. It is important to recognize that the filler of THEME cannot be "relaxed" indefinitely. To mark the boundaries of abductive relaxation, the RELAXABLE-TO facet is used (see below).

DEFAULT: The filler of a DEFAULT facet is the most frequent or expected constraint for a particular property in a given concept. This filler is always a subset of the filler of the SEM facet. In many cases, no DEFAULT filler can be determined for a property. PAY, however, does have a clear DEFAULT filler for its THEME property:

```
PAY
      DEFINITION     value     "to compensate somebody for goods or
                               services rendered"
```

```
AGENT          sem      HUMAN
THEME          default  MONEY
               sem      COMMODITY
PATIENT        sem      HUMAN
```

RELAXABLE-TO: This facet indicates to what extent the ontology permits violations
of the selectional constraints listed in the SEM facet—for example, in nonliteral usage
such as a metaphor or metonymy. The filler of this facet is a concept that indicates
the maximal set of possible fillers beyond which the text should be considered anomalous. Continuing with ever-finer description of the semantics of PAY, we can arrive at
the following specification:

```
PAY
     DEFINITION    value         "to compensate somebody for
                                 goods or services rendered"
     AGENT         sem           HUMAN
                   relaxable-to  ORGANIZATION
     THEME         default       MONEY
                   sem           COMMODITY
                   relaxable-to  EVENT
     PATIENT       sem           HUMAN
                   relaxable-to  ORGANIZATION
```

The DEFAULT, SEM, and RELAXABLE-TO facets are used in the procedure for matching
what amounts to multivalued selectional restrictions. In cases when multiple facets
are specified for a property, the program first attempts to perform the match on
the selectional restrictions in DEFAULT facet fillers, where available. If it fails to find
a match, then the restrictions in SEM facets are used and, failing that, those in
RELAXABLE-TO facets.

NOT: Fillers introduced through this facet should be excluded from the set of acceptable fillers of a slot, even if other facets, such as, for instance, SEM, list fillers of
which the fillers of NOT are a subset. This is just a shorthand device (essentially, representing set difference) to allow the developers of the ontology to avoid having to
enumerate long lists of acceptable fillers (see an example in the discussion of inheritance in section 7.1.2).

DEFAULT-MEASURE: This facet is used for the rather special purpose of specifying
a measuring unit for the number or numerical range that fills the VALUE, DEFAULT,
SEM, or RELAXABLE-TO facet of the same slot. It is needed to keep the types of numerical fillers to a minimum—they can still be only a number, a set of numbers, or a
numerical range. If dimensionality is added to the fillers, then there will be at least as
many different types of such fillers as there are measuring units (actual measuring

units are defined as concepts in the ontology). In other words, the number *five* could stand for five meters, five dollars, or five degrees Kelvin. The example below shows a typical use of the facet DEFAULT-MEASURE:

```
MONEY
    ...
    AMOUNT      default-measure   MONETARY-UNIT
                sem               >=0
    ...
```

This specification of the content of the AMOUNT property of MONEY allows us to correct, once again, the deliberate simplification in the specification of the semantics of PAY—the filler of the default facet of its theme is actually an amount of money, not simply the concept MONEY. In the corrected example, we use the shorthand notation MONEY.AMOUNT to represent the filler of a particular property of a concept:

```
PAY
    DEFINITION    value        "to compensate somebody for
                                goods or services rendered"
    AGENT         sem          HUMAN
                  relaxable-to ORGANIZATION
    THEME         default      MONEY.AMOUNT
                  sem          COMMODITY
                  relaxable-to EVENT
    PATIENT       sem          HUMAN
                  relaxable-to ORGANIZATION
```

As can be seen from the DEFAULT-MEASURE facet, the facet facility can be used not only to list specific constraints but also to qualify those constraints in various ways. In fact, in the Mikrokosmos implementation of ontological semantics, the facet facility was used, for example, to specify the saliency of a particular property for the identity of a concept (e.g., that a table has a flat top is a more salient fact than the number of legs it has) or the tolerance of a particular value that shows how strict or fuzzy the boundaries of a certain numeric range are. Eventually, saliency came to be represented as a kind of MODALITY (see section 8.5.3) and the semantics of tolerance was subsumed by RELAXABLE-TO. The above developments underscore the complexity and the need to make choices of expressive means in building a metalanguage for representing meaning in texts (TMR), in the world (the ontology and the FR), and in the lexis of a language (the lexicon).

The INV facet is used to mark the fact that a particular filler was obtained by traversing an inverse relation from another concept. Fillers of INV are never recorded manually but rather are calculated by the acquisition environment and presented to

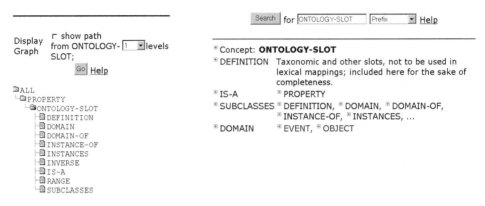

Figure 7.3
The auxiliary slots in the ontology, the ONTOLOGY-SLOT subtree.

the user for browsing. TIME-RANGE is a facet used only in facts—that is, concept instances—and specifies the temporal boundaries within which the information listed in the fact is correct. The value of this facet is used to support truth-maintenance operations. The INFO-SOURCE facet is used to record the source of the particular information element stored in a slot. It may be a URL or a bibliographical reference.

ONTOLOGY-SLOTS, as already mentioned, are special properties, in that they do not have a world-oriented semantics. In other words, they are used to record auxiliary information as well as information about the topology of the ontological hierarchy rather than semantic constraints on concepts. The small ontological subtree of ONTOLOGY-SLOT is illustrated in figure 7.3.

```
ONTOLOGY-SLOT ::= ONTOLOGY-SLOT-NAME DEF-SLOT TIME-STAMP-SLOT
      ISA-SLOT [SUBCLASSES-SLOT] DOMAIN-SLOT ONTO-RANGE-SLOT
      INVERSE-SLOT
DEF-SLOT ::= DEFINITION value "an English definition string"
TIME-STAMP-SLOT ::= time-stamp value time-date-and-username+
IS-A-SLOT ::= IS-A value { ALL | CONCEPT-NAME+ | RELATION-NAME+ |
      ATTRIBUTE-NAME+ }
SUBCLASSES-SLOT ::= subclasses value {CONCEPT-NAME+ |
      RELATION-NAME+ | ATTRIBUTE-NAME+}
INSTANCES-SLOT ::= instances value instance-name+
INSTANCE-OF-SLOT ::= instance-of value concept-name+
DOMAIN-SLOT ::= domain sem concept-name+
INVERSE-SLOT ::= inverse value relation-name
ONTO-RANGE-SLOT ::= REL-RANGE-SLOT | ATTR-RANGE-SLOT
```

The semantics of the properties that are children of ONTOLOGY-SLOT is as follows:

DEFINITION: This slot is mandatory in all concepts and instances. It has only a VALUE facet whose filler is a definition of the concept in English intended predominantly for human consumption during the knowledge-acquisition process—for instance, to help establish that a candidate for a new ontological concept is not, in fact, synonymous with an existing concept.

TIME-STAMP: This is used to encode a signature showing who created this concept and when, as well as an update log for the concept. In some applications of ontological semantics this information is stored in a separate set of log files that are not part of the ontology proper.

IS-A: This slot is mandatory for all concepts except ALL, which is the root of the hierarchy. Instances do not have an IS-A slot. This slot has only a VALUE facet filled by the names of the immediate parents of the concept. A concept missing an IS-A slot is called an orphan. Ideally, only ALL should be an orphan in the ontology.

SUBCLASSES: This slot is mandatory for all concepts except the leaves (concepts that do not have children). Note that instances do not count as ontological children. This slot also has only a VALUE facet filled by the names of the children of the concept.

INSTANCES: This slot is present in any concept that has remembered instances associated with it in the FR. A concept may naturally have both SUBCLASSES and INSTANCES. There is no requirement that only leaf concepts have instances. This slot also has only a VALUE facet filled by the names of the instances of this concept. This and the next slot provide cross-indexing capabilities between the ontology and the FR.

INSTANCE-OF: This slot is mandatory for all instances and is present only in instances—that is, in the TMR and FR. It has only a VALUE facet that is filled by the name of the concept of which the FR element, where the INSTANCE-OF slot appears, is an instance.

INVERSE: This slot is present in all relations and only in relations. Only a VALUE facet is defined for it, which is filled by the name of the RELATION that is the inverse of the relation in which the INVERSE slot appears. For example, the inverse of the relation PART-OF is the relation HAS-PARTS. The INVERSE slot is used to cross-index relations.

DOMAIN: This slot is present in all properties and only in them. It has only a SEM facet filled by the names of concepts that can be in the domain of this property—that is, the concepts in which such properties can appear as slots. A DOMAIN slot uses a VALUE facet only when a property is riffed—that is, made into a freestanding frame in the TMR, usually because it is the head of a proposition or because there is a need to add a qualifying constraint to it, which in the representation language we have used cannot be done for a slot. (Incidentally, this is also the formal reason why a property, if not riffed, cannot become head of a TMR proposition—see section 8.2.1.) However, typically a property enters a text-meaning representation (TMR) as a slot in an instance of an OBJECT, EVENT, or other TMR construct (e.g., DISCOURSE-RELATION).

RANGE: This slot is also present in all properties and only in properties. It too has only a SEM facet. In relations, the SEM facet is filled with the names of concepts that are in the range of this relation—that is, that can be its values. In an attribute, the SEM facet can be filled by any of the possible literal or numerical values permissible for that attribute. The filler can also be a numerical range specified using appropriate mathematical comparison operators (such as >, <, and so on). Again, the RANGE slot usually does not use its VALUE facet since typically instances of a property in a TMR are recorded in a slot in some other instance.

```
RELATION ::= RELATION-NAME DEF-SLOT TIME-STAMP-SLOT IS-A-SLOT
        [SUBCLASSES-SLOT] DOMAIN-SLOT REL-RANGE-SLOT INVERSE-SLOT
ATTRIBUTE ::= ATTRIBUTE-NAME DEF-SLOT TIME-STAMP-SLOT IS-A-SLOT
        [SUBCLASSES-SLOT] DOMAIN-SLOT ATTR-RANGE-SLOT
REL-RANGE-SLOT ::= RANGE SEM CONCEPT-NAME+
ATTR-RANGE-SLOT ::= RANGE SEM { number | literal }*
```

The above definitions introduce RELATIONS and ATTRIBUTES as freestanding concepts, as opposed to properties (slots) in other concepts (frames). The difference between RELATIONS and ATTRIBUTES boils down to the nature of their fillers: RELATIONS have references to concepts in their RANGE slots; RANGE slots of ATTRIBUTES can contain elements from specific value sets. These values can be individual, sets, or ranges. They can also be either numerical or symbolic; see below.

```
CONCEPT-NAME ::= name-string
INSTANCE-NAME ::= name-string
ONTOLOGY-SLOT-NAME ::= name-string
RELATION-NAME ::= name-string
ATTRIBUTE-NAME ::= name-string
NAME-STRING ::= alpha {alpha | digit}* {- {alpha | digit}+ }*
```

A word is in order about naming conventions. While, syntactically, names of concepts and instances are arbitrary name strings, semantically, further conventions are introduced in any implementation of ontological semantics, to maintain order and uniformity in representations. All concept names in the ontology are alphanumeric strings with the addition of only the hyphen character. No accents are permitted on any of the characters. Such enhancements are permitted only in lexicons. As far as ontology development is concerned, all symbols that we encounter can be classified into one of the following types:

• Concept names: typically English phrases with at most four words in a name, separated by hyphens

• Instance names: following the standard practice in AI, an instance is given a name by appending the name of the concept of which this instance is INSTANCE-OF with a hyphen followed by an arbitrary but unique integer

• References: fillers of the format concept.property[.facet] or instance.property that indicate that a filler is bound by reference to the filler in another concept or instance—for example,

```
CAR-32
      COLOR CAR-35.COLOR
```

which says that the color of CAR-32 is the same as that of CAR-35

• Literal (nonnumeric) constants: these are also usually English words, in fact single words most of the time

• The special symbols: NONE, NIL, UNKNOWN, NOTHING, NOT, AND, OR, REPEAT, UNTIL, as described below

• Other miscellaneous symbols used in the various implementations of ontological semantics, including:

  − TMR symbols

  − Lexicon symbols

  − Numbers and mathematical symbols

A (real) number is any string of digits with an optional decimal point and an optional +/− sign; a literal is any alphanumeric string starting with an alphabetical symbol. We will not formally define them any further. As mentioned above, the legal format of a filler in any implementation of ontological semantics can be a string, a symbol, a number, a numerical (scalar), or a literal (symbolic) range. Strings are typically used as fillers (of VALUE facets) of ontology slots representing user-oriented, nonontological properties of a concept, such as DEFINITION or TIME-STAMP. A symbol in a filler can be an ontological concept. This signifies that the actual filler can be either the concept in question or any of the concepts that are defined as its subclasses. In addition to concept names and special keywords (such as facet names and so on), we also allow symbolic value sets as legal primitives in a world model. For instance, we can introduce symbolic values for the various colors—RED, BLUE, GREEN, and so forth—as legal values of the property COLOR, instead of defining any of the above color values as separate concepts. Numbers, numerical ranges, and symbolic ranges (e.g., APRIL–JUNE) are also legal fillers in the representation language. Note that symbolic ranges are only meaningful for ordered value sets and that, for numerical range values, one can locally specify a measuring unit. The measuring unit is introduced in

the ontology through the filler of the DEFAULT-MEASURE facet. If no DEFAULT-MEASURE
is specified locally, the system will use the (default) unit listed in the definition of each
scalar attribute in the ontology. In the Dionysus implementation there was another
syntactic convention: to prepend the ampersand, &, to symbolic value-set members
in order to distinguish them from ontological entity names, which were marked by
the asterisk, and instances from the FR, which were marked with the percent symbol,
%. In the Mikrokosmos implementation, value-set members receive names different
from concept names, and instances are recognized by the unique number appended
to the concept name.

Individual numerical values, numerical value sets, and numerical (scalar) ranges
are fillers of the range slot for SCALAR-ATTRIBUTES. The values can be absolute and
relative. If the input text to be processed contains an overt reference to a quantity—
for example, *a ten-foot pole*—then the filler of the appropriate property, LENGTH-
ATTRIBUTE, is represented as a number with a measuring unit specified. In this
case, the number will be 10, and the measuring unit, feet (this value is the filler of
the DEFAULT-MEASURE facet on LENGTH-ATTRIBUTE). A property that can be measured
on a scale can also be described in an input in relative terms. We can say *The temperature is 90 degrees today* or *It is very hot today*. Relative references to property
values are represented in ontological semantics using abstract scales, usually running
from 0 (the lowest possible value) to 1 (the highest possible value). Thus, the meaning
of *hot* in the example above will be represented as the range [0.75–1] on the scale of
temperature (we often notate this as $>= .75$). If we want to compare two different
relative values of a property, we will need to consult the definitions of the corresponding concepts where the ranges of acceptable absolute values of such properties
for a given concept are listed. For example, the temperature of water runs between
0 and 100 degrees centigrade, so hot water, if represented on an abstract scale as
above, will, in fact, translate into an absolute, measured scale as the range between
75 and 100 degrees. At the same time, the temperature of bathwater would range
between, say, 20 and 50 degrees centigrade. Therefore, *a hot bath* will be represented
in absolute terms as a range between 42.5 and 50 degrees.

Literal symbols in the ontology are used to stop unending decomposition of meanings. These symbols are used to fill certain slots (namely, they are fillers of LITERAL-
ATTRIBUTES) and are defined in the ontology in the range slots of the definitions of
their respective LITERAL-ATTRIBUTES. Some characteristics of literal symbols worth
noting include:

• Literal symbols are used in our representations in much the same way as the qualitative values used in qualitative physics and other areas of AI that deal with modeling and design of physical artifacts and systems (de Kleer and Brown 1984; Goel
1992).

• Literal symbols are either binary or refer to (approximate) positions along an implied scale—that is, over an ordered set of symbols. Examples include days of the week or planets of the solar system, counted from Mercury to Pluto, whose status as a planet has, as a matter of fact, been recently thrown into doubt. For binary values, it is often preferable to use attribute-specific literal symbols rather than a generic pair (such as YES or NO, or ON or OFF).

• Literal symbols are often used when there is no numerical scale in common use in physical or social models of the corresponding part of the world. For example, OFFICIAL-ATTRIBUTE has in its range the literals OFFICIAL and UNOFFICIAL. Although one can talk about an event or a document being more official than another, there is no obvious scale in use in the world for this attribute. The two literals seem to serve well as the range of this attribute.

• It is not always true that literal attributes are introduced in the absence of a numerical scale in the physical or social world. A classic example of this is COLOR. Although several well-defined numerical scales for representing color exist in models of physics (such as the frequency spectrum, hue and intensity scales, and so on), such a scale does not serve our purposes well at all. First of all, it would make our TMRs more or less unreadable for a human if it has a frequency, a hue range, and a value of intensity in place of a literal such as RED or GREEN. Moreover, it makes lexicon acquisition more expensive: lexicographers will have to consult a physics reference to find out the semantic mapping for the word *red* instead of quickly using their own intuitive understanding of its meaning. The above consideration is strongly predicated, however, on the expected granularity of description. It would be, in fact, far preferable to use a nonliteral representation of color to support processing of texts in which color differences are centrally important.

Four special fillers—NIL, UNKNOWN, NONE, and NOTHING—are used in the various implementations of ontological semantics. NIL means that the user has not specified a filler and there is no filler to be inherited. UNKNOWN means that a filler exists but is not (yet) specified. NONE means that there can be no filler, and the user (or the system) overtly specified this. For instance, if for a certain property in a certain concept there cannot be found a default filler—that is, when several potential fillers are equally probable—then the user will have to enter NONE as the filler of this default facet. The special symbol NOTHING has been introduced to block inheritance. It will be discussed, together with other issues concerning inheritance, in the next section.

7.1.2 Inheritance

When talking about inheritance, we only concentrate on content-related issues relating to the expressive power of the ontology metalanguage. We see ontological semantics as guided by the theory of inheritance (e.g., Touretzky 1984, 1986;

Thomason, Horty, and Touretzky 1987; Touretzky, Horty, and Thomason 1987; Thomason and Touretzky 1991) but do not aspire to contribute to further development of the theory of inheritance. Our approach to inheritance is fully implementation oriented.

The inheritance hierarchy, which is implemented using IS-A and SUBCLASSES slots, is the backbone of the ontology. When two concepts, X and Y, are linked via an IS-A relation (that is, X IS-A Y), then X inherits slots (with their facets and fillers) from Y according to the following rules:

- All slots that have not been overtly specified in X, with their facets and fillers, but are specified in Y, are inherited into X.
- ONTOLOGY-SLOTS (IS-A, SUBCLASSES, DEFINITION, TIME-STAMP, INSTANCE-OF, INSTANCES, INVERSE, DOMAIN, RANGE) are excluded from this rule. They are not inherited from the parent.
- If a slot appears both in X and Y, then the filler from X takes precedence over the fillers from Y.
- The filler NOTHING is used to locally block inheritance on a property. If a parent concept has a slot with some facets and fillers and if some of its children have NOTHING as the filler of the SEM facet for that same slot, then the slot will not be inherited from the parent. Since the local slot in the child has NOTHING as its filler, no instance of any OBJECT or EVENT or any number or literal will match this symbol. As such, no filler is acceptable to this slot and this slot will never be present in any instance of this concept. This has the same effect as removing the slot from the concept. For example, ANIMAL has the property MATERIAL-OF filled by AGRICULTURAL-PRODUCT; HUMAN IS-A ANIMAL and it inherits the slot MATERIAL-OF from ANIMAL; however, the filler of this slot in HUMAN is, for obvious reasons, NOTHING. Note that in descendants of HUMAN it is entirely possible to reintroduce fillers other than NOTHING in the MATERIAL-OF slot—for instance, in news reports about transplants or cloning.
- Inheritance of a filler that is introduced through the NOT facet is blocked. Thus, the filler HUMAN will be introduced through the facet NOT in the THEME slot of BUY, while the SEM facet will list OBJECT as its filler (and HUMAN is a descendant of OBJECT). This is our way of saying that, in the extant implementations of ontological semantics, people cannot be bought or sold (which, incidentally, may turn out to be a problem for processing news reports about slavery in the Sudan or buying babies for adoption).

Regular inheritance of a slot simply incorporates all fillers for the slot from all ancestors (concepts reached over the IS-A relation) into the inheriting concept. For example, a kitchen has a stove, a refrigerator, and other appliances. A room has walls, a ceiling, a floor, and so on. A kitchen, being a room, has the appliances as well as a floor, and so forth. Blocking inheritance indicates that a slot or slot/filler combination that appears in an ancestor should not be incorporated into the inheriting concept.

There are two reasons for blocking inheritance using NOTHING. First, in a subtree in the ontology, all but a few concepts might have a particular property (slot). It is much easier to put the slot at the root of the subtree and block it in those few concepts (or subtrees) that do not have that slot rather than putting the slot explicitly in each of the concepts that do take the slot. For example, all EVENTs take the agent slot except PASSIVE-COGNITIVE-EVENTS and INVOLUNTARY-PERCEPTUAL-EVENTS. We can put the AGENT slot (with the SEM constraint ANIMAL) in EVENT and put a SEM NOTHING in PASSIVE-COGNITIVE-EVENT and INVOLUNTARY-PERCEPTUAL-EVENT. This will effectively block the AGENT slot in the subtrees rooted under these two classes of EVENT, while all other EVENTs will still automatically have the AGENT slot.

A second, stronger reason for introducing this mechanism comes from the needs of lexical semantics. Sometimes the SEM-STRUC zone of the lexicon entry for certain words (see section 7.2) will have to refer to a property (slot) defined for an entire class of concepts, even though a few concepts in that class do not actually feature that property. For example, in the SEM-STRUC of the Spanish *activo*, "asset," we must refer to the AGENT of EVENT without knowing what EVENT it is. This requires us to add an AGENT slot to EVENT even though there are two subclasses of EVENT that do not have AGENT slots. An alternative would be to list every type of EVENT other than the above two in the SEM-STRUC of the lexicon entry for this word. This, however, is not practical at all. In a sense, this mechanism is introducing the power of default slots just like we have a DEFAULT facet in a slot. We can specify a slot for a class of concepts that acts like a default slot: it is present in every concept unless there is an explicit SEM NOTHING filler in it.

While multiple inheritance is allowed and is indicated by the presence of more than one filler in the IS-A slot in a concept, no extant implementation of ontological semantics has fully developed sufficiently formal methods for using multiple inheritance.

7.1.3 Case Roles for Predicates

Semantic properties help to describe the nature of objects and events. Some of these properties constrain the physical properties of OBJECTS (e.g., TEXTURE, LENGTH or MASS), or EVENTS (e.g., INTENSITY). Some others introduce similar "inherent" properties of nonphysical—that is, social or mental—objects or events (e.g., PRECONDITION, DESCRIBES, or HAS-GOVERNMENT). Still others are applicable to the description of any kind of OBJECT or EVENT (e.g., HAS-PARTS). There is, however, a group of relations that has a special semantics. These relations describe connections between events and objects or other events that the "main" events are in some sense "about." In other words, they allow one to contribute to the description of the semantics of propositions through the specification of their semantic arguments. These arguments are typical roles that a predicate can take; they appear as properties of events in the TMR, as well as in the ontology and the FR.

The first descriptions of similar phenomena in linguistics were independently proposed in the 1960s by Gruber (1965) and Fillmore (1968, 1971, 1977), who called his approach *case grammar*. Since then, case grammar has had a major impact on both theoretical and computational linguistics (e.g., Bruce 1975; Grimshaw 1990; Levin and Rappaport Hovav 1995) and has found its way, in varying forms, into knowledge representation for reasoning and natural language processing systems. An overview and comparison of several theories of case grammar in linguistics can be found in Cook 1989, and reviews of case systems as they are used in natural language processing, for example, in Bruce 1975, Winograd 1983, or Somers 1986.

In case grammar, a case relation (or case role, or simply case) is a semantic role that an argument (typically, a noun) can have when it is associated with a particular predicate (typically, a verb). While many linguistic theories of case have been proposed, all of them have in common two primary goals: to provide an adequate semantic description of the verbs of a given language, and to offer a universal approach to sentence semantics (see Cook 1989, ix). Unfortunately for our purposes, most approaches to case grammar in linguistics remain, at base, syntactic, and indeed talk about language-dependent arguments of verbs and nouns, not of language-independent properties of events, general declarations about the universality of the approach notwithstanding.

Another issue is the actual inventory of the case roles. It has been amply noted that there are about as many systems of case roles as there are theories and applications that use them. We view this state of affairs as necessary and caused by the difficulty of balancing the grain size of description against coverage and ease of assignment of case-role status to semantic arguments. The case roles must be manipulated by people during the knowledge-acquisition stage of building an implementation of ontological semantics—that is, when the ontology and the lexicons are constructed. This makes it desirable to use a small inventory of case roles—or risk the acquirers spending long minutes selecting and constraining an appropriate set of case roles to describe an event. It is equally imperative that the case roles are defined in a straightforward way and correspond to a clear-cut and identifiably coherent subset of reality—or else the acquirers will find it difficult to assign semantic arguments to specific case roles. As a result, they would freely indulge in metaphorically or metonymically extending the semantics of some roles beyond their intended purview. The above trade-off has been, consciously or subconsciously, on the mind of many lexical and computational semanticists. Some proposals completely eschew

Table 7.1
Agent

Definition	The entity that causes or is responsible for an action.
Semantic constraints	Agents are either intentional—that is, in our judgment, humans or higher animals—or forces.
Syntactic clues	The subject in a transitive sentence is often, but not always, the agent. In languages with grammatical cases, a nominative, ergative, or absolutive case marker often triggers an agent. Here and in the rest of the specifications of case roles, the syntactic clues are presented as defeasible heuristics rather than strong constraints.
Examples	**Kathy** ran to the store.
	The storm broke some windows.
	Du Pont Co. said **it** agreed to form a joint venture in gas separation technology with **L'Air Liquide S.A.**, an industrial gas company based in Paris.
Notes	1. *Du Pont Co.* and *l'Air Liquide S.A.* are metonymical agents—see section 8.4.2.
	2. After the resolution of coreference (see section 8.6.1), *it* will be assigned appropriate semantic content that will fill the agent case role of the event corresponding to *agree*.
	3. In the last example, the two companies are both treated as agents of the event corresponding to *forming a joint venture*—see section 7.1.4.

naming case roles and even use numerical indices to refer to them (cf. Mel'čuk 1974). Some others (e.g., Fillmore, Wooters, and Baker 2001) define separate individual case roles for every event (e.g., "sayer" and "sayee"). This latter approach helps with any problems of case-role assignment but makes it much more difficult to encode any inference rules in terms of case roles, due to the suddenly very large number of them. Our approach, similarly to that of Jackendoff (1983), prefers to stress paucity (and, therefore, generality of inference-rule formulation) at the expense of ease of case-role assignment.

In what follows, we describe the set of case roles defined in the CAMBIO/CREST implementation of ontological semantics. This set has been the subject of much development and modification over the years, because the earlier implementations of ontological semantics used distinctly different inventories. We expect that any future applications, with their specific goals, sublanguage and subworld, and granularity,

Table 7.2
Theme

Definition	The entity manipulated by an action.
Semantic constraints	Themes are seldom human.
Syntactic clues	Direct objects of transitive verbs; subjects in intransitive sentences and verbal complements are often themes. In languages with grammatical cases, nominals in accusative often trigger themes.
Examples	John kicked **the ball**.
	The price is high.
	The ball rolled down the hill.
	John said **that Mary was away**.
	Bridgestone Sports Co. has set up **a company** in Taiwan with a local concern and a Japanese trading house.
Notes	While not particularly hard to detect, probably because of the relative reliability of syntactic clues, this case role ends up covering probably more heterogeneous phenomena than it should—there is a clear intuitive difference between the themes realized in language by objects and those realized by (sentential) complements; similarly, there is a difference between the themes realized by direct objects and by subjects.

will involve further modifications to the inventory of case roles. In the examples that accompany the specification of the case roles (tables 7.1 through 7.9), we take the liberty of marking with **boldface** the textual elements whose semantic description will fill the corresponding case-role slot in the semantic description of the appropriate event in the TMR.

7.1.4 Choices and Trade-offs in Ontological Representations

In section 6.6, we established that, for a given state of static resources, including ontology, a given format of the TMR, and a given analysis procedure, there is no paraphrase in TMRs. That is, a given textual input, under the above conditions, will always result in the same TMR. This is the result of all the choices made at definition and acquisition time of both static and dynamic knowledge sources. As a matter of policy, at definition time, ontological semantics strives to make a single set of choices on every phenomenon that is perceived by the developers as allowing in principle several different ways of treatment. Of course, one is never guaranteed that the onto-

Table 7.3
Patient

Definition	The entity that is affected by an action.
Semantic constraints	Typically, patients are human.
Syntactic clues	Indirect objects often end up interpreted as patients, when the above semantic constraint holds; subjects of verbs whose meanings are involuntary perceptual events and subjects of nonagentive verbs (e.g., *feel, experience, suffer*) are interpreted as patients. In languages with grammatical cases, dative forms often trigger patients.
Examples	Mary gave a book to **John**. **Fred** heard music. **Bill** found **himself** entranced.
Notes	Relatively easy to identify when a theme is also present, as in the first example above. The definition of this role is admittedly difficult to distinguish from that of theme. Early implementations of ontological semantics, instead of a single patient role, used several: experiencer (for *Fred* in the second example and *Bill* in the third) and beneficiary (for *John* in the first example). Unlike the second example, in *Fred listened to music*, Fred is interpreted as the AGENT of the underlying event because the event implies intentionality—indeed, one hears music much too often when one would rather not hear it.

Table 7.4
Instrument

Definition	The object or event that is used in order to carry out an action.
Semantic constraints	None.
Syntactic clues	Prepositions *with* and *by*, in their appropriate senses, may trigger the case-role instrument. In some languages there is a special case marker that is a clue for instrument—for example, the instrumental case in Russian.
Examples	Seymour cut the salami with **a knife**. Armco will establish a new company by **spinning off its general steel department**.
Notes	Sometimes, across languages, instruments are elevated syntactically to the subject positions, as in *The knife cut the salami easily*.

Table 7.5
Source

Definition	A starting point for various types of movement and transfer (used with verbs of motion, transfer of possession, mental transfer, and so on).
Semantic constraints	Sources are primarily objects.
Syntactic clues	Prepositional clues are often available (see Nirenburg 1980 for details)—for example, the English *from* in one of its senses; in some languages there is a special case marker that is a clue for SOURCE, as with the ablative in Latin or elative in Finnish; however, one cannot, as with AGENT, THEME, or PATIENT, expect a clue for SOURCE on the basis of grammatical function, such as subject or direct object.
Examples	The goods will be shipped from **Japan**. Susan bought the book from **Jane**. TWA Flight 884 left **JFK** at about 11 P.M.
Notes	We avoid treating events as sources in sentences like *John went from working twelve hours a day to missing work for weeks at a time* by interpreting the events in the corresponding TMR as freestanding propositions, with a discourse relation between them. One can envisage making the opposite choice and thus relaxing the above semantic constraint. One rationale for our choice comes from the application of MT: we cannot count on the availability of the *go from* construction used in this way in languages other than English. Therefore, we analyze the input further, stressing not the way the two propositions are connected in the source language but rather reporting the actual sequence of events.

Table 7.6
Destination

Definition	An end point for various types of movement and transfer (used with verbs of motion, transfer of possession, mental transfer, and so on).
Semantic constraints	Destinations are primarily objects.
Syntactic clues	Prepositional clues may be available, such as the English *to* or *toward* in one of their senses; in some languages there is a special case marker that is a clue for destination—for example, allative (or destinative) in Finnish; however, one cannot, as with AGENT, THEME, or PATIENT, expect a clue for SOURCE on the basis of grammatical function, such as subject or direct object.
Examples	John took his mother to **the theater**. Cindy brought the money to **me**. Hilda gave **John** an idea.
Notes	Considerations parallel to those in the notes on the case-role source apply here.

Table 7.7
Location

Definition	The place where an event takes place or where an object exists.
Semantic constraints	Locations are typically objects.
Syntactic clues	Prepositions that have locative senses (*in, at, above*, and so on) and, in some languages with grammatical cases, special case values, like locative in East Slavic languages or essive in Finnish.
Examples	The milk is in **the refrigerator**. The play by Marlowe will be performed at **the Shakespeare Theater**.
Notes	The meaning of location (as well as time, treated parametrically—see section 8.5.2) must be posited whenever an instantiation of an event or an object occurs. In fact, imparting spatiotemporal characteristics to an event type can be considered a defining property of instantiation (as well as in indexation in the philosophy of language). If no candidate for a filler is available, either in the input text or in the FR, abductively overridable DEFAULT or SEM values can be propagated from the corresponding concepts or, alternatively, through contextual inferences.

Table 7.8
Path

Definition	The route along which an entity (i.e., a theme) travels, physically or otherwise.
Semantic constraints	Paths are typically objects.
Syntactic clues	Some prepositions, such as *along, down, up, through, via, by way of, around*, and so on, in their appropriate senses, trigger the case role PATH.
Examples	Mary ran down **the hill**. The plane took **the polar route** from Korea to Chicago. He went through **a lot of adversity** to get to where he is now.
Notes	The meanings that can be represented using PATH can also be specified by other means—for instance, by proliferating the number of freestanding propositions in the TMR and connecting them with overt discourse relations (cf. the notes to the case role SOURCE where this device was mentioned for the situation in which the candidate for the case role's filler was an event). It can be argued that such means are available for all case roles. It is, however, a matter of a trade-off between the parsimony of the case-role inventory and ease of assigning an element of input to a particular case role, at acquisition time or at processing time.

Table 7.9
Manner

Definition	The style in which something is done.
Semantic constraints	Manner is typically a scalar attribute.
Syntactic clues	Manner is triggered by some adverbials.
Examples	She writes **easily**. Bell Atlantic acquired GTE **very fast**.
Notes	This case role accommodates some typical scalars comfortably, treating their semantics along the lines of adjectival semantics (see Raskin and Nirenburg 1995, 1998); the grain size of the definition is deliberately coarse—otherwise, assignment will be complicated; this case role is used as a hold-all in ontological semantics to link any event modifier that cannot be assigned to one of the above case roles.

logical semantic knowledge sources will not contain means for expressing a particular content in more than one way. In fact, checking that this is not the case is far from trivial, and it might well be impossible to avoid such an eventuality. Obviously, ontological semantics attempts to preclude this from happening in every case when this possibility is detected.

Eliminating multiple representation possibilities involves making a number of choices and trade-offs. We already alluded to some such choices in the notes for the case roles in the previous section. Here we would like to illustrate some further and more generally applicable decisions of this kind.

In the Dionysus implementation of ontological semantics, the set of case roles included several "co-roles," such as CO-AGENT, CO-THEME, or ACCOMPANIER. These were defined as entities that behaved like agents or themes but always in conjunction with some other agent or theme, thus fulfilling, in some sense, an auxiliary role—for instance, *John* (AGENT) *wrote a book with Bill* (CO-AGENT) or *The Navy christened the new frigate* (THEME) *The Irreversible* (CO-THEME). In the former case, the choice taken, for example, in the Mikrokosmos and CAMBIO/CREST implementations of ontological semantics is to make the grain size of description somewhat more coarse and declare that the AGENT and the CO-AGENT are members of a set that fills the AGENT role of WRITE. What we lose in granularity here is the shade of meaning that John was somehow more important as the author of the book than Bill. However, this solution is perfectly acceptable in most subject domains.

In the case of the purported case role CO-THEME, when a solution similar to that we just suggested for CO-AGENT is impossible, and this is, indeed, the case in the second example above, a treatment may be suggested that avoids using exclusively case roles for connecting elements of meaning in the TMR. In this example, the lexicon entry for *christen* uses the ontological concept GIVE-NAME:

```
GIVE-NAME
...
      THEME default HUMAN
                      HAS-NAME   sem   NAME
             sem      OBJECT
                      HAS-NAME   sem   NAME
          ...
```

The corresponding part of the TMR is filled by the input sentence as follows:

```
GIVE-NAME-20
      ...
      THEME value  SHIP-11
                   HAS-NAME   value   The Irreversible
...
```

The problem of representing the meaning of the example accurately is solved this way not at the level of such general properties as case roles but rather at the level of an individual ontological concept, GIVE-NAME, whose semantics uses both a case role (THEME) of the event itself and a non-case-role property (HAS-NAME) of that case role's filler. This kind of solution always invites itself when it is necessary to avoid the introduction of a possibly superfluous general category. Because CO-THEME would have to be introduced for a small set of phenomena and its presence would make the processes of knowledge acquisition and text analysis more complicated, it is preferable to provide for the ontological representation of the phenomena without generalization—that is, in the definitions of individual lexical items (namely, *christen*) and ontological concepts (i.e., GIVE-NAME).

As a result of reasoning along these lines, the inventory of case roles was shrunk at least twofold from the Dionysus to the Mikrokosmos implementation of ontological semantics. This was done mostly at the expense of co-roles and case roles that were judged to be better interpreted in an alternative preexisting manner—as discourse relations, defined in the ontology and used in TMRs (see the notes for the case role SOURCE in the previous section; see also section 8.6.3 on discourse relations). This is not only parsimony, at its purest, but also elimination of a possibility for paraphrase in TMR: leaving those case roles in would have made it possible to represent the same meaning either with their help or using the discourse relations.

7.1.5 Complex Events

To represent the meaning of connected text, not simply that of a sequence of ostensibly independent sentences, several things must happen. One of the most obvious connections across sentence boundaries is coreference. The TMR in ontological semantics allows for the specification of coreference, and special procedures exist for treating at least facets of this phenomenon in extant applications of ontological semantics (see section 8.6.1). Discourse relations among propositions can also hold across sentence boundaries, and ontological semantics includes facilities for both detecting and representing them.

There are, however, additional strong connections among elements of many texts. These have to do with the understanding that individual propositions may hold well-defined places in "routine," "typical" sequences of events (often called complex events, scripts, or scenarios; see section 3.7) that happen in the world, with a well-specified set of object-like entities that appear in different roles throughout that sequence. For example, if the sequence of events describes a state visit, the "actors" may, under various circumstances, include the people who meet (the "principals"), their handlers, security personnel, journalists, and possibly a guard of honor; the "props" may include airplanes, airports, meeting spaces, documents, and so on. All these actors and props will fill case roles and other properties in the typical component events of the standard event sequence for a state visit, such as travel, arrival, greetings, discussions, negotiations, press conferences, joint statements, and so forth. The component events are often optional; alternatively, some component events stand in a disjunctive relation with some others (that is, of several components only one may actually be realized in a particular instantiation of the overall complex event), and their relative temporal ordering may be fuzzy.

Such typical scripts can be expressed in natural language using expository texts or narratives, sets of the above (indeed, one conceptual story can be "gathered" from several textual sources), plus text in tables, pictures, TV and movie captions, and so on. The notion of script is clearly recursive, because every component event can itself be considered a script, at a different level of granularity. The notion of script, under a variety of monikers, was popularized in computer science by Minsky (1975), Schank and Abelson (1977), Charniak (1972), and their colleagues in the 1970s. However, at that time, no realistic-size implementation of natural language processing using scripts could be undertaken, in part, because there was no clear idea about the required inventory of knowledge sources and their relations and content. Script-based theories of semantics were proposed in theoretical linguistics (Fillmore 1985; Raskin 1986) but were overshadowed by the fashion for formal semantics (see section 3.5.1). Moreover, the size of the task of creating the ontological semantic knowledge sources was at the time underestimated by the practitioners and overestimated by critics. It can be said that ontological semantics is a descendant of the script-oriented approach to natural language processing, especially in the strategic sense of accentuating semantic content—that is, the quantity and quality of stored knowledge required for descriptions and applications. Ontological semantics certainly transcends the purview and the granularity levels of the older approach, as well as offering an entirely different take on coverage of world and language knowledge and on its applicability.

In the complex-event-based approach to processing text inputs, the complex events in the ontology that get instantiated from the text input provide expectations for processing further sentences in a text. Indeed, if a sentence in a text can be seen as instantiating, in the nascent TMR, a complex event, the analysis and disambiguation of subsequent sentences can be aided by the expectation that propositions contained in them are instantiations of event types that are listed as components of the activated complex event. Obviously, the task of activating the appropriate complex event from the input is far from straightforward. Also, not all sentences and clauses in the input text necessarily fit a given complex event. There can be deviations and fleeting extraneous meanings that must be recognized as such and connected to other elements of the TMR through regular discourse relations—that is, through a weaker connection than that among the elements of a complex event.

Complex events usually describe situations with multiple agents. Each of these agents can be said, in some sense, to carry out their own plans that are made manifest through the reported component events in a complex event. Plans are special kinds of complex events that describe the process of attaining a goal by an agent or its proxies. Goals are represented in ontological semantics as postconditions (effects) of events (namely, steps in plans or components of general complex events). For example, if an agent's goal is to own a TV set, this goal would be attained after successful completion of one of a number of possible plans. In other words, it will be listed in the ontology as the postcondition (effect) of such events as BUY, BORROW, LEASE, STEAL, MANUFACTURE. Note that the plans can be activated only if all the necessary preconditions for their triggering hold. Thus, the ontology, in the precondition property of BUY, for example, will list the requirement that the agent must have enough money (see McDonough 2000).

Manipulating plans and goals is especially important in some applications of ontological semantics—for instance, in advice-giving applications where the system is entrusted with recognizing the intentions (goals) of an agent or a group of agents based on processing texts about their behavior. Goal- and plan-directed processing relies on the results of the analysis of textual input, as recorded in the basic TMR, as well as on the complementary knowledge about relevant (complex) events and objects and their instances, stored in the ontology and the FR, and instantiated in the extended TMR. It is clear that reasoning based on the entire amount of knowledge in the extended TMR can be much richer than if only those facts mentioned in the input texts were used for inference making. Richer possibilities for reasoning would yield better results for any NLP application, provided it is supplied with the requisite inference-making programs—for instance, for resolving translation mismatches. Our basis for making a distinction among NLP applications is the extent to which an application depends on such capabilities. For example, MT practitioners have typically assumed that this application does not really need machinery for inference making. This belief is clearly based on the perception that acquiring the knowledge necessary to support reasoning is prohibitively expensive or even outright infeasible, and therefore one must make do with simpler approaches. Of course, should MT developers be able to obtain such resources, they would use them. Ontological semantics has among its goals that of supplying application builders with exactly this kind of knowledge.

Of course, as mentioned above, in addition to the knowledge, efficient reasoning procedures must be developed. Such procedures must conform to a number of constraints, an example of which is the following. It is common knowledge that, unless a limit is imposed on making inferences from knowledge units in rich knowledge bases, the inferencing process can go too far or even not halt at all. In advanced applications—for example, advice giving—a good candidate for such a limit is deriving the active goals and plans of all relevant agents in the world. However, even applications that involve more or less direct treatment of basic text meaning, such as machine translation, will benefit from making fewer inferences. There will always be difficult cases, such as the need to understand the causal relation in *The soldiers fired at the women and I saw some of them fall* in order to select the correct reference for *them*. In Hebrew, for example, the choice of the pronoun (the masculine *otam* or the feminine *otan*) will depend on the gender of the antecedent. Such cases are not overly widespread, and a prudent system would deliberately trigger the necessary inferences when it recognizes that there is a need for them. In general, any event is, in fact, complex—that is, one can almost always find subevents of an event; whether and to what extent it is necessary to develop its HAS-PARTS property is a matter of grain size dictated by whether an application needs this information for reasoning.

Complex events are represented in ontological semantics using the ontological property HAS-PARTS. It has temporal semantics if it appears in events, and spatial semantics if it appears in physical objects—for example, to indicate that an automobile consists of an engine, wheels, the chassis, and so on. The properties PRECONDITION and EFFECT also carry information necessary for various kinds of reasoning and apply to any events, complex or otherwise. Complex events require an extension to the format of meaning representation. The reason for that is the need to bind the case roles and other property values in component events to establish coreference. Also, the HAS-PARTS slot of complex events should allow for the specification of rather advanced combinations of component events. Therefore, the format of the filler of HAS-PARTS in complex events should allow the Boolean operators **and**, **or**, and **not**, as well as loop statements. Complex events also need statements about partial temporal ordering of their components. For this purpose, a special new property, COMPONENT-RELATIONS, is introduced.

Component events in a complex event have a peculiar status. They are not regular instances of concepts, because in the ontology no instantiation occurs. (Instantiation is one of the two main operations in generating TMRs, the other being matching selectional restrictions in order to combine individual concept instances.) But the meanings of these instances are different from those of the general concepts to which they are related. In other words, asking questions in the context of a class at school is clearly different from the general idea of asking questions. To represent this difference, the notion of ontological instance is introduced. In an ontological instance, some properties are constrained further as compared to their "parent" concept. The constraints typically take the form of a cross-reference to the filler of another component event in the same complex event.

For reasons of clarity and convenience, instead of describing the component events and component relations directly in the fillers of corresponding slots in the concept specification for the complex event, we use the device of reification by just naming them in a unique way in that location and describe their content separately, at the same level as the main complex event. (We identify ontological instances by appending letters, not numbers as in the case of real instances.) As a result, the format of the ontological description of a complex event is a set of ontological concept frames.

Reification in ontological semantics is a mechanism for allowing the definition of properties on properties by elevating properties from the status of slots in frames to the level of a freestanding concept frame. It is desirable from the point of view of nonproliferation of elements of metalanguage to avoid introducing a concept of, say, DRIVER if it could always be referred to as DRIVE.AGENT. However, this brings about certain difficulties. For example, if we want to state that somebody is a DRIVER of TRUCKs, we would have to say that there is an instance of DRIVE in which the THEME is TRUCK and the AGENT is the person in question. There is no direct relationship between THEME and AGENT, and it would take a longer inference chain to realize that TRUCK is, in fact, the value of a property of DRIVER, too, not only of DRIVE. The more properties one would want to add to DRIVER and not to DRIVE, the more enticing it would be to reify the property DRIVE.AGENT and treat it as a separate concept. In principle, we can use reification on the fly, while building a TMR, when we need to add a property to a property, which is prohibited in the static knowledge sources such as the ontology and the lexicon. As we will see in the example below, reification also facilitates the specification of complex events.

In the example below, we present a simplified view of the complex event TEACH. As illustrated, TEACH has as PRECONDITION two EVENTS—that the teacher knows the material and the students do not; as EFFECT, it has the EVENT that the students (now) know the material. The process of teaching is presented as follows: the teacher presents the material to the students, the students ask the teacher questions about this material, and the teacher answers these questions. The above is admittedly a gross simplification of the actual state of affairs but will serve well for purposes of illustration.

The ontological instances introduced in the process are: TEACH-KNOW-A, -B, and -C, TEACH-DESCRIBE, TEACH-REQUEST-INFO, TEACH-ANSWER, TEACH-AFTER-A and -B. The constraints in these instances are all references to fillers of slots in other components of the complex event or the complex event itself. Reference is expressed using the traditional dot notation (m.s[.f] is read as "the filler of the [facet f of the] slot s of the frame m"). Ontological instances are not indexed in the FR. They appear in HAS-PARTS slots of complex events and their fillers are all references to fillers of other ontological instances within the same complex event or the complex event itself. They are PART-OF (INVERSE of HAS-PARTS) of the complex event in which they are listed but INSTANCE-OF their corresponding basic concept—that is, TEACH-DESCRIBE-A is the first ontological instance of DESCRIBE that is at the same time PART-OF TEACH.

```
TEACH
      IS-A             value    COMMUNICATIVE-EVENT
      AGENT            sem      HUMAN
                       default  TEACHER
      THEME            sem      KNOWLEDGE
      DESTINATION      sem      HUMAN
                       default  STUDENT
      PRECONDITION     default  TEACH-KNOW-A TEACH-KNOW-B
      EFFECT           DEFAULT  TEACH-KNOW-C
      HAS-PARTS        value    TEACH-DESCRIBE
                                repeat    TEACH-REQUEST-INFORMATION
                                          TEACH-ANSWER
                                until TEACH-KNOW-C
      COMPONENT-RELATIONS       value   TEACH-AFTER-A
                                        TEACH-AFTER-B
      COMPONENT-MODALITIES value    TEACH-MODALITY-A

TEACH-KNOW-A
      INSTANCE-OF      value    KNOW
      PATIENT          value    TEACH.AGENT.sem
      THEME            value    TEACH.THEME.sem

TEACH-KNOW-B
      INSTANCE-OF      value    KNOW
      PATIENT          value    TEACH.DESTINATION.sem
      THEME            value    TEACH.THEME.sem

TEACH-MODALITY-A
      modality-type    value    EPISTEMIC
      modality-scope   value    TEACH-KNOW-B
      modality-value   value    0

TEACH-KNOW-C
      INSTANCE-OF      value    KNOW
      PATIENT          value    TEACH.DESTINATION.sem
      THEME            value    TEACH.THEME.sem

TEACH-DESCRIBE
      INSTANCE-OF      value    DESCRIBE
      AGENT            value    TEACH.AGENT.sem
      THEME            value    TEACH.THEME.sem
      DESTINATION      value    TEACH.DESTINATION.sem
```

```
TEACH-REQUEST-INFORMATION
        INSTANCE-OF    value    REQUEST-INFORMATION
        AGENT          value    TEACH.DESTINATION.sem
        THEME          value    TEACH.THEME.sem
        DESTINATION    value    TEACH.AGENT.sem
TEACH-ANSWER
        INSTANCE-OF    value    ANSWER
        AGENT          value    TEACH.AGENT.sem
        THEME          value    TEACH-REQUEST-INFORMATION.THEME.sem
        DESTINATION    value    TEACH.DESTINATION.sem

TEACH-AFTER-A
        DOMAIN         value    TEACH-DESCRIBE
        RANGE          value    TEACH-REQUEST-INFORMATION

TEACH-AFTER-B
        DOMAIN         value    TEACH-REQUEST-INFORMATION
        RANGE          value    TEACH-ANSWER
```

7.1.6   Axiomatic Definition of Ontology

To summarize the basic decisions made in defining the ontology, we present its axiomatic definition. This definition was originally formulated by Kavi Mahesh (1996) on the basis of the Mikrokosmos implementation of ontological semantics.

The axioms collectively define a correct and consistent representation in the ontology. These axioms define the up-to-date view of the ontology in ontological semantics and provide a precise framework for discussing the implications of introducing additional features and complexities in ontological representations.

The axioms below use the following symbols:

Variables: p, r, s, t, u, v, w, x, y, and z

Metaontological predicates: frame, concept, instance, slot, and ancestor. Frame, concept, and instance are one-place predicates; ancestor is a two-place predicate, indicating whether the second argument is an ancestor of the first. Slot is a four-place predicate, its arguments being the concept, the slot, the facet, and the filler. Slot is the basic predicate. The rest of the metaontological predicates can be derived on its basis with the help of the constants listed below: a frame is a named set of slots; a concept is a frame in whose slots the facets VALUE, SEM, DEFAULT, and RELAXABLE-TO may appear; an instance is a frame in whose slots only the facet VALUE appears. An ancestor of a concept is a concept that is among the fillers of the IS-A slot of the latter (or, recursively, of one of its ancestors).

Other predicates: $=, \neq, \in, \notin, \subset, \cap, \cup$, string, literal, reference, and scalar. The predicate $\in$ is to be read as *belongs to* and indicates membership in a set. The predicate $\subset$ is used in a generic sense and includes the relationship between a scalar range and its subranges. String, literal, and scalar are one-place predicates indicating whether an entity is a string, a scalar (i.e., a number or a range of numbers), or a literal symbol. Reference is a two-place predicate whose arguments are an entity and a slot and whose semantics is that the entity is bound to the filler of the slot.

Logical symbols: $\neg, \wedge, \vee, \forall, \exists, \Rightarrow, \Leftrightarrow$

Constants from the ontology: ALL, OBJECT, EVENT, PROPERTY, RELATION, ATTRIBUTE, LITERAL-ATTRIBUTE, SCALAR-ATTRIBUTE, IS-A, INSTANCE-OF, SUBCLASSES, INSTANCES, DEFINITION, TIME-STAMP, DOMAIN, RANGE, INVERSE, NOTHING, VALUE, SEM, DEFAULT, NOT, RELAXABLE-TO, DEFAULT-MEASURE.

The list of axioms follows:

1. A frame is a concept or an instance.
frame(x) $\Leftrightarrow$ concept(x) $\vee$ instance(x)
concept(x) $\Rightarrow$ $\neg$instance(x)
instance(x) $\Rightarrow$ $\neg$concept(x)
2. Every concept except ALL must have an ancestor.
concept(x) $\Leftrightarrow$ (x = all) $\vee$ ($\exists$y concept(y) $\wedge$ slot(x, is-a, value, y))
3. No concept is an INSTANCE-OF anything.
concept(x) $\Rightarrow$ $\neg\exists$y slot(x, instance-of, value, y)
4. If a concept x IS-A y then it is in the SUBCLASSES of y.
slot(x, is-a, value, y) $\Leftrightarrow$ slot(y, subclasses, value, x)
5. Every instance must have a concept that is its INSTANCE-OF.
instance(x) $\Leftrightarrow$ $\exists$y concept(y) $\wedge$ slot(x, instance-of, value, y)
6. No instance is an IS-A of anything.
instance(x) $\Rightarrow$ $\neg\exists$y slot(x, is-a, value, y)
7. If an instance x is an INSTANCE-OF a concept y, then x is in the instances of y.
slot(x, instance-of, value, y) $\Leftrightarrow$ slot(y, instances, value, x)
8. Instances do not have INSTANCES or SUBCLASSES.
instance(x) $\Rightarrow$ ($\neg\exists$y slot(y, instance-of, value, x)) $\wedge$ ($\neg\exists$y slot(y, is-a, value, x))
9. If y is an ancestor of x, then x and y are concepts and either x = y or x IS-A y or x IS-A z and y is an ancestor of z.
ancestor(x, y) $\Leftrightarrow$ concept(x) $\wedge$ concept(y) $\wedge$ ((x = y) $\vee$ slot(x, is-a, value, y) $\vee$
($\exists$z slot(x, is-a, value, z) $\wedge$ ancestor(z, y)))
10. A concept is either ALL or has one of OBJECT, EVENT, and PROPERTY as an ancestor.
concept(x) $\Leftrightarrow$ (x = all) $\vee$ ancestor(x, object) $\vee$ ancestor(x, event) $\vee$
ancestor(x, property)

11. No concept has more than one of OBJECT, EVENT, and PROPERTY as ancestors.

concept(x) ⇒ ¬(ancestor(x, object) ∧ ancestor(x, event))

concept(x) ⇒ ¬(ancestor(x, object) ∧ ancestor(x, property))

concept(x) ⇒ ¬(ancestor(x, event) ∧ ancestor(x, property))

12. Every frame has a DEFINITION and a TIME-STAMP slot, each filled by a string.

frame(x) ⇒ slot(x, definition, value, y) ∧ string(y) ∧ slot(x, time-stamp, value, z) ∧ string(z)

13. If y is a slot in a concept, then y IS-A PROPERTY.

slot(x, y, w, z) ⇒ ancestor(y, property)

14. Every PROPERTY is either a RELATION or an ATTRIBUTE. No PROPERTY is both.

slot(x, is-a, value, property) ⇒ (x = relation) ∨ (x = attribute)

ancestor(x, relation) ⇒ ¬ancestor(x, attribute)

ancestor(x, attribute) ⇒ ¬ancestor(x, relation)

15. If concept x IS-A ATTRIBUTE and y is a slot in x, then y is one of IS-A, SUBCLASSES, DEFINITION, TIME-STAMP, DOMAIN, or RANGE.

slot(x, y, w, z) ∧ ancestor(x, attribute) ⇒ y ∈ {is-a, subclasses, definition, time-stamp, domain, range}

16. If concept x IS-A RELATION and y is a slot in x, then y is one of IS-A, SUBCLASSES, DEFINITION, TIME-STAMP, DOMAIN, RANGE, or INVERSE.

slot(x, y, w, z) ∧ ancestor(x, attribute) ⇒ y ∈ {is-a, subclasses, definition, time-stamp, domain, range, inverse}

17. Property slots in frames can be filled either directly or by reference to the filler of a slot of another concept—that is, by reference.

∀y slot(x, y, w, z) ⇒ frame(z) ∨ scalar(z) ∨ literal(z) ∨ ∃t (slot(s, t, u, v) ∧ reference(z, slot(s, t, u, v)))

18. Fillers of the INVERSE slot are always RELATIONS.

slot(x, inverse, value, y) ⇒ ancestor(y, relation)

19. If y is the INVERSE of x, then x is the INVERSE of y.

slot(x, inverse, value, y) ⇔ slot(y, inverse, value, x)

20. There is only one INVERSE for every RELATION.

slot(x, inverse, value, y) ⇒ ¬∃z (slot(x, inverse, value, z) ∧ (y ≠ z))

21. Fillers of domain slots must be OBJECTS, EVENTS, or INSTANCES.

slot(x, domain, w, y) ⇒ object(y) ∨ event(y) ∨ instance(y)

22. Fillers of RANGE slots of RELATIONS must be OBJECTS, EVENTS, INSTANCES, or NOTHING.

slot(x, range, w, y) ∧ ancestor(x, relation) ⇒ object(y) ∨ event(y) ∨ instance(y) ∨ nothing

23. If x has a slot y, then x must have an ancestor t that is in the DOMAIN slot of concept y.

slot(x, y, w, z) ⇒ ∃t slot(y, domain, sem, t) ∧ ancestor(x, t)

24. If x has a slot y that is a RELATION filled by z, then z must have an ancestor t that is in the RANGE of the concept y, or z must be NOTHING.

slot(x, y, w, z) ∧ ancestor(y, relation) ⇒ (∃t slot(y, range, sem, t) ∧ ancestor(z, t)) ∨ (z = nothing)

25. An INVERSE slot may be inherited or present implicitly: if x has a slot y that is a RELATION filled by z, then z has a slot u filled by v where v is an ancestor of x, and y has an INVERSE t that is an ancestor of u.

slot(x, y, w, z) ∧ ancestor(y, relation) ∧ (z ≠ nothing) ⇒ (∃u∃v slot(z, u, w, v) ∧ ancestor(x, v) ∧ ∃t (slot(y, inverse, value, t) ∧ (ancestor(u, t) ∧ ancestor(t, u)))) ∨ (∃t∃v slot(y, inverse, value, t) ∧ slot(t, range, sem, v) ∧ ancestor(x, v))

26. Inheritance of RELATION slots: if x has a RELATION y as a slot filled by z, and x is an ancestor of t, then t also has a slot y that is filled by a u that has z as one of its ancestors or is NOTHING.

slot(x, y, sem, z) ∧ ancestor(y, relation) ∧ ancestor(t, x) ⇒ ∃u (slot(t, y, sem, u) ∧ (ancestor(u, z) ∨ (u = nothing)))

27. Inheritance of ATTRIBUTE slots: if x has an ATTRIBUTE y as a slot filled by z, and x is an ancestor of t, then t also has a slot y that is filled by a u that is either z, or a subset of z, or NOTHING.

slot(x, y, sem, z) ∧ ancestor(y, attribute) ∧ ancestor(t, x) ⇒ ∃u (slot(t, y, sem, u) ∧ ((u = z) ∨ (u ⊂ z) ∨ (u = nothing)))

28. Every slot y in an instance x of concept t is also a slot in concept t; in x, y is filled with a narrower range or a lower concept (or an instance thereof), using the value facet.

slot(x, y, w, z) ∧ instance-of(x, t) ⇒ slot(t, y, v, u) ∧ w = value ∧ ((z ⊂ u) ∨ ancestor(z, u))

29. Every slot of a concept has at least one of VALUE, SEM, and DEFAULT facets.

slot(x, y, w, z) ⇒ w ∈ {value, sem, default}

30. Every slot y (other than IS-A, SUBCLASSES, DEFINITION, TIME-STAMP, DOMAIN, RANGE, and INVERSE) of a concept x has one of the following sets of facets: VALUE with or without DEFAULT-MEASURE or NOT, either DEFAULT, SEM, or both, with or without RELAXABLE-TO, NOT, and DEFAULT-MEASURE.

slot(x, y, w, z) ∧ y ∉ {IS-A SUBCLASSES DEFINITION TIME-STAMP DOMAIN RANGE INVERSE} ∧

t ⊂ {not default-measure} ∧ u ⊂ {default sem} ∧ v ⊂ {relaxable-to not default-measure} ⇒ w ⊂ {value t} ∨ w = {u ∪ v}

31. Every attribute is either a SCALAR-ATTRIBUTE or a LITERAL-ATTRIBUTE, but not both.

slot(x, is-a, value, attribute) ⇒ (x = scalar-attribute) ∨ (x = literal-attribute)
ancestor(x, scalar-attribute) ⇒ ¬ancestor(x, literal-attribute)
ancestor(x, literal-attribute) ⇒ ¬ancestor(x, scalar-attribute)

32. The range of a SCALAR-ATTRIBUTE can only be filled by a scalar.

ancestor(x, scalar-attribute) ∧ slot(x, range, w, y) ⇒ scalar(y)

33. The range of a LITERAL-ATTRIBUTE can only be filled by a literal.

ancestor(x, literal-attribute) ∧ slot(x, range, w, y) ⇒ literal(y)

34. If property y is one of PRECONDITION, EFFECT, HAS-PARTS, COMPONENT-RELATIONS, or COMPONENT-MODALITIES, then its filler z is a frame s, the fillers of whose slots are only references.

slot(x, y, w, z) ∧ y ∈ {precondition effect has-parts component-relations component-modalities} ⇒ frame(z) ∧ ∀t∀v∃u (slot(z, t, value, v) ∧ slot(s, u, p, r) ∧ reference(v, slot(s, u, p, r))))

Note: This axiom is needed to define the class of ontological instances.

7.2   Fact Repository

The knowledge required in a world model for ontological semantics includes not only an ontology, as sketched above, but also records of past experiences, both actually perceived and reported, depending on the application. The *lingua mentalis* equivalent of a text is an episode, a unit of knowledge that encapsulates a particular experience of an intelligent agent, and that is typically represented as a TMR, a temporally and causally ordered network of object and event instances.

The ontology and the episodes are sometimes discussed in terms of the contents of two different types of memory: semantic and episodic (e.g., Tulving 1985; in the philosophy of language, a similar distinction is captured by the terms *noncontingent* and *contingent knowledge*—see Bar Hillel 1954). This distinction is reflected in ontological semantics by the opposition between concepts, stored in the ontology, and their instances (episodes, facts), stored in the FR. The presence of a systematic representation and indexing method for episodic knowledge is not only necessary for processing natural language but is also an enablement condition for case-based reasoning (Kolodner and Riesbeck 1986; Kolodner 1984; Schank 1982) and analogical inference (e.g., Carbonell 1983).

Instances in the FR are indexed by the concept they correspond to and can be interrelated on temporal, causal, and other properties. The instances list only those properties of the corresponding concepts that have been given actual fillers as a result of processing some textual input or coreferential specification. The fillers in instances cannot be concepts; instead, they can be concept instances, literal or scalar values or ranges, and references to either other property slot fillers or to even system-external elements, such as, for instance, URLs. The latter facility is useful when a value is constantly changing, like the exchange rate between two currencies. The only facet allowed in instances for specifying a semantic filler is VALUE. Instance frame slots may contain two additional facets—TIME-RANGE and INFO-SOURCE—both introduced in the BNF in section 7.1.1 but used only in specifying the FR.

TIME-RANGE is used for truth maintenance; it marks the beginning and end of the time period during which the datum specified in a particular property is true. For example, informally, if I painted my car blue three years ago and repainted it red yesterday, then the time-range for the property blue of my car would start on that date three years ago and end yesterday. INFO-SOURCE is used to record the source of the particular datum stored in the FR. One reason for having this facet is that it is, in practice, very typical that some property of an object or an event is given different fillers in different source texts (for example, people's ages are habitually reported differently in different stories or newspapers). Since it may be necessary to record different timed values of properties and different data sources, in the CAMBIO/CREST implementation of ontological semantics, instance frames are allowed

Property	Value	Time Range
ABSOLUTE-PLACEMENT	1	(-,+)
ABSOLUTE-RESULT	107	(-,+)
AGENT	Mi-Jin Yun (ATHLETE-3285)	(-,+)
COMPETITION-STAGE	FINAL	(-,+)
DATALINK	file:/home/olympic/spider/nbc_daily/2000-09-19/arw070-4.html	(-,+)
	http://www.nbcolympics.com/results/oly/ar/arw070.html? event=arw070100o.js	(-,+)
DATE	09/19/2000 16:08:00	(-,+)
GENDER	FEMALE	(-,+)
IN-DISCIPLINE	ARCHERY	(-,+)
INDIVIDUAL-OR-TEAM	INDIVIDUAL	(-,+)
INSTRUMENT	ARROW	(-,+)
	BOW	(-,+)
LOCATION	Sydney (CITY-8)	(-,+)
PART-OF	ARCHERY-INDIVIDUAL-WOMEN	(-,+)
PEOPLE-IN-TEAM	ONE	(-,+)
RESULT-MEASURE	GAME-POINT	(-,+)

Figure 7.4
An instance of INDIVIDUAL-SPORTS-RESULT in the CAMBIO/TIDES implementation of ontological semantics; this fact records Mi-Jin Yun's gold medal in women's individual archery.

You are browsing the instance Mi-Jin Yun (ATHLETE-3285)

List all the instances of ATHLETE

Property	Value
AGE	17
AGENT-OF	Archery Individual Women Final plcmt 1 (SPORTS-INDIVIDUAL-RESULT-0
	ARCHERY-INDIVIDUAL-WOMEN
	ARCHERY-TEAM-WOMEN
DATALINK	file://home/olympic/spider/sydney/www.olympics.com/eng/athletes/KOR/
	http://www.olympics.com/eng/athletes/KOR/0207616/
GENDER	FEMALE
HAS-BIRTHPLACE-CITY	Taechon (CITY-1052)
HAS-COACH	In-Taek Im (TRAINER-1103)
HAS-NATIONALITY	South Korea (NATION-183)
HEIGHT	165 cm
WEIGHT	55 kg

Figure 7.5
The personal profile of Mi-Jin Yun in the CAMBIO/TIDES FR.

to have as many slots of the same name as there are differences in their fillers on either TIME-RANGE or INFO-SOURCE facets. An alternative solution would have been to create a new instance for each unique combination of TIME-RANGE and INFO-SOURCE fillers.

Figures 7.4 through 7.6 show some typical facts from the CAMBIO/CREST FR.

In early implementations, in contrast to ontological concepts, instances in FR were given both formal names (generated by appending a unique numerical identifier to their corresponding concept name) and, optionally, names by which they could be directly referred to in the onomasticon (see section 7.4). Thus, in the Spanish onomasticon, there was an entry *Estados Unidos de America* that pointed to the named instance USA (aka NATION-213). In most later implementations, the onomasticon of any language refers the appropriate name to NATION-213 directly. Thus, names of instances remain squarely within onomasticons.

7.3   The Lexicon

In any natural language processing system, the lexicon supports the processes of analysis and generation of text or spoken language at all levels—tokenization (that

You are browsing the instance South Korea (NATION-183)

```
List all the instances of NATION
```

Property	Value	Time Range	Source
BORDERS-ON	North Korea (NATION-148)	(-,+)	CIA World Factbook
HAS-CURRENCY	Won (MONETARY-UNIT-124)	(-,+)	CIA World Factbook
HAS-MEMBER	Korean (HUMAN-130)	(-,+)	CIA World Factbook
HAS-REPRESENTATIVE	Kim DaeJung (GOVERNMENTAL-ROLE-200)	(-,+)	CIA World Factbook
NATIONALITY-OF	Bae-Young Lee (ATHLETE-3254)	(-,+)	http://www.olympics.com
	Bang-Hyun Kim (ATHLETE-3178)	(-,+)	http://www.olympics.com
	Bo-Eun Lee (ATHLETE-3179)	(-,+)	http://www.olympics.com
	Bo-Ra Cho (ATHLETE-3167)	(-,+)	http://www.olympics.com
	Bong-Ju Lee (ATHLETE-3371)	(-,+)	http://www.olympics.com
	Bu-Kyung Jung (ATHLETE-	(-,+)	http://www.olympics.com

Figure 7.6
This is an excerpt from what the CAMBIO/TIDES FR knows about South Korea.

is, roughly, lexical segmentation); part-of-speech tagging and morphological analysis; proper-name recognition; syntactic, semantic, and discourse/pragmatic analysis; lexical selection, syntactic structure generation, and morphological-form generation.

The lexicon for a given language is a collection of superentries that are indexed by the citation form of the word or phrasal lexical unit (set expression). A *superentry* includes all the lexemes that have the same base written form, regardless of syntactic category, pronunciation, or sense. Each lexicon *entry* is comprised of a number of *zones* corresponding to the various types of lexical information. The zones containing information for use by an NLP system are: CAT (lexical category), ORTH (orthography—abbreviations and variants), PHON (phonology), MORPH (morphological irregular forms, class or paradigm, and stem variants or "principal parts"), SYN (syntactic features such as *attributive* for adjectives), SYN-STRUC (indication of sentence- or phrase-level syntactic dependency, centrally including subcategorization), and SEM-STRUC (lexical semantics, meaning representation). The following scheme, in a BNF-like notation, summarizes the basic lexicon structure. Some additional information is added for human consumption in the ANNOTATIONS zone.

```
SUPERENTRY ::=
      ORTHOGRAPHIC-FORM: "FORM"
      ({SYN-CAT}: <LEXEME>*)*
LEXEME ::=
      CATEGORY: {SYN-CAT}
      ORTHOGRAPHY:
            VARIANTS: "VARIANTS"*
            ABBREVIATIONS: "ABBS"*
      PHONOLOGY: "PHONOLOGY"*
      MORPHOLOGY:
            IRREGULAR-FORMS: ("FORM"
                                 {IRREG-FORM-NAME})*
            PARADIGM: {PARADIGM-NAME}
            STEM-VARIANTS: ("FORM" {VARIANT-NAME})*
      ANNOTATIONS:
            DEFINITION: "DEFINITION IN NL"*
            EXAMPLES: "EXAMPLE"*
            COMMENTS: "LEXICOGRAPHER COMMENT"*
            TIME-STAMP: {LEXICOG-ID DATE-OF-ENTRY}*
      SYNTACTIC-FEATURES: (FEATURE VALUE)*
      SYNTACTIC-STRUCTURE: F-STRUCTURE
      SEMANTIC-STRUCTURE: LEX-SEM-SPECIFICATION
```

The following example illustrates the structure and content of the lexicon. The example shows not a complete superentry but just the first verbal sense of the English lexeme *buy*:

```
buy-v1
    cat    v
    morph stem-v  bought v+past
                  bought v+past-participle
    anno  def     "when A buys T from S, A acquires possession of T
                  previously owned by S, and S acquires a sum of
                  money in exchange"
          ex      "Bill bought a car from Jane"
          time-stamp    dha; 12-13-94 ;the acquirer and the date
    syn-struc
          root    buy
          subj    root    $var1
                  cat     n
```

```
            obj      root    $var2
                cat    n
            oblique  root    from
                     cat     prep
                     opt     +
                     obj     root    $var3
                             cat     n
   sem-struc
        BUY

                AGENT    value  ^$var1
                         sem    HUMAN
                THEME    value  ^$var2
                         sem    OBJECT
                SOURCE   value  ^$var3
                         sem    HUMAN
```

The above states that the verb *buy* takes a subject, a direct object, and a prepositional adjunct; that its meaning is represented as an instance of the ontological concept BUY; that the AGENT of the concept BUY, which constitutes the meaning of the
verb's subject, is expected to be a HUMAN; that the THEME of the concept BUY, which
is the meaning of the verb's direct object, can be any OBJECT; and that the SOURCE of
the concept BUY, which constitutes the meaning of the verb's prepositional adjunct,
can be a HUMAN. (Semantic constraints on the case roles of the predicate are overtly
specified in the example above. In practice, when they directly correspond to the
constraints stored in the ontology for the corresponding concepts, they are not
overtly listed in the lexicon entries. Overt constraints in lexicon entries are used for
modifying—and overriding—the ontological constraints for the concept or concepts
used to represent the meaning of the lexical unit in question.)

The presence of variables (*$varN*) in the SYN-STRUC and SEM-STRUC zones of the
lexicon is obviously intended to establish a kind of coindexing. Indeed, it links syntactic arguments and adjuncts of the lexeme (if any) with the case roles and other
ontological properties that the meanings of these syntactic arguments and adjuncts
fill. ^*$varN* reads "the meaning of *$varN*."

The meaning of the lexeme is established separately. For most open-class lexical
units, the specification of meaning involves instantiating and often constraining one
or more ontological concepts and/or values of parametric elements of TMR (e.g.,
modality, style, aspect, and so on). The case of *buy-v1* is rather simple, because all
the constraints from the ontological concept that forms the basis of its meaning description will remain unchanged in the lexical meaning. To describe the meaning of

the English words *acquire-v2* and *acquire-v3*, the senses used to refer to corporations buying corporations, the ontological concept BUY will be used as well, but in both these cases, it will be further constrained:

```
acquire-v2
        cat     v

        anno    def     "when company A buys company, division,
                        subsidiary, etc. of company T from the
                        latter"
                ex      "Alpha Inc acquired from Gamma Inc the
                        latter's candle division"

        syn-struc
                root    acquire
                subj    root    $var1
                        cat     n
                obj     root    $var2
                        cat     n
                oblique root    from
                        cat     prep
                        opt     +
                        obj     root    $var3
                                cat     n
        sem-struc
                BUY
                        AGENT   value   ^$var1
                                sem     CORPORATION
                        THEME   value   ^$var2
                                sem     ORGANIZATION
                        SOURCE  value   ^$var3
                                sem     CORPORATION

    acquire-v3
        cat     v
        anno    def     "when company A buys company T"
                ex      "Bell Atlantic acquired GTE"
        syn-struc
                root    acquire
                subj    root    $var1
                        cat     n
                obj     root    $var2
                        cat     n
```

```
sem-struc
        BUY
                AGENT   value  ^$var1
                        sem    CORPORATION
                THEME   value  ^$var2
                        sem    CORPORATION
                SOURCE  value  ^$var2.OWNED-BY
                        sem    HUMAN
```

The constraints on the properties of BUY as used in the lexicon to specify the meaning of *acquire-v2* have been changed from the ontological concept to its occurrence in the lexicon entry. In AGENT and SOURCE, HUMAN was replaced by CORPORATION. In THEME, OBJECT was narrowed down to ORGANIZATION. This mechanism—allowing the lexical meaning in lexicon entries to be specified using modified values of fillers in the concept that forms the basis of the meaning of the lexeme—is an important capability that keeps the ontology as a language-independent resource, while specifying lexical idiosyncrasies within the lexicon of a language. The alternative to this solution would lead to a separate concept for specifying the meaning of *acquire-v2* (and *acquire-v3*, too) and consequently, to separate concepts for meanings of lexemes from different languages. This would entirely defeat the goal of language-independent meaning specification, because it would require establishing bilingual correspondences of meanings, essentially the same way as semantics-free transfer MT systems establish correspondences of strings in various languages, sometimes with further constraints of a syntactic nature. It is because of considerations such as the above that we fail to recognize the merits of developing different ontologies for different languages (e.g., Vossen 1998).

The above example illustrates an additional point. The SOURCE case role typically does not have a syntactic realization. However, the ontological concept BUY that we use, again, economically, to represent the meaning of *acquire-v3*, stipulates the presence of SOURCE and constrains it to HUMAN. The meaning of *acquire-v3* actually includes the (world-knowledge) information about the source: it is the stockholders or, generally, owners of the corporation that is the meaning of the source of *acquire-v3*. The lexicon entry, correspondingly, lists this information, using the dot notation to refer to the filler of the OWNED-BY slot of the frame for CORPORATION.

The attentive reader will have noticed by now that the above formulation of *acquire-v3* leads to a violation of a precept of ontological semantics, specifically, that instances in the basic TMR do not contain those properties of the corresponding concept that are not overtly specified, either in an input text or, in some applications, by a human user. If the information about the source property is not mentioned, it should not be a part of the lexical entry. If it is mentioned, its value should not be specified by reference, but rather directly as the meaning of an appropriate syntactic constituent in the input text. The information in the SEM-STRUC zone of the above entry simply will remain recorded in the ontology as the filler of the default facet of the property OWNED-BY. That is, we will retain the capability of making the inference that companies are sold by their owners should such an inference (which will be licensed by the extended TMR) be called for by a reasoning module of an application.

There is an important reason why this information should be recorded in the ontology and not in the lexicon. If it is recorded in the lexicon, as shown in the entry for *acquire-v3* above, and an input containing *acquire* has no explicit information about ownership, *acquire* will be assigned its *acquire-v3* sense and the TMR will have the OWNED-BY property filled not with an actual value but rather with the potential, ontological filler for OWNED-BY of the THEME of BUY. Now, should further input contain a direct mention of ownership, the procedure will have to substitute the new filler for the old one. If, on the other hand, the information is recorded in the ontology, it will not be instantiated in the TMR until there is an explicit mention of ownership in the input or if the application calls for the use of information in the extended TMR. As a reminder for the reader, extended TMRs contain those properties of the ontological concepts instantiated in the basic TMR that are not explicitly mentioned in the input—properties whose fillers are listed in SEM and DEFAULT facets and are, therefore, abductively defeasible.

In the ontological concept BUY the ownership information that we discuss above is recorded as follows:

```
BUY
    ...
    THEME   default      COMMODITY
            sem          OBJECT
    SOURCE  default      THEME.OWNED-BY
            sem          HUMAN
            relaxable-to ORGANIZATION
    ...
```

We will return to the important issue of the proper place for recording semantic constraints—the ontology or the lexicon—in section 9.1 in the context of knowledge acquisition.

On the whole, all of the above examples were quite straightforward with respect to the linking relations: the grammatical subject is a natural clue for agency; direct objects very often signal themes, and so on.[2] The relations between the syntactic and the semantic information in the ontological semantic lexicon can, however, be much more complicated. Thus, two values of the SYN-STRUC zone may appear in a single entry, if they correspond to the same meaning, as expressed in the SEM-STRUC zone of the entry (19); syntactic modification, as recorded in the SYN-STRUC zone, may not yield a parallel semantic modification in the SEM-STRUC zone (20); the semantics of a lexicon entry may be linkable to a component of the syntactic structure by reference rather than directly (25).

```
(19)
big-adj1
        cat     adj
        syn-struc
                1    root   $var1
                     cat    n
                     mods   root    big
                2    root   big
                     cat    adj
                     subj   root    $var1
                     cat    n
        sem-struc
                1 2  SIZE-ATTRIBUTE
                     DOMAIN value          ^$var1
                            sem            PHYSICAL-OBJECT
                     RANGE  value          >0.75
                            relaxable-to   >0.6
```

In the above example, there are two subcategorization patterns, marked 1 and 2, listed in the SYN-STRUC. The former pattern corresponds to the attributive use of the adjective: the noun it modifies is assigned the variable $var1$, and the entry head itself appears in the modifier position. The latter pattern presents the noun, bound to $var1$, in the subject position and the adjective in the predicative position. Once again in the SEM-STRUC zone, instead of variables bound to syntactic elements, the meanings of the elements referred to by these variables (and marked by a caret, "^") are used. Thus, $^{\wedge}var1$ reads as "the meaning of the element to which the variable $var1$ is bound." Among the constraints listed in the SEM-STRUC zone of an entry are selectional restrictions (the noun must be a physical object) and relaxation information, which is used for the treatment of unexpected ("ill-formed") input during processing.

Thus, an entry like the above should be read as follows:

• The first line is the head of the superentry for the adjective *big* (in our terminology, an "entry" is a specification of a single sense, while the "superentry" is the set of such entries).

• The second line assigns a sense number to the entry within its superentry.

• Next, the adjective is assigned to its lexical category.

• The first subcategorization pattern in the SYN-STRUC zone describes the Adj-N construction; the second subcategorization pattern describes the N-Copula-Adj construction.

• The SEM-STRUC zone defines the lexical semantics of the adjective by assigning it to the class of SIZE adjectives, stating that it is applicable to physical objects and that its meaning is a high-value range on the SIZE scale/property.

The two subcategorization patterns in the SYN-STRUC zone of the entry correspond to the same meaning. There is an even more important distinction between this lexical entry and those for the verbs *buy* and *acquire*. The meanings of entries for words that are heads of syntactic phrases or clauses—that is, predominantly verbs and nouns—are typically expressed by instantiating ontological concepts that describe their basic meaning, with optional further modification in the lexicon entry itself, by either modifying property values of these concepts or introducing additional, often parametric, meaning elements from the ontology. In the case of modifiers—mostly adjectives and adverbs—the meaning is, in the simplest case, expressed by the filler of a property of another concept, namely, the concept that forms the basis for the meaning specification of the modifier's syntactic head. Thus, in the entries for verbs, the concepts that form the basis of specifying their meanings appear at the top level of the SEM-STRUC zone. In the entries for modifiers, such as *big*, the reference to the concept that is, in fact, the meaning of *big*, is introduced as the value of the domain of the property SIZE-ATTRIBUTE that forms the basis of the meaning of *big*. This distinction is further marked notationally: in the verb entries the main concept refers to the syntactic constituent corresponding to the lexeme itself; in the entries for modifiers, the main concept refers to the syntactic constituent marked as *$var1*, the head of the modifier.

In the lexicon entries, the facet VALUE is used to refer to the meanings of the syntactic constituents mentioned in the SYN-STRUC zone, while the ontology provides the semantic constraints (selectional restrictions; see section 8.2.2), recorded in the DEFAULT, SEM, and RELAXABLE-TO facets of its concepts. As was already shown, these constraints may be modified during the specification of the lexical meaning.

```
good-adj1
      cat       adj
      syn-struc
               1   root   $var1
                   cat    n
                   mods   root      good
```

```
2  root   $var0
   cat    adj
   subj   root    $var1
          cat     n
sem-struc
     modality
          modality-type          evaluative
          modality-value         value  >0.75
                                 relaxable-to  >0.6
          modality-scope         ^$var1
          modality-attributed-to *speaker*
```

The meaning of *good* is entirely parameterized—that is, the sem-struc zone of its entry does not contain any ontological concept to be instantiated in the TMR. Instead, the meaning of *good* is expressed as a value of modality on the meaning of the element that *good* modifies syntactically. The meaning of *good* is also noncompositional (see sections 3.5.2 and 3.5.3) in the sense that it deviates from the usual adjectival-meaning function of highlighting a property of the noun the adjective modifies and—in the typical case—assigning a value to it.

The meaning of *good* presents an additional problem: it changes with the meaning of the noun it modifies. This phenomenon is often referred to as *plasticity* (see Marx 1983; Raskin and Nirenburg 1995). We interpret *good* in a sentence like (21) as, essentially, (22). We realize that, in fact, *good* in (21) may have a large variety of senses, some of which are illustrated in the possible continuations of (21) in (23). Obviously, *good* may have additional senses when used to modify other nouns (24).

(21) This is a good book.

(22) The speaker evaluates this book highly.

(23) ... because it is very informative.
     ... because it is very entertaining.
     ... because the style is great.
     ... because it looks great on the coffee table.
     ... because it is made very sturdily and will last for centuries.

(24) This is a good breadmaker.
     He is a good teacher.
     She is a good baby.
     Rice is good food.

In each case, *good* selects a property of a noun and assigns it a high value on the evaluation scale associated with that property. The property changes not only from noun to noun but also within the same noun, depending on the context. The finest grain-size analysis requires that a certain property of the modified noun be contextually selected as the one on which the meaning of the noun and that of the adjective are connected. This is what many psychologists call a "salient" property.

Now, it is difficult to identify salient properties formally, as is well known, for instance, in the scholarship on metaphor, where salience is the determining factor for the similarity dimension on which metaphors (and similes) are based. (See, for instance, Black 1954–55, 1979; Davidson 1978; Lakoff and Johnson 1980; Lakoff 1987; Searle 1979; on salience, specifically, see Tversky and Kahnemann 1983.) It is, therefore, wise to avoid having to search for the salient property, and the hypothesis of practical effability for MT (see section 9.3.6) offers a justification for this. What this means, in plainer terms, is that if we treat the meaning of *good* as unspecified with regard to the noun property it modifies, there is a solid chance that there will be an adjective with a matching generalized, unspecified meaning like that in the target language as well.

In the extant implementations of ontological semantics, the representation solution for *good*, as illustrated in the entry, deliberately avoids the problem of determining the salient property by shifting the description to a coarser grain size—that is, scoping not over a particular property of an object or event but over an entire concept. This decision has so far been vindicated by the expectations of the current applications of ontological semantics—none so far has required a finer grain size. In MT, for example, this approach "gambles" on the availability across languages of a "plastic" adjective corresponding to the English *good*, in conformance with the principle of practical effability that we introduce in the context of reducing polysemy (see Raskin and Nirenburg 1995 and section 9.3.5).

Note that the issue of plasticity of meaning is not constrained to adjectives. It affects the analysis of nominal compounds and indeed testifies to its being as notoriously difficult as it has proven to be over the years. In fact, analyzing nominal compounds—for example, *the IBM lecture*—is even more difficult than analyzing adjectival modification because in the former case there is no specification of any property on which the connection can be made, even at the coarse grain size that we use in describing the meaning of *good*. Indeed, IBM may be the filler of the properties OWNED-BY, LOCATION, and THEME, as well as many others (cf. section 8.2.2, especially examples (42)–(44)).

Returning to the issues of linking, we observe that noncompositional adjectives also include temporal adjectives, such as *occasional* (see one possible entry for it in (25)) as well as Vendler's (1968) classes A_5–A_8 of adjectives that "ascribe the adjective ... to a whole sentence." The concept introduced in the SEM-STRUC zone of the entry in (25) corresponds neither to the lexeme itself nor to the noun the latter modifies syntactically. Rather, it introduces a reference to the EVENT concept that is

the meaning of the typical event of which the noun modified by *occasional* is the
AGENT. Adjectives such as *occasional* are as difficult to analyze as nominal modifiers
because they can signify fillers of a variety of properties. Indeed, while (25) will serve
well for *occasional cook* (the typical event of which a cook is agent is cooking), the
linking in the SEM-STRUC should be on ^$var1.patient-of in *occasional honoree* and on
the event as a whole (^$var1) in *occasional storm*.

```
occasional-adj1
      cat         adj
      syn-struc
                  root    $var1
                  cat     n
                  mods    root        occasional
      sem-struc
                  ^$var1.AGENT-OF
                        aspect    phase        b/c/e
                                  iteration    multiple
```

The above treatment amounts essentially to treating adjectives such as *occasional* as
sentential adverbs, as if through the following transformation: He is an occasional
cook → He cooks occasionally.

  The next example is even more complex and well illustrates the expressive power
of ontological semantics. In the current ontology, there is no concept TRY or, for that
matter, FAIL or SUCCEED. The corresponding meanings, when expressed in natural
language, are represented parametrically, as values of the epiteuctic modality (see
section 8.5.3).

```
try-v3
      syn-struc
                  root    try
                  cat     v
                  subj    root    $var1
                          cat     n
                  xcomp   root    $var2
                          cat     v
                          form    OR infinitive gerund
      sem-struc
                  set-1           element-type    refsem-1
                                  cardinality     >=1
                  refsem-1        sem    EVENT
                          AGENT    ^$var1
                          EFFECT   refsem-2
```

```
modality
        modality-type    epiteuctic
        modality-scope   refsem-2
        modality-value   <1
refsem-2        value    ^$var2
                sem      EVENT
```

The SEM-STRUC zone of the above example is interpreted as follows. SET-1 consists of
one or more events whose properties are presented using the internal coreference
device REFSEM. This device, to which we referred in the section on ontology as reification, is necessary in the lexicon for the same reason: because property fillers in the
format of our ontology must be strings or references in the dot notation. In other
words, if these strings refer to concepts, then no properties of these concepts can be
constrained in the fillers. So, the REFSEM mechanism is needed to reify the concept
that would serve as a filler and constrain its properties in the freestanding specification of the concept instance in the TMR. The agent of each of the events in SET-1 is
the meaning of the subject of the input sentence, essentially the entity that does the
trying. These events have an effect that is the meaning of the XCOMP in the source text
and that must be an EVENT (once again, we must reify the filler of effect because it has
a property of its own, being an EVENT). The meaning of *try* includes the idea that the
event that was attempted was not achieved. This is, as mentioned above, realized in
ontological semantics parametrically as a value on the epiteuctic modality. It scopes
over the desired effect of the agent's actions and its value, <1, records the lack of
success.

To further clarify the meaning of *try*, as represented in the above entry, let us look
at the sentence *I tried to reach the North Pole*. In it, *try* is used in the sense described
above and has the following meaning:

• The agent performs one or more actions that are not specified in the sentence.
• Each of these actions (all of them, in reality, complex events) have the event of
reaching the North Pole as their EFFECT.
• The epiteuctic modality value states that the goal is not reached (that is, the
speaker has not reached the North Pole).

Our philosopher colleagues may object at this point that the example above does
not necessarily imply the failure of each of the attempts and may quote a sentence
like *I tried and, moreover, succeeded in reaching the North Pole* as a counterexample.
Leaving aside the marginal acceptability of such a sentence (nobody talks like that
unless deliberately wanting to make a humorous effect through excessive ped-
antry), this sentence should be actually characterized as a repair—that is, *I tried, no,
actually, I succeeded in reaching the North Pole. Moreover* functions as a mark to

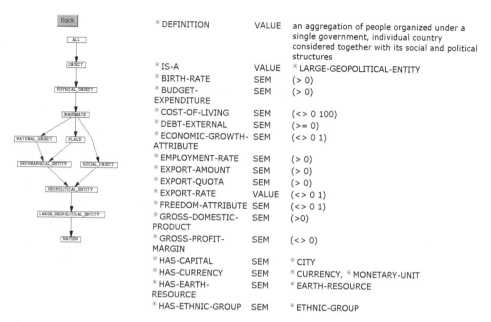

⊞ DEFINITION	VALUE	an aggregation of people organized under a single government, individual country considered together with its social and political structures
⊞ IS-A	VALUE	⊞ LARGE-GEOPOLITICAL-ENTITY
⊞ BIRTH-RATE	SEM	(> 0)
⊞ BUDGET-EXPENDITURE	SEM	(> 0)
⊞ COST-OF-LIVING	SEM	(<> 0 100)
⊞ DEBT-EXTERNAL	SEM	(>= 0)
⊞ ECONOMIC-GROWTH-ATTRIBUTE	SEM	(<> 0 1)
⊞ EMPLOYMENT-RATE	SEM	(> 0)
⊞ EXPORT-AMOUNT	SEM	(> 0)
⊞ EXPORT-QUOTA	SEM	(> 0)
⊞ EXPORT-RATE	VALUE	(<> 0 1)
⊞ FREEDOM-ATTRIBUTE	SEM	(<> 0 1)
⊞ GROSS-DOMESTIC-PRODUCT	SEM	(>0)
⊞ GROSS-PROFIT-MARGIN	SEM	(<> 0)
⊞ HAS-CAPITAL	SEM	⊞ CITY
⊞ HAS-CURRENCY	SEM	⊞ CURRENCY, ⊞ MONETARY-UNIT
⊞ HAS-EARTH-RESOURCE	SEM	⊞ EARTH-RESOURCE
⊞ HAS-ETHNIC-GROUP	SEM	⊞ ETHNIC-GROUP

Figure 7.7
The ontological concept NATION, a view of the inheritance paths from the root of the ontology, and a partial view of the properties of the concept.

cancel the meaning of the beginning of the sentence, similarly to the way *but* does in *I tried to reach the North Pole several times but succeeded only once.* A different way of expressing the same position on the issue is to say that the meaning of *succeed* automatically subsumes any attempts to succeed, thus making a mention of those attempts redundant. What is at issue is, of course, simply how to define the meaning of *try*—as allowing for successful attempts or not—and the argument we have presented supports the latter choice.

We have established so far that the meaning of a lexeme can be represented as an ontological concept, as the property of an ontological concept, or as the value of a parameter—that is, in a manner unrelated to any ontological concept other than the name of the parameter. This does not exhaust all the possibilities. Thus, many closed-class lexemes enjoy special treatment: personal pronouns, determiners, possessives, and other deictic elements, such as *here* or *now*, as well as copulas are treated as triggers of reference-finding procedures; some conjunctions may introduce discourse relations in the TMR; numerals and some special adjectives—for example, *every* and *all*—characterize set relations. Of course, the emphasis in ontological lexical semantics is on open-class lexical items.

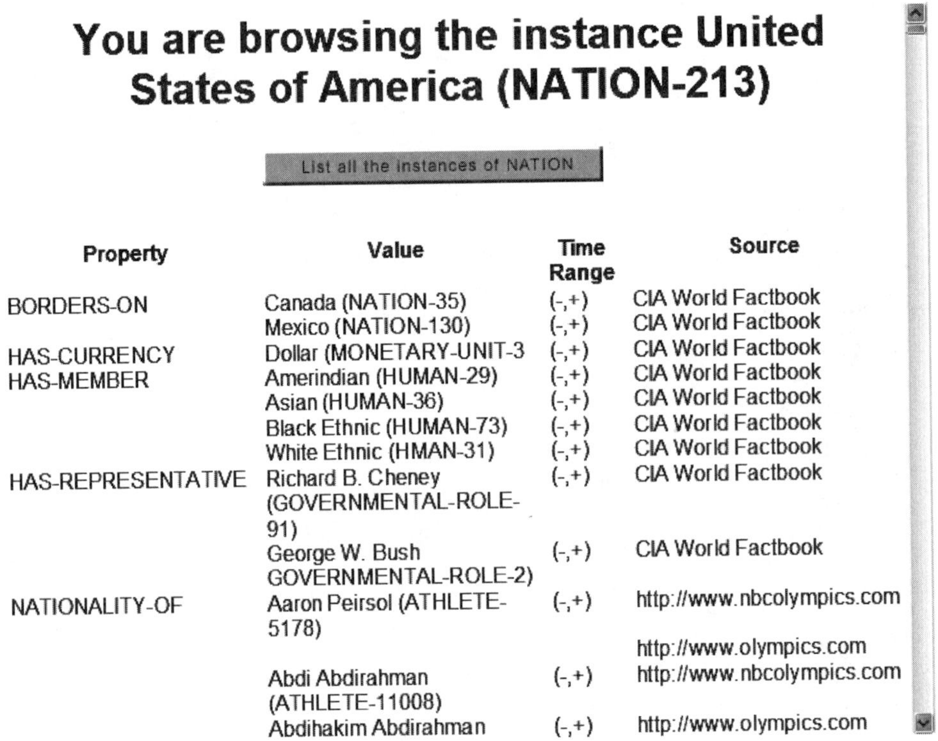

You are browsing the instance United States of America (NATION-213)

List all the instances of NATION

Property	Value	Time Range	Source
BORDERS-ON	Canada (NATION-35)	(-,+)	CIA World Factbook
	Mexico (NATION-130)	(-,+)	CIA World Factbook
HAS-CURRENCY	Dollar (MONETARY-UNIT-3	(-,+)	CIA World Factbook
HAS-MEMBER	Amerindian (HUMAN-29)	(-,+)	CIA World Factbook
	Asian (HUMAN-36)	(-,+)	CIA World Factbook
	Black Ethnic (HUMAN-73)	(-,+)	CIA World Factbook
	White Ethnic (HMAN-31)	(-,+)	CIA World Factbook
HAS-REPRESENTATIVE	Richard B. Cheney (GOVERNMENTAL-ROLE-91)	(-,+)	CIA World Factbook
	George W. Bush GOVERNMENTAL-ROLE-2)	(-,+)	CIA World Factbook
NATIONALITY-OF	Aaron Peirsol (ATHLETE-5178)	(-,+)	http://www.nbcolympics.com
			http://www.olympics.com
	Abdi Abdirahman (ATHLETE-11008)	(-,+)	http://www.nbcolympics.com
	Abdihakim Abdirahman	(-,+)	http://www.olympics.com

Figure 7.8
A partial view of the fact UNITED STATES OF AMERICA.

Table 7.10
Ontological concepts used in the onomasticon

Animate	Name of a living being (human, animal, plant, or imaginary character like *Zeus* or *Bucephalus*)
Organization	Name of an organization, real (e.g., *Toyota Corp., U.S. Senate, NATO, The U.S. Republican Party, Harvard University, McDonald's*) or imaginary (e.g., *RUR*)
Time period	Name of an event (e.g., *Christmas 2005*) or a period (e.g., *The Middle Ages*)
Geographical entity	Name of a geographical entity: river, valley, mountain, lake, sea, ocean, astronomical entity, and so on. May contain a common noun identifying some geographical feature contained within a geographical name, such as *valley, mount*, and so forth (*The Mississippi, The Mississippi River*)

7.4   The Onomasticon

Nouns can be common (*table, sincerity*) or proper (*World War II, Mr. Abernathy*). The common nouns are listed in the lexicon, where their meanings are typically explained in terms of the ontology. Proper nouns, or names, in ontological semantics are listed in the onomasticon, where their meanings are explained in terms of both the ontological categories to which they belong, and facts from the FR to which they refer. Each such fact is, by definition, an instance of an ontological concept. Therefore, entries in the onomasticon name instances—specific and unique objects and events, not their types. For example, a Toyota Corolla with a specific Indiana license plate is an instance. But Toyota Corolla is a class of all the instances of this particular model of this particular car make and as such is not listed in the onomasticon but rather in the ontology. However, *Toyota* will be listed in the onomasticon because it refers to the name of a unique corporation, say, CORPORATION-433, in the FR. Similarly, Passover 2000 is an instance of an event, while Passover is a concept.

In the CAMBIO/CREST implementation of ontological semantics, the phrasal entry *United States of America* is listed in the onomasticon as NATION and refers to FR element NATION-213. In the case of proper names, the extended TMR is obtained by including information about it from the FR, in addition to its ontological information. Thus, an input text might just mention the name (or alias, such as *USA* or *US of A*) of the phrase, but its extended TMR will include both information on NATION (see figure 7.7) and NATION-213 (figure 7.8).

Ontological concepts used in categorizing entries in the onomasticon are given in table 7.10.

CHAPTER 8

Basic Processing in Ontological Semantic Text Analysis

Text analysis is only one of the processes supported by ontological semantics, albeit a central one. An ontology replete with the representations of complex events and objects can also support reasoning in such applications as information extraction, question answering, and advice giving. The various applications differ in the measure in which text should be processed in them, from extended coverage in question answering to full coverage in MT to spot coverage in IE and summarization to, possibly, no text analysis in planning applications.

The proclaimed goal of ontological semantics as applied to text analysis is to input a text and output a formal expression that is declared to be its meaning representation. This process requires many diverse knowledge sources. This means that building ontological semantic analyzers and generators may take longer than NLP applications that use other methods. One must bear in mind, however, that no task that requires generation of representations can completely bypass the need for compiling extensive knowledge sources. Only when no representations are sought can modules even consider relying on purely corpus-based statistical methods as the backbone of processing (cf. section 2.6.2.1).

In this chapter, we present the process of text analysis in ontological semantics. We will remain at the conceptual level and will not go into the details and issues related to potential or actual implementations of these processes. In other words, for each process we will describe the task that it performs, as well as specifying its input and output data and the requirements this processing module imposes on static knowledge sources in the system, such as lexicons or the ontology. We will pay special attention to the issue of potential failure of every processing module and ways of recovering from such failures.

8.1 Preprocessing

While ontological semantics concentrates on issues of meaning, no serious NLP application can afford to avoid dealing with nonsemantic processing, such as

<!-- Yahoo TimeStamp: 950652115 -->
Tuesday February 15 5:01 PM ET
<title>'American Beauty' Leads Oscar Nods</title>
<h2>'American Beauty' Leads Oscar Nods</h2>
<!-- TextStart -->

<p><font size ="-1">By DAVID GERMAIN AP Entertainment Writer </font><p>BEVERLY HILLS, Calif. (AP) - The
Oscars embraced dysfunction and darkness Tuesday, bestowing a leading eight nominations on the suburban burlesque
"<a href="http://movies.yahoo.co/ shop?d=hv&cf=info&id=1800018623">American Beauty</a>" and honoring movies about
abortion, death row and the tormented souls of the dead.<p>The top nominees included "<a href="http://movies.yahoo.com/
shop?d=hv&cf=info&id=1800025331">The Cider House Rules</a>" set in a combination orphanage and abortion mill;
"<a href="http://movies.yahoo.com/shop?d=hv&cf=info&id=1800019665">The Sixth Sense</a>" about
a boy from a broken home who can see ghosts; and
"<a href="http://movies.yahoo.com/shop?d=hv&cf=info&id=1800025551">The Green Mile</a>" about the bonds between prison
guards and condemned men.<p>Those four movies, along with "<a href="http://movies.yahoo.com/
shop?d=hv&cf=info&id=1800025632">The Insider</a>" a film about a
tobacco industry whistle-blower, were nominated for best picture.<p>The top acting categories also were heavy on family dysfunction.<p>The best-actor candidates included
<a href="http://search.yahoo.com/bin/search?p=Kevin%20Spacey">Kevin Spacey</a> in "American
Beauty" as a dad who blackmails his boss, smokes pot with a neighbor kid and flirts with his daughter's
cheerleading friend.
<!-- TextEnd -->

Figure 8.1
A document with HTML encodings. Only a part of this material must be processed by an
NLP system.

morphology or syntax. The output of these modules provides input and background
knowledge to the semantic modules of any ontological semantic application.

8.1.1 Tokenization and Morphological Analysis

Input text comes in many guises: as plain text or as text with some kind of markup,
such as SGML, HTML, or XML (see figures 8.1 and 8.2). Text—for instance, some
newspaper headlines—may come in all caps. Some languages, like Chinese and Hebrew, do not make a distinction between capital and lowercase letters. Languages
vary in their use of punctuation; thus Spanish uses inverted exclamation marks at the
beginning of exclamatory sentences. Languages use different means of rendering
dates; alternatives include May 13, 2000, and the thirteenth of May, 2000. Usage
also varies with respect to numbers (for instance, Japanese breaks numbers into units
of 10,000 and not 1,000, like most European languages) as well as acronyms (e.g.,
pur for *pursuit*, *Mr.* for *Mister*, and *U.N.* for *United Nations*). An NLP system must
recognize all this material and present it in a standardized textual form. The module
responsible for this functionality is often called the *tokenizer*.

The next stage in preprocessing is morphological analysis of the results of tokenization. A morphological analyzer accepts a string of word forms as input and for
each word form outputs a record containing its citation form and a set of morphological features and their values that correspond to the word form from the text. (A

'American Beauty' Leads Oscar Nods

By DAVID GERMAIN AP Entertainment Writer

BEVERLY HILLS, Calif. (AP) - The Oscars embraced dysfunction and darkness Tuesday, bestowing a leading eight nominations on the suburban burlesque "American Beauty" and honoring movies about abortion, death row and the tormented souls of the dead.

The top nominees included "The Cider House Rules" set in a combination orphanage and abortion mill; "The Sixth Sense" about a boy from a broken home who can see ghosts; and "The Green Mile" about the bonds between prison guards and condemned men.

Those four movies, along with "The Insider" a film about a tobacco industry whistle-blower, were nominated for best picture. The top acting categories also were heavy on family dysfunction.

The best-actor candidates included Kevin Spacey in "American Beauty" as a dad who blackmails his boss, smokes pot with a neighbor kid and flirts with his daughter's cheerleading friend.

Figure 8.2
The text from figure 1.1 that will undergo NLP.

number of detailed descriptions of approaches to morphological analysis exist, e.g., Sproat 1992; Koskenniemi 1983; Sheremetyeva, Jin, and Nirenburg 1998; Megerdoomian 2000.)

Both the tokenizer and the morphological analyzer rely on static resources:

• "Ecological" rules for each language that support tokenization (one example of this would be to understand a sequence of a number followed by a period (.) in German as an ordinal numeral—for example, *2.* means *zweite*, "second")
• Morphological declension and conjugation paradigms (e.g., all the possible sets of forms of French verbs, indexed by the value of corresponding features), morphophonological information about stem alternations, and other types of knowledge needed to produce a record, such as {"*vendre*, Past Indefinite, Third Person, Singular"} from the word form *vendait*

As usual in NLP, there is no guarantee that the static knowledge sources are complete—in fact, one can practically guarantee that they will be incomplete at any given time! In addition, the set of processing rules can contain omissions, ambiguities, and errors. For example, the German tokenization rule above will fail when the symbol *2* is put at the end of a sentence. The rule will tokenize the input sequence *2.* as ⟨number-ordinal second⟩ while the correct tokenization may, in fact, be ⟨number: 2⟩ ⟨punctuation: period⟩.

Morphological analyzers often produce ambiguous results that cannot be disambiguated without some further, syntactic or even semantic processing. For instance, if the English string *books* is input to a morphological analyzer, it will correctly produce at least the following two variants: "book, Noun, Plural" and "book, Verb, Present, Third Person, Singular." Of course, there will also be errors due to the incompleteness of static knowledge; processing rules can be insufficiently general or, on the contrary, too generalizing. While unknown words (that is, words not in the system's lexicon) can be processed by some morphological analyzers, there is no protection against spelling errors (unless an interactive spell-checker is integrated in the system). This situation will bring additional problems at the lexical lookup stage.

Improvement of tokenization and morphological analysis is obtained through manual correction of the static resources as well as through the integration of additional tools, such as spell-checkers and methods for treating unexpected input (see section 8.4.3).

8.1.2 Lexical Lookup

Once the morphological analyzer has generated the citation forms for word forms in a text, the system can look them up in its lexicons, including the onomasticon for names, and thus activate the relevant lexical entries. These lexical entries contain, as the reader knows by now, a variety of types of information, including information concerning syntax and lexical semantics, but also morphology. The latter information is used to double-check and, if necessary, help to disambiguate the results of morphological analysis.

Lexical lookup can produce wrong results for misspellings and fail to produce results for both misspellings and bona fide words that are not in the lexicon. For example, many English texts may have Latin (*exeunt*), French (*frisson*), German (*Angst*), Spanish (*paella*), Italian (*dolce*), Russian (*perestroika*), and other words, not all of which would have been accepted as English words and therefore listed in a typical English lexicon. Still more problematic are proper names. Even if large onomasticons are built, one can be virtually certain that many names will not have been collected there. In some cases, there will be ambiguity between proper and common readings of words—the name *Faith*, when starting a sentence, will be ambiguous with the common reading of the word. Additional difficulties will be brought about by multiword lexical units, both set phrases (*there is*) and words with discontinuous components (*look up*). Conversely, some words are compound, spelled as a single word (*legroom*, *spatiotemporal*), or hyphenated (*well-known*). One cannot expect to find all of them in the lexicon. Indeed, listing all such entities in the lexicon may not be an option. If a word is not attested in the lexicon, one recovery procedure is to hypothesize that it is compound and to attempt to look up its components. However, at least for Swedish, as reported by Dura (1998), serious difficulties exist for automatic resolution of compounds, which means that the lexicons for Swedish (and, most probably, other compounding languages, such as Hungarian) will have to include the compounds, complicating lexical acquisition.

There are two basic ways of dealing with the failures of lexical lookup. First, a system may insist that all unknown words be checked manually and either corrected (if they were misspelled) or added to the lexicon. Second, a system of dealing with unknown words can be built that not only processes compounds but also carries out all the processing that is possible without knowing the stem or root of the word in question (for instance, guessing morphological features, often the part of speech and other syntactic properties but never the meaning). For example, in the Mikrokosmos implementation of ontological semantics, unknown words are treated very casually—all of them are assigned the part of speech Noun and their meaning is constrained trivially: they are declared to be children of the root ontological concept ALL, which amounts to saying that they carry no meaningful semantic constraints. Remarkably, even this simplistic treatment helps (see Beale, Viegas, and Nirenburg 1997 for details).

8.1.3   Syntactic Analysis

The task of syntactic analysis in ontological semantics is essentially to determine clause-level dependency structures for an input text and assign syntactic valency values to clause constituents (that is, establish subjects, direct objects, obliques, and adjuncts). Because it is expected that the results of syntactic analysis within ontological semantics will never constitute the final stage of text processing, it has an auxiliary status in the approach. One corollary is that in ontological semantics work on optimization of syntactic parsing is not a high priority.

At the same time, ontological semantics does not dismiss syntactic knowledge out of hand, as was done in early computational semantics (cf. Schank 1975; Wilks 1972). While those authors chose to concentrate on proving how far "pure" semantic approaches can take text analysis, we believe in basing text analysis on as much knowledge as it is possible to obtain, from whatever source. Syntactic analysis is supported by a syntactic grammar and syntax-related zones (SYN-STRUC; see section 7.2) of the lexicon entries. In addition, the ontological semantic lexicon supports syntax-to-semantics linking, mapping between syntactic valencies and semantic case roles.

Just as with other modules (and other syntactic-analysis systems), syntactic analysis can fail due to a lack of complete coverage or errors in either grammar or lexicon or both, resulting in inappropriate input-sentence chunking, incorrect syntactic dependencies, mislabeling of constituent heads, and outright failures to produce output. An additional reason for this latter eventuality may be the ill-formedness of an input text.

Besides, realistic grammars are typically ambiguous, leading to the production of multiple syntactic readings, in which case a special ranking function must be designed and built for selecting the best candidate. Fortunately, within ontological semantics, one can defer this process until after semantic analysis is underway—in many cases semantic constraints will impose enough preferences for the correct choice to be made. At no time will there be a declared goal of selecting the "most appropriate" syntactic reading for its own sake. The ultimate goal of ontological semantics is producing text-meaning representations using all available means. Semantic resources and processors are, naturally, a central component of such a system, and they should not be misused by applying them to determining the best out of a candidate set of syntactic readings of some input. Rather, they can be expected to help at least with some types of the above-mentioned failures.

Thus, example sentence (1), repeated below as (26), shows a syntactic irregularity in that the tense of *expect* should agree with that of *say* (the "sequence of tenses" rule in English) and be Past rather than Present. No syntactic repair will be necessary, however, because the semantic component of ontological semantics will not process *expects* as a tensed element but will assign its meaning to a timeless modality. In fact, one can probably speculate that this "deverbed" status of *expects* in the sentence allows for this syntactic laxness in the first place.

8.2   Building Basic Semantic Dependency

In chapter 7, we illustrated, on the example of (1), repeated here as (26), the basic processes involved in generating TMRs.

(26) Dresser Industries said it expects that major capital expenditure for expansion of U.S. manufacturing capacity will reduce imports from Japan.

The initial big step in semantic analysis is building basic semantic dependencies for the input text. Proceeding from the lexical, morphological, and syntactic information available after the preprocessing stage for a textual input, on the one hand, and an empty TMR template, on the other, we establish the propositional structure of the future TMR, determine the elements that will become heads of the TMR propositions, and fill out the property slots of the propositions by matching case-role inventories and selectional restrictions on sets of candidate fillers. In this section, we will follow the flowchart in figure 8.3 in describing the various processes involved in ontological semantic text analysis.

8.2.1   Establishing Propositional Structure

Example (26) contains three syntactic clauses. A syntactic clause generally corresponds to a TMR proposition. A TMR proposition is, most commonly, an instance of an event in the ontology. No TMR is well formed if it does not contain at least one proposition. A TMR proposition is represented essentially as a template that combines a specification of the basic semantic dependency structure consisting of a

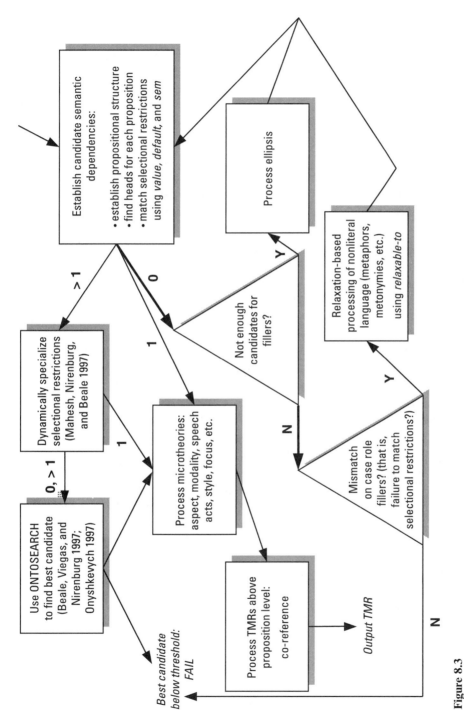

Figure 8.3
A schematic view of the processes involved in the semantic analysis of text in ontological semantics.

head and its properties as well as such parameterized meaning components as aspect, time, modality, style, and others. The boundary between parameterized and non-parameterized meaning will fluctuate with different implementations of ontological semantics. Different decisions concerning parameterization of meaning components will result in differences in the size and the content of the ontologies and lexicons involved (see section 6.3).

It might appear paradoxical, then, that the TMR for (26) involves six, not three propositions (see (18)). This means that no one-to-one correspondence exists between syntactic clauses and TMR propositions. There are six propositions in (26) because the SEM-STRUC zones of exactly six lexical entries contain ontological event instances. This is the simplest of the possible heuristics for establishing the propositional structure. In the case of (26), it was sufficient. As a result of the decision to establish six propositions, six propositional templates are instantiated in the TMR working space, with the heads of the propositions filled by the six event instances and the rest of the property slots yet unfilled. It would have been easier to formulate the above heuristic in morphosyntactic rather than ontological terms: that a proposition should be instantiated in the TMR working space for each verb in the source text. Unfortunately, there is no isomorphism between syntactic verbs and semantic event instances. Indeed, there are four verbs in (26)—*say*, *expect*, *manufacture*, and *reduce*—but they engender only three propositions because, in our definition of TMR, the meaning of *expect* is parametrical. The other three propositions are engendered by nouns in (26), namely, those whose semantics is described by event instances: *expenditure*, *expansion*, and *import*.

The choice of propositional structure can be complicated by the fact that some SEM-STRUCS can contain more than one event instance—for example, the lexicon entry for the English *fetch* contains GO and BRING. This lexicon entry will engender two propositions in the TMR. Fortunately, the routine (at least in English, where virtually every noun can convert to a verb, e.g., *book*, *table*, *floor*, and so on) ambiguity between word senses involving event instances and senses of the same word not involving them is not a problem for ontological semantic analysis, because this ambiguity is syntactic and is expected to be eliminated during preprocessing.

In practice, establishing propositional structure of natural language input proceeds by determining semantic dependencies among elements of input at different levels. Semantic dependencies are represented by having the dependent elements as fillers of slots in the governing elements. For example, OBJECT property values depend on OBJECT instances, OBJECT instances on EVENT instances in which they fill case roles, and so on.

Before the construction of such basic dependencies is attempted, the candidates for proposition headship are checked to ascertain whether their meanings are parametric—that is, whether they should be treated not as proposition heads but rather as values of aspect, time, modality, or other parameters inside the representation of propositions or TMRs. Once such parametric entities are accounted for, all remaining argument-taking entities are declared heads of TMR propositions. We expect that such remaining material will include event instances and, more seldom, object instances that cannot be claimed as fillers of any of the case roles of the event instances. When such "freestanding" object instances are present in nonelliptical contexts, they become heads of propositions. Syntactic predication may be present, as in (27), or absent, as in (28), but this difference will not influence ontological semantic representation. A special and interesting case is when syntactic predication is present but serves to mark coreference, as in (29).

(27) The car is blue.

(28) The blue car.

(29) My son John is a teacher.

Examples (27) and (28) get the same propositional structure, where the head of the proposition is the concept instance evoked by *car*, and BLUE is the (literal) filler of the property COLOR defined for CAR as a descendant of PHYSICAL-OBJECT. The difference in meaning between (27) and (28) is captured by the value of a parameter—the saliency modality—that is used in ontological semantics to deal with the phenomenon of focus, scoping over the filler of the property COLOR of the concept CAR in (30) and the entire instance of CAR in (31). Example (31) also illustrates how TMR treats existential quantification.

```
(30)
proposition
      head   CAR-i
             COLOR              blue
modality-j
      modality-type    saliency
      modality-scope   CAR-I.COLOR
      modality-value   1

(31)
proposition
      head   CAR-i
             COLOR              blue
modality-j
      modality-type    saliency
      modality-scope   CAR-i
      modality-value   1
```

The index *i* means the *i*th instance of the concept CAR in the TMR whose existence is posited. An object instance is assigned the head position in a TMR proposition as a stand-in in the absence of any event instances among the meanings of the clause constituents.[1] The corresponding rule for proposition head selection is, then, as follows: if one of exactly two open-class lexical entries in the input clause stands for an object and the other for its property, and there is no event involved, the object gets elevated to proposition headship.

The above procedure for finding heads of propositions effectively defines what is considered a proposition in the latest implementation of ontological semantics. Note that according to this definition, neither syntactic nor logical predication guarantees propositionhood. Thus, the difference between syntactically predicated (27) and unpredicated (28)—unless the latter is used elliptically—can be ignored in ontological semantics without any penalty. This would depend on the needs of a particular application of ontological semantics. For example, in a machine-translation application it may be considered important to retain in the target text the sentence boundaries of the source text; in this case, we will need to go through with the head-selection rules as illustrated above. However, in a variety of knowledge-management applications the rhetorical structure of the text is of much less importance; in these cases, one can avoid introducing separate propositions in the cases of absence of predicates provided the same object instance is mentioned in the text elsewhere as an argument of a predicate. Clearly, this requires facilities for reference resolution.

Both (27) and (28) can be treated as propositions if a text or an application licenses it. For instance, if a text introduces a parameter value not claimed by any other proposition, this will elevate the meaning of (28) to the status of a proposition. Thus, in *the car was blue* the necessity of assigning the TIME parameter ensures that the TMR representation of this sentence is a proposition. It may appear, at first sight, that in reality the propositionhood of the above example is due to the presence of syntactic predication expressed by the copula. While syntactic predication may be a sufficient condition for propositionhood, it is most certainly not a necessary one. In some languages, the above sentence will lack a copula and contain a lexicalized realization of the TIME parameter (e.g., *yesterday*).

Examples (27) and (28) illustrate that the much-touted distinction between predicative (27) and attributive (28) syntactic constructions in the linguistic literature on adjectives (see Raskin and Nirenburg 1995, 1998) loses its significance in ontological semantics. This phenomenon further corroborates our tenet that semantic distinctions are not isomorphic to syntactic distinctions (see section 4.2).

While syntactic predication often signals propositionhood in ontological semantic representations, its absence does not preclude it. In ontological semantics, the meaning of *The blue car is parked in the driveway* is identical to that of *The car is parked in the driveway. The car is blue.* It is quite possible that the exaggeration of the role of syntactic predication in establishing propositional structure is due to constraints imposed by the metalanguage of logic. Of course, it does not help either that most formal linguistic theories have been developed based on the material of languages, such as English, where complete sentences always expect predication to be expressed lexically (for comparison, Russian omits present tense copulas, so that *the car is blue* will be glossed as *car blue*). The meaning of (29) is represented as follows:

```
(32)
proposition
      head    TEACHER-m
proposition
      head    HAS-SON-k
                      domain *speaker*
                      range  HUMAN-j
                                    NAME John
modality-j
      modality-type   saliency
      modality-scope  TEACHER-m
      modality-value  1
coreference  HUMAN-j HUMAN-l TEACHER-m
```

Ontological description allows one to avoid introducing the separate concept TEACHER and makes it possible instead to always refer to it as the habitual agent of the event TEACH. Should such a decision be taken (and in the Mikrokosmos implementation of ontological semantics this was, in fact, not done; see section 7.1.5), the TMR would be as follows:

```
(33)
proposition
      head    TEACH-m
              aspect
                      iteration multiple
proposition
      head    HAS-SON-k
                      domain *speaker*
                      range  HUMAN-j
                                    NAME John
modality-j
      modality-type   saliency
      modality-scope  TEACH-m.AGENT
      modality-value  1
coreference  HUMAN-j TEACH-m.AGENT
```

where the values of the properties of the aspect parameter carry the meaning of habituality.

There is no event instance involved in (29). This is similar to (27) and (28). However, in (27) and (28) there is only one candidate for head. In the current case, there is no evidence in the input for selecting a single head from among the two OBJECT instances evoked by the words *teacher* and *John* or the relation instance evoked by the word *son*. Therefore, we posit that all three become heads of three (eventless) propositions, with the semantics of existential quantification. This outcome is predetermined by the fact that there is no way any one of the three elements can be "folded" into any other as a value of one of its properties—in contrast to the situation with events present, when instances of objects and relations are accounted for by filling the property slots of events, thus obviating the need to treat them as heads.

8.2.2 Matching Selectional Restrictions

The input to this stage of processing consists of the results of syntactic analysis of input and of the lexical lookup. For example, for sentence (34), the results of syntactic analysis are in (35), while the results of the lexical lookup relevant to semantic dependency building are summarized in (36). In the specification of the lexical entries, direct use is made of the ontological concepts. Example (37) illustrates the relevant properties of the concept we need to use in explaining the process of matching selectional restrictions.

(34) John makes tools.

```
(35)
root    manufacture
        cat             verb
        tense           present
        subject
                root            john
                cat             noun-proper
        object
                root            tool
                cat             noun
                number          plural
(36)
make-v1
        syn-struc
                root    make
                cat     v
```

```
                 subj    root    $var1
                         cat     n
                 object  root    $var2
                         cat     n
        sem-struc
                 MANUFACTURING-ACTIVITY
                         AGENT  value   ^$var1
                         THEME  value   ^$var2
John-n1
        syn-struc
                 root    john
                 cat     noun-proper
        sem-struc
                 HUMAN
                         NAME            value   john
                         GENDER          sem     male
tool-n1
        syn-struc
                 root    tool
                 cat     n
        sem-struc
                 TOOL
(37)
MANUFACTURING-ACTIVITY
...
        AGENT   sem   HUMAN
        THEME   sem   ARTIFACT
```

The lexicon entry for *make* establishes that the meaning of the syntactic subject of *make* is the main candidate to fill the AGENT slot in MANUFACTURING-ACTIVITY, while the meaning of the syntactic object of *make* is the main candidate to fill the THEME slot. The lexicon entry for *make* refers to the ontological concept MANUFACTURING-ACTIVITY without modifying any of its constraints in the lexicon entry. This states that the meaning of its subject should be constrained to any concept in the ontological subtree with the root at the concept HUMAN; and the meaning of its object, to an element of the ontological subtree rooted at ARTIFACT. These constraints are selectional restrictions, and the lexicon entries for *John* and *tool* satisfy them.

Because the meanings of *John* and *tool* have been found to be dependent on the meaning of *make* (or, more precisely, because MANUFACTURING-ACTIVITY was established as an argument-taking concept), the semantic analyzer establishes that the instance of the event MANUFACTURING-ACTIVITY, listed in the lexicon as the semantic representation of the first sense of *make*, must be considered as the head of the proposition. Because there is no other remaining material in the input, this is the only proposition.

Selectional restrictions in ontological semantics are used at all levels of building semantic dependencies—not just between predicates and their arguments but also between all the other pairs of governing and dependent elements in the input. In particular, adverbial meanings are folded into verbal (38) or adjectival (40) meanings, and meanings of nominal modifiers, including adjectives (39) and other nouns (41), are folded into those of the heads of noun phrases.

(38) John makes tools quickly.

(39) John makes expensive tools.

(40) John makes very expensive tools.

(41) John makes power tools.

Unlike in the case of predicate-argument selectional restrictions, where, as we could see, the input offers both syntactic and semantic clues for matching, in the case of other modifications, the system must often rely only on semantics in deciding to which of the properties of the governing concept it must add a filler corresponding to the semantics of the modifier. Thus, in (39) above, it is only the meaning of the adjective that makes it a candidate filler for the COST property of the concept TOOL. In *John makes large tools* the adjective will be connected on the property SIZE, while the syntax remains the same for both. Because meanings of nouns typically do not correspond to properties, in cases like (41), even this clue is not available. This is the reason the problem of nominal compounding is so confounding in English: *the IBM lecture* in (42) can mean a lecture given by IBM employees, a lecture sponsored by IBM, a lecture about IBM, a lecture given at IBM, as well as many other things. This means that in different contexts the connection of *IBM* to *lecture* occurs on different properties (cf., e.g., Finin 1980; Isabelle 1984).

(42) The IBM lecture will take place tomorrow at noon.

In such cases there are several courses of action for the system to take, all costly and error-prone. For example, the system can look for a prior co-occurrence of the meanings of *IBM* and *lecture* in the TMR, establish how they are connected, and use this knowledge in resolving the current occurrence. If an antecedent is found, information in it may serve to disambiguate the current input. Thus, the information in the first sentence of (43) weakly suggests that in the second sentence, *IBM* should be connected to *lecture* through the latter's LOCATION property. Of course, the heuristics for such disambiguation are error-prone, as, for instance, in the garden-path case of (44).

(43) John went to the IBM facility to give a lecture. The IBM lecture started at noon.

(44) IBM sponsored a series of lectures on early computer manufacturers. Naturally, the IBM lecture was the most interesting.

8.2.3   Multivalued Static Selectional Restrictions

If the above lexical entry for *make* is used, (45) will violate selectional constraints, in that gorillas are not humans and, according to the lexical and ontological definition above (see (36) and (37)), are unsuitable as fillers for the AGENT slot of MANUFACTURING-ACTIVITY.[2]

(45) The gorilla makes tools.

We know, however, that (45) is meaningful. To account for this, we must modify the knowledge sources. There are two ways this can be done. One could do this locally, in the lexicon entry for *make* in (36), by changing the filler for the AGENT property to PRIMATE. It is preferable, however, to initiate this modification in the ontological concept MANUFACTURING-ACTIVITY. An immediate reason for that is that a meaning modification such as the one suggested above ignores the fact that most tools are manufactured by people. Indeed, this is the reason why most people would assume that *John* in (38) refers to a human male. It was in order to capture this knowledge that we introduced the ontological facet DEFAULT (see section 7.1.1). The relevant part of the ontological concept MANUFACTURING-ACTIVITY should become as illustrated in (46) while the lexical entry for *make* remains unchanged—no matter that it actually means a slightly different thing now.

```
(46)
MANUFACTURING-ACTIVITY
      ...
      AGENT       default HUMAN
                  sem     PRIMATE
      ...
```

The semantic analyzer first attempts to match inputs against the fillers of the DEFAULT facet and, if this fails, against those of the SEM facet. If it succeeds, then the task of basic semantic dependency building is completed, and the system proceeds to establish the values of other components of TMRs (see sections 6.2 through 6.5). Success in building basic semantic dependencies means that there remains, after the application of basic selectional restrictions, exactly one candidate word or phrase sense for every open-class input word or phrase used in specifying the semantic dependency. In other words, it means that the word-sense disambiguation process for the propositional part of the analysis has been successful.

Two more outcomes are possible in this situation: first, the basic procedure that applies selectional restrictions does not result in a single answer but rather returns more than one candidate word or phrase sense; second, none of the candidate senses of a word or phrase match the selectional restrictions, and the basic procedure of applying selectional restrictions returns no candidate senses for some words or phrases.

In both cases, the first remedy that comes to mind is to try to modify the selectional restrictions on the various senses so that a match occurs, and to do this in such a way as to minimize the overall amount of modification to the static knowledge. Such dynamic adaptation of selectional restrictions has not, to our knowledge, been proposed before. It is discussed in some detail below (section 8.3.1).

An important methodological note is appropriate here. The many approaches to analysis using selectional restrictions imply the availability of ideal lexicons and other resources. Since discussions of selectional restrictions are usually centered around one example, such as *The man hit the colorful ball* in Katz and Fodor 1963, all that they require is to develop only a small fraction of the lexicon, and the constant temptation is to make the example work by presenting the senses exactly as needed for the example. If such discussions aimed at any significant coverage of the lexicon (see sections 4.1 and 4.4), they would encounter serious practical difficulties having to do with the limitations and inaccuracies of resources, with complex trade-offs in the decisions taken while specifying different lexical entries and elements of their representations, and with maintaining consistency in the grain size of descriptions (see section 9.3.6). As a result of these difficulties, the descriptions created for the purpose of illustrating a few selectional restrictions will often fail when facing new selectional restrictions, for which they were not intended in the first place. In other words, the descriptions created for isolated examples are ad hoc and likely to fail when significant coverage becomes a factor, which is always the case in practical applications. The goal of practical word-sense disambiguation, then, is to eliminate as many inappropriate word senses in running text as possible, *given a particular set of static knowledge sources.*

The most common practical methods for resolving word-sense ambiguities are based on statistical collocations (e.g., Gale et al. 1992; Yarowsky 1992, 1995) or selectional restrictions between pairs of word senses. Of these two, the former is necessary when the method for word-sense disambiguation does not rely on meaning representation (see section 2.6.2.1) and extraction. Selectional restrictions provide stronger disambiguation power and, therefore, ontological semantics concentrates on selectional restrictions as the main disambiguation knowledge source, additionally so because we have acquired a source of selectional-restriction knowledge of nontrivial size, namely, the ontology and lexicon complex.

However, neither a static ontology nor a static lexicon helps to achieve good disambiguation results all by itself. The real power of word-sense selection lies in the ability to tighten or relax the semantic constraints on senses of a lexeme, or superentry, on the basis of choices made by a semantic analyzer for other words in the dynamic context. In other words, the selectional restrictions are not taken from the static knowledge sources directly but rather are calculated by the dynamic knowledge sources on the basis of both the existing static selectional restrictions and the interim results of semantic processing. Moreover, the resulting selectional restrictions are not recorded in the static knowledge sources, at least not until a method is developed for economically recording, prioritizing, and indexing the entire fleeting textual and conceptual context for which they have been generated.

One often hears that context is crucial for semantic analysis. It is exactly in the above sense that one can operationalize this rather broad statement to make it practically applicable. Very few nontoy experiments have been carried out to investigate how this might be done in practice and on a realistic scale. Ontological semantics can be said to aspire to make realistic operational use of the notion of textual and conceptual context. We argue that:

· Individual constraints between the head of a proposition and each of its arguments typically available in static knowledge sources (lexicons) are often not strong enough or too strong for effective selection of word senses.
· In addition to traditional selectional restrictions that check constraints between proposition heads and their semantic arguments, knowledge of constraints and conceptual relationships among the arguments of a proposition is critical because it is often not possible to determine a diagnostic context statically—that is, before any decisions are made for the current sentence.
· Effective sense disambiguation is helped by the availability of rich knowledge with a high degree of cross-dependence among knowledge elements.
· While representations such as semantic networks (including both simple labeled hierarchies, e.g., SENSUS (Knight and Luk 1994) and ontological concept networks (e.g., the Mikrokosmos ontology (Mahesh 1996; Mahesh and Nirenburg 1995)) can capture such constraints and relationships, processing methods currently applied to semantic networks such as marker passing (e.g., Charniak 1983a, 1986) and spreading activation (e.g., Waltz and Pollack 1985) do not facilitate selection of word senses based on dynamic context.
· Marker passing and spreading activation are effective on well-designed and sparse networks but become less and less effective as the degree of connectivity increases (for details, see Mahesh, Nirenburg, and Beale 1997; Mahesh et al. 1997).

8.3   When Basic Procedure Returns More Than a Single Answer

When the basic selectional-restriction matching procedure returns more than a single candidate for each lexeme in the input, this means that the process of word-sense disambiguation is not complete. The reason for that in this case is that the selectional restrictions are too loose. Additional processing is needed to bring the set of candidate word or phrase senses down to exactly one candidate for each lexeme—that is, to tighten the restrictions.

8.3.1 Dynamic Tightening of Selectional Restrictions

We will now demonstrate how dynamic tightening of selectional restrictions helps to resolve residual ambiguities. We will do this using the results of an experiment run in the framework of the Mikrokosmos implementation of ontological semantics, with the static and dynamic knowledge sources at a particular stage of their development (see Mahesh, Nirenburg, and Beale 1997 for the original report).

Let us consider the sentence *John prepared a cake with the range*. Leaving aside, for the sake of simplicity, the PP-attachment ambiguity, let us concentrate on lexical disambiguation. In this sentence, several words are ambiguous, relative to the static knowledge sources. The lexical entry for *prepared* contains two senses, one related to the ontological concept PREPARE-FOOD, and the other, to PREPARE-DOCUMENT. The lexical entry for *range* has a number of different senses, referring to a mathematical range, a mountain range, a shooting range, a livestock grazing range, as well as to a cooking device. In the latter sense, *range* can be related either to the ontological concept OVEN or the ontological concept STOVE. The lexical entry for *cake* is unambiguous: it has the ontological concept CAKE as the basis of its meaning specification. However, the ontological concept CAKE has two parents, BAKED-FOOD and DESSERT. The entry for *John* is found in the onomasticon and unambiguously recognized as a man's name. The entry for *with* establishes the type of relation on which the appropriate sense of *range* is connected to the appropriate sense of *prepare*. The possibilities include AGENT, with the filler that is a set (*Bill wrote the paper with Jim*), and INSTRUMENT (*Bill opened the door with a key*). The meanings of *a* and *the* will have "fired" in the process of syntactic analysis (see, however, section 8.5.3 on additional meanings of the English articles related to the saliency modality).

After the sentence is analyzed according to the procedure illustrated in detail in chapter 7, it will be determined that the meaning of *prepare* will become the head of the proposition describing the meaning of this sentence. The selectional restriction on *prepare* in the sense of PREPARE-FOOD matches the candidate constraint provided by the meaning of its direct object *cake*, while the selectional restriction on *prepare* in the sense of PREPARE-DOCUMENT does not. This disambiguates *prepare* using only static selectional restrictions. *John*, in fact, matches either of the senses of *prepare*. So, while this word does not contribute to the disambiguation of *prepare*, at least it does not hinder it.

Next, we establish that the correct sense of *with* is the one related to INSTRUMENT rather than AGENT because none of the senses of *range* are related to concepts that

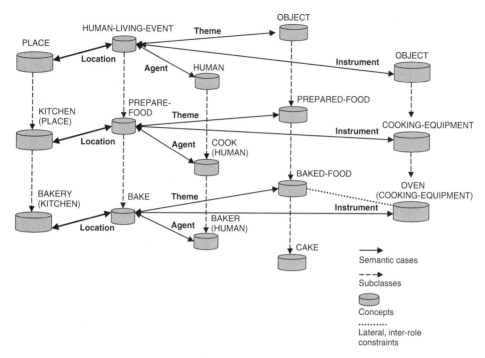

Figure 8.4
A fragment of the ontology showing main properties and constraints for PREPARE-FOOD. The properties are marked on arrows, their values marked on the circles representing concepts. The values in parentheses refer to those in SEM facets, whereas the rest of the values denote the fillers of DEFAULT facets.

are descendants of HUMAN, which is a requirement for being AGENT of PREPARE-FOOD. At this point, we can exclude all those senses of *range* that are not compatible with the remaining sense of *with*, namely, all but the two kitchen-related ones, whose meanings are related to STOVE and OVEN. Static selectional restrictions already disambiguated everything but the remaining two senses of *range*. No static selectional restrictions are available in the lexicon to help us complete the disambiguation process. We are now at the main point of our example, namely, a demonstration of the utility of dynamic selectional restrictions.

As shown in figure 8.4 (cf. Mahesh, Nirenburg, and Beale 1997), the ontological concept PREPARE-FOOD has PREPARED-FOOD as its THEME; COOK as its DEFAULT AGENT (and HUMAN as its SEM AGENT); and COOKING-EQUIPMENT as its INSTRUMENT. PREPARED-FOOD has many descendants, including BAKED-FOOD, which, in turn, has many descendants, one of which is CAKE, the ontological concept defining the meaning of the English *cake* (or, for that matter, Russian *pirog* or Hebrew *uga*).

The last remaining task for disambiguation is to choose either OVEN or STOVE (signaled in the input by the corresponding word senses of *range*) as the INSTRUMENT of the proposition head PREPARE-FOOD. Without context, this determination is not possible. However, once it is known that the THEME of this instance of PREPARE-FOOD is CAKE, a dynamic selectional restriction can be computed to make the choice. Because CAKE IS-A BAKED-FOOD, it also meets the selectional restriction on the theme of *bake*. BAKED-FOOD is the THEME of BAKE, a direct descendant of PREPARE-FOOD, whose INSTRUMENT is constrained to OVEN but not STOVE. To make this disambiguation, we must, for the given context, specify PREPARE-FOOD as BAKE. In other words, we successfully dynamically apply the tighter selectional restriction on the INSTRUMENT of BAKE instead of whatever restriction is stated for the INSTRUMENT of PREPARE-FOOD. See figure 8.5 for an illustration of this process.

An important point is that *bake* was not explicitly mentioned in the sentence. Nevertheless, once CAKE is determined to be a kind of BAKED-FOOD, the processor should be able to infer that the meaning of *prepared* should be, in this context, analyzed as BAKE since that is the only descendant of PREPARE-FOOD that takes BAKED-FOOD as THEME. This information is used by the procedure that computes dynamic selectional restrictions only after it is determined that the meaning of *cake* refers to BAKED-FOOD by virtue of CAKE being a descendant of BAKED-FOOD. Once this dynamic context is inferred, the selectional restriction is tightened.

The dynamic selectional restriction is necessary because one cannot realistically expect an English lexicon to contain a static selectional constraint associated with the INSTRUMENT role of PREPARE-FOOD that enables the system to distinguish between OVEN and STOVE, both direct ontological descendants of COOKING-EQUIPMENT, because any kind of cooking equipment can be an instrument of preparing food. Processing dynamic selectional restrictions is not a simple operation. Is it possible either to avoid it or at least to record its successful results in some way so that the next time a similar situation occurs, there would be no need to compute the restriction dynamically again?

One way of recording this information is to introduce yet another kind of selectional restriction—the interrole *lateral* selectional restriction, which is not anchored at the head of a proposition but holds between two properties of the proposition head. Some lateral selectional restrictions, including the one between BAKED-FOOD and OVEN, are marked in figures 8.4 and 8.5 with a dotted line. There is, of course, an alternative way that allows one to avoid introducing a new type of selectional restriction. The failure of dynamic selectional restrictions could trigger a request to add to the ontology a direct descendant of a concept that will have the needed, tighter, selectional restrictions. In other words, if BAKE were not already in the ontology and the English *range* required the disambiguation between OVEN and STOVE, this could trigger a request to add to the ontology a direct descendant of PREPARE-FOOD with the

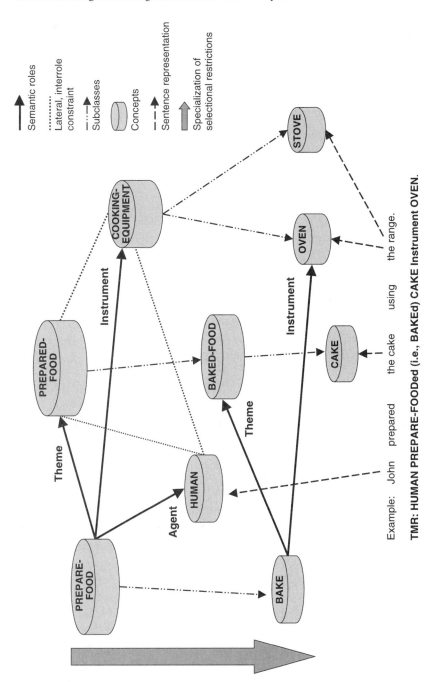

Figure 8.5
Dynamic selectional restrictions in action. Specialization is needed, since checking selectional restrictions on PREPARE-FOOD retains the ambiguity between OVEN and STOVE, while the restrictions on BAKE lead to the desired disambiguation.

INSTRUMENT value of OVEN and the value of THEME, CAKE. In fact, there will be additional values in the various case roles of BAKE, but the above will "seed" the process of acquiring this concept.

It is reasonably clear that adding descendants to ontological concepts and recording lateral selectional restrictions in the ontology are different methods for doing essentially the same thing. At the same time, trying to avoid the processing of dynamic selectional restrictions by fixing the ontology statically involves the familiar time-space trade-off: if the information is not recorded, it will need to be computed every time a need arises. We also noted elsewhere (see sections 5.3.1 and 5.3.2) that the occurrence in the input of a word with a specific type of ambiguity should not necessarily add concepts to the ontology.

Obviously, for a given time-stamped ontology and lexicons, neither the appropriate descendants nor lateral selectional restrictions can be expected to be available for every input. In fact, NLP systems that depend on always having such information have not been successful in domain-independent word-sense disambiguation because there is no way to establish the necessary grain size of description a priori and, therefore, any realistic NLP system must expect unattested elements in its input and have a means of processing them (see also section 8.4.3).

One must assume that knowledge sources for NLP are always incomplete and inaccurate, due to limitations of all acquisition methods as well as to unavoidable errors, including errors in judgment about grain size of description or a particular form that the description takes (see a discussion of synonymy in TMRs in section 6.6). Our example showed how contextual processing, realized through dynamic selectional restrictions, helps to resolve the ambiguity even in the absence of complete background knowledge (such as a direct lateral selectional restriction between OVEN and BAKED-FOOD).

Our example described a successful application of dynamic selectional restrictions. The reason for success was the presence of BAKE, which featured appropriately tight selectional restrictions, among the descendants of PREPARE-FOOD. Had BAKE not been available, the system would not have given up, though it would have taken a different route to the solution. This alternative solution would fail to resolve the ambiguity of *range* between OVEN and STOVE; it would accept this loss and fill the property of instrument for PREPARE-FOOD with the lowest common ancestor for OVEN and STOVE, namely, COOKING-EQUIPMENT. For many practical applications, this is an acceptable solution if, to put it plainly, the ambiguity is not important either for the text or for the application. The former means that this information is accidental and not elaborated on. This usually indicates that the corresponding concept instance is not likely either to be in the scope of a high-valued saliency modality filler in any proposition or to recur in many propositions in the TMR. An information item would not be important for a particular application if, for example, in MT, its translation is not ambiguous or there is no mismatch (e.g., Dorr 1994; Viegas 1997) between the source and target language on this word or phrase. In IE, importance can be judged by whether an information element is expected to be a part of the filler of an IE template slot.

Note that the main computational problem we are dealing with while trying to resolve the lexical ambiguity of *range* is one of controlling the search for appropriate constraints, not the correctness of propagating those constraints that are already available from the static knowledge sources. Do we need to devise our own procedure for this purpose, or can such well-known computational methods as marker passing or spreading activation also accomplish this task? The answer depends on whether one can expect to solve this problem by using only heuristics based on the topology of the network, or also include the knowledge stored in the network. Marker passing and spreading activation, in their pure form, are too weak to guarantee that a selected context is the right one given all available knowledge. This is because these methods are adversely influenced by uninterpreted topological knowledge in the network that is not relevant to the current context. They do not reach into the semantics of the nodes and links.

As argued in detail in Mahesh, Nirenburg, and Beale 1997, in the case of marker passing, there may be paths of lengths equal or shorter than the one at which the procedure should aim, though not going through nodes in the desired context, such as BAKE. In figure 8.4, for example, there is an alternative path from BAKED-FOOD to PREPARE-FOOD via PREPARED-FOOD, not via BAKE. This path consists of a THEME segment and an IS-A (SUBCLASS) segment, like the one going through BAKE. Thus, any choice in a marker-passing algorithm will be hampered, because these two paths are equally preferable in this approach.

Let us follow the standard marker-passing procedure in our example. The following nodes become the origins for marker passing: HUMAN, PREPARE-FOOD, the ontological concepts representing the other senses of *prepare*, the ontological concepts BAKED-FOOD, OVEN, STOVE, and the ontological concepts representing the other senses of *range*. The goal of marker passing is to find the shortest path between each pair of origins. In pure marker passing, there are no weights on links; they carry a unit cost. Some candidates for shortest paths are illustrated in figure 8.6. It is clear from the figure that COOKING-EQUIPMENT and PREPARED-FOOD are strong intermediate nodes that could be chosen as elements of the path selected by the marker-passing algorithm. BAKE might lose against these two and if so, the path from OVEN to BAKED-FOOD via BAKE may be rejected and the competing path via PREPARED-FOOD selected in order to maximize measures such as the total number of shared nodes among the selected paths. As a result, OVEN and STOVE turn out to be equally likely. Although BAKE had created a shorter path between OVEN and BAKED-FOOD than between STOVE and BAKED-FOOD, other parts of the network had an undue advantage over BAKE as a

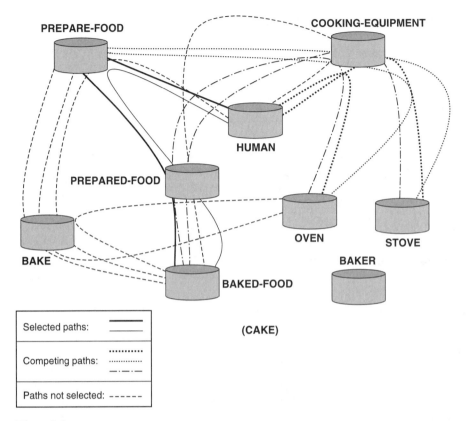

Figure 8.6
Shortest-path candidates for pure marker passing in the semantic network for the example sentences.

result of the above well-intentioned heuristics. In this situation, it is only by luck that OVEN might get selected, or even that the heuristics would discriminate between competing word senses sufficiently for any selection to take place at all.

We illustrated a small fragment of a conceptual network, with only a few types of available links listed. Any realistic model will have a much larger network with many other types of links between concepts, further decreasing the chances that the desired path through BAKE will be the least-cost path in the context of a sentence such as the one above. Moreover, these networks are almost always hand coded and may include spurious links that eventually bypass certain desired paths. Processing mechanisms such as marker passing and spreading activation are simple and have a cognitive appeal, but their lack of reference to the content of the nodes makes them too weak for making the kinds of inferences needed for effective word-sense disambiguation.

Our basic disambiguation method checks selectional constraints exhaustively, examining all the pairwise constraints on all word senses in a sentence, encoded statically in the ontological network or in the lexicon, using a very efficient search mechanism, called Hunter-Gatherer, based on constraint satisfaction, branch-and-bound, and solution-synthesis methods (Beale, Nirenburg, and Mahesh 1995; Beale 1997). To augment this method to process dynamic selectional restrictions, we introduce the *context specialization operator* (CSO) with the following content:

If a sense *P* is selected for a word *w*, and the rest of the word senses in the environment satisfy the constraints on *P*, examine the constraints on children of *P*; if exactly one child *C* of *P* satisfies the constraints, then infer that the correct sense of *w* is *C*; apply the constraints on *C* to other words.

The semantic analyzer checks selectional restrictions and applies the CSO iteratively, thereby resolving word-sense ambiguities successively. Using the notion of CSO, the processing of our example sentence can be described as follows: CAKE is first determined to be a kind of BAKED-FOOD. Then, using this information, *prepared* is disambiguated to PREPARE-FOOD. Applying the CSO at this point shows that BAKE is the only ontological descendant of PREPARE-FOOD that satisfies the selectional restriction that the THEME must be BAKED-FOOD and the INSTRUMENT, one of the senses of *range*. Hence BAKE is included in the dynamic context—that is, the selectional restrictions have been dynamically tightened from those in PREPARE-FOOD to those in BAKE, and the latter's constraints are applied to *range*, thereby excluding STOVE and selecting OVEN.

The methods outlined above were implemented for semantic analysis in a Spanish-English MT system based on the Mikrokosmos implementation of ontological semantics. The system employed an ontology represented as a network of 5,000 concepts, where each node had an average connectivity of 16. A Spanish lexicon of about 37,000 word senses mapped them to nodes in this network.

It is certainly possible to fine-tune the ontological network or introduce and manipulate weights on the links to obtain the selection of OVEN over STOVE without resorting to dynamic selectional restrictions. However, such an approach does not guarantee that desired results will be obtained for inputs outside training corpora. Moreover, such fine-tuning invariably has a catastrophic effect on processing other inputs. For example, if we fixed the network so that OVEN were somehow closer to BAKED-FOOD than STOVE, then OVEN would be selected even in an example such as *John ate the cake on the range*. There is, in fact, no information in this sentence that leads to a preference for either the STOVE or the OVEN sense of *range*. In general, these difficulties boil down to the following simple observation: any method that is oriented essentially toward manipulating uninterpreted strings does not have—and cannot be realistically expected to have—a sufficient amount of disambiguating heuristics for the task of text processing.

Statistical methods based on sense-tagged corpus analysis are subject to the same limitations as the network search methods. In a sufficiently general corpus, ample collocations of word senses may lead to irrelevant interference in sense disambiguation. For example, a high degree of collocation between the phrases *baked food* or *baked foods* or *bakery products*, on the one hand, and *oven*, on the other, helps to select the right sense of *range* in the the example sentence. But just as with marker passing, the same statistical preference can mislead the processor into selecting the OVEN sense of *range* in *John ate the cake on the range*.

In general, any of the above disambiguating procedures, including those using dynamic selectional restrictions, may fail not because of their own faults but because the input is genuinely ambiguous.

8.3.2   When All Else Goes Wrong: Comparing Distances in Ontological Space

When the procedure for applying dynamic selectional restrictions fails and the alternative solutions for some reason do not work either—for instance, because the lowest common ancestor of the candidate fillers for a property is judged too general—we can apply a technique that uses the ontology as a search space to find weighted distances between pairs of ontological concepts and thus to establish preferences for choice. Such a method, called Ontosearch, was developed in ontological semantics (Onyshkevych 1997) and applied in the Mikrokosmos implementation of ontological semantics (Mahesh, Nirenburg, and Beale 1997; Mahesh et al. 1997).

Ontosearch is different from the standard marker-passing and spreading activation techniques in that it uses the semantics of links and nodes in the ontological networks. This method is also different from the procedure for applying selectional restrictions. The latter consists in simply determining that the candidate for filling a property slot in an ontological concept instance is a descendant of the ontological concept listed as a constraint there. Ontosearch undertakes to establish the weighted distance between the constraint and the candidate not only along the hierarchical (IS-A) backbone of the ontological network but following any and all links from every node—the node where the constraint originates (the constraint node), the candidate node, and each of the intermediate nodes. Controlled constraint satisfaction in Ontosearch is managed by considering all relations and levying a cost for traversing any relations other than IS-A. The ontology is treated as a directed (possibly cyclic) graph, with concepts as nodes and relations as arcs. Constraint satisfaction consists in finding the cheapest path between the candidate concept node and the constraint nodes.

The cost assessed for traversing an arc may be dependent on the previous arcs traversed in a candidate path, because some arc types should not be repeatedly traversed, while other arcs should not be traversed if certain other arcs have already been seen. Ontosearch uses a state transition table to assess the appropriate cost for traversing an arc (based on the current path state) and to assign the next state for each candidate path being considered. The weight assignment transition table has about 40 states, and has individual treatment for 40 types of arcs; the other arcs (out of the nearly 300 total property types available in the ontology at the time when Ontosearch was first introduced) are treated by a default arc-cost determination mechanism.

The weights that are in the transition table are critical to the success of the method. An automatic training method has been used to train them (see Onyshkevych 1997). After building a training set of inputs (candidate fillers and constraints) and desired outputs (the "correct" paths over the ontology—that is, the preferred relation), Ontosearch used a simulated annealing numerical optimization method (Kirkpatrick, Gelatt, and Vecchi 1983; Metropolis et al. 1953) for identifying the set of arc costs that resulted in the optimal set of solutions for the training data. A similar approach is used to optimize the arc costs so that the cheapest cost reflects the preferred word sense from a set of candidates.

Let us walk through a simple example of the operation of Ontosearch. Suppose the ontological semantic analyzer is processing the following sentence: *El grupo Roche, a través de su compañía en España, adquirió el laboratorio farmacéutico Dr. Andreu, se informó hoy aquí*, "It was reported here today that the Roche Group, through its subsidiary in Spain, has acquired the pharmaceutical laboratory Dr. Andreu." We will concentrate on resolving just two potential ambiguities in this sentence. It is marginally possible to translate *adquirió* as *learned* in addition to the more common translation *acquired*. *Dr. Andreu* can be understood to refer to a company or to a person. Throughout the analysis, we assume that the static or dynamic selectional restrictions have not succeeded in disambiguating these cases.

A fragment of the ontological network used by Ontosearch to resolve the above ambiguities is illustrated in figure 8.7. After the Ontosearch procedure has finished its operation, it has assigned the values for quality of transitions to the individual arcs (the higher the value, the more preferable the transition). In the figure, we can see that (a) ORGANIZATION (which is the conceptual basis of the meaning of *the Roche Group*) is a better candidate to fill the AGENT property of LEARN than of ACQUIRE, (b) there is no penalty for having ORGANIZATION (the conceptual basis for one of the meanings of *Dr. Andreu*) fill the THEME of ACQUIRE, and (c) the somewhat awkward meaning of "learning an organization" represented by the path between LEARN and the ORGANIZATION sense of *Dr. Andreu* is penalized. The overall preferred path is the one highlighted in bold in the figure. Incidentally, "learning a person" gets the same penalty as "learning an organization," while "acquiring a person" is simply prohibited in our ontological model of the world (see section 7.1.2).

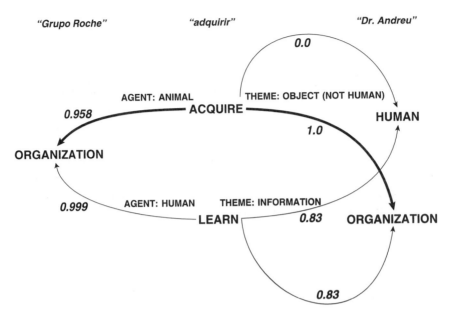

Figure 8.7
Applying the general calculation of ontological distances for lexical disambiguation.

8.4 When Basic Procedure Returns No Answer

In the previous section, we considered the situation when the static selectional restrictions recorded in the lexicons and the ontology select more than one candidate from among the word senses of a word for each property of the proposition head. That introduces indeterminacy and a need for further disambiguation. In this section, we are considering the opposite situation—when a selectional restriction fails to find any candidate for filling the value of a property. There can be two reasons for such a contingency: the candidate lexeme is available in the lexicon but has no sense that matches the selectional restriction, or there is no recognizable candidate in the input on which a match attempt could be made. The former case involves either what is known in the philosophy literature as sortal incongruity, or incorrectness (e.g., Thomason 1972) or the use of nonliteral language. There are also two possible reasons for a candidate being unavailable: ellipsis or the presence of unattested words or phrases in the input.

8.4.1 Relaxation of Selectional Restrictions

We are already familiar with the use of the facets DEFAULT and SEM (see sections 6.2 and 7.1.1). Thus, for instance, PREPARE-FOOD has COOK as the value of its AGENT property on the DEFAULT facet and HUMAN on the SEM facet. Unlike in example (45), the use of GORILLA as a candidate for the filler of AGENT of PREPARE-FOOD cannot be accommodated by the constraint in the SEM facet: all primates make tools but not all primates cook. Nevertheless, the sentence *The gorilla cooked dinner* can be given an interpretation by using the facet RELAXABLE-TO on the AGENT property of PREPARE-FOOD.

This facet is the main resource for dealing with the case when no sense of an available lexeme matches a selectional restriction. The sentence *The baby ate a piece of paper* illustrates a typical case of sortal incongruity: in ontological semantics, this is reflected in the fact that INGEST, the ontological basis of the meaning of *eat*, requires a descendant of EDIBLE as a filler of its THEME. PAPER is not a descendant of EDIBLE; it is a descendant of MATERIAL. The facet RELAXABLE-TO ensures that this meaningful sentence obtains its interpretation.

8.4.2 Processing Nonliteral Language

A similar relaxation technique is used to accommodate nonliteral language. Nonliteral language is understood in ontological semantics as having lexemes carry derivable but unrecorded senses. For example, in the sentence *The pianist played Bach*, the selectional restriction on the SEM facet of the THEME property of PLAY-MUSICAL-INSTRUMENT, the concept on which the appropriate meaning of *play* is based, is MUSIC-COMPOSITION, which is the basis for specifying the meaning of such English words as *sonata, concerto, symphony*, and so on. The entry for *Bach* in the onomasticon characterizes it as HUMAN. The discrepancy in the selectional restriction is due to fact that the filler of the theme property is realized as a standard metonymy of the "author for creation" type. In the case of metonymy, the same simple treatment that we used for the case of sortal incongruity will not work.

The difference between treating sortal incongruity and metonymy is that in the former case the analyzer, after establishing a match between the candidate filler concept and the selectional restriction on the RELAXABLE-TO facet for a property, directly fills the corresponding slot of the TMR concept with an instance of this same candidate filler concept. In the case of metonymy, the match takes place similarly to the above case, but what becomes the filler of the property in TMR is the instance of a different concept. This concept, the expansion of the metonymy, cannot be derived dynamically in the current microtheory of nonliteral language processing used in ontological semantics. Until and unless such a theory becomes available (and it is not at all clear whether such a theory is, in fact, feasible—see Fass 1991; Barnden et al. 1994; Onyshkevych and Nirenburg 1994; Beale, Viegas, and Nirenburg 1997), a stopgap measure is to directly list the expansions of metonymies in the static selectional restrictions, namely, in the RELAXABLE-TO slots of corresponding properties.

The facet RELAXABLE-TO, when used for treating nonliteral language, will necessitate a modification to the format of ontological specification beyond the level in
extant implementations of ontological semantics. When applied to the THEME of
PLAY-MUSICAL-INSTRUMENT, in order to account for metonymies such as that in *The
pianist played Bach*, the RELAXABLE-TO facet will have to refer to both the literal
interpretation that will be needed for matching the input and the expansion that is
needed to include the appropriate meaning in the TMR:

```
PLAY-MUSICAL-INSTRUMENT
...
    THEME   sem                MUSICAL-COMPOSITION
            relaxable-to  match    HUMAN-1
                                   AGENT-OF  COMPOSE-MUSIC
                          expansion MUSICAL-COMPOSITION
                                   AUTHORED-BY value HUMAN-1.NAME
```

The analyzer will fail to match the SEM selectional restriction and will proceed to the
RELAXABLE-TO one. Here it will make a match on the value HUMAN and proceed to
instantiate the concept MUSICAL-COMPOSITION with its COMPOSED-BY property filled by
the same-named instance of HUMAN (marked as coindexical in the ontological specification of PLAY-MUSICAL-INSTRUMENT). The property COMPOSED-BY has as its domain
LITERARY-COMPOSITION, in addition to MUSICAL-COMPOSITION.

The ontological semantic analyzer will carry out more work on the sentence *The
pianist played Bach* than described above. This is because the English *play* has another sense, the one related to sports. It is represented using the ontological concept
SPORTS-ACTIVITY, the AGENT property of which (the meanings of both the subject
and the direct object of *play* will be connected on the AGENT property of the concept
SPORTS-ACTIVITY) has the selectional restriction that matches HUMAN, among other
concepts—for example, TEAM. The analyzer will prefer the musical reading of the
sentence because the default value of AGENT of PLAY-MUSICAL-INSTRUMENT will be
matched by the meaning of *pianist*, namely, MUSICIAN, while the latter will not be a
DEFAULT value of AGENT for the SPORTS-ACTIVITY sense of *play* (it will match the
SEM facet). This underscores, again, the general rule that DEFAULT constraints have
priority over SEM constraints, which, in turn, are preferred to the RELAXABLE-TO constraints. Let us not forget that, as always, this analysis may be overturned by text-
level context.

If the example sentence is followed in a text, as in the well-known joke, by *Bach
lost*, the analyzer will have to dynamically revise the preferences derived during the
processing of the first sentence due to the requirements of text coherence (captured in
ontological semantics, still only partially in the extant implementations, through dis-

course relations in TMRs—see section 8.6.3). The second sentence makes sense only if the overall context is sports. The analyzer (possibly, in a simplification) follows the rule that a text belongs to a single conceptual context or domain (cf. Gale, Church, and Yarowsky 1992 about one sense per discourse). This rule is triggered in this example because the second sentence is elliptical (see section 8.4.4 for the ontological semantics take on ellipsis processing), and for elliptical sentences there is a strong expectation that they describe another component of the same complex event whose description was begun in earlier sentence(s). The clue is especially strong if this sequence of sentences is contiguous. One of the factors contributing to our perception of the text as humorous is that people who analyze it follow the same path of "priming"—that is, selecting a particular complex event and expecting to stay with it in the immediate continuation of a text (for additional factors dealing with juxtaposing the primed event against the competing one, see Raskin 1985c; Attardo and Raskin 1991; Attardo 1994).

The switch to the different sense of the event in the above example occurred in a situation where that sense was already recorded in the lexicon. When input contains metaphorical language, the other kind of nonliteral language processed by ontological semantics, such a switch must be made without the benefit of a previously recorded sense. Consider the sentence *Mary won an argument with John*. No sense of *argument* matches the selectional restrictions on the THEME of WIN, which are MILITARY-ACTIVITY, SPORTS-ACTIVITY, and GAME-ACTIVITY. If the selectional restriction on the RELAXABLE-TO facet of the THEME property of WIN matches ARGUE, this case can be treated as metonymy. It is more interesting, however, at this point, to consider a situation in which the selectional restriction on the RELAXABLE-TO facet of the THEME of WIN does not have a value. It is in this situation that the analyzer must process a metaphor, which in our environment means searching for an event whose selectional restrictions match the fillers of the case roles in the proposition obtained from the above sentence. Specifically, for this example, such an event should match the selectional restriction HUMAN on the fillers of the AGENT (*Mary* and *John*) properties and ARGUE on the THEME property of WIN. One good solution would be the concept CONVINCE: the sentence *Mary convinced John in an argument* is indeed a nonmetaphorical rendering of the original example. Unfortunately, there is no theory of metaphor, in ontological semantics or elsewhere, that is capable of guaranteeing that such a result could be procedurally obtained.

A microtheory of metaphor in ontological semantics would need to search through the entire set of events looking for matches on inverse selectional restrictions. This must be done in an efficient manner. If the algorithm is designed to check this search space exhaustively (discarding only those candidates that at any given moment can be proved not to fit the bill), then it is likely that it will return more than one candidate

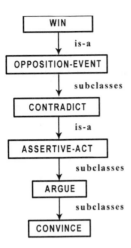

Figure 8.8
The most economical path between two concepts in the ontology may be multidimensional.

solution. Then a special routine will have to be written to establish a preference structure over this set of candidate solutions, which is not a trivial task. If, however, the algorithm is designed on the basis of satisficing—that is, if it will halt when the first appropriate candidate is found—the main issue, which may be equally complex, becomes how to establish the satisficing threshold so as to diminish the probability of an erroneous choice.

Intuition suggests that the best strategy for fitting the inverse selectional restrictions to the events is by relaxing the restrictions in the events themselves—that is, by moving from the source domain of the metaphor, the origin of the search, toward the root of the ontological tree. Even a cursory manual examination of several examples immediately shows that such hopes are unjustified. Indeed, continuing with the assumption that CONVINCE is a good literal substitute for WIN in the above example, we can see in figure 8.8 that the most economical path between the two concepts in the ontology is multidirectional. In *The ship plowed the waves*, the path between the metaphorical PLOW and the literal MOVE-WATER-VEHICLE is even more convoluted (see figure 8.9). Whether the hope for the microtheory of metaphor in ontological semantics lies in figuring out how to navigate such paths or in applying other algorithms, the best ontological semantics can do at this point is to define the problem and the search space in which to look for an answer. It is clear then that until such a microtheory is available, it is advisable to reduce metaphor to metonymy by specifying fillers for RELAXABLE-TO facet values of event properties in the ontology, whenever possible.

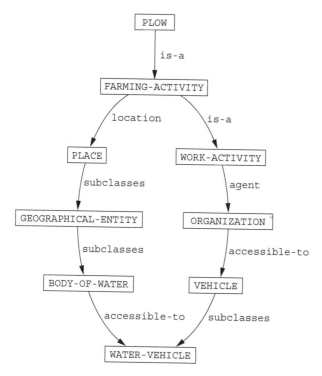

Figure 8.9
The convoluted path between the metaphorical PLOW and the literal MOVE-WATER-VEHICLE.

8.4.3 Processing Unattested Inputs

Used in real-life conditions, any NLP system must expect inputs that contain words and phrases for which there are no entries in the lexicons or the onomasticons. Such inputs fall into several categories. In certain text types, most prominently, in journalistic prose, one should expect proper names to form the largest single category of unattested input elements. The preprocessing component of the analyzer (see section 8.1) contains routines for recognizing unattested proper names. Because they are used at an early stage in the processing, such routines use only textual context elements as clues—for instance, if a phrase ends in *Inc.*, *GmbH*, *Corp.*, *Cie*, *NA*, or *Ltd.*, it is the name of a company, and so on. This process, incidentally, was among the tasks assigned for the Seventh Message Understanding Conference (MUC-7; see Chinchor 1998). A number of experimental systems for the purpose of detecting names, both based on onomasticons (see Cowie, Nirenburg, and Molina-Salgado 2000c; Stevenson and Gaizauskas 2000; Pastra et al. 2002) and attempting to bypass the need for them, have been developed and can be adapted as a module of ontological semantic preprocessing (e.g., Bikel, Schwartz, and Weischedel 1999; Mikheev, Moens, and Grover 1999; Fleischman and Hovy 2002).

Unattested material that is not recognized and categorized as a kind of proper name is also processed by the special routine that uses the available morphological, syntactic, and semantic analyzers to assign as many features to the unknown word as is possible when no lexicon entry is there. Morphologically, this routine attempts to assign a part of speech and other grammatical features (such as gender or person) to the unknown word on the basis of its form as well as its syntactic context. Syntactically, it establishes this word's or phrase's position in the syntactic dependency structure generated by the syntactic analyzer for the input text. Semantically, the procedure uses the syntactic dependency and the knowledge available in the lexicon entry to link syntactic and semantic dependencies to weave the meaning of this word into the TMR. Humans perform exactly the same operations, quite successfully, when faced with texts like Lewis Carrol's *Jabberwocky*: *"Twas brillig and the ..."*

Because the meaning of an unattested word is not reliably available, the procedure does its best to constrain this meaning by assuming that, when the word is a semantic modifier, the selectional restrictions on the properties that the unknown word must match to be the appropriate filler in the semantic dependency structure define the meaning of the unattested word. When the unknown word is a semantic head, the selectional restrictions in its lexicon definition will exactly match the constraints on the senses of elements that fill the corresponding properties in the TMR for the sentence in which the unattested word appears. As we demonstrated in section 8.2.2, the algorithms for processing selectional restrictions involve matching two values—that of the constraint on the property and that of the candidate filler for that property. In the "regular" case, this is, then, reciprocal matching. When unattested words occur, one of the values for the match is unavailable, so that the match is trivial and always succeeds, because it is a match of a constraint against a general set of possible candidates. Let us first consider an example of processing an unattested modifier, then that of an unattested head.

Thus, in the sentence *Fred locked the door with the **kheegh***, the highlighted string is an unattested word. Its position between a determiner and the end of the sentence easily identifies it as a noun. The prevalent sense of *with* combined with the availability of the INSTRUMENT property in the meaning of *lock*, links the meaning of *kheegh* to the filler of this property in the concept LOCK-EVENT. The selectional restriction on INSTRUMENT in LOCK-EVENT is KEY on the DEFAULT facet and ARTIFACT on the SEM facet. At this point, a TMR emerges, whose relevant part is shown in (47). The filler of the INSTRUMENT property is an instance of ARTIFACT, which means that the procedure used the SEM constraint of the property rather than committing itself to the DEFAULT constraint (and using the concept KEY in the TMR) on insufficient evidence—after all *kheegh* may mean "credit card." A side effect of this processing is that a tentative lexicon entry for *kheegh* (48) can be automatically constructed with the content determined by the above results.

```
(47)
...
LOCK-EVENT-6
      AGENT         value   HUMAN-549
      THEME         value   DOOR-23
      INSTRUMENT    value   ARTIFACT-71
...

(48)
kheegh-n1
      syn-struc
              root   kheegh
              cat    n
      sem-struc
              ARTIFACT
                     INSTRUMENT-OF   value   LOCK-EVENT
```

Now consider the sentence *Fred **lauched** the door with the key*. A lexicon entry will be created for the unattested event with selectional restrictions provided by the meanings of the case-role fillers:

```
lauch-v1
      syn-struc
              root     lauch
              cat      v
              subject root    $var1
                      cat     n
              object  root    $var2
                      cat     n
              oblique root    with
                      cat     prep
                      object  root $var3
                              cat  n
      sem-struc
              EVENT
                     AGENT          value   ^$var1
                                    sem     HUMAN
```

```
        THEME           value   ^$var2
                        sem     DOOR
        INSTRUMENT      value   ^$var3
                        sem     KEY
```

The above means that the event realized by *lauch* has a human agent, a theme that is a door and an instrument that is a key. This is all the information that can be reliably gleaned from the input sentence. While it is not expected that the lexicon entry can be completed without inspection and further tightening by a human knowledge acquirer, recording the results of processing unattested input reduces the amount of manual acquisition work. The procedure described above can be seen as a mechanism for generating word senses "on the fly" and thus reducing the level of dependence of the analysis process on a given preacquired lexicon (cf. Wilks 1997).

A different, and more subtle, case of unattested input is when an input word matches the head of a superentry in the lexicon but does not really match any of the entries (word senses) in it. This case can be ultimately reduced to that of processing totally unknown words after the "regular" process of sense attribution (a part of the general semantic dependency building process through matching selectional restrictions) is declared to fail. This recognition of failure is implemented by introducing an empirical minimum threshold of quality for the results returned by the ultimate relaxation procedure (Ontosearch; see section 8.3.2), for otherwise that procedure will always return a preference, albeit not always a useful one.

8.4.4 Processing Ellipsis

Sometimes the basic procedure for processing selectional restrictions returns no result because the input does not contain a sufficient supply of candidates for filling the case roles of the proposition head—for example,

(49) Nick went to the movies and Paul to the game.

(50) I finished the book.

(51) The book reads well.

(52) John shaved.

Example (49) is probably the most standard case of syntactic ellipsis, where the second clause follows the syntactic structure of the first and does not repeat a certain word, in this case, the verb. Most of the literature on ellipsis in theoretical and computational linguistics concentrates on this symmetrical type of ellipsis. But it is clearly not true that ellipsis is an exclusively syntactic phenomenon (see Baltes 1995 and references there). Examples (50) through (52) are not elliptical syntactically and, in fact, many natural language processing programs (or theoretical linguists) will not treat them as elliptical. From the point of view of ontological semantics, however, some of them are. In each of the three examples, the failure to match a selectional restriction due to the lack of lexical material in the input to fill a case role, signals the need for processing semantic ellipsis. Analysis of (50) must involve instantiation of an ontological concept not directly referred to in the input, namely, *read* or *write* (or, at a stretch, *bind* or *copy*). Similarly, there is no lexical element in (51) that can be considered as a candidate filler for the AGENT property of the meaning of *read. Shave* in (52) is the intransitive sense of the verb. In ontological semantics, however, the transitive and intransitive senses of the verb *shave* are defined in terms of one concept. This concept expects an AGENT and a PATIENT. In the surface form of (52) there is no separate candidate for the filler of PATIENT, after the meaning of *John* is selected to fill the AGENT slot. However, in the lexicon entries for all reflexive verbs, we record that the meaning of the single NP constituent that they require fills both the property of AGENT and of PATIENT. The intransitive sense of *shave* is treated as a reflexive verb, making semantic ellipsis in this example illusory.

Semantic ellipsis is often triggered by the occurrence of a verb like *finish* in (50). This verb belongs to a class of verbs that take other verbs as their complements. In their lexicon entries, these verbs require an EVENT as the filler of their THEME property. Moreover, in some cases such verbs constrain the semantics of their themes, which obviously helps to recover their meanings when in the input text the verbs corresponding to these events are elided, as in the example. When it is not possible to impose a strong constraint on the filler of THEME, the recovery procedure is more complex. For example, the THEMEs of *enjoy* in the sentences *Mary enjoyed the movie*, *Mary enjoyed the book*, and *Mary enjoyed the cake* can be recovered as SEE, READ, and INGEST. This is because the ontological concepts for *movie*, *book*, and *cake* contain the above concepts in the DEFAULT facet of their THEME-OF property. Similarly, the example we briefly referred to in section 3.4.2, *fast motorway*, is treated as a regular case of ellipsis: the missing event DRIVE is recovered as the filler of the DEFAULT facet of the property LOCATION-OF on the concept ROAD, which is the basis of the meaning of *motorway*. The meaning of *fast* is a region on the scale that is the range of the property VELOCITY on the concept DRIVE.

The ontological concept for *lizard*, however, does not contain a DEFAULT value in its THEME-OF property because there is no typical EVENT that can be enjoyed concerning lizards. This makes the recovery of the ellipsis in *Mary enjoyed the lizard* a more difficult task: Is the required event INGEST or SEE or something else? The natural procedure here is to weaken the constraint on the EVENT by defining it as belonging to the ontological subtree rooted at the filler of the SEM facet of the THEME-OF property of LIZARD. If the EVENT contains a set of values, the procedure will use the lowest common ancestor of all of them in the ontology. This makes it clear that the treatment of this kind of semantic ellipsis has a great deal in common with the treatment of unattested verbs. In both cases, the semantics of the EVENT realized by the verb, either elided or unattested, is determined, to the degree possible, by the constraints on the content of the inverse case-role properties (THEME-OF, INSTRUMENT-OF, AGENT-OF, and so on) in the meanings of the arguments of these verbs.

Some of the verbs that trigger semantic ellipsis have additional senses that are not elliptic. Thus, *I finished the bench* is genuinely ambiguous between the nonelliptic sense "I covered the bench with varnish" and the elliptic sense "I finished making/ repairing/painting/ ... the bench." Such cases must be treated both as potentially ambiguous and potentially elliptic. This means that the procedure that matches selectional restrictions must expect at the same time to obtain the state of affairs with more than one candidate solution (if the input is to be treated as ambiguous) or no candidate (the case of ellipsis). Because the above eventualities are quite frequent, the procedure becomes quite complex.

8.5 Processing Meaning Beyond Basic Semantic Dependencies

When selectional restrictions are matched successfully and thus the basic semantic dependency for an element of input is established, it is time to establish the values of the various parameters defined in TMR, both alongside basic semantic dependencies within a proposition and alongside propositions in the TMR for an entire text (see example (18) and section 6.3). Each propositional parameter characterizes a specific proposition; it has a set of values that contribute standardized meaning components and belong to instances, but not to ontological concepts.

Suprapropositional parameters characterize an entire TMR. They come in three varieties. The first type involves instantiation of ontological relations with propositions filling their DOMAIN and RANGE slots. In other words, it establishes relations among propositions. The second type groups TMR elements from different propositions according to the semantics of the particular parameter—for example, into COREFERENCE chains or into a partial ordering of time references. The third type of suprapropositional parameter is given a value through the application of a function over the values of specific propositional parameters; this is the way the STYLE of an entire text is calculated on the basis of style values generated for individual propositions.

In what follows, we describe the specific parametric microtheories that have been developed for the Mikrokosmos implementation of ontological semantics. There may be other implementations, based on different approaches to building the specific microtheories (see section 1.7 for a discussion of the microtheory approach). In other words, the microtheories may, in principle, be replaced with other, better, microtheories at any time and, we believe, with a minimum of disturbance for the entire complex of static and dynamic knowledge sources in an ontological semantic application. The emphasis in this section is on the content of the semantic microtheories and nature of clues for assigning values of properties defining the microtheory, not on the many ways languages express the meanings captured by the various parametric microtheories.

8.5.1 Aspect

Aspectual meanings in ontological semantics are represented using a set of two properties—PHASE and ITERATION. PHASE has four values—BEGIN, CONTINUE, END, and BEGIN/CONTINUE/END. The latter value covers events perceived as momentary on a human-oriented time scale. Technically, of course, these events will, in fact, have duration, albeit a very short one (see Comrie 1976, 41–44, for an attempt to analyze this distinction at a finer grain size; we believe that this would serve no useful purpose in ontological semantics). ITERATION, which, predictably, refers to the repetitiveness of a process, is represented using an actual number or the indefinite value MULTIPLE. The meaning of PHASE refers to the temporal stage in a process—whether the input talks about the initial (BEGIN) or the final (END) stage or about neither (CONTINUE).

The examples in table 8.1 show that clues for the assignment of aspectual values in our microtheory will, in the general case, be composite. This finding corroborates the conclusions one can reach from the material presented in Comrie 1976 that a

Table 8.1
Clues for assignment of aspectual values

Phase	Iteration	Examples
begin	1	Ivan zapel ("Ivan started singing")
begin	multiple	Obychno Ivan nachinal pet' ("Usually, Ivan started singing")
end	1	Ivan dostroil dom ("Ivan finished building the house")
end	multiple	Ivan stroil po domu kazhdyj mesjac ("Ivan built a house every month")
continue	1	Ivan sidel na skam'e ("Ivan sat on a bench" or "Ivan was sitting on a bench")
continue	multiple	Ivan sidel na skam'e po sredam ("On Wednesdays Ivan sat on the bench")
b/c/e	1	Ivan vyigral gonku ("Ivan won the race") Ivan vyigryval gonku odin raz ("Ivan won the race once")
b/c/e	4	Ivan vyigral gonku chetyre raza ("Ivan has won the race four times") Ivan vyigryval gonku chetyre raza ("Ivan won the race four times")

given morphological marker of aspect in a language does not necessarily predict the aspectual meaning of a proposition. For example, in the last two rows of table 8.1, Russian verbs with different morphological aspectual markers contribute to the same semantic value of ASPECT (that is, to the same combination of values of PHASE and ITERATION).

The microtheory of aspect proposed here is not the first one used in ontological semantics (e.g., Pustejovsky and Nirenburg 1988). In earlier implementations, aspect was described using a superset of the properties we use here. In particular, the properties of duration and telicity were used in addition to PHASE and ITERATION. Duration distinguished momentary and prolonged events (for example, *he woke up* vs. *he slept*). Telicity distinguished between resultative and nonresultative events (for example, *he built a house* vs. *he slept for ten hours*).

Because the main motivation for parameterizing a component of meaning is economy of ontological knowledge acquisition (see section 6.3), it is only worth our while to parameterize duration or telicity if there exists a sufficient number of pairs of lexical items (possibly, different senses of the same word) whose meanings differ only in the values of these parameters. In such a case the meaning of N such pairs ($2N$ lexical items) could be expressed with, at most, N ontological concepts plus the values of one TMR parameter. The alternative, nonparameterized approach may lead to up to $2N$ ontological concepts. In the case of duration, we have failed to detect any significant body of event realizations that feature such a dichotomy. Whatever examples of variation of duration actually exist (e.g., the momentary *he sat down* vs. the prolonged *he sat for an hour*) can be readily captured by the appropriate values of the PHASE parameter—BEGIN/CONTINUE/END and CONTINUE, respectively.

Telicity, similarly, does not seem to warrant parameterization. While the phenomenon of telicity is real enough, and information about resultativity of an activity should be included in the EFFECT property of ontological events (see section 6.7),[3] once again, we do not see a critical enough mass of pairs in the lexical stock of many languages to suggest parameterization of this meaning component.[4]

In what follows, we illustrate the assignment of aspectual values in the microtheory of aspect in the Mikrokosmos implementation of ontological semantics for analyzing English. Of course, in analyzers for other languages there may be additional kinds of clues (e.g., verbal prefixation in Slavic languages, as in the Russian *zapel*). Still, English examples are sufficiently representative. First, there is a class of what we would call phasal verbs—*begin, cease, commence, stop, finish, desist from, carry on, keep, continue,* and so on—whose contribution to the overall meaning of the sentence in which they appear is aspectual. The aspectual value for the proposition in which a phasal verb like *begin* appears will be obtained from the SEM-STRUC zone of the lexical entry for the appropriate sense of *begin*:

```
begin-v2
      syn-struc
              root    begin
              cat     v
              subj    root    $var1
                      cat     n
              xcomp   root    $var2
                      cat     v
                      obj     root    $var3
                              opt     +
      sem-struc
              EVENT
                              AGENT   value    ^$var1
                              THEME   value    ^$var3
                  aspect
                          phase begin
```

The ASPECT property in the SEM-STRUC of *begin-v2* appears at the level of proposition whose head (marked as *^$var2*) is the meaning of the (syntactic) head of the infinitival or gerundive construction occupying the xcomp position in the syntactic dependency of *begin-v2*—that is, the meaning of *sing* in *John began to sing*. Phasal verbs do not have any meaning other than aspectual. The next example illustrates how phasal value can be contributed not by a special verb but by a closed-class lexical morpheme (either free, a preposition or a particle, or bound, an affix). In this case, the word governing the closed-class morpheme contributes a nonaspectual meaning to the TMR. The example below is the English phrasal verb *drink up* that combines the nonaspectual meaning INGEST with the phasal value END and iteration meaning 1. The lexicon entry treats *drink up* as one of the senses of *drink*, specifically, the one subcategorizing for the literal *up* rather than for the category of preposition. The direct object of this verb is optional—both *Drink up!* and *Drink your milk up!* are well formed.

```
drink-v23
      syn-struc
              root      drink
              cat       v
              subj      root    $var1
                        cat     n
              obj       root    $var2
                        cat     n
                        opt     +
              oblique root    up
```

```
sem-struc
    INGEST
                AGENT value   ^$var1
                THEME value   ^$var2
                      sem     LIQUID
        aspect
                phase         end
                iteration     1
```

Up in *drink up* may be treated as a derivational morpheme. An inflectional closed-class morpheme—for instance, the marker of verbal tense—may also contribute to aspectual meaning. In combination with the lexical meanings of many verbs (e.g., *lose, arrive, contribute, hide, refuse*), the syntactic meaning of simple past tense in English adds the phasal value of BEGIN/CONTINUE/END and the iteration value 1. The progressive tense forms, for those verbs that have them, would contribute the phasal value CONTINUE but will not provide a clue for the value of the iteration feature.

Aspectual values are contributed to the meaning of a proposition not only through verbs. A number of adverbials denoting time have aspectual meaning as well. Compare *he sat on the bench on Wednesday* and *he sat on the bench every Wednesday*. The aspectual value of the former is PHASE: CONTINUE, ITERATION: 1; that of the latter is PHASE: CONTINUE, ITERATION: MULTIPLE.

```
wednesday-n1
    syn-struc
        root    wednesday
        cat     n
    sem-struc
        TIME    get-proposition-time
        aspect iteration       1
```

In the SEM-STRUC above, *get-proposition-time* is the call to a function that returns an absolute value of time that maximally includes the full date, the day of the week, and the time of day. The above meaning of *wednesday* captures such usages as *on Wednesday, last Wednesday,* or *next Wednesday*. We expect to be able to establish rather accurately the time relation between the time when the text is written or read (as can be determined, for example, from the dateline of a newspaper article) and the Wednesday that is the time of the proposition in the sentence. We separate the second nominal meaning of *Wednesday* to account for iterative events that happen on Wednesdays—that is, to capture such usages as *(he goes to the park) every Wednesday, on Wednesdays,* or simply *Wednesdays*. This meaning is realized using three different syntactic constructions and uses the ontological concept WEDNESDAY, a descendant of TIME-PERIOD.

```
wednesday-n2
   syn-struc
        1        root     wednesday
                 cat      n
                 mods     root     OR every each
        2        root     wednesday
                 cat      n
                 number plural
        3        root     on
                 cat      prep
                 object root     wednesday
                        cat      n
                        number plural
   sem-struc
        1 2 3  WEDNESDAY
               aspect
                      iteration multiple
```

We present only the temporal meaning of *every*, which is reflected in the value of the element-type property of the set that is used to represent universal quantification. The syntactic constraints in this entry include a reference to the word that *every* modifies (represented as *$var1*). It is the meaning of that word that is quantified—that is, is listed as the value of the element type of the set. The filler of the SEM facet of the element type property of the format of set is present to constrain the meaning of that word to temporal units, so that if the input is *every table* instead of *every Wednesday*, this sense of *every* will not be selected.

```
every-adj2
     syn-struc
           root   $var1
           cat    n
           mods   root    every
     sem-struc
           TIME
                 set-1
                       element-type value  ^$var1
                                     sem    temporal-unit
                       complete      value yes
```

The multiple value of ITERATION may be contributed by an adverb such as *often*. *Often* modifies a verb (represented as *$var1*). The meaning of *often* is represented in exactly the same way as the meaning of *many*—the difference between these words is

syntactic, because *many* modifies nominals. The meaning of *often* is represented as
follows. There is a set, set1, of all possible occurrences of the EVENT marked by *$var1*.
A subset, set2, of this set refers to all the occurrences of this EVENT that are referred
to in the input. The property MULTIPLE of this subset represents the relative cardinality of the subset and the entire set in terms of the standard abstract scalar range
{0,1} used in ontological semantics. The particular numbers in the lexicon entry
represent the meaning of *many* (for comparison, the numbers 0.6–0.9 would represent the meaning of *most*).

```
often-adv1
      syn-struc
              root       $var1
              cat        v
              mods       root     often
sem-struc
      set-1
         element-type value    ^$var1
                       sem      event
         complete      value    yes
      set-2
         subset-of     value    set-1
         multiple      sem      0.33—0.66
      aspect
         iteration multiple
```

The following two entries describe two of the meanings of *time*. Both meanings
are triggered when the word is preceded by a number or a word with the meaning of
a number—as in *seven times* or *one time*—that supplies the filler for the aspectual
property of ITERATION.

```
time-n5
      syn-struc
              root       $var1
              cat        v
              mods       root     time
                         cat      n
                         number   singular
                         mods     root      OR one single
            sem-struc
                    ^$var1
                    aspect
                            iteration        1
```

```
time-n6
     syn-struc
              root     $var1
              cat      v
              mods     root     time
                       cat      n
                       number   plural
                       mods     root     $var2
                                cat      number
     sem-struc
              ^$var1
              aspect
                       iteration        ^$var2
```

Processing of aspectual values consists of instantiating the meanings of aspect present in the lexical entries for all the input words and unifying them among themselves and with the clues present in the results of syntactic analysis of the input. We posit that the absence of aspectual clues in the lexical entries for the words in the input should lead to the assignment of the aspectual features PHASE: CONTINUE, ITERATION: 1.

8.5.2 Proposition Time

Propositions in the ontological semantic TMR have the property of time—indicated through reference to the start and/or end times of the event that is the head of the proposition. The values of time in this version of the ontological semantic microtheory of time can be absolute and relative. Absolute times (e.g., June 11, 2000) may be either directly reported in the input, or it might be possible to calculate them based on the knowledge of the time of the speech act in the input sentence using the procedure GET-PROPOSITION-TIME first introduced in the discussion of the lexical entry for *Wednesday* in section 8.5.1.

Speech acts can be either explicit (*IBM announced that it would market applications of voice recognition technology*) or implicit (*IBM will market applications of voice recognition technology*). The time of an explicit speech act is marked on the meaning of the communicative verbs (*announce*, in the example). The time of an implicit speech act must be derived using ellipsis processing—the simplest clue, if available, is the dateline of the article or message containing the statement.

If absolute times cannot be determined, a significant amount of information about temporal relations among the various propositions and speech acts in the input text can still be extracted and represented. In fact, one and the same function can be used for determining the absolute and the relative temporal meanings. In the former case, the values will be actual, though possibly partial (for example, referring only to dates, not times of the day), absolute specifications of times. Relative times, which are partial orderings on times of events in a text, are represented in the TMR using the operators "after" ($>$), "before" ($<$), and "at" ($=$) applied to start and end points of other events, even if the absolute times of these referent events are unknown. As a shorthand notation, we allow the "$=$" operator to apply to time intervals. In such cases, the semantics of the operator is cotemporaneity of those intervals.

A detailed example of calculating propositional temporal meaning at the grain size of dates is given below. This procedure will allow the specification of absolute times if the time of speech is known to the system and relative times otherwise. The function given in the example details how to determine the temporal meaning of the sentence *he will leave on* ⟨*day-of-the-week*⟩, where ⟨day-of-the-week⟩ is any of {*Monday,..., Sunday*}. The function is described in pseudocode for legibility.

```
get-proposition.time :=
  case day-of-the-week
    monday
    case get-speech-act.time
      tuesday      = speech-act.time.date + 6⁵
      wednesday    = speech-act.time.date + 5
      thursday     = speech-act.time.date + 4
      friday       = speech-act.time.date + 3
      saturday     = speech-act.time.date + 2
      sunday       = speech-act.time.date + 1⁶
      monday       = speech-act.time.date + 7⁷
      undetermined AND (> speech-act.time.date + 1)
                       (< speech-act.time.date + 7)
    tuesday
    case get-speech-act.time
      tuesday      = speech-act.time.date + 7
      wednesday    = speech-act.time.date + 6
      thursday     = speech-act.time.date + 5
      friday       = speech-act.time.date + 4
      saturday     = speech-act.time.date + 3
      sunday       = speech-act.time.date + 2
      monday       = speech-act.time.date + 1
      undetermined AND (> speech-act.time.date + 1)
                       (< speech-act.time.date + 7)
    wednesday
    case get-speech-act.time
```

```
    tuesday      = speech-act.time.date + 1
    wednesday    = speech-act.time.date + 7
    thursday     = speech-act.time.date + 6
    friday       = speech-act.time.date + 5
    saturday     = speech-act.time.date + 4
    sunday       = speech-act.time.date + 3
    monday       = speech-act.time.date + 2
    undetermined AND > (speech-act.time.date + 1
                        < speech-act.time.date + 7)
  thursday
    case get-speech-act.time
    tuesday      = speech-act.time.date + 2
    wednesday    = speech-act.time.date + 1
    thursday     = speech-act.time.date + 7
    friday       = speech-act.time.date + 6
    saturday     = speech-act.time.date + 5
    sunday       = speech-act.time.date + 4
    monday       = speech-act.time.date + 3
    undetermined AND (> speech-act.time.date + 1)
                     (< speech-act.time.date + 7)
  friday
  case get-speech-act.time
    tuesday      = speech-act.time.date + 3
    wednesday    = speech-act.time.date + 2
    thursday     = speech-act.time.date + 1
    friday       = speech-act.time.date + 7
    saturday     = speech-act.time.date + 6
    sunday       = speech-act.time.date + 5
    monday       = speech-act.time.date + 4
    undetermined AND (> speech-act.time.date + 1)
                     (< speech-act.time.date + 7)
  saturday
  case get-speech-act.time
    tuesday      = speech-act.time.date + 4
    wednesday    = speech-act.time.date + 3
    thursday     = speech-act.time.date + 2
    friday       = speech-act.time.date + 1
    saturday     = speech-act.time.date + 7
    sunday       = speech-act.time.date + 6
```

```
    monday        = speech-act.time.date + 5
    undetermined AND (> speech-act.time.date + 1)
                     (< speech-act.time.date + 7)
  sunday
  case get-speech-act.time
    tuesday       = speech-act.time.date + 5
    wednesday     = speech-act.time.date + 4
    thursday      = speech-act.time.date + 3
    friday        = speech-act.time.date + 2
    saturday      = speech-act.time.date + 1
    sunday        = speech-act.time.date + 7
    monday        = speech-act.time.date + 6
    undetermined AND (> speech-act.time.date + 1)
                     (< speech-act.time.date + 7)
```

The above function can be extended for treating such sentences as *he left on ⟨day-of-the-week⟩*, *he leaves next week/month/year*, *he returns in ⟨number⟩ minutes/hours/days/weeks/months/years*, and so on.

Proposition time is assigned not only when there is an overt lexical reference to time in the input, as in the above examples. In fact, most sentences and clauses in input texts will contain references to times through tense markers on verbs. In such cases, relative time values will be introduced in the propositions, with time marked with reference to the time of speech. Thus, simple past tense forms will engender time values < SPEECH-ACT.TIME in the TIME property of the relevant proposition.

If both a tense marker and an overt lexical time reference are present in the input, the temporal information can be recorded in the TMR multiply, both as an absolute and a relative reference to time filling the TIME property of the same proposition. Usually, they will be in agreement with each other—for example, a statement issued on June 12, 2000, that the president left for Camp David on June 9, 2000. Occasionally, however, there may be a discrepancy, as in a statement issued on June 12, 2000, which reads as follows: *It may turn out on June 15, 2000, that the president left for an emergency Middle East summit on June 14.* In the case when the temporal meanings clash, the absolute reference gets priority.

While the above examples involve time references to points (or at least are interpreted as such), overt references to time intervals are equally frequent in texts—for example, *the meeting lasted for five hours* or *the meeting lasted from 10 A.M. until 3 P.M.* In such cases, temporal meanings are encoded using the start and end points of the intervals. Similarly to the case with point references to time, both relative and absolute (or partial absolute) values are acceptable.

8.5.3   Modality

Consider the following English verbs: *plan, try, hope, expect, want, intend, doubt, be sure, like (to), mean, need, choose, propose, want, wish, dread, hate, loathe, love, prefer, deign, disdain, scorn, venture, afford, attempt, contrive, endeavor, fail, manage, neglect, undertake, vow, envisage.* Their meanings have much in common. They all require complements that are infinitival or gerundive constructions (that is, modifying another verb) and their meanings express an attitude on the part of the speaker toward the content of the proposition headed by the meaning of the verb that the verbs from the above list modify. The syntactic similarity of these verbs is not terribly important. Indeed, there are verbs in English (e.g., *help* or *forget*) with the same syntactic behavior but whose meaning is not attitudinal. As is customary in linguistic and philosophical literature, we refer to these attitudinal meanings as modal (cf., e.g., Jespersen 1924, 313, where the term *mood* is used for modality; Lyons 1977, 787–849). Unlike most linguists and philosophers (Fillmore 1968, 23; Lewis 1946, 49; Palmer 1986, 14–15), ontological semantics limits the category of modality to just these attitudinal meanings, having posited ASPECT and TIME as parameters in their own right. The grammatical counterparts of these, the categories of aspect, tense, and mood, are treated as clearly distinct from the above semantic categories, though they provide clues for assigning various values of the ontological semantic parameters.

As shown in section 7.1.1, modalities in ontological semantics are represented in the following format:

```
modality
  modality-type epistemic | epiteuctic | deontic | volitive
                | potential | evaluative | saliency
  modality-attributed-to *speaker*
  modality-scope          <any TMR element>
  modality-value          [0.0, 1.0]
  modality-time           time
```

Modalities can scope over entire propositions, proposition heads, other concept instances, or even instances of properties. Note that MODALITY.TIME is often different from PROPOSITION.TIME, as in *I was sure they would win*, said about yesterday's game.

Epistemic modality expresses the attitude of the speaker toward the factivity of the proposition in the scope of the modality. As Lyons (1977, 793) correctly points out about epistemic modality, "There is some discrepancy ... between the sense in which philosophers employ the term and the sense in which it has come to be used in linguistic semantics." While "epistemic logic deals with the logical structure of statements which assert or imply that a particular proposition, or set of propositions, is

known or believed," epistemic modality in ontological semantics measures the degree
of certainty with regard to the meaning of a proposition on the part of the speaker.

The values of epistemic modality range from "The speaker does not believe that
X" (value 0) through "The speaker believes that possibly X" (value 0.6) to "The
speaker believes that X" (value 1). In what follows we present examples of the use of
epistemic modality in TMR fragments for actual texts.

Nomura Shoken announced that it has tied up with Credit 109.

```
modality-2
        modality-type            epistemic
        modality-attributed-to   corporation-11
        modality-scope           MERGE-6
        modality-time            <speech-act.time
        modality-value           1.0
```

For every proposition in TMR there will be an epistemic modality scoping over it.
When there are no overt clues for the value of this modality—that is, when a statement
is seemingly made without any reference to the beliefs of the speaker (as, in fact, most
statements are), then it is assumed that the value of the epistemic modality is 1.0. There
may be additional epistemic modalities scoping over parts of the proposition, as mentioned above. For example, in the TMR for the sentence below, two epistemic
modalities are captured. The first modality is practically a default value. It simply says
that somebody actually made the assertion and there are no clues to the effect that
this could not have happened. The second modality is more informative and says that
the amount of investment given in the input sentence is only estimated and not known
for a fact, and we record this by assigning the value of the modality at 0.8–0.9. If the
word *guessed* were used instead of *estimated*, the value would go down to 0.3–0.7.

The amount of investment in the joint venture is estimated at $34 million.

```
modality-5
        modality-type            epistemic
        modality-attributed-to   *speaker*
        modality-scope           INVEST-43
        modality-value           1.0
        modality-time            <speech-act.time
modality-6
        modality-type            epistemic
        modality-attributed-to   *speaker*
        modality-scope           INVEST-43.THEME
        modality-value           0.8—0.9
        modality-time            <speech-act.time
```

Epistemic modality is the device of choice in ontological semantics for representing negation:

The energy conservation bill did not gain a sufficient number of votes in the Senate.

```
modality-7
        modality-type              epistemic
        modality-attributed-to     *speaker*
        modality-scope             MAKE-LAW-33
        modality-value             0.0
        modality-time              <speech-act.time
```

Epiteuctic[8] modality scopes over events and refers to the degree of success in attaining the results of the event in its scope. The values of epiteuctic modality range from complete failure with no effort expended as in *they never bothered to register to vote* (value 0) to partial success in *they failed to recognize the telltale signs of an economic downturn* (value 0.2–0.8) to near success in *he almost broke the world record in pole vaulting* (value 0.9) to complete success in *they reached the North Pole* (value 1.0).

Epiteucticity may be seen as bearing some resemblance to the notion of telicity. In standard examples,

Situations like that described by *make a chair* are called telic, those like that described by *sing* atelic. The telic nature of a situation can often be tested in the following way: if a sentence referring to this situation in a form with imperfective meaning (such as the English Progressive) implies the sentence referring to the same situation in a form with perfect meaning (such as the English Perfect), then the situation is atelic; otherwise, it is telic. Thus from *John is singing* one can deduce *John has sung*, but from *John is making a chair* one cannot deduce *John has made a chair*. Thus a telic situation is one that involves a process that leads up to a well-defined terminal point, beyond which the process cannot continue.   (Comrie 1976, 44–45)

We have several serious problems with telicity. First, is it a property of the meaning of a verb or is it not? *Sing* is atelic but *sing a song* is telic. Worse still, *making a chair* is telic but *making chairs* is atelic. More likely, it is the situation described by a text rather than the semantic property of a verb that can be telic or atelic. Recognizing this, Comrie remarks that "provided an appropriate context is provided, many sentences that would otherwise be taken to describe atelic situations can be given a telic interpretation." However, we cannot accept Comrie's final positive note about telicity: "Although it is difficult to find sentences that are unambiguously telic or atelic, this does not affect the general semantic distinction made between telic and atelic situations." The reason for that is that texts in natural languages are not normally ambiguous with regard to telicity. Because ontological semantics is descriptive in nature, it has a mandate to represent the intended meaning of input texts. If people cannot judge the telicity of most inputs but are still able to understand the sentences correctly, then one starts to suspect that the category of telicity is spurious: it does not contribute any useful heuristics for successful representation of text meaning.[9]

We also have problems with Comrie's test. It works well in English. It does not seem to "translate" well into other languages, such as, for instance, Russian. The Russian equivalent of the English progressive for *pet'* ("sing") is *poju* ("(I) sing" or "(I) am singing"). The equivalent of the English perfect is *spel* ("have sung"), and it is not implied by *poju*. To complicate matters even further, the difference between Russian perfective and imperfective verbs referring to the same basic event is derivational, and therefore lexical rather than inflectional and therefore grammatical. In fact, we suspect that it is the neatness of the above English test that suggested the introduction of the concept of telicity in the first place. As we argued in section 4.2 (see also section 3.5.2), there is no isomorphism between syntactic and semantic distinctions, so we are not surprised that telicity is hard to pin down syntactically.[10]

Epiteucticity also resembles Vendler's (1967) accomplishment and achievement *Aktionsarten*. Vendler associates accomplishments with durative events and achievements with punctual ones. We have found a use for this distinction in ontological semantics, and epiteucticity seems to cover both these *Aktionsarten*. Ontological semantics also easily accommodates the phenomena that gave rise to the discussions of telicity. The content of fillers of the EFFECT property of events in the ontology describes the consequences and results of the successful completion of events. Interestingly, some of these events would be characterized as atelic. For example, one of the effects of the event BUILD is the existence of the THEME of this event; one of the effects of SLEEP, clearly an atelic event, is that the PATIENT of SLEEP is refreshed and is not sleepy anymore.

Unlike telicity, epiteucticity passes the procedural test in ontological semantics—we need this modality to account for the meanings of such English words as *fail, neglect, omit, try, attempt, succeed, attain, accomplish, achieve*, as well as *almost, nearly, practically* (cf. Defrise's 1989 in-depth analysis of the meaning of the French *presque*).

Deontic modality in ontological semantics deals with the semantics of obligation and permission. "Deontic modality," Lyons (1977, 823) writes, "is concerned with the necessity or possibility of acts performed by morally responsible agents" (see section 1.1). This modality is used to express the speaker's view that the agent of the event described in the proposition within the scope of a deontic modality statement is either permitted to carry out the event or is actually under an obligation to do so.

The scale of deontic modality measures the amount of free will in the actions of an agent: unconstrained free will means zero obligation or maximum permissiveness; rigid obligation means absence of free will. The polarity of the scale does not matter much. Ontological semantics defines 0.0 as the value for the situations of unconstrained free will, while the other extreme (value 1.0) of the scale corresponds to the situations of absence of free will, or unequivocal obligation. The values of deonticity in the examples below range from no obligation whatsoever in (53) (value 0.0), to some hint of a nonbinding obligation in (54) (value 0.2), to the possibility of an obligation in (55) (value 0.8), to an absolute obligation in (56) (value 1.0).

(53) British Petroleum may purchase crude oil from any supplier.

(54) There is no stipulation in the contract that Disney must pay access fees to cable providers.

(55) Kawasaki Steel may have to sell its South American subsidiary.

(56) Microsoft must appeal the decision within fifteen days.

To give but one example, the modality for (56) will be recorded as follows:

```
modality-9
        modality-type            deontic
        modality-attributed-to   *speaker*
        modality-scope           APPEAL-6
        modality-value           1.0
        modality-time            >speech-act.time
```

Ontological semantics analyzes negative deonticity as in *I do not have to go to Turkey* as a zero epistemic modality scoped over the deontic modality value of 1.0 (deduced from the lexical clue *have to* in the input).

Volitive modality expresses the degree of desirability of an event. Among the English words that provide lexical clues for volitivity are: *want, hope, plan, wish, desire, strive, look forward to, be interested in*, and so on. The scale of the volitive modality corresponds to the intensity of the desire. For example, in *also angling for a solid share in the Philippine rolled steel market is Nissho Iwai Corp.*, the volitive modality value is as follows:

```
modality-19
        modality-type            volitive
        modality-attributed-to   *speaker*
        modality-scope           ACQUIRE-8
        modality-value           >0.7
        modality-time            >speech-act.time
```

Potential modality deals with meanings that describe the ability of the agent to perform an action. These meanings are carried by modal verbs such as *can* and *could*, as well as other lexical clues, such as *be capable of, be able to*, and so on. The scale of the potential modality goes from "Action is not doable by Agent" (value 0) through "Action is definitely doable by Agent" (value 1.0). For example, in *less than 90% of*

California's power demand can be met by in-state utilities the value of the potential modality is as follows:

```
modality-21
        modality-type           potential
        modality-attributed-to  *speaker*
        modality-scope          PROVIDE-67
        modality-value          <.9
        modality-time           =speech-act.time
```

Evaluative modality expresses attitudes toward events, objects, and properties. One can also evaluate another modality. Evaluation goes from the worst, from the speaker's point of view (value 0.0), to the best (value 1.0). English lexical clues evoking evaluative modality include such verbs as *like, admire, appreciate, praise, criticize, dislike, hate, denigrate,* and so on as well as such adjectives as *good* or *bad.* As we have shown elsewhere (Raskin and Nirenburg 1995, 1998), such adjectives provide one of the clearest examples of syntactic modification being distinct from semantic modification: the meanings of these adjectives express evaluative modality and do not modify the meaning of the nouns they modify syntactically. The meanings of *John said that he liked the book he had finished yesterday* and *John said that he had finished a good book yesterday* are identical and contain the following element:

```
modality-23
        modality-type           evaluative
        modality-attributed-to  *speaker*
        modality-scope          BOOK-3
        modality-value          >0.7
        modality-time           <speech-act.time
```

Saliency modality expresses the importance that the speaker attaches to a component of text meaning. Unlike most of the other modalities, saliency does not usually scope over an entire proposition. This is made manifest in the paucity of verbal clues for saliency scoping over propositions. Indeed, this list seems to be restricted to constructions in which *important, unimportant,* and their synonyms introduce clauses— for example, *It is unimportant that she is often late for work,* where a low value of saliency scopes over *she is often late for work.* There are many more cases in which saliency scopes over objects, as manifested by dozens of adjectives with meanings synonymous or antonymous to *important.*

Ontological semantics also uses saliency to mark the focus/presupposition (or topic/comment, or given/new, or theme/rheme) distinction (see section 3.6). In the sentence *the man came into the room, the man* is considered the given and *came into the room,* the new. In the sentence *a man came into the room* the given and the new are reversed. English articles thus provide lexical clues for the given/new distinction.

Not every sentence is as easy to analyze in terms of the given/new distinction. Some sentence elements cannot be categorized as either given or new—for example, *works as* in *my father works as a teacher*. While *my father* and *a teacher* may change places as given and new depending on the context, *works as* always remains "neutral." The most serious difficulty with recognition and representation of this distinction is, however, its contextual dependence and the complexity and variety of textual clues for it as well as its wandering scope. Indeed, the clues can be present outside the sentence, outside the paragraph, and even outside the entire discourse. Clearly, ontological semantics expends a limited amount of resources for the recovery of this distinction; specifically, it relies on the lexical clues that are readily available.

The saliency modality is also used to represent special questions. As we indicated above (see section 6.7), some fillers of TMR properties remain unbound after the analysis of a text—because there was no mention of such a property or filler there. For example, the TMR for the phrase *the brick house* will bind the property of MATERIAL but will leave the properties such as SIZE or COLOR of the concept instance of HOUSE unfilled. To formulate the question *What color is this house?* we include a saliency modality with a high value scoped over the property of COLOR in the frame for HOUSE. Note that this question may either appear in the text or be posed by the human interlocutor in a human-computer question-answering system.

8.6 Processing at the Suprapropositional Level

When both the basic semantic dependencies and the proposition-level microtheories have been processed, it is time to take care of those properties of the text that scope over multiple propositions, possibly over the entire text. In the present implementation of ontological semantics, we have identified the following microtheories at this level: reference, discourse, and style. The comparatively tentative tone of the sections that follow reflects reality: in spite of many attempts and a number of proposals, the state of the art offers little reliable knowledge of these phenomena and few generally applicable processing techniques for them. The current implementations of ontological semantics do not include fully blown microtheories of reference, discourse, and style, either. We do believe, however, that ontological semantics enhances the chances for these phenomena to be adequately treated computationally. This hope is predicated on the fact that no other approach benefits from overt specification of lexical and compositional meaning as clues for determining the values for these phenomena.

8.6.1 Reference and Coreference

The creation of a TMR is a proximate goal of text analysis in ontological semantics. The TMRs contain instances of ontological concepts—events and objects. These instances may be mentioned for the first time in the sum total of texts processed by an ontological semantic processor. Alternatively, they can refer to instances that have already been mentioned before.

In the discussion that follows we assume that the particular ontological semantic system opts to retain the knowledge accumulated during its operation, and we expect most of the systems to follow this route. In this regard, ontological semantics seems to be the first semantic theory that understands the importance of retaining knowledge for accurate meaning representation. In general, it is fair to say that descriptive linguistics is not interested in the actual usages of linguistic expressions, limiting itself to their potential rather than realized meanings. It is hard to imagine in linguistic literature a situation where the description of the sentence *The cat is black* includes any information about the identity of the cat, those of the speaker and the hearers, the time and place, and other parameters of the actual utterance.

Specific utterances of linguistic expressions have never been in the center of linguistic interest even though studying the use of the definite and indefinite articles in English and of the equivalent devices in other languages (see Raskin 1980) calls for the introduction of the notion of instantiation. Bally's (1950) venture into "articulation," his term for instantiation, is a rare exception. The use of object instances would provide a much better explanation of determiner usage than those offered in literature, most of it prescriptive and, therefore, marginal to linguistics. The philosophy of language (see, e.g., Lewis 1972) has attempted to accommodate instantiation by indexing such arguments as speaker, hearer, time, place, and so on in the propositional function. And while the difference between variables and indexed constants has seeped into formal semantics (see section 3.5.1), no actual descriptions have been produced, because neither the philosophy of language nor formal semantics are interested in implementing linguistic descriptions.

Instantiation is, of course, very much in the purview of natural language processing. It is precisely because ontological semantics deals both with standard linguistic descriptions that never refer to instances and the description of specific utterances that it claims standing in both theoretical and computational linguistics.

If an unattested instance appears in a text, a knowledge-retaining ontological semantic processing system would store it in the FR, giving it a new unique identifier. When an instance has already been mentioned before, it is appropriate to coindex a new mention of the same concept instance with the previous mentions of the same instance. The former process establishes reference, the latter, coreference.

We define coreference as identity of two or more instances of ontological concepts appearing in TMRs. Instantiation in ontological semantics is the device for expressing the phenomenon of reference. Thus, for us, coreference is a kind of reference. References to instances of objects and events can be made using such expressive means as:

• Direct reference by name, as in *Last week <u>Secretary of State Colin Powell</u> went to Belgium*
• Pronominalization and other deictic phenomena, as in *The goal of <u>his</u> visit <u>there</u> was to take part in a meeting of the foreign ministers of the NATO countries*
• Indefinite and definite descriptions of various kinds, as in *This was <u>the Secretary's</u> third overseas trip in less than two months*
• Ellipsis, as in *Defense Secretary Rumsfeld planned to travel [to Belgium] with him but had to cancel [his trip] at the last moment*
• Nonliteral language (that is, metaphors, metonymies, and other tropes), as in *<u>The White House</u>* (metonymy) *hopes that the visit will <u>tip the balance</u>* (metaphor) *of European opinion in favor of sending NATO forces to Iraq*

The literature on coreference (Hobbs 1979; Aone and Bennett 1995; Shelton 1997; Baldwin 1997; Azzam, Humphreys, and Gaizauskas 1998; Mitkov 2000) tends to focus centrally on objects, usually realized in language as noun phrases. We extend the bounds of the phenomenon of coreference to event instances. In the current format of the TMR, objects and events are the only independently instantiated ontological entities. Therefore, in our approach, coreference can exist only among independent instances of ontological concepts and can also be defined as reference to the same concept instance, which entails the identity of all properties and their values. Identical attribute values introduced by reference (as in *My street is as broad as yours*) are represented by direct inclusion of the actual value, in this case, street width, in the TMR for both streets. At the same time, the techniques that languages use to introduce coreference and, therefore, the processing techniques with regard to coreference, are also used for marking reference of this and other kinds. These techniques are based on economical devices that natural language has for establishing property values in one concept instance by saying that they are the same as those in another. This is not reference proper, if by reference we understand a relationship between language expressions and instances of ontological events or objects. Here we have a relationship between language expressions and properties of ontological instances.

For instance, in (57), *then* refers to June 1985; therefore, the time of Mary not knowing the fact that John was thinking of leaving the army is also set to June 1985. What this means is that the value of the time property for the first event, John's thinking about leaving the Army, is mentioned directly, in absolute terms (see section 8.5.2); the time property for the second event, Mary's not knowing this, gets the same value by virtue of a correct interpretation of the meaning of *then*.

(57) In June 1985, John was already thinking of leaving the army, and Mary did not know it then.

The examples in (58) and (59) illustrate how the same mechanism works for other parametric properties—aspect and modality. Both sentences introduce two event instances, for one of which the values of modality and aspect are established directly, while for the other, the same values are recorded through a correct interpretation of the meaning of *so did*.

(58) Every Wednesday Eric sat in the park, and so did Terry.

(59) Brian wanted to become a pilot, and so did his brother.

Processing reference involves first identifying all the potentially referring expressions in textual inputs. This is carried out in ontological semantics by the basic semantic dependency builder (see section 8.2), which, when successful, generates all the object and event instances licensed by the input. The next step is to decide for each instance whether it appears in the input text for the first time or whether it has already been mentioned in it. The final result of this process is establishing the chains of coreference relations within a single text.

Next, for each coreference chain or single reference found in the text we need to establish whether the ontological semantic system already knows about this instance—that is, whether it is already listed in the nascent TMR or the FR. If the latter contains the appropriate instance, the information in the input text is used to update the knowledge about that instance. For example, if the TMR or the FR already contains information about Eric from (58), then we will only need to add the knowledge about his park-visiting habits—unless that information is already listed there. If no such instance exists, it is created for the first time. In general, as schematically illustrated in figure II.1, the content of the FR is used, together with that in the nascent TMR, as background world knowledge in routine semantic analysis. That is, the previously recorded information is made available to the analyzer, the inference maker, or the generator when they process a new mention of the same ontological instance. It is noteworthy, however, that in practical implementations of ontological semantics, information is recorded in the FR selectively, to suit the needs of the application at hand (see section 9.4).

The processing of reference relies on a variety of triggers and clues. The most obvious triggers in natural language are pronouns, certain determiners, and other indexical expressions (Bar Hillel 1954; Lewis 1972). Once such a trigger is found in a text, a text-level procedure for reference resolution is called. Less obviously, any language expression that refers to an event or object instance triggers the text-level reference-resolution procedure. As usual, ontological semantics includes available clue systems in its microtheory of reference resolution—for example, the numerous heuristics proposed for resolving deixis, anaphora, and cataphora in natural languages (Partee 1984b; Reinhart 1983; Webber 1991; Fillmore 1997; Nunberg 1993; Mitkov and Boguraev 1997). Most of these proposals cannot use semantic information. Most systems and approaches simply disregard semantics and base their clues on morphological and syntactic properties (e.g., matching grammatical gender between a personal pronoun and a noun casts a vote for their coreferentiality). Approaches that include semantics in their theoretical frameworks uniformly lack any descriptive coverage for developing realistic semantic clues for reference resolution.

What triggers the FR-level reference-resolution procedure is the set of single references and coreference chains established as a result of text-level reference resolution. The clues for determining coreference here include matching or congruency values of all ontological properties. For example, if a FR entry says about John Smith that he resides at 123 Main St. in a certain town and the new text introduces an instance of John Smith at the same address, this state of affairs licenses coreference. Coreference may be established not only by exact matching but also by subsumption: if the instance in the FR says about John Smith that he is between sixty and seventy-five years of age while the instance obtained from a new text says that he is between sixty-five and seventy, this difference will not necessarily lead to refusing coreference.

Database-level reference-related operations involve not only resolution but also inference-making routines typically used when a system (e.g., a question-answering or an MT system) seeks additional information about a fact, specifically, information that was not necessarily present in an input text (in the case of question answering, the text of a query). Such information may be needed for several purposes—for example, to find an answer to a question or to fill an information-extraction template or to find the most appropriate way to refer to an entity in the text that a system is generating. For instance, the FR stores many event instances in which a particular object instance participates, so that if a system seeks a definite description to refer to George W. Bush, it might find the fact that he won the 2000 presidential election, and generate the definite description "the winner of the 2000 election."

In the TMR of a text, reference is represented as a set of coreference chains found in this text by the reference-resolution routine. Each such chain consists of one (reference) or more (coreference) concept instances. The instances in a chain may come either from the same proposition or, more frequently, from different propositions. It is because of the latter fact that reference and coreference phenomena have been assigned to the suprapropositional level (see section 6.4).

8.6.2   TMR Time

This suprapropositional parameter is organized similarly to reference in the sense that it also contains sequences of proposition-level values. While in the case of coreference, each chain establishes the identity of its links, each chain in TMR time states a partial temporal ordering of proposition-level time values. In the literature on processing temporal expressions (Allen 1984; Allen and Hayes 1987;

Shoham 1987; Gabbay, Hodkinson, and Reynolds 1994; Gabbay, Reynolds, and Finger 2000) less attention has been paid to TMR time than to proposition time. Moreover, this literature typically does not focus on any discovery procedures or heuristics for extracting time values from text, concentrating instead on the formalism for representation of those values, once they are determined. Establishing and representing partial temporal orderings is a complex task, because usually there are few explicit clues in texts about the relative order of events.

The process of determining TMR time takes a set of proposition-level times as input and attempts to put all of them on a time axis or at least order them temporally relative to each other, if none of the time references is absolute. Because it is not expected that an absolute ordering of time references is attainable—texts typically do not specify such an absolute ordering, since it is seldom critical to text understanding—the output may take one of two forms. For those chains that include absolute time references, an attempt would be made to place them on a time axis, so that the result of TMR-level time processing will be a set of time axes, with several time references marked on each. Alternatively, if a connected sequence of time references does not include a single absolute time reference, the output takes the form of a relative time chain.

No chain can contain two temporal references for which the temporal ordering cannot be established. For example, consider the following text: *Pete watched television and Bill went for a walk before they met in the pub*. Three event instances will be generated by the semantic analyzer. The proposition-level time microtheory will establish two temporal relations stating that the meeting occurred after Pete watched TV and that it also occurred after Bill went for a walk. There is no way of determining the relative temporal ordering of Pete's and Bill's individual actions. Therefore, the TMR time microtheory will yield two partial temporal ordering chains, not one.

8.6.3 Discourse Relations

Discourse relations are also a suprapropositional phenomenon. However, they are treated and represented in an entirely different way from reference. Unlike reference, discourse relations are ontological concepts. They form a subtree of the RELATION tree in the PROPERTY branch in the ontology. The incomplete but representative set of discourse relations in figure 8.10, with their properties specified, has been developed by Lynn Carlson at NMSU CRL in the framework of the discourse-relation microtheory within ontological semantics (see also Carlson and Nirenburg 1990 and Nirenburg and Defrise 1993 for earlier versions).

The approach of ontological semantics to discourse analysis differs from that taken by current and recent research in this field (Grosz and Sidner 1986; Mann and Thompson 1988; Webber 1991; Marcu 1999). That research, by necessity, establishes

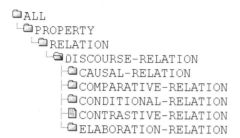

```
⊡ALL
 └⊡PROPERTY
    └⊡RELATION
       └⊟DISCOURSE-RELATION
          ├⊡CAUSAL-RELATION
          ├⊡COMPARATIVE-RELATION
          ├⊡CONDITIONAL-RELATION
          ├⊟CONTRASTIVE-RELATION
          └⊡ELABORATION-RELATION
```

Figure 8.10
The top level of the subtree of discourse relations in the CAMBIO/TIDES implementation of
the ontology.

discourse relations over elements of text—sentences and clauses; in ontological semantics the fillers for the domain and range of discourse relations are TMR propositions. Like all the other approaches, however, in defining and using discourse
relations, ontological semantics seeks to establish connectivity over an entire text by
connecting meanings of individual propositions with the help of discourse relations.

Discourse relations in a text are established using both textual and conceptual
clues. Like all the approaches to discourse analysis, the current ontological semantic
microtheory of discourse analysis uses all the well-known lexical and grammatical
clues. Lexically, it is done using the meanings of words like the English *so, finally,
therefore, anyway, however,* most prepositions ranging over clauses (e.g., *After John
finished breakfast he drove off to work*), and others. Grammatically, the clues can be
found, for instance, in the relative tense and aspect forms of verbs in the matrix and
a subordinate clause: *Having finished breakfast, John drove off to work.* Ontological
semantics adds the opportunity to use conceptual-expectation clues. If, for example,
two or more propositions are recognized as components in the same complex event
stored in the ontology, then even if the overt textual clues are missing, the discourse-
analysis module will establish discourse relations among such propositions based on
the background world knowledge from the ontology or the FR, in the case when the
corresponding complex event was already instantiated and recorded there. Additional discourse-analysis clues are provided by the coreference chains in the TMR.

It is well known both in theoretical and computational discourse analysis that the
current state of the art fails to supply comprehensive and definitive solutions for the
problem. Specifically for the purposes of developing computational applications,
there are far too few reliable and broadly applicable discovery procedures for establishing discourse-relation values. While the blame for that may be assigned by some
to insufficient effort, we believe that the asemantic approaches are inherently doomed
to fail in supplying the necessary results. We hope that the addition of conceptual
clues will facilitate progress in discourse analysis.

8.6.4   Style

Style is a suprapropositional parameter that is given a value through the application of a function over the values of specific propositional parameters. In other words, the style of an entire text is calculated on the basis of style values generated for individual propositions. Just as in the case of discourse analysis, the clues for establishing style may be textual or conceptual, with only the former familiar from literature on stylistics (e.g., DiMarco and Hirst 1988; Hovy 1988; Tannen 1980; Laurian 1986). With respect to textual clues, the literature on text attribution (e.g., Somers 1998) contains methods that can be helpful for determining the values of style properties. These methods tend to operate with the help of a predefined limited set of clues (or a small set of statistical regularities to watch), not systematically connected with the lexicon. In ontological semantics, however, the stylistic zone of the lexicon provides blanket coverage of constituent stylistic values that are supplied as arguments to the style-computation function. The stylistic zone of the lexicon was present in the Mikrokosmos implementation of ontological semantics but did not make it into the CAMBIO/CREST one—only because in neither implementation did the application call for a procedure that used the knowledge in that zone. Note that grammatical information contributing to the determination of style values, from such obvious phenomena as the length and complexity of sentences to the more subtle case of the persistent use of passive voice in a text that signifies a higher level of formality than the use of active voice, can be used both in asemantic and ontological semantic approaches.

Acquisition of Static Knowledge Sources for Ontological Semantics

In chapter 2, we define theory as a set of statements that determine the format of descriptions of phenomena in the purview of the theory. A theory is effective if it comes with an explicit methodology for acquiring these descriptions. A theory associated with an application is interested in descriptions that support the work of an application. We illustrated these relationships in figure 2.9. In figure 9.1 we reproduce a modified version of that figure that specifies how that schema applies not to any application-oriented theory but concretely to ontological semantics.

To recapitulate, the *theory* of ontological semantics includes the format and the semantics of the TMR, the ontology, the FR, the lexicons, and the onomasticons as well as the generic processing architecture for analysis of meaning and its manipulation, including generation of text off of it. The *description* part in ontological semantics includes all the knowledge sources, both static and dynamic (generic procedures for extraction, representation, and manipulation of meaning), implemented to provide full coverage for a language (or languages) and the world. In practice, ontological semantic description is always partial, covering only a subset of subject domains and sublanguages, and constantly under development, through the process of acquisition and as a side effect of the operation of any applications based on ontological semantics.

The *methodology* of ontological semantics consists of acquisition of the static knowledge sources and of the procedures for producing and manipulating TMRs. We addressed the latter in chapter 8. Here, we focus on the former. In our presentation, we will not focus on the methodology of specific applications of ontological semantics beyond restating (cf. section 6.7) that TMRs may be extended in a well-defined way to support a specific application and that such an extension may require a commensurate extension and/or modification of the static resources used by the application. We will start with a general discussion of the attainable levels of automation for acquiring static knowledge sources in ontological semantics. We will then address the specific techniques of acquisition for each of the static resources: ontology, FR, lexicon, and onomasticon.

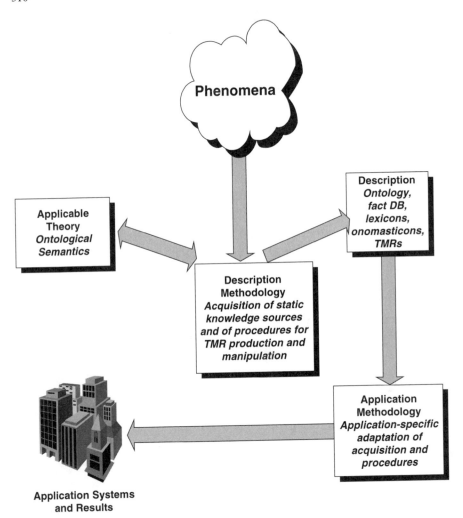

Figure 9.1

Interrelationships between theory, methodology, descriptions, and applications in ontological semantics.

9.1   Automating Knowledge Acquisition in Ontological Semantics

Knowledge-based applications involving natural language processing have traditionally carried the stigma of being too expensive to develop, difficult to scale up and to reuse, as well as incapable of processing a broad range of inputs.[1] The opinion about the high price of development was due to the perceived necessity to acquire all knowledge manually, using highly trained and, therefore, expensive, human acquirers. The difficulty in scaling up was believed to reflect the deficiencies in description breadth, or coverage of material, in the acquisition task for any realistic application. The all-too-real failure of knowledge-based processors on a broad range of inputs was attributed to the lack of depth (or, using our terminology, coarseness of the grain size) in the specification of world and language knowledge used by the meaning-manipulation procedures.

In the consecutive implementations of ontological semantics, the above problems have been progressively addressed. While we cannot claim to have completely eliminated the need for retaining human control over the acquisition process, we are satisfied that ontological semantics uses about as much automation in the acquisition process as is practical within the state of the art in statistical methods of text processing and human-computer interaction. In addition to that, the acquisition methodology takes advantage of all and any possibilities for minimizing human acquisition effort and maximizing the automatic propagation of semantic information recorded earlier over newly acquired material, as applicable. The use of inheritance in ontology, of information-extraction engines in acquiring facts for the FR, as well as of lexical rules and class-oriented syntactic dependency templates in the lexicon, provides examples of such facilities. We have had numerous opportunities to port the resources of ontological semantics across applications, and found this task feasible and cost-effective, even within small projects. In the rest of this section, we briefly review the methodology of knowledge acquisition that has emerged over the years in ontological semantics.

Before a massive knowledge-acquisition effort by teams of acquirers can start, there must be a preparatory step that includes, centrally, the specification of the formats and of the semantics of the knowledge sources—that is, the development of a theory. Once the theory is initially formulated (it is fully expected that the theory will be undergoing further development between implementations), the development of a toolkit for acquisition can start. The toolkit includes acquisition interfaces, statistical corpus-processing tools, a set of text corpora, a set of machine-readable dictionaries (MRDs), a suite of pedagogical tools (knowledge source descriptions, an acquisition tutorial, a help facility), and a database-management system to maintain the data acquired. In many ontology-related projects, the work on the knowledge-specification format, on portability, and on the acquisition interfaces becomes the focus of an entire enterprise (for a view from one particular research tradition, see, for instance, Ginsberg 1991; Genesereth and Fikes 1992; Gruber 1993; Farquhar, Fikes, and Rice 1997). In such format-oriented efforts, it is not unusual to see descriptive coverage sufficient only for bootstrapping purposes. Ontological semantics fully recognizes the importance of fixed and rigorous formalisms as well as good human-computer interaction practices. However, in the scheme of priorities, the content always remains the prime directive of an ontological semantic enterprise.

The preparatory step is in practice interleaved with the bootstrapping step of knowledge acquisition. Both steps test the expressive power of the formats and tools and seed the ontology and the lexicon in preparation for the massive acquisition step.

The bootstrapping of the ontology consists of:

• Developing the specifications of the concepts at top levels of the ontological hierarchy—that is, the most general concepts
• Acquiring a rather detailed set of properties, the primitives in the representation system (for example, case roles, properties of physical objects, of events, and so on), because these will be used in the specifications of all the other ontological concepts
• Acquiring representative examples of ontological concepts that provide models (templates) for specification of additional concepts
• Acquiring examples of ontological concepts that demonstrate how to use all the expressive means in ontology specification, including the use of different facets, of sets, the ways of specifying complex events, and so on, also to be used as a model by the acquirers

The bootstrapping of the lexicon for the recent implementations of ontological semantics involved creating entries exemplifying:

• All the known types of syntax-to-semantics mapping (linking)
• Using every legal kind of ontological filler—from a concept to a literal to a numerical or abstract range
• Using multiple ontological concepts and nonpropositional material, such as modalities or aspectual values, in the specification of a lexical entry
• Using such expressive means as sets, refsems, and other special representation devices

The main purpose of this work is to allow the acquirer during the massive acquisition step to use the example entries as templates instead of deciding on the representation scheme for a meaning from first principles. As usual, practical acquisition leads to the necessity of revising and extending the set of such templates. This means that bootstrapping must be incremental—that is, one cannot expect for it to finish before the massive acquisition step. The preparatory step and bootstrapping are the responsibility of ontological semanticists, who are also responsible for training acquirer teams and validating the results of massive knowledge acquisition. The complete set of types of work that ontological semanticists must do to facilitate a move from pure theory to an actual description includes:

- Theory specification
- Acquisition tool design
- Resource collection
- Bootstrapping
- Management of acquisition teams:
  - Training
  - Work-process organization
  - Quality control

At the step of massive knowledge acquisition, the acquirers use the results of the bootstrapping stage to add ontological concepts and lexicon entries to the knowledge base. It is important to understand that, in the acquisition environment of ontological semantics, acquirers do not manually record all the information that ends up in a static knowledge source unit—an ontological concept, a lexical entry, or a fact. Following strict regulations, they attempt to minimally modify existing concepts and entries to produce new ones. Very typically, in the acquisition of an ontological concept, only a small subset of properties and property values are changed in a new definition compared to the definition of an ancestor or a sibling of a concept that is used as a starting template. Similarly, when acquiring a lexical entry, the most difficult part of the work is determining what concept(s) to use as the basis for the specification of the meaning of a lexical unit. The moment such a decision is made, the nature of the work becomes essentially the same as in ontological acquisition—determining which of the property values of the ontological concept to modify to fit the meaning. With respect to facts, the prescribed procedure is to use an information-extraction system to fill ontologically inspired templates that become candidate entries in the fact repository, so that the task of the acquirer is essentially just to check the consistency and validity of the resulting facts. At the end of the day, only a fraction of the information in the knowledge unit that is acquired at the massive acquisition step is recorded manually by the acquirer, thus imparting a rather high level of automation to the overall acquisition process.

The lists of candidate ontological concepts and lexicon entries to be acquired are included in the toolkit and are manipulated in prescribed ways. Acquirers take items off these lists for acquisition, but as a result of at least some acquisition efforts, new candidates are also added to these lists. For example, when a leaf is added to an ontological hierarchy, it often becomes clear that a number of its conceptual siblings are worth acquiring. When a word of a particular class is given a lexicon entry, it is enticing to immediately add the definitions of all the other members of this class.

The above mechanism of augmenting candidate lists can be called deductive, paradigmatic, or domain driven (see section 9.3.2). The alternative mechanism would be inductive, syntagmatic, and corpus driven and will involve adding words and phrases newly attested in a corpus to the list of lexicon-acquisition candidates. Because the description of the meaning of some of such new words or phrases will require new concepts, the list of candidates for ontology acquisition can also be augmented inductively.

The results of the acquisition must be validated for breadth and depth of coverage as well as for accuracy. Breadth of coverage relates to the number of lexical entries; depth of coverage relates to the grain size of the description of each individual entry. The appropriate breadth of coverage is judged by the rate at which an ontological semantic application obtains inputs that are not attested in the lexicon. The depth of coverage is determined by the disambiguation needs and capabilities of an application that determine the minimum number of senses that a lexeme should have. In other words, the specification of meaning should not contain elements that cannot be used by application programs. Accuracy of lexical and ontological specification can be checked effectively only by using the acquired static knowledge sources in a practical application and analyzing the failures in such applications. Many of these failures will have to be eliminated by tightening or relaxing constraints on the specification of the static knowledge sources.

9.2   Acquisition of Ontology

Acquisition of ontology involves the following basic tasks:

• Determining whether a word sense warrants the introduction of a new concept
• Finding a place for the concept in the ontology—that is determining which of the existing concepts in the ontology would best serve as the parent or sibling of the newly acquired concept
• Specifying properties for the new concept, making sure that it is different from its parents, children, and siblings not only on ONTOLOGY-SLOT properties but rather in a more contentful way, through other ontological properties

The main considerations in deciding on whether a new concept is warranted are:

• The desired grain size of description—for instance, if in a question-answering system we do not expect questions concerning a particular property or set of properties (or, which amounts to the same thing, are content with the system failing on such questions), then the corresponding property becomes too fine grained for inclusion in the ontology; for example, in the CAMBIO/CREST implementation of ontological semantics for the application of question answering, in the domain of sports, no information was included about the regulation sizes and weights of the balls used in various games—baseball, basketball, and so on, for the reason that we did not expect such questions to be asked of the system

• The perception of whether a meaning is generic and language independent (and, therefore, should be listed in the ontology) or a language-specific "fluctuation" of some basic meaning (and should, therefore be described in the lexicon for the language in question)

• The perception of whether a meaning is that of a concept (a type, a class of entities, a meaning, a *significatum* ("signified"), a "variable") or a fact (an instance, a token, an individual, a reference, a *denotatum*, a "constant"); for example, US-PRESIDENT is a concept, while *John Kennedy* is the name (stored in the onomasticon) of an instance of US-PRESIDENT, namely, US-PRESIDENT-35; CORPORATION is a concept; *Ford Motor Company* is the name of an instance of corporation; FORD-FOCUS, however, is a concept, a child of CAR-MAKE and CAR-MODEL; my cousin Phyllis's Ford Focus is an instance of the concept FORD-FOCUS; incidentally, if she calls her car Preston, this will probably not be general or useful enough knowledge to warrant being included in the onomasticon of an ontological semantic application

• The perception of when the analysis and other meaning-processing procedures would fail if particular concepts were not present in the ontology—for instance, the judgment that a particular disambiguation instance cannot be handled using dynamic selectional restrictions (see section 8.3.1)

With respect to language specificity, consider the example of the German *Schimmel* ("white horse"). There seems to be no reason to introduce an ontological concept for *white horse*, because this meaning is easily described in the lexicon by including in the SEM-STRUC field of the corresponding entry an instance of HORSE, with the property of COLOR constrained to WHITE. Also, if this concept is introduced, the considerations of symmetry would lead to suggesting as many siblings for this concept as there are colors in the system applicable to horses.

To generalize further, it is a useful rule of thumb in ontology acquisition not to add an ontological concept if it differs from its parent only in the fillers of some of its attributes because, as we showed in section 7.2, this is precisely the typical action involved in specifying a lexical meaning in the lexicon on the basis of a concept. It is a vote for introducing a new ontological concept if, in the corpus-driven mode of knowledge acquisition, no way can be found of relating a candidate lexeme or candidate sense of an attested lexeme to an existing concept or concepts by constraining some or all of its/their property values.

In other words, it is best to introduce new ontological concepts in such a way that they differ from their parents in the inventory of properties, not only in value sets on the properties that they share. Barring that, if the difference between a concept and

Figure 9.2
The top level of the ontology in all the implementations of ontological semantics.

its parent is in the values of relations other than the children of ONTOLOGY-SLOT (e.g.,
IS-A or INSTANCES), then a new concept may also be warranted. Barring that, in turn,
if there are differences between a concept and its ancestor on more than one attribute, a new concept should be favorably considered. Finally, if the constraint on an
attribute in the parent is an entire set of legal fillers or if a relation has as its filler a
generic constraint "OR EVENT OBJECT," and the child introduces stricter constraints,
one may consider a new ontological concept. Experience in acquisition for ontological semantics shows that applying these rules can be learned relatively reliably,
and compliance with them is easy to check.

The task of finding the most appropriate place to "hook" a concept in the ontology is also complicated. Let us assume that we have already determined, using the
above criteria, that TEACH deserves to be a new ontological concept. The next task is
to find one or more appropriate parents or siblings for the concept. Acquirers use a
mixture of clues for placing this concept in the ontological hierarchy. Experienced
acquirers, well familiar with many branches of the ontological hierarchy, may think
of an appropriate place or two right off the top of their heads, based on clues inherent in concept names. In some cases, this actually does save time. The reliance on
name strings is, however, dangerous, because, as we explained in sections 2.6.2.2 and
7.1.1, the names are elements of the ontological metalanguage and have a semantics
of their own that is different from the lexical meaning of the English words that they
may resemble. Therefore, when this clue is used, the acquirer must carefully read the
definition of the concept and scan its properties and values to determine its actual
meaning. The more reliable, though slower, procedure involves playing a version
of the game of twenty questions—comparing the intended meaning of the candidate
concept with concepts at the top of the ontological hierarchy and then descending
this hierarchy to find the most appropriate match.

At the very top level of the ontological hierarchy of the CAMBIO/CREST implementation of the ontology (figure 9.2), the choice is relatively easy: TEACH is an
EVENT. There are three types of events (figure 9.3). Let us check whether TEACH fits
into the mental-event branch (figure 9.4). Out of all the subclasses of mental events,
COMMUNICATIVE-EVENT (figure 9.5) seems to be the most suitable. COMMUNICATIVE-

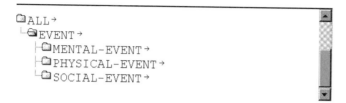

Figure 9.3
The top level of the event hierarchy.

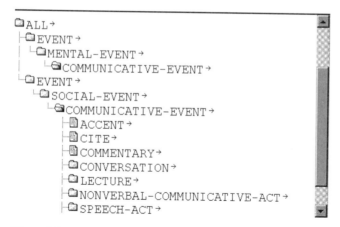

Figure 9.4
Some types of mental events.

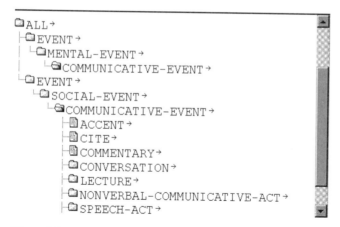

Figure 9.5
Multiple inheritance of COMMUNICATIVE-EVENT and some types of communicative events.

```
□ALL→
 └□EVENT→
    └□SOCIAL-EVENT→
       ├□ABSTRACT-SOCIAL-ACTIVITY→
       ├□ACADEMIC-EVENT→
       ├□ARTISTIC-ACTIVITY→
       ├□COMMUNICATIVE-EVENT→
       ├□CONTROL-EVENT→
       ├□COOPERATIVE-EVENT→
       ├□CRIMINAL-ACTIVITY→
       ├□ENTERTAIN-EVENT→
       ├□FINANCIAL-EVENT→
       ├□NON-WORK-ACTIVITY→
       ├□OPPOSITION-EVENT→
       ├□POLITICAL-EVENT→
       ├□POSSESSION-EVENT→
       ├□RELIGIOUS-ACTIVITY→
       ├□SPORTS-ACTIVITY→
       └□WORK-ACTIVITY→
```

Figure 9.6
Some types of social events.

```
□ALL→
 └□EVENT→
    └□PHYSICAL-EVENT→
       ├□APPLY-FORCE→
       ├□ARTIFACT-EVENT→
       ├▤BE-AVAILABLE→
       ├□CHANGE-LOCATION→
       ├□CHANGE-STATE→
       ├□DISASTER-EVENT→
       ├□DISPLAY→
       ├□ENERGY-EVENT→
       ├□LIVING-EVENT→
       ├▤MIRACLE→
       ├□NATURAL-EVENT→
       ├□NONVERBAL-COMMUNICATIVE-ACT→
       ├□PERCEPTUAL-EVENT→
       ├▤PRODUCE→
       ├▤WAIT→
       └□WAVE-ENERGY-EVENT→
```

Figure 9.7
Some types of physical events.

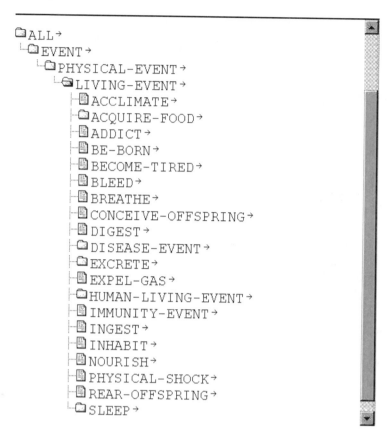

```
□ALL→
  └□EVENT→
     └□PHYSICAL-EVENT→
        └□LIVING-EVENT→
           ├▤ACCLIMATE→
           ├□ACQUIRE-FOOD→
           ├▤ADDICT→
           ├▤BE-BORN→
           ├▤BECOME-TIRED→
           ├▤BLEED→
           ├▤BREATHE→
           ├▤CONCEIVE-OFFSPRING→
           ├▤DIGEST→
           ├□DISEASE-EVENT→
           ├□EXCRETE→
           ├▤EXPEL-GAS→
           ├□HUMAN-LIVING-EVENT→
           ├▤IMMUNITY-EVENT→
           ├▤INGEST→
           ├▤INHABIT→
           ├▤NOURISH→
           ├▤PHYSICAL-SHOCK→
           ├▤REAR-OFFSPRING→
           └□SLEEP→
```

Figure 9.8
Some types of living events.

EVENT has another parent, SOCIAL-EVENT (figure 9.6). A quick check shows that no other children of SOCIAL-EVENT are appropriate to serve as parents of TEACH.

We need to check now whether the third child of event, PHYSICAL-EVENT, or any of its descendants can also serve as a parent of TEACH. On inspection of the concept names of children of PHYSICAL-EVENT (see figure 9.7), we may wish to check whether LIVING-EVENT has children that could be siblings of TEACH because the semantics of the concept name, *living event*, may suggest that it is appropriate. Inspection (see figure 9.8) quickly demonstrates, however, that the name is, in fact, misleading in this case, as the subclasses of LIVING-EVENT do not seem to be appropriate as siblings or parents of TEACH (REAR-OFFSPRING also turns out to be a false lead). At this point, the decision can be safely made: to add TEACH as a child of COMMUNICATIVE-EVENT.

The next task is to describe the semantics of TEACH—that is, to check whether the fillers of the properties it inherits from COMMUNICATIVE-EVENT can be let stand or must be modified (60).

```
(60)
COMMUNICATIVE-EVENT
        AGENT        sem       ANIMAL
        THEME        sem       OR EVENT OBJECT
        INSTRUMENT   default   OR COMMUNICATION-DEVICE NATURAL-
                               LANGUAGE
        DESTINATION  sem       OR ANIMAL SOCIAL-EVENT
        EFFECT       sem       OR EVENT OBJECT
        PRECONDITION sem       OR EVENT OBJECT
```

TEACH does, indeed, simply inherit all the above properties. The actual constraints (fillers) for them were shown in section 7.1.5 and repeated here partially as (61). Besides the properties in (60), TEACH has an additional property, HAS-PARTS, which establishes it as a complex event (descriptions of the components of TEACH are also given in section 7.1.5).

```
(61)
TEACH
        IS-A         value     COMMUNICATIVE-EVENT
        AGENT        sem       HUMAN
                     default   TEACHER
        THEME        sem       KNOWLEDGE
        DESTINATION  sem       HUMAN
                     default   STUDENT
        PRECONDITION default   TEACH-KNOW-a TEACH-KNOW-b
        EFFECT       default   TEACH-KNOW-c
        HAS-PARTS    value     TEACH-DESCRIBE
                               repeat (TEACH-REQUEST-INFO
                               TEACH-ANSWER)
                               until TEACH-KNOW-c
```

Finding the appropriate fillers, if any, for the various facets of a property is a separate acquisition task. For example, if there is a candidate filler that is strongly implied when no explicit reference to it is present in the input text, it should be listed in the DEFAULT facet of the property. Thus, for the AGENT property of TEACH, the default facet will be filled with TEACHER, because in a sentence like *Math was not taught well in his high school*, the implied AGENT of TEACH is clearly a subset of instances of the concept TEACHER. Of course, one example of this kind does not prove the point, but when combined with the acquirer's knowledge of the world, it supports a useful rule of thumb. The acquirer also knows that any (adult) human can at times perform the social role of teacher—for example, parents teaching their teenage children to drive. Therefore, one should expect many inputs in which the constraint on the agent of TEACH is more relaxed than the one in the DEFAULT facet. This most commonly occurring constraint is recorded in the SEM facet of the property. If an input like the sentence *Gorillas teach their offspring essential survival skills* can be expected in an application system, the constraint on the AGENT should be further relaxed to ANIMATE on the RELAXABLE-TO facet (cf. section 8.2.3). However, any attempt to relax the constraint on this property further—for example, in order to accommodate the sentence *Misfortune taught him a good lesson*—should be denied, because the property AGENT in ontological semantics is constrained to HUMAN or FORCE, and rather than coercing misfortune into FORCE, the meaning of this sentence should be represented, roughly, as that of the sentence *He learned a good lesson as a result of a misfortune*, thus reducing the different sense of *teach* in this sentence to a metonymic shift on the appropriate sense of *learn*.

The above procedure of finding the best place to connect a concept into the ontology is not as straightforward as may be deduced from the example. The procedure is predicated on the assumption that the constraints in the ontology become monotonically and progressively stricter as one descends the hierarchy. This was, indeed, the situation with TEACH on every one of the properties inherited. It is legal, however, for constraints in a child to be, in fact, looser than those in an ancestor. In fact, an ancestor may have inheritance on a property completely blocked using the special filler NOTHING, but a child could revert to a contentful filler. This state of affairs makes it dangerous to stop the search for the most appropriate place to include a new concept the moment some constraints become narrower than those expected in this concept. However, in practice, the monotonicity property holds in a much greater majority of cases.

Ontology acquisition may involve not only manipulation of property fillers. Sometimes (preferably, as seldom as possible, though), it is necessary to add a new property to the system. This might be necessary when a concept cannot be described using the extant inventory of properties; this typically, though not exclusively, happens when describing new subject domains. If indeed new properties must be introduced, it is highly desirable that they contain as many concepts as possible in the domain property of their definition. For example, when extending the Mikrokosmos implementation of ontological semantics to accommodate the subject domain of sports in the CAMBIO/CREST implementation, it became necessary to introduce the literal attribute COMPETITION-STAGE, whose domain property was filled with SPORTS-RESULT (a central concept for the domain) and whose range was filled with the useful constants CLASSIFICATION, FINAL, PRELIMINARY, QUALIFICATION, QUARTER-FINAL,

RANKING, REPECHAGE, ROUND-OF-16, ROUND-OF-32, ROUND-OF-64, and SEMIFINAL. The nature of the application dictates this grain size—we do not need to know any information about the above constants than just their names and the corresponding words or phrases in the languages processed by the system.

9.3   Acquisition of Lexicon

Acquisition of lexical knowledge is another crucial component of building natural language processing applications. The requirements for lexical knowledge and the grain size of the specification of lexical meaning also differ across different applications. Some of the applications require only a small amount of information. For example, a lexicon supporting a spelling checker must, at a minimum, only list all the possible word forms in a language. Some other applications require vast quantities of diverse kinds of data. For instance, a comprehensive text-analysis system may require information about word-boundary determination (useful for compounding languages, such as Swedish, where the lexical entries would often match not complete words but parts of compound words). Information about the inflectional and derivational morphology, syntax, semantics, and pragmatics of a lexical unit as well as possible connections among knowledge elements at these levels would also be needed.

In what follows, we will describe some of the lexical acquisition procedures used over the years in the various implementations of ontological semantics.

9.3.1   General Principles of Lexical Semantic Acquisition

The ability to determine the appropriate meaning of a lexical entry or, for that matter, any language unit that has meaning, is something that the native speaker is supposed to possess subconsciously and automatically. However, an ordinary native speaker and even a trained linguist will find it quite difficult to explain what that meaning is exactly and how to derive it. As we showed in section 6.1, it is often hard to separate meaning proper from presuppositions, entailments, and other inferences, often of an abductive or even probabilistic nature. Thus, for a lexical entry such as *marry* it is easy to let into the lexicon all kinds of information about love, sex, fidelity, common abodes, common property, children, typical sleeping arrangements (double beds), and so on. The meaning of the entry, however, includes only a legal procedure, recognized by the society in question, making, typically but not exclusively, one adult man and one adult woman into a family unit. As we discussed in section 6.7, the information supporting inference resides largely in the PRECONDITION and EFFECT properties of EVENTs in the ontology, not in the lexicon. We are discussing these matters in more detail in the section on semantic heuristics.

Another difficulty in lexical acquisition emerges from the commitment in ontological semantics—in keeping with Hayes's (1979) admonition to stem the growth of the ratio of vocabulary size in a metalanguage to that in its object language—to the paucity of the ontological metalanguage. Numerous difficult decisions must be made on the lexical side—for example, whether to go with a potentially cumbersome representation of a sense within the existing ontology, on the one hand, or to revise the ontology by adding concepts to it, to make the representation easier and, often, more intuitively clear. The additions to ontology and the balance and trade-offs between an ontology and a lexicon have already been discussed (see sections 9.1 and 9.2; cf. Mahesh 1996 or Viegas and Raskin 1998), but if such a choice must be made, ontological semantics would tend to produce complicated entries in the lexicon rather than in the ontology, and to this effect it provides lexicon acquisition with more expressive means and looser metasyntactic restrictions than the ontology. As we demonstrated in section 7.2, entire stories can be "told" in lexical entries using such devices as the various TMR parameters, refsems, and the ability to use more than one ontological concept in the specification of lexical meaning.

9.3.2 Paradigmatic Approach to Semantic Acquisition I: "Rapid Propagation"

The principle of complete coverage, to which ontological semantics is committed (see Nirenburg and Raskin 1996), means that every sense of every lexical item should receive a lexical entry—that is, should be acquired. *Every* in this context means every word or phrase sense in a corpus on which an application is based. There is, however, an alternative interpretation of *every* as in "every word in the language." This does not seem very practical or implementable. There is, however, a way to move toward this goal quite rapidly and efficiently. We refer to this approach as "rapid propagation" (see, for instance, Raskin and Nirenburg 1995). The linguistic principle on which it is based can be called "paradigmatic," or "thesaurus-based." The procedure for its implementation involves having a "master acquirer" produce a single sample entry for each class of lexemes, such that the remainder of the acquisition work will involve copying the "seed" entry and modifying it, often very slightly. One problem here might be that some of the classes will prove to be relatively small; in some cases of the most frequent and general words, these might be classes of one. However, this observation does not refute the obvious benefit of using a ready-made template for speedy and uniform acquisition of items in a class. And some such classes are quite large.

One example of a large lexical class (over 250 members) whose acquisition can be rapidly propagated is that of the English adjectives of size. The meaning of all of these adjectives is described as a range on the size-attribute scale, and many of them differ from each other only in the numerical value of that range, while all the rest of the constraints in the semantic part of their entries remain the same as those in a sample entry, say, that for *big* (see example (19) in section 7.2). Thus, the entries for

enormous and *tiny* differ from that for *big* in this way (as well as by the absence of the
RELAXABLE-TO facet):

```
enormous-adj1
      cat      adj
      syn-struc
      1        root   $var1
               cat    n
               mods   root    $var0
      2        root   $var0
               cat    adj
               subj   root    $var1
                      cat     n
      sem-struc
      1 2      SIZE-ATTRIBUTE
                      DOMAIN value   ^$var1
                             sem     PHYSICAL-OBJECT
                      RANGE  value   >0.9

tiny-adj1
      cat      adj
      syn-struc
      1        root   $var1
               cat    n
               mods   root    $var0
      2        root   $var0
               cat    adj
               subj   root    $var1
                      cat     n
      sem-struc
      1 2      SIZE-ATTRIBUTE
                      DOMAIN value   ^$var1
                             sem     PHYSICAL-OBJECT
                      RANGE  value   <0.2
```

A slight variation of the template can be also used to account for many more adjectives. Thus, one sense of *fat* (see below), as in *fat man*, essentially utilizes the same
template with a different scale, MASS, substituted for SIZE, and an appropriate SEM
facet specified for ^$var1:

```
fat-adj1
      cat      adj
      syn-struc
```

```
1          root    $var1
           cat     n
           mods    root    $var0
2          root    $var0
           cat     adj
           subj    root    $var1
                   cat     n
sem-struc
1 2        MASS-ATTRIBUTE
                   DOMAIN  value       ^$var1
                           sem         ANIMAL
                   RANGE   value       >0.75
                           relaxable-to  >0.6
```

By varying the scales and the classes of modified nouns in the appropriate slots of the SEM-STRUC, as illustrated above, the semantic representations of many other types of adjectival senses based on numerical scales—quantity-related (e.g., *abundant, scarce, plentiful*), price-related (e.g., *affordable, cheap, expensive*), human-height-related (e.g., *tall, short, average-height*), human-mass-related (e.g., *fat, thin, emaciated, buxom, chubby*), container-volume-related (e.g., *capacious, tight, spacious*), and others—were produced in the Mikrokosmos implementation of ontological semantics, 318 adjective senses all in all. All these senses were acquired, basically at an average rate of 18 entries per hour, counting in the several hours spent on the formulation and refinement of the template.

Similarly, by taking care of *good* (see example (20) in section 7.2), we facilitate the acquisition of all adjectives whose meanings invoke evaluative modality, such as *bad, excellent, terrible, mediocre,* and so on. The creation of yet another versatile template, which is copied for each new adjective of the same class (116 adjective senses in the Mikrokosmos implementation of ontological semantics), has also made it possible to account for such senses as that of *comfortable,* with respect to clothing, furniture, and so on, representing their meanings as "good for wearing" or "good for sitting":

```
comfortable-adj1
      cat       adj
      syn-struc
      1          root    $var1
                 cat     n
                 mods    root    $var0
      2          root    $var0
                 cat     adj
                 subj    root    $var1
                         cat     n
```

```
sem-struc
1 2      ^$var1 sem      OR CLOTHING FURNITURE
         modality
                  modality-type    evaluative
                  modality-value value              >0.75
                                  relaxable-to       >0.6
                  modality-scope               ^$var1
                  modality-attributed-to  *speaker*
```

An additional advantage of this approach is that it can use synonymy, antonymy, and other paradigmatic relations among words to generate lists of entries that can be acquired on the basis of a single lexical-entry template. Availability of thesauri and similar online resources facilitates this method of acquisition. It also facilitates the acquisition of entries across languages. The single word senses acquired the way demonstrated for the adjectives above were all reused, without any semantic changes, in the Spanish lexicon and those for other languages. This, in fact, was an empirical corroboration of the principle of practical effability discussed in section 9.3.6: each of the English word senses was found to have an equivalent sense expressed in another language; what varies from language to language is, essentially, how these single senses will be grouped in a superentry. This capability underscores the rather high level of portability of ontological semantics across languages and applications.

9.3.3   Paradigmatic Approach to Lexical Acquisition II: Lexical Rules

The other paradigmatic approach to lexical acquisition finds economies in automatic propagation of lexicon entries on the basis of systematic relationships between classes of lexical entries—for example, between verbs, such as *abhor* (62), and corresponding deverbal adjectives (63), such as *abhorrent*. Lexical rules came into fashion in computational lexical semantics in the early 1990s (see section 4.1). Ontological semantics uses the facility of lexical rules for actual massive lexical acquisition, always paying special attention to the relative effort expended in formulating the rule versus that needed for specifying lexical entries for a class of words manually (see Viegas et al. 1996; Raskin and Nirenburg 1999). As a result, fewer lexical rules are proposed and those that are, generate numerous entries.

```
(62)
abhor-v1
     cat      v
     syn-struc
              root    abhor
              obj     root    $var1
                      cat     n
```

```
sem-struc
        modality
                modality-type            evaluative
                modality-value           <0.1
                modality-scope           ^$var1
                modality-attributed-to   *speaker*
(63)
abhorrent-adj1
    cat    adj
    syn-struc
            1      root    $var1
                   cat     n
                   mods    root    abhorrent
            2      root    abhorrent
                   cat     adj
                   subj    root    $var1
                           cat     n
    sem-struc
            modality
                    modality-type            evaluative
                    modality-value           <0.1
                    modality-scope           ^$var1
                    modality-attributed-to   *speaker*
```

The lexical entry for *abhorrent* is generated from that for *abhor* using the following lexical rule:

```
LR-v-adj-1
    lhs
            syn-struc
                    root    $var0
                    obj     root    $var1
                            cat     n
            sem-struc
                    modality
                            modality-type            evaluative
                            modality-value           <0.1
                            modality-scope           ^$var1
                            modality-attributed-to   *speaker*
```

```
rhs
        syn-struc
        1       root    $var1
                cat     n
                mods    root    adj($var0)
        2       root    adj($var0)
                cat     adj
                subj    root    $var1
                        cat     n
        sem-struc
        1 2     modality
                        modality-type              evaluative
                        modality-value             <0.1
                        modality-scope             ^$var1
                        modality-attributed-to     *speaker*
```

Lexical rules overtly put in correspondence two types of lexical entry: that for the source entry and that for the target one. The binding of variables scopes over the entire rule, both its left-hand side (lhs) and the right-hand side (rhs). The above rule establishes that the semantics of *abhor* and *abhorrent* is identical (this is not always the case; see the example of *criticize/critical* below) but that the syntactic dependency changes from the verb to the adjective, because the direct object of the former becomes the head that the adjective modifies. The expression *adj($var0)* stands for the adjective whose entry is generated by the rule. In the lexicon entry for the verb, an additional zone, LR, will be created, in which each lexical rule applicable to this verb is listed with the string that is the lexeme of the target entry. A practical consideration for the economy of acquisition effort is whether it is preferable to populate the LR zone of a lexical entry or immediately create the target entry or entries.

```
criticize-v1
        cat     v
        syn-struc
                root    criticize
                subj    root    $var1
                        cat     n
                obj     root    $var2
                        cat     n
        sem-struc
                CRITICIZE
                        AGENT   value   ^$var1
                                sem     HUMAN
```

```
                    THEME     value ^$var2
                              THEME OR EVENT OBJECT
            modality

                              modality-type          evaluative
                              modality-value          <0.5
                              modality-scope           ^$var2
                              modality-attributed-to  *speaker*

critical-adj2
    cat     adj
    syn-struc
            1     root     critical
                  cat      adj
                  oblique root   of
                          cat    prep
                          obj    root  $var1
                                 cat   n
            2     root     critical
                  cat      adj
                  oblique root   of
                          cat    prep
                          xcomp  root  $var1
                                 cat   v
    sem-struc
    1 2     modality

                              modality-type          evaluative
                              modality-value          <0.1
                              modality-scope           ^$var1
                              modality-attributed-to  *speaker*
```

The lexical rule for the above pair differs from *LR-v-adj-1* in several respects. The semantics of the verb includes a reference to an ontological concept with some of its properties listed. One of these properties, THEME, plays a central role in the relationship between the meaning of the verb and that of the adjective derived from it: the scope of the modality in the meaning of the adjective is the filler of the THEME property.

Note that the entry for *critical* has a different content of the SYN-STRUC zone compared to that of *abhorrent* or other standard adjectives. The lexical rule will thus connect lexical elements similar to those in the examples with *criticize/critical*: *John criticized the film/John was critical of the film* (corresponding to the first SYN-STRUC variant) or *Lucy criticized China's handling of the spy plane crisis/Lucy was critical of China's handling of the spy plane crisis* (corresponding to the second syn-struc variant).

```
LR-v-adj-2
     lhs
               syn-struc
                      root      $var0
                      obj       root   $var2
                                cat    n
               sem-struc
                      ^$var0
                                theme value    ^$var2
                      modality
                                modality-type            evaluative
                                modality-value           <0.5
                                modality-scope           ^$var2
                                modality-attributed-to   *speaker*
     rhs
               syn-struc
               1      root      adj($var0)
                      cat       adj
                      oblique root   of
                              cat    prep
                              obj    root   $var2
                                     cat    n
               2      root      adj($var0)
                      cat       adj
                      oblique root   of
                              cat    prep
                              xcomp root   $var2
                                     cat    v
               sem-struc
               1 2    modality
                                modality-type            evaluative
                                modality-value           <0.5
                                modality-scope           ^$var2
                                modality-attributed-to   *speaker*
```

The role played by THEME in the above rule will be assumed by other properties
(typically, case roles) in other rules. Thus, for the pair *abuse/abusive*, the adjective
in *abusive behavior* modifies the EVENT itself and in *abusive parent*, the AGENT of the
EVENT. This means that the LR zone in the entry for *abuse* will contain a reference to
two different lexical rules for the production of the corresponding adjective entries.

An alternative approach to specifying the format of the lexical rules would have been to try to formulate all the verb-adjective lexical rules as a single rule, with disjunctions in the text of the rule. It would have afforded some people the pleasure of making formal generalizations at the expense of clarity.

9.3.4 Steps in Lexical Acquisition

The steps in lexical acquisition may be presented as follows:

- *Polysemy reduction*. Decide how many senses for every word must be included into a lexicon entry: read the definitions of every word sense in a dictionary and try to merge as many senses as possible, so that a minimum number of senses remains
- *Syntactic description*. Describe the syntax of every sense of the word
- *Ontological matching*. Describe the semantics of every word sense by mapping it into an ontological concept, a property, a parameter value, or any combination thereof
- *Adjusting lexical constraints*. Constrain the properties of the concept property or parameter, if necessary
- *Linking*. Link syntactic and semantic properties of a word sense

9.3.5 Polysemy Reduction

We have basically two resources for capturing meaning, and their status is quite different: one of them, the speaker's intuition, works very well for humans but not at all for machines (it is difficult to represent it explicitly); the other, the set of human-oriented published dictionaries, represents meaning explicitly but is known to be faulty and unreliable and, moreover, does not contain sufficient amounts of information to allow automatic capturing of word meaning from them (e.g., Wilks et al. 1990; Wilks, Slator, and Guthrie 1996; Guo 1995). From the point of view of computational applications, dictionaries also typically list too many different senses. In a computational lexicon that recognizes the same number of senses, it would be very difficult formally to specify how each of them differs from the others, and the human-oriented dictionaries do not always provide this information. Thus, in a computational application, it becomes important to reduce the number of senses to a manageable set.

In his critique of Katz and Fodor 1963, Weinreich (1966) accused them of having no criteria for limiting polysemy—that is, for determining when a sense should no longer be subdivided. Thus, having determined that one of the senses of *eat* is "ingest by mouth," should we subdivide this sense of *eat* into eating with a spoon and eating with a fork, which are rather different operations? Existing human-oriented dictionaries still do not have theoretically sound criteria for limiting polysemy of the sort Weinreich talked about. It might be simply not possible to formulate such criteria at any but the coarsest levels of accuracy. Dictionary compilers operate with their own implicit rules of thumb and under strict editorial constraints on overall size, but still the entries of a dictionary vary in grain size of description. And, again, the number of senses listed for each entry is usually quite high for the purposes of computational applications—after all, the more senses in an entry, the more complex the procedure for their disambiguation.

It is often difficult to reduce the number of senses for a word even in a computationally informed lexical resource, as can be illustrated by an example from WordNet, a popular online lexical resource (Miller et al. 1988; Fellbaum 1998). In WordNet, each sense in an entry is determined by a "synset," a set of synonyms, rather than by a verbal definition. The list below contains the twelve synsets WordNet lists for the adjective *good*:

SENSE 1:   good (vs. evil)—(morally admirable)

⇒ angelic, angelical, saintly, sainted—(resembling an angel or saint in goodness)
⇒ beneficent, benevolent, gracious—(doing or producing good)
⇒ white—("white magic")

Also See → good, moral, right, righteous, virtuous, worthy

SENSE 2:   good (vs. bad)—(having positive qualities, esp. those desirable in a thing specified: "good news"; "a good report card"; "a good joke"; "a good exterior paint"; "a good secretary")

⇒ bang-up, bully, cool, corking, cracking, dandy, great, keen, neat, nifty, not bad (predicate), peachy, swell, smashing—((informal) very good)
⇒ fine—(very good of its kind or for its purpose: "a fine gentleman"; "a fine mind"; "a fine speech"; "a fine day")
⇒ redeeming (prenominal), saving (prenominal)—(offsetting some fault or defect: "redeeming feature"; "saving grace")
⇒ safe, sound—("a good investment")
⇒ satisfactory—(meeting requirements: "good qualifications for the job")
⇒ suitable—(serving the desired purpose: "Is this a good dress for the office?")
⇒ unspoiled—("the meat is still good")
⇒ well-behaved—("when she was good she was very good")

Also See → best, better, favorable, genuine, good, obedient, respectable, sound, well (predicate)

SENSE 3:   benevolent (vs. malevolent), good—(having, showing, or arising from a desire to promote the welfare or happiness of others)

⇒ beneficent, charitable, generous, kind—("a benevolent contributor")

⇒ good-hearted, kindly, openhearted—("a benevolent smile"; "take a kindly interest")

Also See → beneficent, benefic, charitable, kind

SENSE 4:   good, upright, virtuous—(of moral excellence: "a genuinely good person"; "an upright and respectable man"; "the life of the nation is secure only while the nation is honest, truthful, and virtuous"—Frederick Douglass; "the ... prayer of a righteous man availeth much"—James 5:16)

⇒ righteous (vs. unrighteous)

SENSE 5:   estimable, good, honorable, respectable—("all reputable companies give guarantees"; "ruined the family's good name")

⇒ reputable (vs. disreputable)

SENSE 6:   good, right, seasonable, timely, well-timed—(occurring at a fitting time: "opportune moment"; "a good time to plant tomatoes"; "the right time to act"; "seasonable summer storms"; "timely warning"; "the book's publication was well timed")

⇒ opportune (vs. inopportune)

SENSE 7:   good, pleasing—(agreeable or pleasant: "we had a nice time"; "a nice day"; "nice manners")

⇒ nice (vs. nasty)

SENSE 8:   good, intact—(not impaired in any way: "I still have one good leg")

⇒ unimpaired (vs. impaired)—(not damaged or diminished)

SENSE 9:   good—(not forged: "a good dollar bill")

⇒ genuine (vs. counterfeit)

SENSE 10:   good—("good taste")

⇒ discriminating (vs. undiscriminating)

SENSE 11:   good, Sunday, Sunday-go-to-meeting (prenominal)—(used of clothing: "my good clothes"; "his best suit"; "her Sunday-go-to-meeting clothes")

⇒ best (vs. worst)—(superlative of "good": "the best film of the year")

SENSE 12:   full, good—("gives full (good) measure"; "a good mile from here")

⇒ ample (vs. meager)—(more than enough in size or scope or capacity)

The first thing one notices about the twelve senses is that the noun classes which they modify vary a great deal in size. Sense 2 dwarfs all the other senses in this respect.

Senses 1 and 3–5 all pertain to humans and their actions and are very similar to each other: the association of one of these senses with a noun strongly entails or presupposes the association of the others with the same noun. The meaning of *good* in the examples below can be in any of the WordNet senses 1 or 3–5, as it seems difficult for speakers to tell them apart:

Fred is a good man.
Fred's behavior in that difficult situation was very good.
Mom & Pop, Inc. is a good company

This intuition is the basis for a procedure that Weinreich sought for determining the required levels of polysemy. A group of individuals, if defined as *good*, is indeed more likely to be understood in WordNet sense 5, but none of the other three can be excluded either. In fact, other than in the context of at least several sentences, if not paragraphs, it is very hard to use *good* specifically in one of these similar senses and not simultaneously in the others. This observation can serve as an operational criterion for limiting polysemy: if it is hard to pinpoint a sense within a one-sentence example, the status of the meaning as a separate sense in the lexical entry should be questioned. One cannot understand that the sense of *good* in *Fred is a good man* signifies "of good moral character" unless the text also says something like *he lives by the Bible*.

One observes that if there are different shades of meaning in the above examples, they are due not the meaning of *good* as such but rather to the differences in the meanings of the noun it modifies—for instance, when the latter is not an individual but a group. The influence of the syntactic head on the meaning of *good* is even more obvious in the other WordNet senses for the adjective. Starting with sense 6, the noun classes to which these senses apply shrink in size, and with senses 8–12 come dangerously close to phrasals consisting of *good* and the corresponding nouns. That these senses are listed at all is probably because, in these near-phrasals, the meaning of *good* varies significantly. In ontological semantics, such a situation—when the classes of phenomena are very narrow—always calls for treatment of a construction as a separate phrasal lexical entry instead of adding more small senses to those already existing for the components of the construction.

WordNet itself recognizes some of the observations above by reducing, in one version of the resource, the twelve senses of *good* to the following three senses in response to a different set of parameter settings:

SENSE 1:   good (vs. evil)—(morally admirable)

⇒ good, virtue, goodness—(the quality of being morally excellent or admirable)

SENSE 2:   good (vs. bad)—(having positive qualities, esp. those desirable in a thing specified: "good news"; "a good report card"; "a good joke"; "a good exterior paint"; "a good secretary")

⇒ goodness—(being of positive value)

SENSE 3: benevolent (vs. malevolent), good—(having, showing, or arising from a desire to promote the welfare or happiness of others)

⇒ benevolence—(an inclination to do kind or charitable acts)

This "short list" of the main senses of *good* is still rather unbalanced with respect to the size of noun classes they modify, and the distinction between senses 1 and 3 remains perhaps only slightly less problematic than the distinction among senses 1 and 3–5 of the longer list. It is the long WordNet list rather than the short one that is closer to typical dictionary fare: compare the entries for *good* from the online *Merriam-Webster's* (1963) and the *American Heritage Dictionary* (1992)—we list only meaning-related information from each entry.

(*Merriam-Webster's*)

1. good ...

1a1: of a favorable character or tendency {~ news}

1a2: BOUNTIFUL, FERTILE {~ land}

1a3: COMELY, ATTRACTIVE {~ looks}

1b1: SUITABLE, FIT {~ to eat}

1b2: SOUND, WHOLE {one ~ arm}

1b3: not depreciated {bad money drives out ~}

1b4: commercially reliable {~ risk}

1b5: certain to last or live {~ for another year}

1b6: certain to pay or contribute {~ for a hundred dollars}

1b7: certain to elicit a specified result {always ~ for a laugh}

1c1: AGREEABLE, PLEASANT

1c2: SALUTARY, WHOLESOME {~ for a cold}

1d1: CONSIDERABLE, AMPLE {~ margin}

1d2: FULL {~ measure}

1e1: WELL-FOUNDED, COGENT {~ reasons}

1e2: TRUE {holds ~ for society at large}

1e3: ACTUALIZED, REAL {made ~ his promises}

1e4: RECOGNIZED, HONORED {in ~ standing}

1e5: legally valid or effectual {~ title}

1f1: ADEQUATE, SATISFACTORY {~ care}

1f2: conforming to a standard {~ English}

1f3: DISCRIMINATING, CHOICE {~ taste}

1f4: containing less fat and being less tender than higher grades—used of meat and esp. of beef

2a1: COMMENDIBLE (sic!), VIRTUOUS, JUST {~ man}

2a2: RIGHT {~ conduct}

2a3: KIND, BENEVOLENT {~ intentions}

2b: UPPER-CLASS {~ family}

2c: COMPETENT, SKILLFUL {~ doctor}

2d: LOYAL {~ party man} {~ Catholic}: in effect: VIRTUALLY {as good as dead}: VERY, ENTIRELY {was good and mad}

(*American Heritage Dictionary*)

good

1. Being positive or desirable in nature; not bad or poor: a good experience; good news from the hospital.

2.a. Having the qualities that are desirable or distinguishing in a particular thing: a good exterior paint; a good joke. b. Serving the desired purpose or end; suitable: Is this a good dress for the party?

3.a. Not spoiled or ruined: The milk is still good. b. In excellent condition; sound: a good tooth.

4.a. Superior to the average; satisfactory: a good student. b. Used formerly to refer to the U.S. Government grade of meat higher than standard and lower than choice.

5.a. Of high quality: good books. b. Discriminating: good taste.

6. Worthy of respect; honorable: ruined the family's good name.

7. Attractive; handsome: good looks.

8. Beneficial to health; salutary: a good night's rest.

9. Competent; skilled: a good machinist.

10. Complete; thorough: a good workout.

11.a. Reliable; sure: a good investment. b. Valid or true: a good reason. c. Genuine; real: a good dollar bill.

12.a. In effect; operative: a warranty good for two years; a driver's license that is still good. b. Able to continue in a specified activity: I'm good for another round of golf.

13.a. Able to pay or contribute: Is she good for the money that you lent her? b. Able to elicit a specified reaction: He is always good for a laugh.

14.a. Ample; substantial: a good income. b. Bountiful: a good table.

15. Full: It is a good mile from here.

16.a. Pleasant; enjoyable: had a good time at the party. b. Propitious; favorable: good weather; a good omen.

17.a. Of moral excellence; upright: a good person. b. Benevolent; kind: a good soul; a good heart. c. Loyal; staunch: a good Republican.

18.a. Well-behaved; obedient: a good child. b. Socially correct; proper: good manners.

19. Sports. Having landed within bounds or within a particular area of a court: The first serve was wide, but the second was good.

20. Used to form exclamatory phrases expressing surprise or dismay: Good heavens! Good grief!

Ontological semantics promulgates both content- and computation-related guidelines for justifying the inclusion of a word sense for a lexeme. From the point of view of content, we are solidly with Weinreich in his concern about unlimited polysemy that would make any semantic theory indefensible and the semantic description determined by such a theory infeasible. Disambiguation at runtime will be greatly facilitated by the small number of senses for a lexeme. We cannot make a symmetrical claim that a small number of senses is easier to acquire, because the task of "bunching" senses is not simple. Thus, the guidelines for adding another sense to an adjective lexeme in ontological semantics are:

- That the candidate sense be clearly distinct from those already in the entry
- That set of nouns that the adjective in this sense can modify not be small

The first of these guidelines calls for a significant difference in the properties and their fillers in the SEM-STRUC zone of the lexical entries. This guideline applies equally to all types of lexemes. The second guideline, to be applicable to the other types of lexemes, should watch for dependency of a candidate sense on the meanings of its syntactic arguments. It would be unwise, for instance, to say that *join* in *join the Army* and *join the country club* belong to different senses, on the tenuous ground that the former event involves relocation, while the latter does not. In other words, whatever difference in the shade of meaning exists, it depends on the meaning of the direct object of *join* rather than on the meaning of the verb itself.

The rules of thumb to be used by lexicon acquirers for reducing polysemy can then be summarized as follows:

- Check whether the candidate sense requires further disambiguation if used in a short text example; if you need to provide additional context to recognize what sense is used, this sense should be rejected and subsumed by one of the existing senses in the entry
- Check whether there is a property of the candidate sense that can be filled only with a member of a small set of fillers; if so, reject this sense: its meaning will be either subsumed by one of the existing senses in the entry or will become a part of the meaning of a phrasal

A comment is in order with respect to the first of the above rules. If *He is good* cannot be understood in the moral sense without additional lexical material present; and *He likes to join* cannot be understood exclusively in the sense of involving relocation; then the argument that *I went to the bank* cannot be disambiguated without further detail between the topographic and the repository senses is not relevant because both senses of *bank* are present in the example. In other words, we accept the views of Firth (1957) and Zvegintzev (1968) that words, as a matter of rule, change their meanings when appearing in collocation with other words. What we do not do is declare that each such shade of meaning warrants a separate sense in a lexicon. On this issue, ontological semantics differs from human-oriented lexicography, as exemplified above by WordNet and the two MRDs. In ontological semantics, the shades of lexical meaning yielding unique interpretations of collocations are reflected in the equally unique combinations of properties and their values in the results of the semantic analysis of text, namely, in TMRs. There is no doubting Firth's claim that the meaning of *dark*, for instance, in *dark ale* is different from that in *dark coat*, and this is how that difference is reflected in the corresponding portions of the TMRs for inputs in which these expression may occur (64). The relevant parts of the lexicon entries for *ale*, *coat*, and *dark* are as follows:

```
(64)
ale-n1
   ...
   beer
   ...
       color   value   OR yellow pale-yellow reddish-brown black
                        dark-brown
                           ...

coat-n1
   ...
   coat
   ...                   ...
       color   value   OR white yellow red green blue navy-blue
                        dark-grey black dark-brown
...
                         ...

dark-adj1
   ...
   1 ^$var1
   ...
       color   value   OR black navy-blue dark-grey dark-brown
                        brown dark-green
   ...
   2 ...
   ...
```

The following are fragments of the TMR for *dark ale* and *dark coat*.

```
beer
       ...
       color   value   OR black dark-brown
       ...
```

```
coat
    ...
    color   value   OR black navy-blue dark-brown dark-green
                    dark-grey
    ...
```

The above clearly shows the difference in the meaning of *dark* in the two colloca-tions: while both senses of *dark* have the effect of restricting the choice of fillers for the COLOR property, the resulting ranges are different. There is no need to add senses to the superentry for *dark* in the lexicon to reflect this difference.

The above is a manifestation of a general linguistic principle of complementary distribution, or commutation, widely used for establishing variance and invariance of entities in phonology and morphology: if two different senses of the same word can only be realized when used in collocation with different words, they should be seen as variants of the same sense. In a way, some dictionaries try to capture this in their entries by grouping all senses into a small number of "main" ones, which are further divided, often recursively. Thus, as shown above, *Merriam-Webster's* has only two main senses for *good* and two levels of specification under them, but *American Heri-tage* prefers putting twenty senses at the top level, with minimum further subdivision. Both from the point of view of theoretical linguistics and of natural language pro-cessing, entries like that in the *American Heritage Dictionary* are the least helpful.

The objections to the entry in the *American Heritage Dictionary* push us in an obvious direction: we see *good* as having one sense, which takes different shades, depending on the meaning of the modified nouns. This sense of *good* is something like "assigning a high positive value range" to a selected property of the noun. Our entry for *good* (20) captures this meaning but refuses to specify the noun property, and we have a good reason for doing that. *Good* is, of course, an adjective with a very broadly applicable meaning, but the same objections to excessive polysemy hold for other adjectives as well. The same principle of polysemy reduction pertains to other lexical categories: thus, in Nirenburg, Raskin, and Onyshkevych 1995, we reduced fifty-two listed senses for the Spanish verb *dejar* to a manageable set of just seven.

9.3.6   Grain Size and Practical Effability
Reducing the number of senses in a polysemous lexical item affects the grain size of its semantic representation: the fewer the number, the larger the grain size. It would be beneficial for ontological semantics, both in acquisition and in processing, to keep the number of entries in a superentry as low as possible. Particular applications, however, may dictate a finer grain size for some superentries. Thus, the corporate sense of *acquire*, repeated here as (65), differs from the general sense of *acquire* only in the meaning of the filler for the THEME property of BUY, namely, ORGANIZATION as

opposed to OBJECT. According to the principle of reducing polysemy in the lexicon, this sense of *acquire* should not have been defined as a separate entry. The reason it was defined in the Mikrokosmos implementation of ontological semantics is that the implementation supported the application of processing texts about mergers and acquisitions, where this special sense of *acquire* was very prominent. Similarly, in the CAMBIO/CREST lexicon, the sports and the currency exchange domains were represented in much greater detail than in the Mikrokosmos lexicon.

```
(65)
acquire-v2
  cat  v
  anno def        "when a company buys another company, or its
                  division or subsidiary"
       ex         "Alpha Inc acquired from Gamma Inc the latter's
                  candle-making division"
  syn-struc
       root       acquire
       subj       root      $var1
                  cat       n
       obj        root      $var2
                  cat       n
       oblique root        from
                  cat       prep
                  opt       +
                  obj       root      $var3
                            cat       n
  sem-struc
       BUY
                  agent     value     ^$var1
                            sem       CORPORATION
                  theme     value     ^$var2
                            sem       ORGANIZATION
                  source    value     ^$var3
                            sem       CORPORATION
```

In the application of ontological semantics to machine translation, such as Mikrokosmos, meaning analysis and text generation at a certain grain size presuppose lexicons for the source and target languages which represent enough different word and phrase senses to give serious credence to a hope that a meaning expressed in one language will be largely expressible in another language, and at the same grain size. There are, however, cases when this presupposition will fail, and it is those cases that require a finer grain size of semantic analysis than the others. As a result, ontological semantics has variable grain-size meaning descriptions in its various implementations (see Nirenburg and Raskin 1986 for an early discussion of variable depth semantics).

One such case would be a situation when one word in a source language can be translated into a target language as either one of two words, and the decision as to which word to use requires additional information that the source text may not contain at all or at least not in an easily extractable way. For example, the English *corner* can be rendered in Spanish as either *rincón* "(inside) corner, nook" or as *esquina* "(outside) corner, street corner"; the English *blue* can be rendered in Russian as either *siniy* "dark blue, navy blue" or *goluboy* "light blue, baby (sky) blue." As a result, it is difficult to translate the sentences: *He could see the corner clearly* and *She wore a blue dress* into Spanish and Russian, respectively.

Refining the grain size for *corner* and *blue* in their lexical entries—by adding to their lexicon definitions appropriate distinguishing properties in order to accommodate Spanish and Russian—is possible, though often practically useless. This is because the data on which lexical constraints can be checked may not be present in either the text or extralinguistic context. The decision to maintain a grain size of certain coarseness will result in failing many of such cross-language mismatches when no additional lexical clues are available to help disambiguation. Such situations are notably also difficult for human translators, who often have to resort to guesses or arbitrary rules or conventions, such as the common practice of using a form of *goluboy* to translate *blue dress* when worn in the daytime and a form of *siniy* otherwise. The lack of specificity in language is a normal state of affairs because language always underdetermines reality (cf. Barwise and Perry 1983, 30): any sentence leaves out numerous details of the situation described in it, and in the case of the above examples, English underdetermines it more than Spanish or Russian.

In general, when one considers the entire gamut of applications requiring treatment of meaning, it becomes clear that no preset level of detail, or grain size in semantic description will be failproof. In fact, it is not reasonable even to pursue setting a priori grain size as an R&D goal. What is essential is to anticipate what information an application will require and be able to utilize and adjust the grain size of description accordingly, while fully realizing that there is much more that can be said or that, occasionally, the system may require more information than is available. For example, in the CAMBIO/CREST implementation of ontological semantics, the grain size of describing the sports domain is certainly not even the finest that the knowledge acquisition procedure could manage on the basis of the available inputs. It is rather coarser than that of sports page reports, especially box scores, in a newspaper. Thus, the CAMBIO/CREST FR contains information on goal scorers in soccer but not the individual statistics of, say, players on a basketball team. So, the system, as it stands, will not be able to answer directly the question who scored the most points in the Lithuania-USA basketball game at the Sydney Olympics. The best the system would be able to do is to refer the questioner to an online report about the game.

Whether or not it was reasonable to have established the cutoff in acquisition at that particular level, it is important to understand that some such cutoff will be necessary in any application, no matter how fine the grain size of description actually is. There can always be an expectation of a question that refers to a data item that was not recorded in the static knowledge sources of an ontological semantic application. What makes systems with natural language input and output, such as MT, different is that, apparently, the linguistic universals make all natural languages in some sense "self-regulating" in maintaining roughly similar levels of grain size in deciding on what becomes a lexeme, and this is reflected in the principle of effability.

We use the principle of effability, or mutual intertranslatability of natural languages, in Katz's (1978, 209) formulation: "Each proposition can be expressed by some sentence in any natural language" (see also Katz 1972/1974, 18–24; Frege 1963, 1; Tarski 1956, 19–21; Searle 1969, 19–21). This is, of course, a view which is opposite to that famously formulated by Quine (1960, 26–30) in his *gavagai* discourse. In our work, we have to assume a stronger form of this principle. The generic formulation of this stronger form, expressed in the terms of the philosophical debate on effability, is as follows:

Hypothesis of practical effability.   Each sentence can be translated into another natural language on the basis of a lexicon compiled at the same level of granularity, which is made manifest by the roughly comparable ratio of entries per superentry.

A version more attuned to the environment of computational applications can be formulated as follows:

Hypothesis of practical effability for computational applications.   Any text in the source language can be translated into the target language in an acceptable way on the basis of a lexicon for the source language and a lexicon for the target language with a comparable ratio of entries per superentry.

We have consistently been able to use fewer than ten, very often, fewer than five senses per lexeme. The limitation does not, of course, affect the scope of the word meaning: all the possible senses of a lexical item are captured in the superentry. The small number of these senses simply means a larger grain size. In a limited domain, however, some senses of the same word can be ignored because they denote concepts that are not used in the domain, are not part of the sublanguage that serves the domain, and thus are unlikely to occur in the corresponding corpora (see Nirenburg and Raskin 1987c; Raskin 1971, 1987a, 1987b, 1990).

The practical effability hypothesis was successfully tested on a corpus of English with 1,506 adjective senses. Let us see how exactly it is reflected in the choices forming the lexical entries. The adjective *good* is, again, a good example. We will show how, for this adjective, we settled on a grain size of description coarser than the most detailed semantic analysis possible. We will then see how the principle of not specifying in detail the specific noun property modified by an adjective applies to all the other adjectives as well. And we will briefly discuss the conceptual and computational status of those properties which are introduced by the scales we need to postulate for adjective entries.

We interpret *good* in a sentence like *This is a good book* as, essentially, *The speaker evaluates this book highly*. We realize that in this sentence *good* may have a large variety of senses, some of which are illustrated in the possible continuations of the sentence (cf. example (23) in section 7.2):

- ... because it is very informative.
- ... because it is very entertaining.
- ... because the style is great.
- ... because it looks great on the coffee table.
- ... because it is made very sturdily and will last for centuries.

In each case, *good* selects a property of a noun and assigns it a high value on the evaluation scale associated with that property. The property changes not only from noun to noun but also within the same noun, depending on the context. The finest grain-size analysis requires that a certain property of the modified noun be contextually selected as the one on which the meaning of the noun and that of the adjective is connected. This is what many psychologists call a "salient" property. In our approach, the representation solution for *good* would be to introduce an evaluation modality, with a high value and scoped over this property.

Now, it is difficult to identify salient properties formally, as is well known, for instance, in the scholarship on metaphor, where salience is the determining factor for the similarity dimension on which metaphors, and similes, are based (see, for instance, Black 1954–55, 1979; Davidson 1978; Lakoff and Johnson 1980; Lakoff 1987; Searle 1979; on salience, specifically, see Tversky and Kahnemann 1983). It is, therefore, wise to avoid having to search for the salient property, and the hypothesis of practical effability offers a justification for this. What this means, in plainer terms, is that if we treat the meaning of *good* as unspecified with regard to the nominal property it modifies, there is a solid chance that there will be an adjective with a matching generalized, unspecified meaning like that in the target language as well.

In fact, however, we go one step further with the lexical entry of *good* and other adjectives from the same scale and remove their meaning from the nouns they modify, making them contribute instead to an evaluative modality pertaining to the whole sentence. It can be argued, of course, that since the scope of the modality remains the modified noun, all that changes is the formalism and not the essence of the matter. We do not wish to insist, therefore, that this additional step constitutes a step towards an even larger grain size.

Non-modality-based scalars are treated in a standard fashion: their lexicon entries effectively execute the following, informally defined, procedure: insert the scale name and scale value for an adjective as a property-value pair in the frame describing the meaning of the noun the adjective modifies.

If *house*, in one of its senses, has the following lexicon entry:

```
house-n2
      cat     n
      syn-struc
              root    house
              cat     n
      sem-struc
              PRIVATE-HOME
```

then the meanings of the phrases *big house* and *red house* will be represented in TMRs as follows:

```
PRIVATE-HOME
      ...
      SIZE-ATTRIBUTE          value   >0.75
      ...

PRIVATE-HOME
      ...
      COLOR-ATTRIBUTE         value   red
```

In the former example, the attribute is selected rather high in the hierarchy of attributes—in the ontology SIZE-ATTRIBUTE is the parent of such properties as LENGTH-ATTRIBUTE, WIDTH-ATTRIBUTE, AREA-ATTRIBUTE, WEIGHT-ATTRIBUTE, and so on. If the context does not allow the analyzer to select one of those, a coarser-grain solution is preferred. In other words, we represent the meaning of *big house* without specifying whether *big* pertains to the length, width, height or area of a house. Such decisions, affecting all types of lexemes not only adjectives, are made throughout the ontological lexicon acquisition.

9.3.7 Ontological Matching and Lexical Constraints

Leaving the syntactic description step in lexical acquisition to the end, in order to discuss it together with linking, we will focus here on the basic question, What does this word mean? In some sense, this is the most important question in lexical acquisition. It is remarkable, therefore, how relatively little is written in semantic literature about it. Most authors prefer to discuss details of representation formalisms for meaning specifications, with no apparent interest in showing how one arrives at the content of meaning specification that is stated in examples. This is true with respect not only to lexical semantics but also to compositional semantics, the study of deriving meaning representations of texts on the basis, among other factors, of lexical meaning (see sections 3.5.2, 3.5.3, and 3.7).

In this section, we discuss, then, two related but distinct issues in lexical acquisition, namely, how a lexicon acquirer can discover what a lexeme means and how the choice is made of the way to represent this meaning. The commitment to using the ontology in lexical meaning specification helps to determine the actual representation of a lexical entry but it does not make it a deterministic process: there are further choices to make that require a theoretical underpinning. These choices form the basis of a procedure that a human acquirer follows for lexical acquisition. The first step of this procedure, polysemy reduction, was discussed in section 9.3.5. The following steps relate to the determination of meaning of one particular sense of a lexeme.

The next step is checking whether the meaning of a word can be fully, or almost fully, reduced to that of another. We showed above that a word may be a member of a class, such as that of adjectives of size, for which a single meaning template can be used. That was grouping by meaning. Orthogonally, the acquirer must check whether a morphological cognate of the word being acquired is already in the lexicon, to establish whether the new meaning can be derived from that of the cognate, either with the help of a lexical rule (see section 9.3.3) or directly. Thus, the acquirer will correctly determine that the meaning of the adjective *abhorrent* (63) is the same as that of the verb *abhor* (62).

If the candidate sense does not belong to a semantic class some of whose members have already been given lexical descriptions, or when there are no useful morphological cognates with lexicon entries, a new lexicon entry must be created from scratch. In that case, the next step must be to determine whether there is an element in the ontology or the TMR specification that should be used in the representation of the entry being acquired. We describe at length elsewhere (see section 7.2) what factors determine the decision to relate a lexical entry directly to an existing ontological concept or property in another concept or to describe it in parametric terms. Here we will focus on the former option, that is, finding a suitable ontological concept.

Remember that at this stage, the acquirer already has the name of the lexical entry and its lexicographical definition, borrowed and/or adapted from an MRD or another source. Looking for the most appropriate ontological concept, the acquirer attempts to match the name and/or the most information-laden, in his opinion, part(s) of the word meaning definition with a concept name or the fillers of the DEFINITION property. Let us consider the word *shirt* in its "garment" sense. The

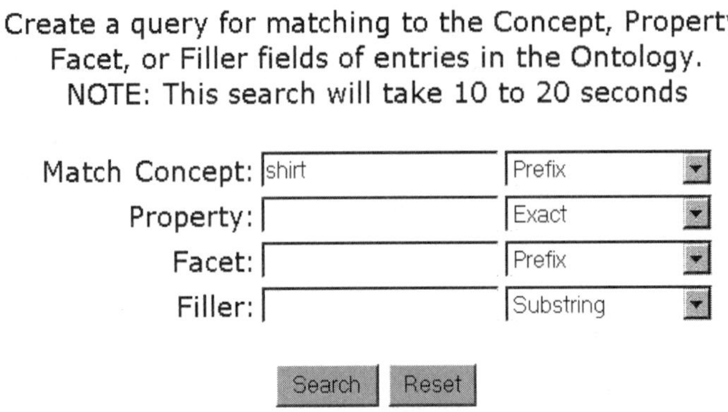

Create a query for matching to the Concept, Property,
Facet, or Filler fields of entries in the Ontology.
NOTE: This search will take 10 to 20 seconds

Match Concept: |shirt| | Prefix   ▾|
Property: | | | Exact   ▾|
Facet: | | | Prefix   ▾|
Filler: | | | Substring ▾|

[Search] [Reset]

Figure 9.9
The main window of the search tool in the CAMBIO/CREST implementation of ontological
semantics.

CAMBIO/CREST implementation of ontological semantics supplies a tool to support this search (figure 9.9).

The search will actually yield two concepts, SHIRT and SHIRT-NUMBER (figure 9.10), because, as shown in figure 9.9, the search mode was "prefix" and thus asked for all concept names that begin with the string "shirt." While the "exact" search mode would yield only SHIRT, the consideration that the name of the concept may not exactly match the word, might make the "prefix" or even "substring" modes of the search preferable. The definition of the concept SHIRT will correspond to the acquirer's lexicographical definition and the SEM-STRUC zone of the entry will contain only a reference to an instance of the concept SHIRT, with no further constraints. This is, of course, the simplest case.

What if the concept SHIRT had not been found? The next option is to use the search tool to look for a string in definitions of ontological concepts. It is reasonable to suppose that the word *garment* is used in the lexicographical definitions available to the acquirer, and the acquirer will choose this as a search string (figure 9.11). The search yields all the concepts that contain *garment* in their definitions (figure 9.12).

If, counterfactually, SHIRT were not among them, the acquirer would look these concepts up and check whether they are appropriate siblings for the meaning of *shirt*. If this is so, which would be the case, the next step would be to add SHIRT as a sibling and make it the meaning of *shirt*. To determine their common parent, the acquirer will click on any sibling, and discover that it is CLOTHING-ARTIFACT (figure 9.13). The new ontological concept SHIRT will then become a child of the latter.

If the above or similar heuristics for quickly finding the ontological concept on which to base the meaning of a lexical entry fail, the fallback procedure is to perform

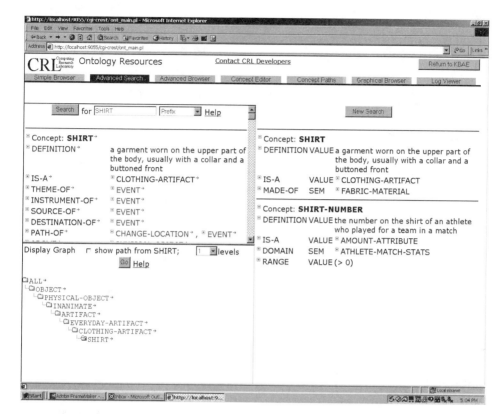

Figure 9.10
A sample screen from the acquisition and browsing tool from the CAMBIO/CREST implementation of ontological semantics. The concept SHIRT.

Create a query for matching to the Concept, Property,
Facet, or Filler fields of entries in the Ontology.
NOTE: This search will take 10 to 20 seconds

Match Concept: [ ] Prefix
Property: definition Exact
Facet: [ ] Prefix
Filler: garment Substring

Search   Reset

Figure 9.11
Search on *garment* in the definition field.

⊕ Concept: **COAT**

⊕ DEFINITION VALUE a sleeved outer garment opening down
                             the front

⊕ Concept: **DRESS**

⊕ DEFINITION VALUE the usual outer garment of women,
                             generally of one piece with a skirt

---

⊕ Concept: **SHIRT**

⊕ DEFINITION VALUE a garment worn on the upper part of
                             the body, usually with a collar and a
                             buttoned front

⊕ Concept: **TROUSERS**

⊕ DEFINITION VALUE a two-legged garment, extending from
                             the waist to the ankles

⊕ Concept: **VEST**

⊕ DEFINITION VALUE a short sleeveless garment, especially
                             worn under a suit coat by men

Figure 9.12
Results of the search on *garment* in the definition field.

a descending traversal of the ontological hierarchy, the way it is done in ontology acquisition (see section 9.2). Unfortunately, there is no guarantee that this procedure will yield an appropriate ontological concept, either for direct specification of meaning or as a possible parent for a new concept that would serve as the basis of the lexical meaning. Such an eventuality can be a clue that the meaning should be formulated in ways other than ontological—that is, parametrically (or, as in the case of *comfortable*, as a hybrid of ontological and parametric representation means).

Thus, reopening the case of *abhor*, its parametric representation in (62) actually historically emerged in the Mikrokosmos implementation of ontological semantics after an earlier attempt to place it in the EVENT branch of the ontology failed: there were no concepts in it that were similar to it, due to the strategic decision not to represent states as EVENTS. As a result of that decision, the lexical entry for *like* was represented parametrically, and the acquirer applied the semantic class membership rule to modify the meaning of *like* to yield that of *abhor*.

Recall that we deliberately referred to the ontological concepts for which we looked in the above step as "the basis of the specification of the lexical meaning." The reason for this pedantic formulation is that, except in the simplest cases, such as that of *shirt*, the accurate specification of lexical meaning will require modifications to the fillers of properties in the concept, such as changing the filler of the THEME of

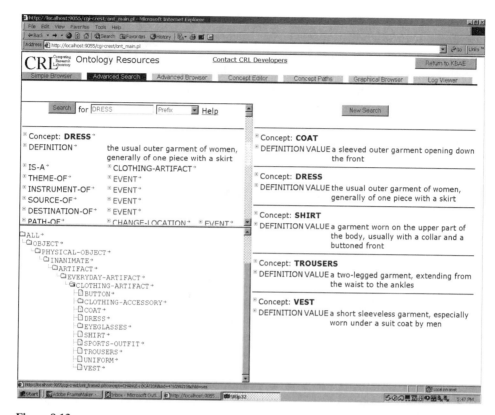

Figure 9.13
The concept DRESS in the CAMBIO/CREST browser.

BUY to accommodate the corporate sense of *acquire* from OBJECT to ORGANIZATION. Sometimes, support for such modifications comes from the lexicographic definitions available to the acquirer.

So far in this section, we have been discussing what amounts to elements of the microtheory of lexical semantics for most open-class lexical entities. There are many other words in the language that must be given a lexical description but whose meanings are not based on an ontological concept or property. Some of these words contribute grammatical information (see sections 6.3 and 7.2) and often serve as triggers for such text analysis procedures as reference resolution (see section 8.6.1). The format of the lexicon in ontological semantics licenses the specification of such items, as it does for phrasals and idioms. While in any practical application of ontological semantics, the coverage of such lexical elements is required (as is the capability to support any morphological and syntactic processing), it is not appropriate to describe here in detail the microtheories that deal with phenomena such as the above. The interested reader will find detailed instructions for the acquisition of all the static resources in ontological semantics, including all the types of lexical entities, in the Ontological Semantics Resources area at the UMBC ILIT website: http://ilit .umbc.edu. The materials there include tutorials for ontology and lexicon acquirers and an updated description of the latest version of the ontology. The area also contains a link to the ontology browser.

The lexicon tutorial concentrates on the acquisition of syntactic and semantic dependency structures as well as the syntax-to-semantics linking. It also contains a large number of richly annotated examples of entries for verbs, nouns, adjectives, and adverbs that provide good guidelines for English and, we believe, are actually applicable—with modifications—to work on other languages. The ontology acquisition tutorial explicates a number of everyday choices that an ontology acquirer must make.

9.4   Acquisition of Fact Repository

Facts in the FR are acquired to support a particular application, and the nature of the acquired facts is dictated by the application's needs. Many of the facts provide the semantics for entries in the onomasticon (see section 7.4). These are *named facts*. Facts that do not have a name property (*unnamed facts*) include those automatically derivable from TMRs as a side effect of the operation of an ontological semantic application. This capability has not yet been implemented in ontological semantics.

Acquisition of both named and unnamed facts can be carried out manually, by people taking specific concepts from the ontology and, on reading a text or several texts, filling an instance of this concept with information, in the metalanguage of ontological semantics and storing it in the FR. For example, a movie star's career can be presented this way, as would be reports about company earnings. What is interesting about acquiring facts is the potential for automating a significant portion of the fact acquisition task. In the CAMBIO/CREST implementation of ontological semantics, the acquisition of FR for the domain of sports has enjoyed significant levels of automation, while the acquisition of the ontology and the lexicon, though considerably automated, still, at the time of writing, contains an irreducible human component.

In the above implementation of ontological semantics, acquisition of facts was partially automated using automatic information extraction. The process has been as follows. First, the ontology was used to generate a set of extraction templates. In the sports domain, these included the templates based on the ontological concepts ATHLETE, NATION, SPORTS-RESULT and some others. A large subset of properties from these concepts were selected for inclusion in the facts. Second, an information extraction program was used on the content of many Web pages devoted to the Sydney Olympics to fill these templates with snippets of text. Third, people converted the text to expressions in the ontological metalanguage, as a result of which candidate facts were produced. Finally, a combined automatic/human step of validation of the syntax (automatically) and content (manually) of the newly acquired facts was carried out. The FR in this implementation was used to support a question answering application.

Even in a book-length account of ontological semantics, many very important issues had to be left out. We have not covered in any detail certain aspects of ontological semantic processing, a number of applications of ontological semantics, and some important methodological issues.

In processing, the most glaring omissions are the lack of attention to text generation and to detail of reasoning (inference-making) processes. With respect to applications, we have not dwelt sufficiently on the considerable potential of ontological semantics for enahncing the quality of human-computer dialog and other higher-end information-processing applications requiring extraction and manipulation of meaning.

Versions of the text generator have been developed in the Dionysus (Nirenburg, Lesser, and Nyberg 1989) and Mikrokosmos (Beale and Nirenburg 1995, 1996; Beale, Viegas, and Nirenburg 1997; Beale et al. 1998) implementations of ontological semantics. Reasoning capabilities were developed, for instance, in the Savona system (Nirenburg 1998b). In text generation, the ontological semantic apparatus helps to choose what to say at the first stage of generation, offers a rich search space for lexical realization options, and provides a convenient control structure (Beale 1997) for combining realization constraints from semantic and nonsemantic sources. Ontological semantics can support generation not only of text but also of text augmented by tables, diagrams, pictures, and other illustrative material.

The richness of the knowledge content in the ontology and the fact repository opens possibilities for enhancing automatic reasoning useful for a variety of desirable applications. The inclusion of complex events in the ontology promises better results in story recognition, in planning dialog responses, and in determining the goals of the text producer. The general idea is not new: in AI it ascends to the script-processing efforts of the 1970s and 1980s (Schank 1975; Schank and Riesbeck 1981). Of course, ontological semantics departs from these early experiments in that it not only presents complex events at a realistic, nontoy grain size but also includes sufficiently fine-grained knowledge content for all the other components needed for processing.

However large the content of all the static and dynamic knowledge sources in ontological semantics may seem, it is quite appropriate to view it as the world and language knowledge within a software-embodied intelligent agent in a society of such intelligent agents. The ontological semantic content of different software agents can be different in a number of details, though in order to maintain communicability among the intelligent agents and between them and human agents in a variety of interesting applications, there must be a significant overlap. Clearly, any, even limited, success in this area promises substantial practical benefits in various applications, notably including Internet-related activities. Once again, the idea as such is not new: people have already talked about avatars and other personal agents (for the latest, see, for instance Agents-98; Agents-99; Cassell and Vilhjálmsson 1999; Woolridge 2002) to help people with their information needs. It is, once again, the detail of content in ontological semantics that promises to bring such applications to a new level of quality.

To support reasoning by intelligent agents, their knowledge bases must include not only their own ontology and FR (we downplay here the role of the language-oriented resources in this process) but also their impressions of the ontologies and FRs of their interlocutors. This capability is important in recognition of goals and plans of other agents. Thus, if agent A relates to agent B that it has finished editing, agent B, using its ontology for agent A, recognizes the complex event of which this instance of editing is a part and then can project what the next activity of agent A should be. Usually in applications this situation is simplified by assuming the same ontology for each agent involved. The ontologies of agents A and B may, in fact, differ. A particular complex event can be simply absent in one of the agents' ontologies. Also, one agent's notion of the ontology and the FR of the other agent may be inaccurate. Many more discrepancies are possible, all resulting in wrong conclusions.

A natural, though possibly spurious issue here is that of infinite regress of models of the ontologies of others' ontologies of oneself, and so on. While some such knowledge may indeed be important in some applications, the complexity inherent in multiply nested ontologies inside each intelligent agent makes reasoning over them prohibitively expensive. It was most probably the realization of this fact that led Ballim and Wilks (1991) to curtail the levels of inclusion of beliefs of others in their model to no more than three turns.

Modeling intelligent agents using the ontological semantic apparatus will also facilitate general experimentation in dialog processing. Among many potential uses, ontological semantics can provide the knowledge and processing substrate for large-scale implementations of the ideas about treating the dialog situation—for example, for studying the levels of similarity between the speaker's and hearer's ontologies and FRs necessary to attain acceptable levels of understanding in a dialog.

Much more development is needed for the module of ontological semantics that deals with the theory and methodology of knowledge acquisition. Throughout the book, we touched on a number of factors relevant to knowledge acquisition, such as the metalanguage of ontological semantic description, the principles of anchoring lexical meaning in ontological concepts, practical recommendations on bunching word senses to simplify the specification of lexical semantics, and so on. Still, additional research is needed into the nature and bounds of the human ability to adequately express internalized knowledge about the world and the language, and to do it in terms of the ontological semantic metalanguage.

With regard to the first point, a distinction must be drawn between having an internalized view of the world and operating on it to carry out a broad variety of cognitive, perception, and motor tasks, on the one hand, and the ability to understand, through introspection, that one has such knowledge and to describe it coherently. All people have a view of the world but very few can express what this view is, and even then the question arises whether that explanation is reliable. One important reason for this inability is the lack of an established and universally accepted metalanguage for such activities. It was this state of affairs that elicited the cry of surprise "I never knew that I was speaking prose" from Molière's Monsieur Jourdain.

Had we predicated knowledge acquisition in ontological semantics on the acquirers' ability (or inability) to express internalized knowledge, a legitimate question could have been raised of the feasibility of this program of work. In fact, what human acquirers in ontological semantics are asked to do is a different, much more attainable task of taking a suggested quantum of knowledge and expressing its semantics (world- or language-related) in terms of small increments to already available static knowledge sources. In other words, the acquirer is given a knowledge element to process and shown how similar elements have already been represented. The mental operations for the acquirer are, then, among the simplest such actions that a person can perform—comparison of two entities and establishing minimum differences between them. The ontology and lexica acquired so far provide a source of candidates for new acquisition, as do text corpora. Thus, our approach is heavily biased toward the empirical end of the methodological scale. Then, introspection, the least reliable knowledge acquisition technique at the opposite end of the methodological scale, becomes highly optional. It is precisely the availability of previously acquired, sufficiently detailed static knowledge sources—that is, ontology and lexicons—that allows us to turn a questionable activity into a feasible task. In a sense, the change is similar to a move from essay-type tests to multiple-choice ones. The first stage of work in ontological semantics on which we report in this book resulted in the development of the initial knowledge sources that license the non-introspective new acquisition phase.

The development of ontological semantics continues in the direction of better coverage and finer grain size. The further refinement and automation of tools and the adaptable, hybrid methodological base of ontological semantics steadily bring down the concomitant acquisition costs and support improvement of the processing components. The emphasis on rich semantic content and the unique division of labor between humans and computers, both in acquisition time and within applications, overcomes the common pessimism about applications based on the representation and treatment of meaning with regard to the attainability of fully automatic, high-quality results at a reasonable cost.

Notes

Chapter 1

1. This assumption follows the well-established views of Newell and Simon (1972) and Miller and Johnson-Laird (1976).

2. The presence of the notions of goal and plan makes this communication model nontrivially distinct from Jakobson's (1960) original speaker-message-hearer scheme, a linguistic adaptation of Shannon and Weaver's (1949) classical model.

3. Agent models for other AI applications, such as general planning and problem solving, may require additional facets and may not need some of the facets we list.

4. As we briefly mentioned above, in early applications of ontological semantics (see, e.g., Nirenburg and Raskin 1987a, 1987b), we maintained that different lexicons have to be produced for analysis and generation. It seems now that this decision was in large part induced by the logistics of knowledge acquisition in a large application project. In fact, the overlap of the knowledge in the two lexicons is quite considerable—even the collocation information that we once considered useful mostly in the lexical selection process in generation appears to be valuable in certain situations in analysis as well.

Chapter 2

1. Of course, language itself has not been ignored by philosophy: much of the philosophy of the twentieth century has been interested precisely in language. Under different historical circumstances, the philosophy of language would have probably come to be known as a strain of linguistics and/or logic rather than a movement in philosophy. This would not pertain to the so-called linguistic turn (cf. Rorty 1967) in philosophy, a sweeping movement from the study of philosophical issues to the study of the utterances expressing these issues.

2. But we have worked on this book for so long that now, on rereading this passage, we can no longer tell which of us was which.

3. Pustejovsky, in his response to the review (Pustejovsky 1998), commented on the differences in the premises, but those, even if valid, would be entailed by the much more essential differences in the purview.

4. In the philosophy of science, especially of AI, Marr's (1982) approach to computational modeling of vision seriously influenced the thinking and writing on computationalism in general—that is, stages, validity, and goals of top-down computer models for mental processes

and activity, mostly on the strong-AI premise (cf. sections 2.4.2.2 and 2.4.3). For various foundational issues with the approach, see Kitcher 1988; Dennett 1991; Horgan and Tienson 1994, 305–307; Hardcastle 1995; Gilman 1996.

5. "It would be fair to say," Moody explains (1993, 2), "that the foundations of a discipline are the concepts and principles most taken for granted in it. In mathematics, for example, a foundational proposition would be, 'There are sets.' The philosopher of mathematics might or might not want to deny this proposition, but would certainly want to ask in a rigorous way what it means." Setless mathematics is definitely a possibility, even if it has not and will not be explored, but, as we will see in section 2.6.2, the computational linguistic premises we have to deal with sound less trivial and impose tough and real choices for the researcher.

6. This group of "antiexperientialists" is not homogeneous: Rorty stands out as accused of an attempt "to discredit, or to replace, the whole analytical enterprise" (Strawson 1993), something neither Popper nor Davidson is usually charged with.

7. Chomsky assumes a similar position as early as *Syntactic Structures* (1957, 49) without any indication that this is a very controversial issue: "A grammar of the language L is essentially a theory of L," he writes. "Any scientific theory is based on a finite number of observations, and it seeks to relate the observed phenomena and to predict new phenomena by constructing general laws in terms of hypothetical constructs such as (in physics, for example) 'mass' and 'electron.' Similarly, a grammar of English is based on a finite corpus of utterances (observations), and it will contain certain grammatical rules (laws) stated in terms of particular phonemes, phrases, etc., of English (hypothetical constructs). These rules express structural relations among the sentences of the corpus and the indefinite number of sentences generated by the grammar beyond the corpus (predictions). Our problem is to develop and clarify the criteria for selecting the correct grammar for each language, that is, the correct theory of this language." But Chomsky took his position much further by letting the theory itself decide certain matters of reality: "Notice that in order to set the aims of grammar significantly it is sufficient to assume a partial knowledge of sentences and non-sentences. That is, we may assume for this discussion that certain sequences of phonemes are definitely sentences, and that certain other sequences are definitely non-sentences. In intermediate cases we shall be prepared to let the grammar itself decide, when the grammar is set up in the simplest way so that it includes the clear sentences and excludes the clear non-sentences" (pp. 13–14). If this sounds too radical—letting a theory decide if a string is a sentence or not, which is a matter of empirical fact for the speaker—he defers to an authoritative source: "To use Quine's formulation, a linguistic theory will give a general explanation for what 'could' be in language on the basis of 'what *is* plus *simplicity* of the laws whereby we describe and extrapolate what is' (Quine [1953], 54)" (p. 14n). Chomsky's position on justification has never changed, largely because he essentially abandoned the issue itself after 1965.

8. This is, of course, rather a cavalier use of the very complex and controversial category. Chomsky does not refer to a vast field of study with regard to the category. See, for instance, Popper 1959 (cf. Simon 1968, 453); Good 1969 (recanted in Good 1983); Rosenkrantz 1976; and especially Sober 1975. According to Richmond 1996, these authors attempted to explain simplicity in terms of the equally complex categories of familiarity and falsifiability, content, likelihood, and relative informativeness.

9. Especially in applications but to some degree also in theoretical work, one must be careful not to yield to the temptation to "show one's ingenuity" by introducing properties, categories,

and relations that might be descriptively adequate but that are not necessary for description. Such a proliferation of terms is generally typical of structuralist work, from which the concern of both the generative and computational approaches about the use of each category in a rule or an algorithm is typically missing. For a contemporary structuralist example see Mel'čuk 1997, 1998. An example of the use of parsimony in transformational grammar (most influentially, perhaps, Postal 1971) has been the long practice of never introducing a new transformational rule for describing a phenomenon unless that rule could be independently motivated by its applicability to a different class of phenomena. In our own work, we discovered that the distinction between the attributive and predicative use of adjectives, widely considered essential, has no bearing on a theory of adjectival meaning and should not therefore be included in it (for details, see Raskin and Nirenburg 1995, 1998)—for lack of any independent motivation.

10. The notion of finiteness brings up the dimension of theory implementation within given resources. We will discuss this issue in detail in section 2.5.

11. Searle (1969) denies chess the status of objective reality because, unlike natural phenomena whose laws may be discovered, chess is a constructed phenomenon "constituted" by its rules. For our purposes, this distinction is immaterial; see a more detailed discussion of the relation of linguistic theories to reality in Nirenburg and Raskin 1996.

12. For early influential work on (un)decidability, see Tarski 1953. For further discussion, see Ackermann 1968 and Gill 1990. On computability, see a good summary in Ershov 1996. On constructibility, very pertinently to our effectiveness, see Mostowski 1969 and Devlin 1984. On decidability in natural language, cf. Wilks 1971.

13. Will, for instance, a syntactic analyzer based on Chomsky's transformational grammar (TG) be tractable? For the sake of simplicity, let us assume its output for each sentence to be a representation, with each constituent phrase bracketed and labeled by the rules that generated the phrase. The input to the analyzer will be simply a string of words, and the analyzer will have to insert the parentheses and labels. Is it computable? It is, but only for grammatical sentences. If the string is ungrammatical, the algorithm will never find a sequence of rules, no matter how long, that will generate the string and will continue to attempt the derivation indefinitely. The noncomputability of the system, if not supplied with an external halting condition, is the killing argument against the TG (or any) formalism as the basis for computational syntactic analysis (parsing). Apparently, no such halting condition could be formulated, so a high-powered effort to develop such an analyzer for TG failed (see Zwicky et al. 1965 and Friedman 1971 on the MITRE project), as did, in fact, a similar effort with regard to Montague grammars (Hobbs and Rosenschein 1977; Friedman, Moran, and Warren 1978a, 1978b; Hirst 1983, 1987; cf. Raskin 1990, 117). In fact, a kind of natural selection occurred early on, when NLP systems started selecting as their syntactic bases simpler and possibly less adequate grammatical models that contained a workable halting condition (see, for instance, Winograd 1971, which deliberately uses a simplified version of systemic grammar—see Berry 1975, 1977; Halliday 1983; cf. Halliday 1985—rather than any version of transformational grammar). Later, several more tractable and NLP-friendly approaches were developed that used many facets of Chomsky's grammar. These include head phrase structure grammar (Pollard 1984; Pollard and Sag 1994), tree-adjoining grammars (Joshi, Levy, and Takabashi 1975; Joshi 1985; Weir, Vijay-Shanker, and Joshi 1986), and unification grammars (Kay 1985; Shieber 1986). NLP-friendliness does not mean just an aspect of formality—it has also to do with literal friendliness. Chomsky's open hostility to computation in linguistics as manifested most publicly in "The Great Debate," aka "the Sloan money battle," mostly by proxy, between

Chomsky and Roger Schank (Dresher and Hornstein 1976, 1977a, 1977b; Schank and Wilensky 1977; Winograd 1977; for a personal memoir, see Lehnert 1994, 148ff; for a related discussion, see Nirenburg 1986), has contributed greatly to the practical disconnect between Chomsky's subsequent theoretical formulations—from standard theory (Chomsky 1965) to extended standard theory (Chomsky 1971) to traces (Chomsky 1973) to government and binding and principles and parameters (Chomsky 1981) and, most recently, to the minimalist position (Chomsky 1995)—and the development of syntactic parsers.

14. The issue of computation on the basis of a theory that is not completely formal is very complex. The content of Nirenburg and Raskin 1996, Mahesh 1996, and Viegas and Raskin 1998 can be considered as a case study and illustration of this issue.

15. Quine (1994, 144) puts it very simply and categorically: "On the philosophical side, the regimentation embodied in predicate logic has also brought illumination quite apart from the technology of deduction. It imposes a new and simple syntax on our whole language, insofar as our logic is to apply. Stripped down to the austere economy that I first described for predicate logic, our simple new syntax is as follows. The parts of speech are: (1) the truth-functional connective, (2) the universal quantifier, (3) variables, and (4) atomic predicates of one and more places. The syntactic constructions are: (1) application of a predicate to the appropriate number of variables to form a sentence; (2) prefixture of a quantifier, with its variable, to a sentence; and (3) joining sentences by the truth-functional connective and the adjusting parentheses. I hesitate to claim that this syntax, so trim and clear, can accommodate in translation all cognitive discourse. I can say, however, that no theory is fully clear to me unless I can see how this syntax would accommodate it. In particular, all of pure classical mathematics can be thus accommodated. This is putting it mildly. The work of Whitehead and Russell and their predecessors and successors shows that the described syntax together with a single two-place predicate by way of extra-logical vocabulary, namely the 'e' of class membership, suffices in principle for it all. Even '=' is not needed; it can be paraphrased in terms of 'e'."

16. This methodological bias is not limited to linguistics. It was for a very similar transgression that Bar Hillel criticized the methodology of logical semanticists: they unduly constrain their purview, and within that limited purview, concentrate primarily on exceptions: "One major prejudice ... is the tendency to assign truth values to indicative sentences in natural languages and to look at those cases where such a procedure seems to be somehow wrong" (Bar Hillel 1970, 203).

17. We understand what Moody means by "philosophical interest," however. On the one hand, it is the fascinating if still tentative philosophy of mind (see, for instance, Simon 1979, 1989; Fodor 1990, 1994; Jackendoff 1994); on the other hand, it is the recurring fashion involving imagination-stimulating, science fiction–inspired punditry in the media about robots and thinking machines and the philosophical ramifications of their future existence.

18. A considerable number of interesting contributions in AI heuristics (see Zanakis, Evans, and Vazacopoulos 1989 for an early survey) developed Newell and Simon's general ideas on problem solving (Newell and Simon 1961; Newell, Shaw, and Simon 1958; Newell and Simon 1972; Simon 1977, 1983), from automating discovery strategy in largely mathematical toy domains (e.g., Lenat 1982, 1983) to a densely populated area of heuristic search techniques (e.g., Lawler and Wood 1966; Nilsson 1971; Pearl 1984; Reeves 1993; Rayward-Smith 1995) to considerable initial progress in automatic theorem solving (see, for instance, Gelernter and Rochester 1958; Gelernter 1959, 1963; Gelernter, Hansen, and Loveland 1963) and machine

learning (see, for instance, Forsyth and Rada 1986; Shavlik and Dietterich 1990; Kearns and Vazirani 1994; Langley 1996; Mitchell 1997).

19. Just as it was easy to believe that we had gone through Dewey's (1910, 74–104) five psychological phases of problem solving—suggestion, intellectualization, the guiding idea, reasoning, and testing hypotheses by action—or Wallas's (1926, 79–107) psychological steps, namely, preparation, incubation, illumination, and verification, or even psychotherapist Moustakas's (1990) six phases of heuristic research: initial engagement, immersion, incubation, illumination, explication, and creative synthesis. Somewhat more substantively, we definitely recognized various forms of guessing and judging under uncertainty—that is, essentially engaging in certain forms of abduction, as explored by Tversky and Kahneman (1973; see also Kahneman, Slovik, and Tversky 1982; cf. Heath and Tindale 1994).

20. In other words, we decline to follow the path, memorably marked by Lakoff (1971), when, in the opening salvos of the official warfare in early transformational semantics, he projected what his foes in interpretive semantics (Katz and Fodor 1963) would do if they made a step they had not made, and proceeded to attack them for that hypothetically ascribed stance.

21. Completeness is understood here relative to a certain given grain size of description. Without this a priori threshold, such descriptions may well be infinite.

22. One can adopt a view that any application is based on a theory, in a trivial sense, namely the theory that underlies it. In NLP practice, such a theory is not usually cognized by the developers, but the point we are making is that that theory will not typically coincide with any single linguistic theory. It will, in the general case, be a hybrid of elements of several theories and a smattering of elements not supported by a theory.

23. A series of interesting but largely inconclusive experiments was conducted within the protocol approach to invention in rhetoric and composition in the 1980s (see, for instance, Flower 1981 and references there; cf. Flower 1994). Writers were asked to comment on their thinking processes as they were composing a new text. On the use of the technique in cognitive science, see Ericsson and Simon 1993.

24. An even more ostentatious attempt in overt theory building is Katz and Postal 1964, where semantic reality was manipulated to fit into an imported premise, later abandoned in revised standard theory (Chomsky 1971), that transformations did not change meaning.

25. As Moody (1993, 3) puts it, "If the sciences are indeed the paradigms of progress, they achieve this status by somehow bypassing the foundational questions or, as was said earlier, by taking certain foundations for granted.... The practical rule in the sciences seems to be: Avoid confronting foundational questions until the avoidance blocks further progress." As this chapter documents, we do believe, on the basis of our practical experience, that we are at the stage in the development of NLP, computational semantics, and perhaps linguistic semantics in general, where "the avoidance blocks further progress."

26. The term *knowledge-based* is used here in a broad sense to mean "relying on overtly specified linguistic knowledge about a particular language," and not in its narrow sense of "machine translation based on artificial intelligence methods."

27. The state of knowledge in this field is still pretheoretical, as a variety of engineering solutions featuring eclectic methodology are propounded for a number of applications. It will be interesting to see whether a theory of merging tools and resources will gradually emerge. The work on computational linguistic architectures (e.g., Cunningham et al. 1997a, 1997b; Zajac,

Casper, and Sharples 1997) is, in fact, a step toward developing a format of a language to talk about such mergers, which can be considered a part of the body of a theory.

28. It is possible to argue that single-meaning entries in the English vocabulary (not, of course, their combinations in complete entries for actual English words—cf. Nirenburg and Raskin 1998; Viegas and Raskin 1998) may serve as crude approximations for universal lexical-semantic parameters. Even on such an assumption, methodologically, the work of acquiring the source-language lexicon remains very much empirical and data driven.

29. Since several different theoretical traditions have been joined in Boas, to expand coverage, a methodological decision was made to include in the list of parameter values different aliases for the same value, to facilitate the work of the user by using terminology to which he or she is habituated by the pertinent grammatical and/or pedagogical tradition.

30. When such acquisition is done semiautomatically, people still check the automatically produced results. If in the future a completely automatic procedure for knowledge acquisition is developed, this procedure will be recognized as a model of human intuition about the world and its connection to the ontology.

31. The paper published in the proceedings of the conference as Searle 1986 is the paper Searle had intended to deliver back in 1982. At the conference itself, however, he chose instead to deliver a philosopher's response to Raskin 1986, the other plenary paper, attacking primarily the compositional aspect of the proposed script-based semantic theory.

32. In contemporary psychology, unlike in science, the deductive cycle is excluded completely in favor of the inductive one. In the dominant methodology, one goes into a series of master-fully designed experiments with the so-called null hypothesis and strives to observe and formulate a theory from clustering the results on the basis of some form of factor analysis or a similar evidence-analysis method. For the best work in the psychology of personality, for instance, see Ruch 1998 and references to his and his associates' work there.

33. Unbeknownst to most scientists, including linguists, the analytical tradition has an increasingly popular competitor in phenomenology, a view of the world from the vantage point of direct firsthand experience. University philosophy departments are usually divided into analytical and phenomenological factions, and the latter see the intensional, explanatory generalizations of the former as, basically, arbitrary leaps of faith, while the former see the anti-generalizational, extensional discussions of the latter as a tortuous and unreliable path to generalizations. Uneasy peace is maintained by not talking with and not reading each other. According to Dupuy (2000, xii–xiii), this is mirrored on a much larger scale in American academia by the phenomenological (poststructuralist, postmodernist) versus analytical split between the humanities and social sciences, respectively. Phenomenology sees itself as having been established by Hegel (1931). Analytical philosophers see it as hijacked by Heidegger (1949, 1980), and notoriously perverted by the likes of Derrida (e.g., 1967, 1987) into an easily reversible, anchorless, relativistic chaos of postmodernism that is easy for a scientist to dismiss offhand. However, the mainstream Husserlian phenomenology (Husserl 1964, 1982) is a serious and respectable alternative philosophical view, except that it is hard for an analytically trained scientist to see how it can be applied. In an occasional offshoot (see, for instance, Bourdieu's 1977 "theory of practice"), phenomenology can even be seen as coming tantalizingly close to the inductive approach within the analytical tradition. On the analytical side, Wittgenstein's "meaning is use" and the ordinary language philosophy (see section 2.6.2.1) come close to the phenomenological side but can be implemented with extensional, non-representational corpus-based statistical methods.

Chapter 3

1. The word *semantics* had, in fact, existed before. In the seventeenth century it was used by philosophers to denote "the science of prediction of Fate on the basis of weather signs." Larousse's French dictionary defined *sémantique* only a century ago as a science of directing troops with the help of signals. See Read 1948 for more information on the term.

2. Frege (1952b) actually used the term *Sinn* ("sense") for meaning and *Bedeutung* ("meaning") for reference.

3. Another foresight of Ogden and Richards that took wing in later years was the idea of expressing meanings using a limited set of primitives ("Basic English"). This idea anticipates componential analysis of meaning (e.g., Bendix 1966). A similar direction of thought can be traced in the works of Hjelmslev (e.g., 1958) and some early contributors to artificial intelligence (Wilks 1972; Schank 1975). The *Longman Dictionary of Contemporary English* (1987) is advertised as using a limited number of primitives (around 2,000)—that is, words used in the explanations of the meanings of the entries.

4. On the one hand, the same proposition can be expressed in a language using any sentence from an often-large set of paraphrases. On the other hand, the same sentence expresses a proposition and all of its logical equivalents.

5. Marconi (1997, 1) seems to make a similar argument: "I concentrated on the understanding of *words*: not words such as 'all,' 'and,' and 'necessarily' but rather words such as 'yellow,' 'book,' and 'kick' [because] the research program generated within the traditional philosophical semantics stemming from Frege ... did not appear to adequately account for word meaning."

6. It is possible, however, that these indices may prove very important, for example, in applications such as systems devoted to question answering based on inferences about facts in the fact repository.

7. Instead, when intension is discussed at all in formal semantics (e.g., Ladusaw 1988; Chierchia and McConnell-Ginet 1990), it is typically limited to the issue of truth values in the so-called opaque contexts, such as the belief sentences.

8. The problem with the category of fact in philosophy has been essentially that any candidate fact could be easily shown to be an aggregate of other facts. This search for the elementary (or primitive) fact stemmed, of course, from the axiomatic theory paradigm, which requires a postulated finite set of primitives.

9. Contrary to the initial implication by Katz and Fodor, paraphrases would not get identical semantic interpretations in the theory, and an additional apparatus would be necessary to establish the appropriate equivalences. Formal semanticists are right in claiming an advantage in this respect because their "semantic representations are logical formulas from an independently defined logic [, which] allows the theory to incorporate all of the familiar logic equivalences" (Ladusaw 1988, 92).

10. The linguistic tradition of rejecting truth-conditional semantics dates back at least to Wilson (1975), who accused it of impoverishing the treatment of meaning in language, of using entailment and truth conditions in ways that are too wide for linguistic semantic purposes, and of being unable to treat nondeclaratives. Even more devastatingly, we think, is the fact that using truth values creates pseudo-problems in linguistic semantics. Thus, the sentence *The present king of France is bald* is seen as highly problematic by formal semantics because it has

no truth value; it is, however, perfectly meaningful and problem-free from the point of view of linguistic semantics.

Chapter 4

1. The works that we consider as belonging to this approach, some more loosely than others, include Asher and Lascarides 1995; Atkins 1991; Briscoe 1993; Briscoe and Copestake 1991, 1996; Briscoe, Copestake, and Boguraev 1990; Briscoe, Copestake, and Lascarides 1995; Briscoe, de Paiva, and Copestake, eds. 1993; Copestake 1990, 1992, 1995; Copestake and Briscoe 1992; Copestake et al. 1994–1995; Johnston, Boguraev, and Pustejovsky 1995; Lascarides 1995; Nunberg and Zaenen 1992; Ostler and Atkins 1991; Pustejovsky 1991, 1993, 1995; Pustejovsky and Boguraev 1993; Saint-Dizier 1995; Sanfilippo 1995; Sanfilippo et al. 1992.

2. See, for instance, Nirenburg, Nirenburg, and Reynolds 1985; Nirenburg, Raskin, and Tucker 1987; Nirenburg, Lesser, and Nyberg 1989; Nirenburg, Raskin, and Onyshkevych 1995; Nirenburg and Raskin 1986, 1987a, 1987c; Raskin 1987a, 1987b, 1990; Carlson and Nirenburg 1990; Meyer, Onyshkevych, and Carlson 1990; Nirenburg and Goodman 1990; Nirenburg and Defrise 1991; Nirenburg and Levin 1992; Onyshkevych and Nirenburg 1992, 1994; Raskin, Attardo, and Attardo 1994a, 1994b; Raskin and Nirenburg 1995, 1996a, 1996b, 1998, 1999; Viegas et al. 1996; Viegas 1999.

3. It is perhaps appropriate here to resort to simple formalism to further clarify this point. Let L be the finite set of all lexical rules, l, used to derive senses from other senses; let T be the finite set of all type-shifting and coercion rules, t; let S be the (much smaller) set of the senses, s, of a lexical entry, e, in the generative lexicon G. Then, $G = \{e_1^G, e_2^G, \ldots, e_n^G\}$ and $S_e = \{s_1^e, s_2^e, \ldots, s_m^e\}$. If $l(s_e)$ is a sense of an entry derived with the help of lexical rule l and $t(s_e)$ is a sense of an entry derived with the help of type-shifting, or coercion, rule t, then let us define V_e as the set of all such derived senses of an entry: $V_e = \{v: \forall v \exists s \exists e \exists l \exists t\, v = l(s_e) \lor v = t(s_e)\}$. Let W^G be the set of all derived senses for all the entries in G: $W^{GLT} = \{w: \forall w \exists s \exists e \exists l \exists t\, w = l(s_e) \lor w = t(s_e)\}$. Finally, let U^{GLT} be the set of all senses, listed or derived, in G: $U^{GLT} == W^{GLT} \cup C^G$, where $C^G = \{c: \forall c \exists s \exists e\, c = s_e\}$. U^{GLT} represents the weak generative capacity of G, given the predefined sets L^G and T^G of lexical and type-shifting rules associated with the generative lexicon.

U^{GLT} is also an enumerable set in the calculus, I, defined by the set of rules $L^G \cup T^G$ applied to C^G in the sense that there is a finite procedure, P, of (typically, one-step) application of a rule to a listed (or, rarely, derived) sense, such that each element in U^{GLT} is generated by P (P includes zero, or nonapplication, of any rule, so as to include C^G in the calculus). In fact, U^{GLT} is also decidable in the sense that for each of its elements, i, there is an algorithm in I, which determines how it is generated—that is, an algorithm that identifies, typically, a listed entry and a rule applied to it to generate i. The set of all those identified pairs of listed entries and rules applied to them determines the strong generative capacity of G.

Then, the only way the lexicon may be able to generate—that is, define—a sense s is if $s \in U^{GLT}$. In what way can such a sense, h, be novel or creative if it is already predetermined in G by L and T? This notion makes sense only if the existence of a proper subset B of U^{GLT} is implied, such that $h \in U^{GLT} \land h \notin B$. Then, a deficient enumerative lexicon, M, would list all the senses of B and not use any lexical or type-shifting rules: $E = \{e_1^e, e_2^e, \ldots, e_k^e\}$, $B = \{b: \forall b \exists s \exists e\, b = s_e\}$ and $L^E = T^E = \varnothing$.

Obviously, if a lexicon, O, does enumerate some senses and derives others in such a way that every sense in U^{GLT} is either listed or derived in O as well, so that both the weak and strong generative capacities of O equal—or exceed—those of U^{GLT}, then G does not generate any novel, creative senses with regard to O. It also follows that the generative lexicon approach must specify explicitly, about each sense claimed to be novel and creative, relative to what corpus or lexicon it is claimed to be novel and creative.

4. See, for instance, Raskin 1977a and references there. The reason for the native speaker's unconscious blocking of ambiguity is that it is a complication for our communication and raises the cognitive processing load (see, e.g., Gibson 1991). So the hearer settles on the one sense that happens to be obvious at the moment (see, again, Raskin 1977a and references there), and blocks the others. There are "non–bona fide" modes of communication based on deliberate ambiguity, such as humor (see, for instance, Raskin 1985c, xiii, 115; cf. Raskin 1992). But functioning in these modes requires additional efforts and skills, and there are native speakers of languages who do not possess those skills without, arguably, being judged incompetent.

5. Coming from a very different disciplinary background, the authors sometimes put forward a line of reasoning similar to ours, but also take unnecessary detours and make some unnecessary claims of their own in the process of pursuing totally different goals—different not only from ours but also from Pustejovsky's. We had a chance to comment on this rather irrelevant review in section 2.3.1.

6. See, for instance, Lewis 1972; Parsons 1972, 1980, 1985, 1990; Stalnaker and Thomason 1973; Montague 1974; Dowty 1979; Barwise and Perry 1983; Keenan and Faltz 1985; Partee, ter Meulen, and Wall 1990; Chierchia and McConnell-Ginet 1990; Cann 1993; Chierchia 1995; Hornstein 1995; Heim and Kratzer 1998.

7. An examination of the Aristotelian roots of the qualia theory fails to fill the vacuum either.

8. Ontological semantic lexicons fit Fillmore and Atkins's (1991, 75) vision of an ideal dictionary of the future: "We imagine, for some distant future, an online lexical resource, which we can refer to as a 'frame-based' dictionary, which will be adequate to our aims. In such a dictionary, ... individual word senses, relationships among the senses of the polysemous words, and relationships between (senses of) semantically related words will be linked with the cognitive structures (or 'frames'), knowledge of which is presupposed by the concepts encoded by the words."

9. The very existence of the distinction between lexical and pragmatic knowledge, the latter equated with "world knowledge" or "encyclopedic knowledge," has been a subject of much debate. (See Raskin 1985a; 1985b; 1985c, 134–135; 2000. For more discussion of the issue—from both sides—see Hobbs 1987; Wilensky 1986, 1991; Peeters 2000; cf. Wilks 1975a, 1975b, 343.)

10. Even in morphology, however, generalization can go overboard. Using a very strict criterion of membership in a declension paradigm, Zaliznyak (1967) demonstrated that Russian has seventy-six declension paradigms for nouns. Traditional grammars define three. These three, however, cover all but a few hundred Russian nouns. One solution is to write rules for all seventy-six paradigms. The other is to write rules only for paradigms with a huge membership and list all the other cases as exceptions.

Chapter 5

1. It is precisely because of this neutrality that text meaning (a form of recording knowledge) is neutral with respect to its truth value. In other words, a sentence may be meaningful even if it

does not have a truth value—that is, for instance, if it talks about unicorns or the present kings of France or even if it states that apples fall upward. The above is a succinct refutation of truth-conditional semantics.

2. Schäfer (1998, 108) even gushes about mereology "provid[ing] two of the elements which were distinguishing for Chomsky's methodological [?!] reform of linguistics: The possibility of rigorous formalisation and a cognitive interpretation of the results." His naïveté in choosing the role model for formal ontology aside (see chapter 2, note 13), the latter "element" is difficult to see as accomplished in Chomskian linguistics, and it remains a problem and a bone of some contention, for instance, between Gruber and Guarino, as we will see shortly.

3. Gruber himself borrows the notion of conceptualization from Genesereth and Nilsson 1987: a body of formally represented knowledge is based on a conceptualization—the objects, concepts, and other entities that are presumed to exist in some area of interest and the relationships that hold between them. This is not so distinct from Guarino's own biases: Quine's view (1953; cf. Guarino 1997, 296) that a logical theory is committed to the entities it quantified over, Newell's definition of knowledge as "whatever can be ascribed to an agent, such that its behavior can be computed according to the principle of rationality" (Newell 1982; cf. Guarino 1995, 1–2), or Wielinga and Schreiber's (1993) similar statement that "[an AI] ontology is a theory of what entities can exist in the mind of a knowledgeable agent." But, Guarino (1998a, 5) claims, "The problem with Genesereth and Nilsson's notion of conceptualization is that it refers to ordinary mathematical relations on [a domain] D, i.e., *extensional* relations. These relations reflect a particular state of affairs: for instance, in the blocks world, they may reflect a particular arrangement of blocks on the table. We need instead to focus on the *meaning* of these relations, independently of a state of affairs: for instance, the meaning of the 'above' relation lies in the *way* it refers to certain couples of blocks according to their spatial arrangement. We need therefore to speak of *intensional* relations."

4. It should be emphasized right away that these "words" are not words of a natural language, something about which Guarino himself and some other scholars are not always careful enough. See section 5.3 for further discussion.

5. Outside of formal ontology proper, in the field of knowledge representation, Doyle and Patil (1991, 289) cast a vote of confidence in the possibility of "general purpose representation systems." They "argue that general purpose knowledge representation systems should provide:

Fully expressive languages,
Tolerance of incomplete classification,
Terminological classification over relevant contingent as well as definitional information,
Nondeductive as well as deductive forms of recognition which permit 'approximate' classification and 'classification' of concepts involving defaults, and
Rational management of inference tools" (p. 266).

These additional properties seem to complement nicely Gruber's more external constraints mentioned in section 5.2.2.

6. Whether lexical ambiguity is accidental or systematic has nothing to do with ontological concepts per se. For example, in the Aquilex and Corelex projects much effort has been expended on treating as many instances of ambiguity as possible in a systematic way. Thus Buitelaar 1998, a Corelex contribution, does not seem to belong in the volume on ontology edited by Guarino.

7. The "slippage" from studying categories of the world in metaphysics to studying human concepts reflecting (or even replacing) these "objective" categories is usually attributed to Kant (1787—cf. Loux 1998, 2).

8. This example was used by Weinreich (1966) in his critique of Katz and Fodor (1963). Weinreich's point was that the semantic theory proposed by Katz and Fodor established no limits for polysemy.

9. Throughout this discussion we have followed Hjelmslev and others in assuming that having a single word in a language to express a certain sense is somehow a privileged state of affairs compared to expressing this sense with a phrase. We have argued elsewhere (Raskin and Nirenburg 1995, 1998—see also section 9.3.6) for the "principle of practical effability" among languages, which removes any distinction between these two alternative ways of expressing a meaning. It was convincingly argued (Zvegintzev 1960) that this priority of single words over phrases is a fallacy and that this fallacy is the cornerstone of the Sapir-Whorf hypothesis. We are not sure that any neurolinguistic or psychological evidence exists for the primacy of the single-word expression in the mind. What we do know is that a computational dictionary can include both words and phrases as entry heads.

10. This is an important desideratum. In fact, a major ontological enterprise was criticized in one evaluation for a lack of strategic direction for achieving a more or less uniform depth and breadth of knowledge coverage—see Mahesh et al. 1996.

Chapter 6

1. The nature and format of morphological and syntactic analyses presented here are outside the purview of ontological semantics and of our narrative. We are fully aware that many other formulations and presentations of these analysis steps are possible. Ontological semantics is neutral with respect to any such formulation and can be adapted to work with any good-quality morphological and syntactic analyzer.

2. We would like to apologize for using a complex, real-life text as our detailed example. Simple examples, often used to illustrate the properties of a representation language, fail to demonstrate in sufficient detail the features of the language or, more importantly, its ability to handle realistic inputs.

3. We use the term *index* in the sense of Bar Hillel 1954 and Lewis 1972 to refer to time, place, possible world, speaker, hearer, and other coordinates that turn an abstract proposition into a real utterance.

4. We will not focus here on what makes this sentence funny—see Raskin 1985c and Attardo 1994 for a discussion of the semantic analysis of humor.

5. Incidentally, this treatment agrees with the theory of latent performatives (Austin 1958; Searle 1989; Bach and Harnish 1992).

Chapter 7

1. They may, however, be instantiated in a TMR by means of a *reification* operation (e.g., Russell and Norvig 1995), thereby making them stand-alone instances in the TMR.

2. A version of LFG has been chosen as the syntactic framework to aid ontological semantics largely because it concentrates on the syntax-to-semantics linking, so that, for instance, we do not have to worry about the passive construction rearranging the above clues.

Chapter 8

1. If the input were *John bought a blue car*, the lexical entry for *buy* (see section 7.2) would instantiate the ontological event BUY, and that instance would assume the headship of the corresponding TMR proposition, obviating the need to elevate an object instance to proposition headship. The logic behind this decision is to avoid using dummy events as heads in TMR propositions. This desire is similar in motivation, though different in content, to Fillmore's (1968) proposal of elevating nonnominative cases to the Subject position in the absence of a more legitimate filler for the latter, thus making syntactic representations of sentences like *The door opened* similar to those for sentences like *John opened the door*.

2. Of course, *John* can be understood as the name of anything, including a gorilla (cf. Schank 1975 about "female fleas called John"). However, there is a reasonable expectation that *John* is a person's name and, in the absence of evidence to the contrary, the system will be wise to stick to this expectation, while fully expecting that it is defeasible, in the spirit of abductive reasoning.

3. The property of effect in the ontological description of events helps to cover a wide variety of important phenomena, such as causality, entailment, and many others, including telicity. Thus, ontological semantics does not require any special device for representing telicity in the lexicon, as proposed by Pustejovsky 1995, 99–101.

4. Many studies of aspect (e.g., Comrie 1976, 44–48; Vendler 1967, 102–104, where telicity was referred to as "accomplishment"; Klein 1974; Dowty 1972; Verkuyl 1972, 1993) have difficulties establishing telicity as a feature distinct from completion. For us, this means that this feature does not have a bona fide semantic aspectual significance (see section 8.5.3 for further discussion).

5. The number added to the speech act time here and elsewhere in the example stands for the number of days.

6. This input is unlikely to occur. The correct input would be "tomorrow."

7. This input is unlikely to occur. If this analysis facility serves a human-computer dialog system, the system should in this state generate a clarification question: "Do you mean today or in a week's time?"

8. From the classical Greek for "success."

9. Another example of a widely promulgated distinction in linguistic theory that we have shown to be devoid of utility for ontological semantics is the dichotomy between attributive and predicative syntactic constructions for adjectives (see Raskin and Nirenburg 1995). Categories like these make us wonder whether the litmus test for introducing a theoretical construct should not be its utility for language processing. In other words, in our work, we oppose introducing distinctions for the sole reason that they can be introduced if this does not help resolve any problems in automatic analysis and synthesis of natural language texts. Theoretical linguistics does not follow this formulation of the Occam's-razor principle.

10. In more recent literature, the term *telic* was reintroduced by Pustejovsky (1995) as the "purpose and function," an "essential aspect of a word's meaning." The examples of English nominal meanings that include the property of telicity show that this property is similar to the lexical function Oper of meaning-text theory (e.g., Mel'čuk 1974), essentially meaning "the typical operation performed with an object." These examples do not make the nature of the

telic/atelic dichotomy clear simply because they do not make use of any such distinction, at least not in Comrie's terms.

Chapter 9

1. "Today's state-of-the-art rule-based methods for natural language understanding provide good performance in limited applications for specific languages. However, the *manual* development of an understanding component using specific rules is costly as each application and language requires its own adaptation or, in the worst case, a completely new implementation. In order to address this cost issue, statistical modeling techniques are used ... to replace the commonly used hand-generated rules to convert the speech recognizer output into a semantic representation. The statistical models are derived from the automatic analyses of large corpora of utterances with their corresponding semantic representations. To port the semantic analyzer to different applications it is thus sufficient to train the component on the application- and language-specific data sets as compared to translating and adapting the rule-based grammar by hand" (Minker, Waibel, and Mariani 1999; xiv).

References

Achinstein, P. 1968. *Concepts of Science*. Baltimore: Johns Hopkins University Press.

Ackermann, W. 1968. *Solvable Cases of the Decision Problem*. Amsterdam: North-Holland.

Agents-98. 1998. *Proceedings of Agents-98*, Minneapolis/St. Paul, MN. New York: ACM Press.

Agents-99. 1999. *Proceedings of Agents-99*, Seattle, WA. New York: ACM Press.

Ahlswede, T. E., M. Evens, K. Rossi, and J. Markowitz. 1985. Building a lexical database by parsing *Webster's Seventh Collegiate Dictionary*. *Advances in Lexicology*, Waterloo, Ontario, Canada, 65–78.

Ajdukiewicz, K. 1935. Die syntaktische Konnexität. *Studia Philosophica* 1, 1–27.

Allen, J. F. 1984. Towards a general theory of action and time. *Artificial Intelligence* 23, 123–154.

Allen, J. F., and P. J. Hayes. 1987. *Moments and Points in an Interval-Based Temporal Logic*. Technical Report TR 180, CS/Philo. Department of Computer Science, University of Rochester, Rochester, NY.

The American Heritage Electronic Dictionary of the English Language. 1992. 3rd ed. New York: Houghton Mifflin.

Amsler, R. 1984. Machine-readable dictionaries. In M. E. Williams, ed., *Annual Review of Information Science and Technology*, vol. 19, 161–209. White Plains, NY: Knowledge Industry Publications for the American Society for Information Science.

Anscombre, J. C., and O. Ducrot. 1983. *L'Argumentation dans la Langue*. Brussels: Pierre Mardaga.

Aone, C., and S. W. Bennett. 1995. Evaluating automated and manual acquisition of anaphora resolution rules. *Proceedings of ACL-95*, 122–129. Cambridge, MA.

Apresyan, Yu. D. 1974. *Leksicheskaya semantika: Sinonimicheskie sredstva yazyka* (Lexical semantics: The synonymic resources of language). Moscow: Nauka.

Apresyan, Yu. D., I. A. Mel'čuk, and A. K. Zholkovsky. 1969. Semantics and lexicography: Towards a new type of unilingual dictionary. In F. Kiefer, ed., *Studies in Syntax and Semantics*, 1–33. Dordrecht: Reidel.

Apresyan, Yu. D., I. A. Mel'čuk, and A. K. Zholkovsky. 1973. Materials for an explanatory combinatory dictionary of Modern Russian. In F. Kiefer, ed., *Trends in Soviet Theoretical Linguistics*, 411–438. Dordrecht: Reidel.

Aristotle. 1968. *Poetics*. London: Cambridge University Press.

Arnold, D., R. L. Humphreys, and L. Sadler, eds. 1993. Special Issue: Evaluation of MT Systems. *Machine Translation* 8, 1–2.

Asher, N., and A. Lascarides. 1995. Metaphor in discourse. In J. Klavans, B. Boguraev, L. Levin, and J. Pustejovsky, eds., *Symposium: Representation and Acquisition of Lexical Knowledge: Polysemy, Ambiguity, and Generativity*, 3–7. Working Notes, AAAI Spring Symposium Series. Stanford, CA: Stanford University, 1995.

Atkins, B. T. S. 1991. Building a lexicon: The contribution of lexicography. In B. K. Boguraev, ed., Special Issue: Building a Lexicon. *International Journal of Lexicography* 4(3), 167–204.

Attardo, D. H. 1996. Lexicographic acquisition: A theoretical and computational study in linguistic heuristics. Unpublished doctoral dissertation, Interdepartmental Program in Linguistics, Purdue University, West Lafayette, IN.

Attardo, S. 1994. *Linguistic Theories of Humor*. Berlin: Mouton de Gruyter.

Attardo, S., and V. Raskin. 1991. Script theory revis(it)ed: Joke similarity and joke representation model. *Humor* 4(3–4), 293–347.

Austin, J. L. 1958. Performatif-constatif. Paper presented at the Royaumont conference. Translated as: The performative-constative distinction. In C. E. Caton, ed., *Philosophy and Ordinary Language*, 22–32. Urbana: University of Illinois Press, 1963.

Austin, J. L. 1961a. The meaning of a word. In J. L. Austin, *Philosophical Papers*. Oxford: Oxford University Press.

Austin, J. L. 1961b. Truth. In J. L. Austin, *Philosophical Papers*. Oxford: Oxford University Press.

Austin, J. L. 1962. *How to Do Things with Words*. Oxford: Clarendon Press.

Awad, E. M. 1996. *Building Expert Systems: Principles, Procedures, and Applications*. Minneapolis–St. Paul, MN: West.

Azzam, S., K. Humphreys, and R. Gaizauskas. 1998. Extending a simple coreference algorithm with a focusing mechanism. In *New Approaches to Discourse Anaphora: Proceedings of the Second Colloquium on Discourse Anaphora and Anaphor Resolution (DAARC2)*, 15–27. Lancaster, UK.

Bach, E. 1984. *Informal Lectures on Formal Semantics*. Albany, NY: SUNY Press.

Bach, K., and R. M. Harnish. 1992. How performatives really work: A reply to Searle. *Linguistics and Philosophy* 15(1), 93–110.

Baldwin, B. 1997. CogNIAC: High precision coreference with limited knowledge and linguistic resources. *Proceedings of the ACL Workshop on Operational Factors in Practical, Robust Anaphora Resolution for Unrestricted Texts*, Madrid, Spain, June, 38–45.

Ballim, A., and Y. Wilks. 1991. *Artificial Believers: The Ascription of Belief*. Hillsdale, NJ: Erlbaum.

Ballim, A., Y. Wilks, and J. Barnden. 1991. Belief ascription, metaphor, and intensional identification. *Cognitive Science* 15(1), 133–171.

Bally, C. 1950. *Linguistique générale et linguistique française*. Berne: A. Francke.

Baltes, P. 1995. Discourse Reduction and Ellipsis: A Semantic Theory of Interpretation and Recovery. Unpublished doctoral dissertation, Department of English, Purdue University, West Lafayette, IN.

Bar Hillel, Y. 1953. A quasi-arithmetical notation for syntactic description. *Language* 29, 47–58. Reprinted in Y. Bar Hillel, *Aspects of Language*, 61–74. Jerusalem: Magnes.

Bar Hillel, Y. 1954. Indexical expressions. *Mind* 63, 359–379.

Bar Hillel, Y. 1967. Dictionaries and meaning rules. *Foundations of Language* 3, 409–414. Reprinted in Y. Bar Hillel, *Aspects of Language*, 347–353. Jerusalem: Magnes, 1970.

Bar Hillel, Y. 1970. Argumentation in natural language. In Y. Bar Hillel, *Aspects of Language*, 202–205. Jerusalem: Magnes.

Barnden, J. A., S. Helmreich, E. Iverson, and G. C. Stein. 1994. An integrated implementation of simulative, uncertain and metaphorical reasoning about mental states. In J. Doyle, E. Sandewall, and P. Torasso, eds., *Principles of Knowledge Representation and Reasoning: Proceedings of the Fourth International Conference*, 27–38. San Francisco: Morgan Kautmann.

Bar-On, D. 1996. Anti-realism and speaker knowledge. *Synthèse* 106(2), 139–166.

Barwise, J., and J. Perry. 1983. *Situations and Attitudes*. Cambridge, MA: MIT Press.

Bateman, J. A. 1990. Upper modeling: Organizing knowledge for natural language processing. *Proceedings of the Fifth International Workshop on Natural Language Generation*, Dawson, PA, 54–60.

Bateman, J. A. 1993. Ontology construction and natural language. In N. Guarino and R. Poli, eds., *Knowledge Representation*. Ladseb-CNR Internal Report 01/93. Padova, Italy, 83–93.

Beale, S. 1997. Hunter-Gatherer: Applying Constraint Satisfaction, Branch-and-Bound and Solution Synthesis to Computational Semantics. Unpublished doctoral dissertation, Language Technologies Institute, School of Computer Science, Carnegie Mellon University, Pittsburgh.

Beale, S., and S. Nirenburg. 1995. Dependency-directed text planning. *Proceedings of the 1995 International Joint Conference on Artificial Intelligence (IJCAI-95), Workshop on Multilingual Text Generation*, Montreal.

Beale, S., and S. Nirenburg. 1996. PICARD, the Next Generator. *Proceedings of the 8th International Workshop on Natural Language Generation*, Herstmonceux, Sussex.

Beale, S., S. Nirenburg, and K. Mahesh. 1995. Semantic analysis in the Mikrokosmos machine translation project. *Proceedings of the Second Symposium on Natural Language Processing (SNLP-95)*, Bangkok.

Beale, S., S. Nirenburg, E. Viegas, and L. Wanner. 1998. De-constraining text generation. *Proceedings of the International Workshop on Natural Language Generation (INLG-98)*, Niagara-on-the-Lake, Ontario, Canada.

Beale, S., and E. Viegas. 1996. Intelligent planning meets intelligent planners. *Proceedings of the Natural Language Generation Workshop at ECAI-96*, Budapest.

Beale, S., E. Viegas, and S. Nirenburg. 1997. Breaking down barriers: The Mikrokosmos generator. In *Proceedings of the Natural Language Processing Pacific Rim Symposium 1997 (NLPRS-97)*, Phuket, Thailand.

Bendix, E. M. 1966. *Componential Analysis of General Vocabulary*. The Hague: Mouton. Also published in *International Journal of American Linguistics* 32(2), pt. 2, and as Indiana

University Research Center in Anthropology, Folklore and Linguistics, Publication 41, Bloomington, IN.

Benveniste, E. 1939. Nature du signe linquistique. *Acta Linguistica* I, 23–29. Reprinted in E. Benveniste, *Problèmes de Linquistique générale*, 49–55. Paris: Gallimard.

Berg, G. 1992. A connectionist parser with recursive sentence structure and lexical disambiguation. *Proceedings of AAAI-92*, 32–37. San Jose, CA.

Bergler, S. 1994–1995. Generative lexicon principles for machine translation: A case for metalexical structure. In B. J. Dorr and J. Klavans, eds., Special Issue: Building Lexicons for Machine Translation II. *Machine Translation* 10(1–2), 155–182.

Bergman, G. 1992. *New Foundations of Ontology*. Madison: University of Wisconsin Press.

Berners-Lee, T. 1998a. Semantic Web Road Map. http://www.w3.org/DesignIssues/Semantic.html.

Berners-Lee, T. 1998b. Web architecture at 50,000 feet. http://www.w3.org/DesignIssues/Architecture.html.

Berners-Lee, T. 1998c. What the Semantic Web Can Represent. http://www.w3.org/DesignIssues/RDFnot.html.

Berners-Lee, T., J. Hendler, and O. Lassila. 2001. The Semantic Web. *Scientific American*, May 17.

Berry, M. 1975. *Introduction to Systemic Linguistics 1: Structures and Systems*. New York: St. Martin's Press.

Berry, M. 1977. *Introduction to Systemic Linguistics 2: Levels and Links*. London: Batsford.

Berwick, R. C., and A. S. Weinberg. 1984. *The Grammatical Basis of Linguistic Performance*. Cambridge, MA: MIT Press.

Bikel, D. M., R. Schwartz, and R. M. Weischedel. 1999. An algorithm that learns what's in a name. *Machine Learning* 34(1–3).

Birner, B. J., and G. Ward. 1998. *Information Status and Noncanonical Word Order in English*. Amsterdam: Benjamins.

Blachowicz, J. 1997. Reciprocal justification in science and moral theory. *Synthèse* 110(3), 447–468.

Black, M. 1954–55. Metaphor. *Proceedings of the Aristotelian Society* 55, 273–294. Reprinted in M. Black, *Models and Metaphors*. Ithaca, NY: Cornell University Press, 1962.

Black, M. 1979. More about metaphor. In A. Ortony ed., *Metaphor and Thought*. Cambridge, U.K.: Cambridge University Press.

Blake, B. J. 1994. *Case*. Cambridge, U.K.: Cambridge University Press.

Bloomfield, L. 1933. *Language*. New York: Holt.

Bobrow, D. G., and T. Winograd. 1977. An overview of KRL, a knowledge representation language. *Cognitive Science* 1(1), 3–46.

Bochman, A. 1990. Mereology as a theory of part-whole. *Logique et Analyse* 129–130, 75–101.

Boden, M. A. 1981. *Minds and Mechanisms: Philosophical Psychology and Computational Models*. Ithaca, NY: Cornell University Press.

Boguraev, B. 1986. Machine readable dictionaries and research in computational linguistics. *Proceedings of the Workshop on Automating the Lexicon*, Grosetto, Italy.

Boguraev, B., ed. 1991. Special issue: Building a lexicon. *International Journal of Lexicography* 4(3).

Boguraev, B., R. Byrd, J. Klavans, and M. Neff. 1989. From machine readable dictionaries to a lexical knowledge base. In U. Zernik, ed., *Proceedings of the First International Lexical Acquisition Workshop (IJCAI-89)*, Detroit.

Bolzano, B. 1930. *Wissenschaftslehre*. Vol. 3. Leipzig: Meiner.

Bonjour, L. 1997. Haack on justification and experience. *Synthèse* 112(1), 13–23.

Botha, R. 1981. *The Conduct of Linguistic Inquiry: A Systematic Introduction to the Methodology of Generative Grammars*. Janua Linguarum, Series Practica 157. The Hague: Mouton.

Bouquiaux, L., and J. M. C. Thomas. 1992. *Studying and Describing Unwritten Languages*. Dallas: Summer Institute of Linguistics Press.

Bourdieu, P. 1977. *Outline of a Theory of Practice*. Cambridge, U.K.: Cambridge University Press.

Brachman, R. J., R. E. Fikes, and H. J. Levesque. 1983. KRYPTON: A functional approach to knowledge representation. *IEEE Computer* 16(10), 67–73.

Braithwaite, R. B. 1955. *Scientific Explanation*. Cambridge, U.K.: Cambridge University Press.

Bréal, M. 1964. *Semantics: Studies in the Science of Meaning*. New York: Dover Publications.

Bresnan, J., ed. 1982. *The Mental Representation of Grammatical Relations*. Cambridge, MA: MIT Press.

Briscoe, E. J., and A. Copestake. 1991. Sense extensions as lexical rules. *Proceedings of the IJCAI Workshop on Computational Approaches to Non-Literal Language*, Sydney, Australia, 12–20.

Briscoe, E. J., A. Copestake, and B. Boguraev. 1990. Enjoy the paper: Lexical semantics via lexicology. *Proceedings of COLING-90*, Helsinki, 42–47.

Briscoe, E. J., A. Copestake, and A. Lascarides. 1995. Blocking. In P. Saint-Dizier and E. Viegas, eds., *Computational Lexical Semantics*, 273–302. Cambridge, U.K.: Cambridge University Press.

Briscoe, T. 1993. Introduction. In T. Briscoe, V. de Paiva, and A. Copestake, eds., *Inheritance, Defaults, and the Lexicon*, 1–12. Cambridge, U.K.: Cambridge University Press.

Briscoe, T., and A. Copestake. 1996. Controlling the application of lexical rules. In Viegas et al. 1996a, 7–19.

Briscoe, T., V. de Paiva, and A. Copestake, eds. 1993. *Inheritance, Defaults, and the Lexicon*. Cambridge, U.K.: Cambridge University Press.

Brooks, R. 1991. Intelligence without representation. *Artificial Intelligence* 47(1–3), 139–159.

Brown, P., J. Cocke, S. Della Pietra, V. Della Pietra, F. Jelinek, J. D. Lafferty, R. L. Mercer, and P. S. Roossin. 1990. A statistical approach to machine translation. *Computational Linguistics* 16(1), 79–85.

Brown, R., and R. Frederking. 1995. Applying statistical English language modeling to symbolic machine translation. *Proceedings of TMI-95*, Leuven, Belgium, July 5–7, 221–239.

Brown, R., and S. Nirenburg. 1990. Human-computer interaction for semantic disambiguation. *Proceedings of COLING-90*, Helsinki, August.

Bruce, B. 1975. Case systems for natural language. *Artificial Intelligence* 6.

Bühler, K. 1907. Über Tatsachen und Probleme zu einer Psychologie der Denkvorgänge. I. Über Gedanken. *Archiv für die gesamte Psychologie* 9, 297–365.

Buitelaar, P. 1998. CoreLex: An ontology of systematic polysemous classes. In N. Guarino, ed., 1998c, 221–235.

Bunge, M. 1967. *Scientific Research*. 2 vols. New York: Springer.

Bunge, M. 1968. The maturation of science. In I. Lakatos and A. Musgrave, eds., *Problems in the Philosophy of Science*. Studies in Logic and the Foundations of Mathematics, vol. 45, 120–137. Amsterdam: North-Holland.

Bylander, T., and B. Chandrasekaran. 1988. Generic tasks in knowledge-based reasoning: The right level of abstraction for knowledge acquisition. In B. R. Gaines and J. H. Boose, eds., *Knowledge Acquisition for Knowledge-Based Systems*. London: Academic Press, 65–79.

Calzolari, N. 1989. Large databases and computational linguistics: Research tools and testbeds. In U. Zernik, ed., *Proceedings of the First International Lexical Acquisition Workshop (IJCAI-89)*, Detroit.

Cann, R. 1993. *Formal Semantics: An Introduction*. Cambridge, U.K.: Cambridge University Press.

Carlson, L., and S. Nirenburg. 1990. *World Modeling for NLP*. Technical Report CMU-CMT-90-121. Center for Machine Translation, Carnegie Mellon University, Pittsburgh. A short version appeared in *Proceedings of the Third Conference on Applied Natural Language Processing*, Trento, Italy, April.

Carnap, R. 1936–1937. Testability and meaning. *Philosophy of Science* 3, 420–268, and 4, 1–40. Reprinted as *Testability and Meaning*. New Haven, CT: Whitlock's, 1950.

Carnap, R. 1937. *The Logical Syntax of Language*. London: Kegan Paul.

Carnap, R. 1939. *Foundations of Logic and Mathematics*. Chicago: University of Chicago Press.

Carnap, R. 1950. *Logical Foundations of Probability*. Chicago: University of Chicago Press.

Cassell, J., and H. Vilhjálmsson. 1999. Fully embodied conversational avatars: Making communicative behaviors autonomous. *Autonomous Agents and Multi-Agent Systems* 2(1), 45–64.

Caton, C. E., ed. 1963. *Philosophy and Ordinary Language*. Urbana: University of Illinois Press.

Caws, P. 1967. Scientific method. In P. Edwards, ed., *Encyclopedia of Philosophy*, vol. 7, 339–343. New York: Macmillan.

Chafe, W. L. 1976. Givenness, contrastiveness, definiteness, subjects, topics, and point of view. In C. Li, ed., *Subject and Topic*, 25–55. New York: Academic Press.

Chafe, W. L. 1977. Creativity in verbalization and its implications for the nature of stored knowledge. In R. O. Freedle, ed., *Discourse Production and Comprehension*, 41–56. Norwood, NJ: Ablex.

Chapell, V., ed. 1964. *Ordinary Language*. Englewood Cliffs, NJ: Prentice-Hall.

Charniak, E. 1972. *Toward a Model of Children's Story Comprehension*. Artificial Intelligence Technical Report 266. Department of Computer Science, MIT, Cambridge, MA, December.

Charniak, E. 1983a. Parsing, how to. In K. Sparck Jones and Y. Wilks, eds., *Automatic Natural Language Parsing*, 156–163. Chichester, U.K.: Horwood.

Charniak, E. 1983b. Passing markers: A theory of contextual influence in language comprehension. *Cognitive Science* 7(3), 171–190.

Charniak, E. 1986. A "neat" theory of marker passing. *Proceedings of AAAI-86*, 584–588. Philadelphia.

Charniak, E., and D. McDermott. 1985. *Introduction to Artificial Intelligence*. Reading, MA: Addison-Wesley.

Charniak, E., and Y. Wilks, eds. 1976. *Computational Semantics*. Amsterdam: North-Holland.

Chierchia, G. 1995. *Dynamics of Meaning: Anaphora, Presupposition, and the Theory of Grammar*. Chicago: University of Chicago Press.

Chierchia, G., and S. McConnell-Ginet. 1990. *Meaning and Grammar: An Introduction to Semantics*. Cambridge, MA: MIT Press.

Chinchor, N. 1998. MUC-7 named entity task definition dry run version, version 3.5 17 September 1997. In *Proceedings of the Seventh Message Understanding Conference (MUC-7)*, Fairfax, VA, San Francisco: Morgan Kaufmann.

Chisholm, R. M. 1996. *A Realistic Theory of Categories: An Essay on Ontology*. Cambridge, U.K.: Cambridge University Press.

Chomsky, N. 1957. *Syntactic Structures*. The Hague: Mouton.

Chomsky, N. 1965. *Aspects of the Theory of Syntax*. Cambridge, MA: MIT Press.

Chomsky, N. 1971. Deep structure, surface structure, and semantic interpretation. In D. D. Steinberg and L. A. Jakobovits, eds., *Semantics: An Interdisciplinary Reader in Philosophy, Linguistics and Psychology*, 183–216. Cambridge, U.K.: Cambridge University Press.

Chomsky, N. 1973. Conditions on transformations. In S. R. Anderson and P. Kiparsky, eds., *A Festschrift for Morris Halle*, 232–286. New York: Holt, Rinehart and Winston. Also included in N. Chomsky, *Essays on Form and Interpretation*, New York: North-Holland, 1977.

Chomsky, N. 1981. *Lectures on Government and Binding*. Dordrecht: Foris.

Chomsky, N. 1986. *Knowledge of Language: Its Nature, Origin, and Use*. New York: Praeger.

Chomsky, N. 1995. *The Minimalist Program*. Cambridge, MA: MIT Press.

Clark, A. 1994. Introduction: Reinventing the connectionist challenge. *Synthèse* 101(3), 301–303.

Clark, H., and S. Haviland. 1977. Comprehension and the given-new contract. In R. O. Freedle, ed., *Discourse Production and Comprehension*, 1–40. Hillsdale, NJ: Erlbaum.

Cole, P., and J. L. Morgan, eds. 1975. *Syntax and Semantics, Vol. 3: Speech Acts*. New York: Academic Press.

Comrie, B. 1976. *Aspect*. Cambridge, U.K.: Cambridge University Press.

Cook, W. A. 1989. *Case Grammar Theory*. Washington, DC: Georgetown University Press.

Copestake, A. 1990. An approach to building the hierarchical element of a lexical knowledge base from a machine readable dictionary. *Proceedings of the First International Workshop on Inheritance in Natural Language Processing*, Toulouse, France, 19–29.

Copestake, A. 1992. The ACQUILEX LKB: Representation issues in semi-automatic acquisition of large lexicons. *Proceedings of ANLP-92*, Trento, Italy, 88–96.

Copestake, A. 1995. Representing lexical polysemy. In J. Klavans, B. Boguraev, L. Levin, and J. Pustejovsky, eds., *Symposium: Representation and Acquisition of Lexical Knowledge: Polysemy, Ambiguity, and Generativity*, 21–26. Working Notes, AAAI Spring Symposium Series. Stanford, CA: Stanford University, 1995.

Copestake, A., and T. Briscoe. 1992. Lexical operations in a unification-based framework. In J. Pustejovsky and S. Bergler, eds., *Lexical Semantics and Knowledge Representation*, 101–119. Berlin: Springer-Verlag.

Copestake, A., T. Briscoe, P. Vossen, A. Ageno, I. Castellon, F. Ribas, G. Rigau, H. Rodríguez, and A. Samiotou. 1994–1995. Acquisition of lexical translation relations from MRD's. In B. J. Dorr and J. Klavans, eds., Special Issue: Building Lexicons for Machine Translation II. *Machine Translation* 10(1–2), 183–219.

Cowie, J., L. Guthrie, and J. Guthrie. 1992. Lexical Disambiguation Using Simulated Annealing. *Proceedings of COLING-92*, 359–365. Nantes, France.

Cowie, J., Ye. Ludovik, H. Molina Salgado, S. Nirenburg, and S. Sheremetyeva. 2000a. Automatic question answering. *Proceedings of the RIAO Conference*, Paris, April.

Cowie, J., Ye. Ludovik, S. Nirenburg, and H. Molina Salgado. 2000b. The week at a glance—cross–language cross document information extraction and translation. *Proceedings of COLING-2000*, Saarbruecken, Germany, 1007–1010.

Cowie J., and S. Nirenburg. 2000. Task-oriented dialogs. *Proceedings of the Workshop on Human-Computer Dialog*, Bellagio, Italy, August.

Cowie, J., S. Nirenburg, and H. Molina Salgado. 2000c. Generating personal profiles. In *Proceedings of the Conference on Machine Translation and Multilingual Applications in the New Millenium*, Exeter, U.K., November.

Crombie, W. 1985. *Process and Relation in Discourse and Language Learning*. London: Oxford University Press.

Cullingford, R. 1981. SAM. In R. Schank and C. Riesbeck, *Inside Computer Understanding*. Hillsdale, NJ: Erlbaum.

Cunningham, H., K. Humphreys, R. Gaizauskas, and Y. Wilks. 1997a. GATE—a TIPSTER-based general architecture for text engineering. *Proceedings of the TIPSTER Text Program Phase III*, Menlo Park, CA: Morgan Kaufmann.

Cunningham, H., K. Humphreys, R. Gaizauskas, and Y. Wilks. 1997b. Software infrastructure for natural language processing. *Proceedings of ANLP-97*, Washington, DC.

Dahlgren, K., J. McDowell, and E. Stabler. 1989. Knowledge representation for commonsense reasoning with text. *Computational Linguistics* 15, 149–170.

Darmesteter, A. 1887. *La Vie des mots etudiée dans leur significations*. Paris: G. Delagrave.

Davidson, D. 1972. On the very idea of a conceptual scheme. *Proceedings of the American Philosophical Association* 47, 1972–73, 5–20.

Davidson, D. 1978. What metaphors mean. *Critical Inquiry* 5(1). Reprinted in S. Saks, ed., *On Metaphor*, 29–45. Chicago: University of Chicago Press, 1979.

Davidson, D. 1983. A coherence theory of truth and knowledge. In D. Henrich, ed., *Kant oder Hegel*. Stuttgart: Klett-Cotta, 423–438. Reprinted in A. R. Malachowski, ed., *Reading Rorty*, 120–134. Oxford: Blackwell, 1990.

Davidson, D. 1984. *Inquiries into Truth and Interpretation*. Oxford: Clarendon Press.

Davidson, D. 1987. Afterthoughts. In A. R. Malachowski, ed., *Reading Rorty*, 134–137. Oxford: Blackwell, 1990.

Defrise, C. 1989. Lexical description for NLP: The case of the french adverb *presque*. *Machine Translation* 4(3), 195–232.

Defrise, C., and S. Nirenburg. 1990a. Meaning representation and text planning. *Proceedings of COLING-90*, Helsinki, August.

Defrise, C., and S. Nirenburg. 1990b. TAMERLAN: A text meaning representation language. *Proceedings of the TKE International Conference*, Trier, Germany.

Democritus. 1717. *Democritus Abderyta Graecus De rebus sacris naturalibus et mysticis*. Norimbergae: Tauberi.

Dennett, D. C. 1979. Artificial intelligence as philosophy and as psychology. In M. Ringle, ed., *Philosophical Perspectives in Artificial Intelligence*, 57–78. Brighton, U.K.: Harvester.

Dennett, D. C. 1991. Cognitive science as reverse engineering: Several meanings of "top-down" and "bottom-up." Paper presented at the Ninth International Congress of Logic, Methodology and Philosophy of Science, Upprala, Sweden.

Derrida, J. 1967. *De la grammatologie*. Paris: Minuit.

Derrida, J. 1987. *Deconstruction and Philosophy: The Texts of Jacques Derrida*. Chicago: University of Chicago Press.

Descartes, R. 1908. *Oeuvres*. Vol. 10. Paris: Léopold Cerf.

Devlin, K. J. 1984. *Constructibility*. Berlin: Springer.

Dewey, J. 1910. *How We Think*. Boston: Heath.

Dillon, G. L. 1977. *Introduction to Contemporary Linguistic Semantics*. Englewood Cliffs, NJ: Prentice-Hall.

Dilworth, C. 1994. Principles, laws, theories and the metaphysics of science. *Synthèse* 101(2), 223–247.

Dilworth, C. 1996. *The Metaphysics of Science: An Account of Modern Science in Terms of Principles, Laws, and Theories*. Dordrecht: Kluwer.

DiMarco, C., and G. Hirst. 1988. Stylistic grammars in language translation. *Proceedings of COLING-88*, Montréal, 148–153.

Dolgopol'skiy, A. B. 1962. Izuchenie leksiki s tochki zreniya transformatsionnogo analiza plana soderzhaniya yazyka (A study of lexics from the point of view of the transformational analysis of the content plane of language). In *Leksikograficheskiy sbornik 5*. Moscow: Nauka.

Dorr, B. J. 1993. Interlingual machine translation: A parameterized approach. *Artificial Intelligence* 63, 429–492.

Dorr, B. J. 1994. Machine translation divergences: A formal description of a proposed solution. *Computational Linguistics* 20(4).

Dorr, B. J., J. Garman, and A. Weinberg. 1994–1995. From syntactic encodings to thematic roles: Building lexical entries for interlingual MT. In B. J. Dorr and J. Klavans, eds., Special Issue: Building Lexicons for Machine Translation II. *Machine Translation* 10(1–2), 221–250.

Dorr, B. J., and J. Klavans, eds. 1994–1995. Special Issue: Building Lexicons for Machine Translation II. *Machine Translation* 10(1–2).

Dorr, B. J., D. Lin, J. Lee, and S. Suh. 1995. Efficient parsing for Korean and English: A parameterized message parsing approach. *Computational Linguistics* 21, 255–263.

Dowty, D. 1972. *Studies in the Logic of Verb Aspect and Time Reference in English*. Studies in Linguistics I. Department of Linguistics, University of Texas, Austin.

Dowty, D. 1978. Applying Montague's views on linguistic metatheory to the structure of the lexicon. In D. Farkas, W. M. Jacobsen, and K. W. Todrys, eds., *Papers from the Parasession on the Lexicon*. Chicago: Chicago Linguistic Society.

Dowty, D. 1979. *Word Meaning and Montague Grammar*. Dordrecht: Reidel.

Dowty, D., R. E. Wall, and S. Peters. 1981. *Introduction to Montague Semantics*. Dordrecht: Reidel.

Doyle, J., and R. Patil. 1991. Two theses of knowledge representation: Language restrictions, taxonomic classification, and the utility of representation services. *Artificial Intelligence* 48(3), 261–298.

Dresher, B. E., and N. Hornstein. 1976. On some supposed contributions of artificial intelligence to the scientific study of language. *Cognition* 4, 321–398.

Dresher, B. E., and N. Hornstein. 1977a. Reply to Schank and Wilensky. *Cognition* 5, 147–149.

Dresher, B. E., and N. Hornstein. 1977b. Reply to Winograd. *Cognition* 5, 379–392.

Dummett, M. 1976. What is a theory of meaning (II)? In G. Evans and J. Mcdowell, eds., *Truth and Meaning*, 67–137. Oxford: Clarendon Press.

Dummett, M. 1991. *The Logical Basis of Metaphysics*. Cambridge, MA: Harvard University Press.

Duncker, K. 1935. *Zur Psychologie des produktiven Denkens*. Berlin: Springer. English Translation: *On Problem Solving*. Psychological Monographs 58, 1945, 1–113.

Dupuy, J.-P. 2000. *The Mechanization of the Mind: On the Origins of Cognitive Science*. Princeton, NJ: Princeton University Press. This is an expanded translation of his *Aux origines des sciences cognitives*. Paris: La Découverte, 1994.

Dura, E. 1998. *Parsing Words*. Göteborg, Sweden: Göteborg University Press.

Durkin, J. 1994. *Expert Systems: Design and Development*. New York: Maxwell-Macmillan.

Ericsson, K. A., and H. A. Simon. 1993. *Protocol Analysis: Verbal Reports as Data*. Cambridge, MA: MIT Press.

Erman, L. D., F. Hayes-Roth, V. R. Lesser, and D. R. Reddy. 1980. The Hearsay-II speech-understanding system: Integrating knowledge to resolve uncertainty. *Computing Surveys* 12(2), 213–253.

Ershov, Yu. L. 1996. *Definability and Computability*. New York: Consultants Bureau.

Evens, M. 1988. *Relational Models of the Lexicon*. Cambridge, U.K.: Cambridge University Press.

Farquhar, A., R. Fikes, W. Pratt, and J. Rice. 1995. *Collaborative Ontology Construction for Information Integration*. KSL-95-63. Knowledge Systems Laboratory, Department of Computer Science, Stanford University, Stanford, CA.

Farquhar, A., R. Fikes, and J. Rice. 1996. *The Ontolingua Server: A Tool for Collaborative Ontology Construction*. KSL-96-26. Knowledge Systems Laboratory, Department of Computer Science, Stanford University, Stanford, CA.

Farquhar, A., R. Fikes, and J. Rice. 1997. *Tools for Assembling Modular Ontologies in Ontolingua*. KSL-97-03. Knowledge Systems Laboratory, Department of Computer Science, Stanford University, Stanford, CA. Also in *Proceedings of AAAI-97*, Providence, 436–441.

Farwell, D., S. Helmreich, W.-Y. Jin, M. Casper, J. Hargrave, H. Molina Salgado, and F.-L. Weng. 1994. PANGLYZER: Spanish language analysis system. *Proceedings of the First Conference of the Association for Machine Translation in the Americas*, Columbia, MO, 56–64.

Fass, D. 1991. met*: A method for discriminating metonymy and metaphor by computer. *Computational Linguistics* 17(1), 49–90.

Fauconnier, G. 1985. *Mental Spaces*. Cambridge, MA: MIT Press.

Fellbaum, C., ed. 1998. *WordNet: An Electronic Lexical Database*. Cambridge, MA: MIT Press.

Féry, C. 1992. *Focus, Topic, and Intonation in German*. Bericht Nr. 20, Arbeitspapiere des Sonderforschungsbereich 340 "Sprachtheoretische Grundlagen für die Computerlinguistik." Stuttgart University, Stuttgart, Germany.

Fillmore, C. J. 1968. The case for case. In E. Bach and R. T. Harms, eds., *Universals in Linguistic Theory*, 1–88. New York: Holt, Rinehart and Winston.

Fillmore, C. J. 1971. Types of lexical information. In D. D. Steinberg and L. A. Jakobovits, eds., *Semantics: An Interdisciplinary Reader in Philosophy, Linguistics and Psychology*, 370–392. Cambridge, U.K.: Cambridge University Press.

Fillmore, C. J. 1977. The case for case reopened. In P. Cole and J. M. Sadock, eds., *Syntax and Semantics 8*, 59–81. New York: Academic Press.

Fillmore, C. J. 1985. Frames and the semantics of understanding. In V. Raskin, ed., Round Table Discussion on Frame/Script Semantics, Part I. *Quaderni di Semantica* 6(2), 222–254.

Fillmore, C. J. 1997. *Lectures on Deixis*. Stanford, CA: CSLI.

Fillmore, C. J., and B. T. Atkins. 1992. Toward a frame-based lexicon: The semantics of RISK and its neighbors. In A. Lehrer and E. Feder Kittay, eds., *Frames, Fields, and Contrasts: New Essays in Semantic and Lexical Organization*, 75–102. Hillsdale, NJ: Erlbaum.

Fillmore, C. J., C. Wooters, and C. F. Baker. 2001. Building a large lexical databank which provides deep semantics. In *Proceedings of the Pacific Asian Conference on Language, Information and Computation*, Hong Kong.

Finin, T. 1980. The semantic interpretation of nominal compounds. *Proceedings of AAAI-80*, Stanford, CA, 310–312.

Firth, J. R. 1957. Modes of meaning. In J. R. Firth, *Papers in Linguistics*, 190–215. London: Oxford University Press.

Fleischman, M., and E. Hovy. 2002. Fine grained classification of named entities. In *Proceedings of the Nineteenth International Conference on Computational Linguistics (COLING-02)*, Taipei, Taiwan, 267–273.

Flower, L. 1981. *Problem-Solving Strategies for Writing*. New York: Harcourt Brace Jovanovich.

Flower, L. 1994. *The Construction of Negotiated Meaning: A Social Cognitive Theory of Writing*. Carbondale: Southern Illinois University Press.

Fodor, J. A. 1990. *A Theory of Content and Other Essays*. Cambridge, MA: MIT Press.

Fodor, J. A. 1994. *The Elm and the Expert: Mentalese and Its Semantics*. Cambridge, MA: MIT Press.

Fodor, J. A., T. G. Beaver, and M. F. Garrett. 1974. *The Psychology of Language*. New York: McGraw-Hill.

Fodor, J. A., and E. Lepore. 1998. The emptiness of the lexicon: Critical reflections on J. Pustejovsky's *The Generative Lexicon*. *Linguistic Inquiry* 29(2), 269–288.

Fodor, J. A., and Z. Pylyshyn. 1988. Connectionism and cognitive architecture: A critical analysis. *Cognition* 28, 3–71.

Fodor, J. D. 1977. *Semantics: Theories of Meaning in Generative Grammar*. Hassocks, U.K.: Harvester.

Forsyth, R., and R. Rada. 1986. *Machine Learning: Applications in Expert Systems and Information Retrieval*. Chichester, U.K.: Horwood-Halsted.

Frawley, W. 1992. *Linguistic Semantics*. Hillsdale, NJ: Erlbaum.

Frederking, R., and S. Nirenburg. 1994. Three heads are better than one. *Proceedings of ANLP-94*, Stuttgart, Germany, October.

Frege, G. 1892. Über Sinn und Bedeutung. *Zeitschrift für Philosophie und philosophische Kritik* 100, 25–50. English translation in P. T. Geach and M. Black, eds., *Translations from the Philosophical Writings of Gottlob Frege*, 2nd ed., 56–78. Oxford: Blackwell, 1966.

Frege, G. 1952a. Frege on Russell's paradox. In M. Black and P. T. Geach, eds., *Translations from the Philosophical Writings of Gottlob Frege*. Oxford: Blackwell.

Frege, G. 1952b. On sense and reference. In M. Black and P. T. Geach, eds., *Translations from the Philosophical Writings of Gottlob Frege*. Oxford: Blackwell.

Frege, G. 1963. Compound thoughts. *Mind* 72, 1–17.

Fridman Noy, N., and M. A. Musen. 2000. PROMPT: Algorithm and tool for automated ontology merging and alignment. *Proceedings of AAAI/IAAI*, Austin, TX, 450–455.

Friedman, J. 1971. *A Computer Model of Transformational Grammar*. New York: American Elsevier.

Friedman, J., D. B. Moran, and D. S. Warren. 1978a. Evaluating English sentences in a logical model: A process version of Montague grammar. *Proceedings of COLING-78*, Bergen, Norway. Also: Paper N-15, Computer Studies in Formal Linguistics, Department of Computer and Communication Sciences, University of Michigan, Ann Arbor.

Friedman, J., D. B. Moran, and D. S. Warren. 1978b. An interpretation system for Montague grammar. *American Journal of Computational Linguistics* 15(1), Microfiche 74, 23–96. Also: Paper N-4, Computer Studies in Formal Linguistics, Department of Computer and Communication Sciences, University of Michigan, Ann Arbor.

Fromkin, V. 1973. *Speech Errors as Linguistic Evidence*. The Hague: Mouton.

Gabbay, D. M., I. Hodkinson, and M. A. Reynolds. 1994. *Temporal Logic: Mathematical Foundations and Computational Aspects*. Vol. 1. Oxford: Clarendon Press.

Gabbay, D. M., M. A. Reynolds, and M. Finger. 2000. *Temporal Logic: Mathematical Foundations and Computational Aspects*. Vol. 2. London: Oxford University Press.

Gale, W. A., K. W. Church, and D. Yarowsky. 1992. Using bilingual materials to develop word sense disambiguation methods. *Proceedings of TMI-92*, Montreal, 101–112.

Gardiner, A. 1951. *The Theory of Speech and Language*. 2nd ed. Oxford: Clarendon Press.

Gelernter, H. 1959. Realization of a geometry theorem-proving machine. *Proceedings of an International Conference on Information Processing*, 273–282. Paris: UNESCO. Reprinted in E. A. Feigenbaum and J. Feldman, eds., 1963. *Computer and Thought*, 134–152. New York: McGraw-Hill.

Gelernter, H., J. R. Hansen, and D. W. Loveland. 1963. Empirical explorations of the geometry theorem proving machine. In E. A. Feigenbaum and J. Feldman, eds., *Computer and Thought*, 153–163. New York: McGraw-Hill.

Gelernter, H., and N. Rochester. 1958. Intelligent behavior in problem-solving machines. *IBM Journal of Research and Development* 2, 336–345.

Genesereth, M. R., and R. E. Fikes. 1992. *Knowledge Interchange Format, Version 3.0 Reference Manual*. Technical Report Logic-92-1. Computer Science Department, Stanford University, Stanford, CA.

Genesereth, M. R., and N. J. Nilsson. 1987. *Logical Foundations of Artificial Intelligence*. San Mateo, CA: Morgan Kaufmann.

Gibson, E. 1991. A Computational Theory of Human Linguistic Processing: Memory Limitations and Processing Breakdown. Unpublished doctoral dissertation, Computational Linguistics Program, Carnegie Mellon University, Pittsburgh.

Gill, R. R. R. 1990. *Deducibility and Decidability*. London: Routledge.

Gilman, D. 1996. Optimization and simplicity: Computational vision and biological explanation. *Synthèse* 107(3), 293–323.

Ginsberg, M. 1991. Knowledge interchange format: The Kif of Death. *AI Magazine*, 163, 5–63.

Givón, T. 1967. *Transformations of Ellipsis, Sense Development and Rules of Lexical Derivation*. SP-2896. Santa Monica, CA: Systems Development Corporation.

Goel, A. 1992. Representation of design functions in experience-based design. In D. Brown, M. Waldron, and H. Yoshikawa, eds., *Intelligent Computer-Aided Design*, 283–308. Amsterdam: North-Holland.

Good, I. J. 1969. Corroboration, explanation, evolving probability, simplicity and a sharpened razor. *British Journal for the Philosophy of Science* 19(1), 123–143.

Good, I. J. 1983. *Good Thinking: The Foundation of Probability and Its Applications*. Minneapolis: University of Minnesota Press.

Goodenough, W. 1956. Componential analysis and the study of meaning. *Language* 32(1).

Goodman, K., and S. Nirenburg, eds. 1991. *KBMT-89: A Case Study in Knowledge-Based Machine Translation*. San Mateo, CA: Morgan Kaufmann.

Goodman, N. 1977. *The Structure of Appearance*. 3rd ed. Dordrecht: Reidel.

Goodman, N. 1983. *Fact, Fiction, and Forecast*. Cambridge, MA: Harvard University Press.

Greenberg, J. 1949. The logical analysis of kinship. *Philosophy of Science* 16(1).

Greenberg, J. H., ed. 1978. *Universals of Language*. Stanford, CA: Stanford University Press.

Greene, G. 1989. *Pragmatics and Natural Language Understanding*. Hillsdale, NJ: Erlbaum.

Grice, H. P. 1957. Meaning. *Philosophical Review* 66, 377–388. Reprinted in D. D. Steinberg and L. A. Jakobovits, eds., *Semantics: An Interdisciplinary Reader in Philosophy, Linguistics and Psychology*, 53–60. Cambridge, U.K.: Cambridge University Press, 1971.

Grice, H. P. 1975. Logic and conversation. In P. Cole and J. L. Morgan, eds., *Syntax and Semantics, Vol. 3: Speech Acts*. New York: Academic Press.

Grimshaw, J. 1990. *Argument Structure*. Cambridge, MA: MIT Press.

Grishman, R., and R. Kittredge, eds. 1986. *Analyzing Language in Restricted Domains: Sublanguage Description and Processing*. Hillsdale, NJ: Erlbaum.

Groner, M., R. Groner, and W. F. Bischof. 1983b. Approaches to heuristics: A historical review. In R. Groner, M. Groner, and W. F. Bischof, eds. *Methods of Heuristics*, 1–18. Hillsdale, NJ: Erlbaum.

Groner, R., M. Groner, and W. F. Bischof, eds. 1983a. *Methods of Heuristics*. Hillsdale, NJ: Erlbaum.

Grossmann, R. 1992. *The Existence of the World: An Introduction to Ontology*. London: Routledge.

Grosz, B. 1977. The representation and use of focus in dialogue understanding. *Proceedings of IJCAI-77*. Reprinted in B. J. Grosz, K. Sparck Jones, and B. L. Webber, eds., *Readings in Natural Language Processing*, 353–362. Los Altos, CA: Morgan Kaufmann.

Grosz, B. J., and C. L. Sidner. 1986. Attention, intentions, and the structure of discourse. *Computational Linguistics* 12(3), 175–204.

Gruber, J. 1965. Studies in Lexical Relations. Unpublished doctoral dissertation, MIT, Cambridge, MA, 1965. A revised and extended version published as *Lexical Structures in Syntax and Semantics*. New York: North-Holland, 1976.

Gruber, T. R. 1993. A translation approach to portable ontology specifications. *Knowledge Acquisition* 5, 199–220.

Gruber, T. R. 1995. Toward principles for the design of ontologies used for knowledge sharing. In N. Guarino and R. Poli, eds., Special Issue: The Role of Formal Ontology in the Information Technology. *International Journal of Human and Computer Studies* 43(5–6), 907–928.

Guarino, N. 1995. Formal ontology, conceptual analysis, and knowledge representation. In N. Guarino and R. Poli, eds., Special Issue: The Role of Formal Ontology in the Information

Technology. *International Journal of Human and Computer Studies* 43(5–6). (Page numbers refer to a downloaded version.)

Guarino, N. 1997. Understanding, building, and using ontologies. *International Journal of Human-Computer Studies* 46, 293–310.

Guarino, N. 1998a. Formal ontology and information systems. In Guarino 1998c, 3–15.

Guarino, N. 1998b. Some ontological principles for designing upper level lexical resources. *Proceedings of the First International Conference on Lexical Resources and Evaluation*, Granada, Spain.

Guarino, N., ed. 1998c. Formal ontology in information systems. *Proceedings of the First International Conference (FOIS-98)*, June 6–8, Trento, Italy. Amsterdam: IOS Press.

Guarino, N., and C. Welty. 2002. Evaluating ontological decisions with OntoClean. *Communications of the ACM* 45(2), 61–65.

Guo, C. 1995. *Machine Tractable Dictionaries: Design and Construction*. Norwood, NJ: Ablex.

Haack, S. 1993. *Evidence and Inquiry: Towards Reconstruction in Epistemology*. Oxford: Blackwell.

Haack, S. 1997. Précis of *Evidence and Inquiry: Towards Reconstruction in Epistemology*. *Synthèse* 112(1), 7–11.

Hajičová, E. 1998. Questions on sentence prosody linguists have always wanted to ask. *Prague Bulletin of Mathematical Linguistics* 70, 23–36.

Hajičová, E., B. Partee, and P. Sgall. 1998. *Topic-Focus Articulation, Tripartite Structures, and Semantic Content*. Dordrecht: Kluwer.

Halliday, M. A. K., ed. 1983. *Readings in Systemic Linguistics*. London: Batsford.

Halliday, M. A. K. 1985. *An Introduction to Functional Grammar*. London: Arnold.

Harabagiu, S. M., and S. J. Maiorano. 1999. Knowledge-lean coreference resolution and its relation to textual cohesion and coherence. In *Proceedings of the ACL Workshop on the Relation of Discourse/Dialogue Structure and Reference*, College Park, MD, 29–38.

Harabagiu, S., and D. Moldovan. 1998. Knowledge processing on extended WordNet. In C. Fellbaum, ed., *WordNet: An Electronic Lexical Database and Some of Its Applications*. Cambridge, MA: MIT Press.

Hardcastle, V. G. 1995. Computationalism. *Synthèse* 105(3), 303–317.

Hašek, J. 1974. *The Good Soldier Švejk and His Fortunes in the World War*. New York: Crowell.

Hausser, R. 1999. *Foundations of Computational Linguistics*. Berlin: Springer.

Hayakawa, S. I. 1975. *Language in Thought and Action*. 3rd ed. New York: Harcourt Brace Jovanovich.

Hayes, P. 1974. Some problems and non-problems in representation theory. *Proceedings of the AISB Conference*, University of Sussex, Falmer, Brighton, UK.

Hayes, P. 1979. The naive physics manifesto. In D. Mitchie, ed., *Expert Systems in the Microelectronic Age*. Edinburgh: Edinburgh University Press.

Hayes-Roth, B. 1985. A blackboard architecture for control. *Artificial Intelligence* 26(3), 251–321.

Heath, L., and R. S. Tindale. 1994. Heuristics and biases in applied settings: An introduction. In L. Heath, R. S. Tindale, J. Edwards, E. J. Posavac, F. B. Bryant, E. Henderson-King, Y. Suarez-Balcazar, and J. Myers, eds., *Applications of Heuristics and Biases to Social Issues*, 1–12. New York: Plenum.

Hegel, G. W. F. 1931. *The Phenomenology of Mind*. London–New York: Allen and Unwin–Macmillan.

Hegel, G. W. F. 1983. *Hegel's Lectures on the History of Philosophy*. Atlantic Heights, NJ: Humanities Press.

Heidegger, M. 1949. *Existence and Being*. Chicago: Regnery.

Heidegger, M. 1980. *Hegel's Phänomenologie des Geistes*. Frankfurt am Main: Klostermann.

Heim, I., and A. Kratzer. 1998. *Semantics in Generative Grammar*. Oxford: Blackwell.

Hempel, C. G. 1965. *Scientific Explanation: Essays in the Philosophy of Science*. New York: Free Press.

Hempel, C. G. 1966. *Philosophy of Natural Science*. Englewood Cliffs, NJ: Prentice-Hall.

Hendler, J. 2001. Agents and the semantic web. *IEEE Intelligent Systems* 16, 30–37.

Hirst, G. 1983. *Semantic Interpretation against Ambiguity*. Technical Report CS-83-25. Department of Computer Science, Brown University, Providence, RI.

Hirst, G. 1987. *Semantic Interpretation and the Resolution of Ambiguity*. Cambridge, U.K.: Cambridge University Press.

Hirst, G. 1991. Existence assumptions in knowledge representation. *Artificial Intelligence* 49, 199–242.

Hirst, G. 1995. Near-synonymy and the structure of lexical knowledge. In J. Klavans, B. Boguraev, L. Levin, and J. Pustejovsky, eds., *Symposium: Representation and Acquisition of Lexical Knowledge: Polysemy, Ambiguity, and Generativity*, 51–56. Working Notes, AAAI Spring Symposium Series. Stanford, CA: Stanford University, 1995.

Hjelmslev, L. 1958. Dans quelle mesure les significations des mots peuvent-elle être considérées comme formant une structure? *Proceedings of the Eighth International Congress of Linguists*, Oslo, 636–654.

Hjelmslev, L. 1961. *Prolegomena to a Theory of Language*. Madison: University of Wisconsin Press.

Hobbs, J. 1979. Coherence and co-reference. *Cognitive Science* 3(1), 67–82.

Hobbs, J. 1987. World knowledge and word meaning. In Y. Wilks, ed., *TINLAP-3: Theoretical Issues in Natural Language Processing-3*, 20–25. Las Cruces, NM: Computational Research Laboratory, New Mexico State University.

Hobbs, J. R., and S. J. Rosenschein. 1977. Making computational sense of Montague's intensional logic. *Artificial Intelligence* 9(3), 287–306.

Hoeksma, J. 1984. *Categorial Morphology*. Dordrecht: Denderen.

Horgan, T., and J. Tienson. 1989. Representations without rules. *Philosophical Topics* 17, 27–43.

Horgan, T., and J. Tienson. 1994. A non-classical framework for cognitive science. *Synthèse* 101(3), 305–345.

Hornstein, N. 1984. *Logic as Grammar*. Cambridge, MA: MIT Press.

Hornstein, N. 1995. *Logical Form: From GB to Minimalism*. Oxford: Blackwell.

Horty, J. F., R. H. Thomason, and D. S. Touretzky. 1990. A sceptical theory of inheritance in nonmonotonic semantic networks. *Artificial Intelligence* 42(2–3), 311–348.

Hovy, E. 1988. *Generating Natural Language under Pragmatic Constraints*. Hillsdale, NJ: Erlbaum.

Hovy, E. 1998. Combining and standardizing large-scale practical ontologies for machine translation and other uses. *Proceedings of the 1st Conference on Language Resources and Evaluation Research*, Granada, Spain.

Hovy, E., and S. Nirenburg. 1992. Approximating an interlingua in a principled way. *Proceedings of the DARPA Workshop on Speech and Natural Language*, New York: Arden House.

Hughes, G. E., and M. J. Cresswell. 1968. *An Introduction to Modal Logic*. London: Routledge.

Humboldt, W. von. 1971. *Linguistic Variability and Intellectual Development*. Philadelphia: University of Pennsylvania Press. English Translation of *Über die Verschiedenheit des menschlichen Sprachbaues und ihren Einfluss auf die geistige Entwicklung des Menschengeschlechts*. Berlin: Royal Academy of Sciences, 1836.

Husserl, E. 1900–1901. *Logische Untersuchungen*. 1st ed., Halle: Niemeyer; 2nd ed., 1913–1921. English translation (of the 2nd ed.): *Logical Investigations*. London: Routledge, 1970.

Husserl, E. 1964. *The Idea of Phenomenology*. The Hague: Nijhoff.

Husserl, E. 1982. *Ideas Pertaining to a Pure Phenomenology and to a Phenomenological Philosophy*. The Hague: Nijhoff.

Hutchins, W. J., and H. L. Somers. 1992. *An Introduction to Machine Translation*. London: Academic Press.

Ide, N., and J. Veronis. 1998. Introduction. Special Issue on Word Sense Disambiguation: The State of the Art. *Computational Linguistics* 24(1), 1–40.

Ingria, R. 1987. Lexical information for parsing systems: Points of convergence and divergence. In D. Walker, A. Zampolli, and N. Calzolari, eds., *Automating the Lexicon 1: Research in a Multilingual Environment*. New York: Oxford University Press.

Isabelle, P. 1984. Another look at nominal compounds. *Proceedings of COLING-84*, Stanford, CA, 509–516.

Jackendoff, R. 1983. *Semantics and Cognition*. Cambridge, MA: MIT Press.

Jackendoff, R. 1994. *Patterns in the Mind: Language and Human Nature*. New York: Basic Books.

Jakobson, R. 1960. Linguistics and poetics. In T. A. Sebeok, ed., *Style in Language*. Cambridge, MA: Technology Press of MIT. Reprinted in R. Jakobson, *Selected Writings*, vol. 3, 18–51. The Hague: Mouton, 1981.

Jakobson, R. 1965. Quest for the essence of language. *Diogenes* 51. Reprinted in R. Jakobson, *Selected Writings*, vol. 2, 345–359. The Hague: Mouton.

Jespersen, O. 1924. *The Philosophy of Grammar*. London: Allen and Unwin.

Johannesson, P., and P. Wohed. 1998. Deontic specification patterns—generalisation and classification. In Guarino, 1998c, 95–107.

Johansson, I. 1998. Pattern as an ontological category. In Guarino, 1998c, 86–94.

Johnson-Laird, P. N. 1983. *Mental Models*. Cambridge, MA: Harvard University Press.

Johnston, M., B. Boguraev, and J. Pustejovsky. 1995. The acquisition and interpretation of complex nominals. In J. Klavans, B. Boguraev, L. Levin, and J. Pustejovsky, eds., *Symposium: Representation and Acquisition of Lexical Knowledge: Polysemy, Ambiguity, and Generativity*, 69–74. Working Notes, AAAI Spring Symposium Series. Stanford, CA: Stanford University, 1995.

Joshi, A. K. 1985. How much context-sensitivity is necessary for characterizing structural descriptions—tree adjoining grammars. In D. R. Dowty, L. Karttunen, and A. M. Zwicky, eds., *Natural Language Parsing: Psychological, Computational, and Theoretical Perspectives*, 206–250. New York: Cambridge University Press.

Joshi, A. K., L. Levy, and M. Takabashi. 1975. Tree adjunct grammars. *Journal of the Computer and System Sciences* 10(1), 136–163.

Jubien, M. 1997. *Contemporary Metaphysics*. Malden, MA: Blackwell.

Kaczmarek, T., R. Bates, and G. Robbins. 1986. Recent developments in NIKL. *Proceedings of the National Conference on Artificial Intelligence*, American Association for Artificial Intelligence, Philadelphia.

Kahneman, D., P. Slovik, and A. Tversky, eds. 1982. *Judgment under Uncertainty: Heuristics and Biases*. Cambridge, U.K.: Cambridge University Press.

Kamp, H. 1984. A theory of truth and semantic representation. In J. Groenindijk, T. Janssen, and M. Stockhof, eds., *Truth, Interpretation, and Information*, 1–41. Cinnaminson, NJ: Foris.

Kant, I. 1787. *Kritik der reinen Vernunft*. English translation: *Critique of Pure Reason*. London: Macmillan, 1929.

Kapitsa, P. L. 1980. *Experiment, Theory, Practice: Articles and Addresses*. Dordrecht: Reidel.

Katz, B., and J. Lin. 2002. Annotating the Semantic Web using natural language. *Proceedings of the Second Workshop on NLP and XML (NLPXML-2002)* at COLING 2002, Taipei, Taiwan.

Katz, J. J. 1972/1974. *Semantic Theory*. New York: Harper and Row.

Katz, J. J. 1978. Effability and translation. In F. Guenthner and M. Guenthner-Reutter, eds., *Meaning and Translation: Philosophical and Linguistic Approaches*, 191–234. London: Duckworth.

Katz, J. J., and J. A. Fodor. 1963. The structure of a semantic theory. *Language* 39(1), 170–210. Reprinted in J. A. Fodor and J. J. Katz, eds., *The Structure of Language: Readings in the Philosophy of Language*, 479–518. Englewood Cliffs, NJ: Prentice-Hall, 1964.

Katz, J. J., and P. M. Postal. 1964. *An Integrated Theory of Linguistic Descriptions*. Cambridge, MA: MIT Press.

Kay, M. 1985. Parsing in functional unification grammar. In D. R. Dowty, L. Karttunen, and A. M. Zwicky, eds., *Natural Language Parsing: Psychological, Computational, and Theoretical Perspectives*, 251–278. New York: Cambridge University Press.

Kay, P. 1971. Taxonomy and semantic contrast. *Language* 47(4), 866–887.

Kearns, M. J., and U. V. Vazirani. 1994. *An Introduction to Computational Learning Theory*. Cambridge, MA: MIT Press.

Keenan, E. L., and L. M. Faltz. 1985. *Boolean Semantics for Natural Language*. Dordrecht: Reidel.

Kehler, A., and S. Shieber. 1997. Anaphoric dependencies in ellipsis. *Computational Linguistics* 23(3), 457–466.

Kemenade, A. van, and N. Vincent, eds. 1997. *Parameters of Morphosyntactic Change*. Cambridge, U.K.: Cambridge University Press.

Kenny, A. 1989. *The Metaphysics of the Mind*. Oxford: Clarendon Press.

Kilgariff, A. 1993. Dictionary word sense distinctions: An enquiry into their nature. *Computers and the Humanities* 26(1–2), 365–387.

Kilgariff, A. 1997a. "I don't believe in word senses." *Computers and the Humanities* 31(1), 91–113.

Kilgariff, A. 1997b. What is word sense disambiguation good for? *Proceedings of the Natural Language Processing Pacific Rim Symposium 1997 (NLPRS-97)*, Phuket, Thailand.

Kilgariff, A., and J. Rosenzweig. 2000. Framework and results for English SENSEVAL. *Computers and the Humanities* 34(1–2), 15–48.

Kim, J. 1993. *Supervenience and Mind*. Cambridge, U.K.: Cambridge University Press.

King, M., and K. Falkedal. 1990. Using test suites in the evaluation of machine translation systems. *Proceedings of COLING-90*, Helsinki, 211–219.

Kirkpatrick, D. G., C. Gelatt, and M. P. Vecchi. 1983. Optimization by simulated annealing. *Science* 220, 621–680.

Kitcher, P. 1988. Marr's computational theory of vision. *Philosophy of Science* 55, 1–24.

Kittredge, R. 1987. The significance of sublanguage for automatic translation. In S. Nirenburg, ed., *Machine Translation: Theoretical and Methodological Issues*, 59–67. Cambridge, U.K.: Cambridge University Press.

Kittredge, R., L. Iordanskaja, and A. Polguère. 1988. Multilingual text generation and the meaning-text theory. *Proceedings of TMI-88*, Pittsburgh, June.

Kittredge, R., and J. Lehrberger, eds. 1982. *Sublanguage: Studies of Language in Restricted Semantic Domains*. Berlin: Walter de Gruyter.

Kittredge, R., A. Polguère, and E. Goldberg. 1986. Synthesis of weather forecasts from formatted data. *Proceedings of COLING-86*, Bonn, 563–565.

Klavans, J., B. Boguraev, L. Levin, and J. Pustejovsky, eds. 1995. *Symposium: Representation and Acquisition of Lexical Knowledge: Polysemy, Ambiguity, and Generativity*. Working Notes, AAAI Spring Symposium Series. Stanford, CA: Stanford University.

Kleer, J. de, and J. S. Brown. 1984. A qualitative physics based on confluences. *Artificial Intelligence* 24, 7–83.

Klein, H. G. 1974. *Tempus, Aspekt, Aktionsart*. Tübingen: Niemeyer.

Knight, K., and S. Luk. 1994. Building a large-scale knowledge base for machine translation. *Proceedings of AAAI-94*, Seattle, 773–778.

Köhler, W. 1921. *Intelligenzprüfungen an Menschenaffen*. Berlin: Springer.

Kornfilt, J. 1997. *Turkish*. London: Routledge.

Korzybski, A. 1933. *Science and Sanity*. Lancaster, PA: International Non-Aristotelian Library Publishing Company.

Koskenniemi, K. 1983. Two-level model for morphological analysis. *Proceedings of IJCAI-83*, Karlsruhe, 683–685.

Krifka, M. 1991. A compositional semantics for multiple focus constructions. In S. Moore and G. Wyner, eds., *Proceedings of SALT I*, Cornell University, Ithaca, NY, 127–158.

Kroeber, A. 1952. Classificatory systems of relationships. In A. Kroeber, ed. *The Nature of Culture*. Chicago: University of Chicago Press.

Kuno, S. 1972. Functional sentence perspective. *Linguistic Inquiry* 3, 269–320.

Ladusaw, W. A. 1988. Semantic theory. In F. J. Newmeyer, ed. *Linguistics the Cambridge Survey I, Linguistic Theory: Foundations*, 89–112. Cambridge, U.K.: Cambridge University Press.

Lakoff, G. 1971. On generative semantics. In D. D. Steinberg and L. A. Jakobovits, eds., *Semantics: An Interdisciplinary Reader in Philosophy, Linguistics and Psychology*, 232–296. Cambridge, U.K.: Cambridge University Press.

Lakoff, G. 1972. Linguistics and natural logic. In D. Davidson and G. Harman, eds., *Semantics of Natural Language*, 545–665. Dordrecht: Reidel.

Lakoff, G. 1987. *Women, Fire, and Dangerous Things*. Chicago: University of Chicago Press.

Lakoff, G., and M. Johnson. 1980. *Metaphors We Live by*. Chicago: University of Chicago Press.

Langley, P. 1996. *Elements of Machine Learning*. San Francisco: Morgan Kaufmann.

Lascarides, A. 1995. The pragmatics of word meaning. In J. Klavans, B. Boguraev, L. Levin, and J. Pustejovsky, eds., *Symposium: Representation and Acquisition of Lexical Knowledge: Polysemy, Ambiguity, and Generativity*, 75–80. Working Notes, AAAI Spring Symposium Series. Stanford, CA: Stanford University, 1995.

Laurian, A.-M. 1986. Stylistics and computing: Machine translation as a tool for a new approach to stylistics. *Computers and Translation* 1, 215–224.

Lawler, E., and D. E. Wood. 1966. Branch-and-bound methods: A survey. *Operations Research* 14, 699–719.

Leeds, S. 1994. Constructive empiricism. *Synthèse* 101(2), 187–221.

Lehnert, W. G. 1978. *The Process of Question Answering*. Hillsdale, NJ: Erlbaum.

Lehnert, W. G. 1994. Cognition, computers, and car bombs: How Yale prepared me for the 1990s. In R. C. Schank and E. Langer, eds., *Beliefs, Reasoning, and Decision-Making: Psycho-Logic in Honor of Bob Abelson*, 143–173. Hillsdale, NJ: Erlbaum.

Lehnert, W. G., and M. H. Ringle, eds. 1982. *Strategies for Natural Language Processing*. Hillsdale, NJ: Erlbaum.

Lehrer, A., and E. Feder Kittay, eds. 1992. *Frames, Fields, and Contrasts: New Essays in Semantic and Lexical Organization*. Hillsdale, NJ: Erlbaum.

Leibniz, G. W. 1880. *Philosophische Schriften*. Vols. 1–7. Berlin: Weidmannsche Buchhandlung.

Lemon, O. 1996. Semantical foundations of spatial logics. In L. C. Aiello, J. Doyle, and S. C. Shapiro, eds., *Proceedings of the Fifth International Conference on the Principles of Knowledge Representation and Reasoning (KR-96)*, Cambridge, MA. Los Altos, CA: Morgan Kaufmann.

Lenat, D. B. 1982. The nature of heuristics. *Artificial Intelligence* 19, 189–249.

Lenat, D. B. 1983. Toward a theory of heuristics. In R. Groner, M. Groner, and W. F. Bischof, eds., *Methods of Heuristics*, 351–404. Hillsdale, NJ: Erlbaum.

Lenat, D. B. 1995. Cyc: A large-scale investment in knowledge infrastructure. *Communications of the ACM* 38(11).

Lenat, D. B., and R. V. Guha. 1990. *Building Large Knowledge Based Systems*. Reading, MA: Addison-Wesley.

Lenci, A., N. Calzolari, and A. Zampolli. 2002. From text to content: Computational lexicons and the Semantic Web. Paper presented at the AAAI Workshop "Semantic Web Meets Language Resources," Edmonton, Alberta, Canada, June.

Levin, B. 1991. Building a lexicon: The contribution of linguistics. In B. Boguraev, ed., Special Issue: Building a Lexicon. *International Journal of Lexicography* 4(3), 205–226.

Levin, B. 1993. *Towards a Lexical Organization of English Verbs*. Chicago: University of Chicago Press.

Levin, B., and S. Pinker, eds. 1991. Special Issue: Lexical and Conceptual Semantics. *Cognition* 41.

Levin, B., and M. Rappaport Hovav. 1995. *Unaccusativity at the Syntax–Lexical Semantics Interface*. Cambridge, MA: MIT Press.

Levin, L. S. 1991. Syntactic theory and processing. In K. Goodman and S. Nirenburg, eds., *KBMT-89: A Case Study in Knowledge-Based Machine Translation*, 49–70. San Mateo, CA: Morgan Kaufmann.

Lewis, C. L. 1946. *An Analysis of Knowledge and Evaluation*. La Salle, IL: Open Court.

Lewis, D. 1972. General semantics. In D. Davidson and G. Harman, eds., *Semantics of Natural Language*, 169–218. Dordrecht: Reidel. Reprinted in Partee 1976, 1–50.

Longman Dictionary of Contemporary English. 1987. Harlow, U.K.: Longman.

Lounsbury, F. 1956. A semantic analysis of the Pawnee kinship usage. *Language* 32(1).

Loux, M. J. 1998. *Metaphysics: A Contemporary Introduction*. London: Routledge.

Ludovik, Ye., J. Cowie, H. Molina Salgado, and S. Nirenburg. 1999. Ontology-based information extraction. *Proceedings of MT Summit*, Singapore.

Lurfle, S. Ya. 1970. *Demokrit. Teksty. Perevod. Issledovaniia* (Democritus. Texts. Translation. Research). Leningrad: Nauka.

Lyons, J. 1977. *Semantics*. Vol. 2. Cambridge, U.K.: Cambridge University Press.

Madhavan, J., P. A. Bernstein, P. Domingos, and A. Halevy. 2002. Representing and reasoning about mappings between domain models. *Proceedings of the Eighteenth National Conference on Artificial Intelligence (AAAI-2002)*, Edmonton, Alberta, Canada.

Mahesh, K. 1996. *Ontology Development for Machine Translation: Ideology and Methodology*. Memoranda in Computer and Cognitive Science MCCS-96-292. Computing Research Laboratory, New Mexico State University, Las Cruces.

Mahesh, K., S. Beale, and S. Nirenburg. 1996. Ontology-based ambiguity resolution and non-literal interpretation. *Proceedings of the International Conference on Knowledge Based Computer Systems (KBCS-96)*, December 16–18, Bombay, India.

Mahesh, K., and S. Nirenburg. 1995. A situated ontology for practical NLP. Paper presented at the IJCAI-95 Workshop on Basic Ontological Issues in Knowledge Sharing, August 19–21, Montreal.

Mahesh, K., S. Nirenburg, and S. Beale. 1997. If you have it, flaunt it: Using full ontological knowledge for word sense disambiguation. *Proceedings of TMI-97*, Santa Fe, NM, 1–9.

Mahesh, K., S. Nirenburg, S. Beale, E. Viegas, V. Raskin, and B. Onyshkevych. 1997. Word sense disambiguation: Why statistics if we have these numbers. In *Proceedings of TMI-97*, Santa Fe, NM, 151–159.

Mahesh, K., S. Nirenburg, J. Cowie, and D. Farwell. 1996. *An Assessment of CYC for Natural Language Processing*. Memoranda in Computer and Cognitive Science MCCS-96-296. Computing Research Laboratory, New Mexico State University, Las Cruces.

Mann, W., and S. Thompson. 1988. Rhetorical structure theory: Toward a functional theory of text organization. *Text* 8, 243–281.

Marconi, D. 1997. *Lexical Competence*. Cambridge, MA: MIT Press.

Marcu, D. 1999. A decision-based approach to rhetorical parsing. *Proceedings of ACL-99*, College Park, MD, 365–372.

Marr, D. 1982. *Vision*. New York: Freeman.

Martin, J. 1992. Computer understanding of conventional metaphoric language. *Cognitive Science* 16(2), 233–270.

Marx, W. 1983. The meaning-confining function of the adjective. In G. Rickheit and M. Bock, eds., *Psycholinguistic Studies in Language Processing*, 70–81. Berlin: Walter de Gruyter.

Mathesius, V. 1947. O tak zvaném aktuálnim cleneni vetném (On the so-called actual articulation of the sentence). In V. Mathesius, *Cestina a obecny jazykepyt*. Prague: Melantrich.

Mayer, A., and J. Orth. 1901. Zur qualitativen Untersuchung der Association. *Zeitschrift für Psychologie und Physiologie der Sinnesorgane* 26, 1–13.

McCarthy, J. 1977. Epistemological problems of artificial intelligence. *Proceedings of IJCAI-77*, Cambridge, MA, 1038–1044.

McCarthy, J., and P. Hayes. 1969. Some philosophical points from the point of view of artificial intelligence. *Machine Intelligence* 4, 463–502.

McCawley, J. D. 1968. The role of semantics in a grammar. In E. Bach and R. T. Harms, eds., *Universals in Linguistic Theory*, 124–169. New York: Holt, Rinehart and Winston.

McCawley, J. D. 1972. A program for logic. In D. Davidson and G. Harman, eds., *Semantics of Natural Language*, 157–212. Dordrecht: Reidel.

McCawley, J. D. 1976. Some ideas not to live by. *Die Neueren Sprachen* 75, 151–165. Reprinted in J. D. McCawley, *Adverbs, Vowels, and Objects of Wonder*, 234–246. Chicago: University of Chicago Press, 1979.

McDermott, D. 1978. Tarskian semantics, or no notation without denotation. *Cognitive Science* 2(3), 277–282. Reprinted in B. J. Grosz, K. Sparck Jones, and B. L. Webber, eds., *Readings in Natural Language Processing*, 167–169. Los Altos, CA: Morgan Kaufmann, 1986.

McDonald, D. D., and E. J. Conklin. 1982. Salience as a simplifying metaphor for natural language generation. *Proceedings of AAAI-82*, Pittsburgh, PA, 75–78.

McDonough, C. J. 2000. Complex Events in an Ontologic-Semantic Natural Language Processing System. Unpublished doctoral dissertation, Department of English, Purdue University, West Lafayette, IN.

McGuinness, D. 2000. Conceptual modeling for distributed ontology environments. *Proceedings of ICCS-2000*, Darmstadt, Germany.

McKeown, K. 1985. *Text Generation: Using Discourse Strategies and Focus Constraints to Generate Natural Language Text*. Cambridge, U.K.: Cambridge University Press.

McShane, M. Forthcoming. *A Theory of Ellipsis*. Oxford University Press.

McShane, M., and S. Nirenburg. 2002. *Reference and Ellipsis in Ontological Semantics*. Memoranda in Computer and Cognitive Science MCCS-02-329. Computing Research Laboratory, New Mexico State University, Las Cruces.

McShane, M., S. Nirenburg, J. Cowie, and R. Zacharski. 2002. Embedding knowledge elicitation and MT systems within a single architecture. *Machine Translation* 17(4), 271–305.

Megerdoomian, K. 2000. Unification-based Persian morphology. *Proceedings of CICLing-2000*, Centro de Investigacion en Computacion-IPN, Cuidad de Mexico, Mexico.

Meillet, A. 1922. *Introduction à l'étude comparative des langues indo-européennes*. Paris: Hachette.

Meinong, A. 1904. Über Gegenstandstheorie. In A. Meinong, ed., *Untersuchungen zur Gegenstandstheorie und Psychologie*. Leipzig: Bart. Reprinted in A. Meinong, *Gesamtausgabe*, vol. 2, 481–535. Graz, Austria: Akademische Druck- und Verlaganstadt, 1969–1978. Translated as The theory of objects, in R. M. Chisholm, ed., *Realism and the Background of Phenomenology*, 76–117. Glencoe, IL: Free Press, 1960.

Mel'čuk, I. A. 1974. *Opyt teorii lingvisticheskikh modeley "Smysl ↔ Tekst"* (An essay on a theory of linguistic models "Sense ↔ Text"). Moscow: Nauka.

Mel'čuk, I. A. 1979. *Studies in Dependency Syntax*. Ann Arbor, MI: Karoma.

Mel'čuk, I. A. 1988. Semantic description of lexical units in an explanatory combinatorial dictionary: Basic principles and heuristic criteria. *International Journal of Lexicography* 1(3), 165–188.

Mel'čuk, I. A. 1997. *Kurs obshchey morfologii* (A course in general morphology). Vol. 1. Moscow-Vienna: Progress–Wiener Slawistischer Almanach.

Mel'čuk, I. A. 1998. *Kurs obshchey morfologii* (A course in general morphology). Vol. 2. Moscow-Vienna: Progress–Wiener Slawistischer Almanach.

Merriam-Webster's Collegiate Dictionary. 1963. 7th ed. Springfield, MA: Merriam-Webster.

Metropolis, N., A. Rosenbluth, M. Rosenbluth, A. Teller, and E. Teller. 1953. Equations of state calculations by fast computing machines. *Journal of Chemical Physics* 21, 1087–1092.

Meyer, I., B. Onyshkevych, and L. Carlson. 1990. *Lexicographic Principles and Design for Knowledge-Based Machine Translation*. Technical Report CMU-CMT-90-118. Center for Machine Translation, Carnegie Mellon University, Pittsburgh.

Mihalcea, R., and D. Moldovan. 1999. A method for word sense disambiguation of unrestricted text. In *Proceedings of the Thirty-Seventh Annual Meeting of the Association for Computational Linguistics*, College Park, MD.

Mikheev, A., M. Moens, and C. Grover. 1999. Named entity recognition without gazetteers. In *Proceedings of the Ninth Meeting of the European Chapter of the Association of Computational Linguistics*. Bergen, Norway, 1–8.

Miller, G. A., C. Fellbaum, J. Kegl, and K. Miller. 1988. Wordnet: An electronic lexical reference system based on theories of lexical memory. *Révue Québecoise de Linguistique* 17, 181–211.

Miller, G. A., E. Galanter, and K. H. Pribram. 1960. *Plans and the Structure of Behavior*. New York: Holt.

Miller, G. A., and P. N. Johnson-Laird. 1976. *Language and Perception*. Cambridge, MA: Harvard University Press.

Minker, W., A. Waibel, and J. Mariani. 1999. *Stochastically-Based Semantic Analysis*. Boston: Kluwer.

Minsky, M. 1975. A framework for representing knowledge. In P. H. Winston, ed., *The Psychology of Computer Vision*, 211–277. New York: McGraw Hill.

Mitchell, T. M. 1997. *Machine Learning*. New York: McGraw-Hill.

Mitchie, D., ed. 1979. *Expert Systems in the Microelectronic Age*. Edinburgh: Edinburgh University Press.

Mitkov, R. 2000. Towards more comprehensive evaluation in anaphora resolution. *Proceedings of LREC-2000*, Athens, 1309–1314.

Mitkov, R., and B. Boguraev, eds. 1997. *Operational Factors in Practical Anaphora Resolution for Unrestricted Texts, Postconference Workshop of ACL/EACL-97*, Madrid.

Mitra, P., G. Wiederhold, and M. Kersten. 2000. A graph-oriented model for articulation of ontology interdependencies. *Proceedings of the Conference on Extending Database Technology (EDBT-2000)*, Konstanz, Germany.

Moldovan, D., S. Harabagiu, M. Pasca, R. Mihalcea, R. Goodrum, R. Giriu, and V. Rus. 2000. Lasso: A tool for surfing the Answer Net. In *Proceedings of the Eighth Text Retrieval Conference (TREC-8)*, NIST Special Publication 500-246, Gaithersburg, MD, 175–183.

Monarch, I., and S. Nirenburg. 1987. The role of ontology in concept acquisition for knowledge-based systems. *Proceedings of the First International Workshop on Knowledge Acquisition*, Reading, England, August.

Monarch, I., and S. Nirenburg. 1988. ONTOS: An ontology-based knowledge acquisition and maintenance system. *Proceedings of the Second Workshop on Knowledge Acquisition*, Banff, Canada, August.

Monarch, I., S. Nirenburg, and T. Mitamura. 1989. Ontology-based lexicon acquisition for a machine translation system. *Proceedings of the Fourth Workshop on Knowledge Acquisition for Knowledge-Based Systems*, Banff, Canada, August.

Montague, R. 1974. *Formal Philosophy: Selected Papers of Richard Montague*. New Haven, CT: Yale University Press.

Moody, T. C. 1993. *Philosophy and Artificial Intelligence.* Englewood Cliffs, NJ: Prentice-Hall.

Moreno Ortiz, A., V. Raskin, and S. Nirenburg. 2002. New developments in ontological semantics. In *Proceedings of the Third International Conference on Language Resources and Evaluation (LREC-2002)*, Las Palmas de Gran Canaria, Spain, May 29–31, 1196–1202.

Mostowski, A. 1969. *Constructible Sets with Applications.* Amsterdam-Warsaw: North-Holland–PWN.

Moustakas, C. E. 1990. *Heuristic Research: Design, Methodology, and Applications.* Newbury Park, CA: Sage.

Müller, G. E. 1911. *Zur Analyse der Gedächtnistätigkeit und des Vorstellungsverlaufs.* Leipzig: Barth.

Muller, P. 1998. SPACE-TIME as a primitive for space and motion. In Guarino, 1998c, 63–76.

Narayanan, S., C. J. Fillmore, C. F. Baker, and M. R. L. Petruck. 2002. FrameNet meets the semantic web: A DAML+OIL frame representation. Paper presented at the AAAI Workshop "Semantic Web Meets Language Resources," Edmonton, Alberta, Canada, June.

Newell, A. 1973. Artificial intelligence and the concept of mind. In R. Schank and K. Colby, eds., *Computer Models of Thought and Language*, 1–60. San Francisco: Freeman.

Newell, A. 1982. The knowledge level. *Artificial Intelligence* 18, 87–127.

Newell, A. 1983. The heuristics of George Polya and its relation to artificial intelligence. In R. Groner, M. Groner, and W. F. Bischof, eds. *Methods of Heuristics*, 195–243. Hillsdale, NJ: Erlbaum.

Newell, A., J. C. Shaw, and H. A. Simon. 1958. Elements of a theory of human problem solving. *Psychological Review* 65, 151–166.

Newell, A., and H. A. Simon. 1961. GPS, a program that simulates human thought. In H. Billing, ed., *Lernende Automaten*. Munich: Oldenbourg. Reprinted in E. Feigenbaum and J. Feldman, eds., *Computers and Thought*. New York: McGraw-Hill, 1963.

Newell, A., and H. A. Simon. 1972. *Human Problem Solving.* Englewood Cliffs, NJ: Prentice-Hall.

Newell, A., and H. A. Simon. 1976. Computer science as empirical inquiry: Symbols and search. *Communications of the ACM* 19, 113–126. Reprinted in J. Haugeland, ed., *Mind Design: Philosophy, Psychology, Artificial Intelligence*, 35–66. Cambridge, MA: MIT Press, 1985.

Nilsson, N. J. 1971. *Problem-Solving Methods in Artificial Intelligence.* New York: McGraw-Hill.

Nirenburg, S. 1980. Application of Semantic Methods in Description of Russian Morphology. Unpublished doctoral dissertation, Hebrew University of Jerusalem, Jerusalem, Israel.

Nirenburg, S. 1986. Linguistics and artificial intelligence. In P. C. Bjarkman and V. Raskin, eds., *The Real-World Linguist: Linguistic Applications in the 1980s*, 116–143. Norwood, NJ: Ablex.

Nirenburg, S. 1989a. Dictionary acquisition and maintenance for a knowledge-based machine translation system. *Proceedings of the First International Language Acquisition Workshop*, Detroit, August.

Nirenburg, S. 1989b. Lexicons for computer programs and lexicons for people. *Proceedings of the Fifth OED Conference*, Oxford, September.

Nirenburg, S., ed. 1994. *The Pangloss Mark III Machine Translation System*. A Joint Technical Report by Computing Research Laboratory, New Mexico State University; Information Sciences Institute, University of Southern California; and Center for Machine Translation, Carnegie Mellon University.

Nirenburg, S. 1998a. Project Boas: "A Linguist in the Box" as a multi-purpose language resource. *Proceedings of the First International Conference on Language Resources and Evaluation*, Granada, Spain.

Nirenburg, S. 1998b. *A Software Environment for Developing Large-Scale Knowledge Bases*. Project C-7-2903, Final Report. Onyx Consulting Inc. Technical Report. Las Cruces, CA: Onyx Consulting Inc.

Nirenburg, S. 2000a. *CAMBIO: Progress Report*. Working Paper, Computing Research Laboratory, New Mexico State University, Las Cruces, NM.

Nirenburg, S. 2000b. *CREST: Progress Report*. Working Paper, Computing Research Laboratory, New Mexico State University. Presented at the DARPA TIDES PI Meeting, Chicago, October.

Nirenburg, S., S. Beale, K. Mahesh, B. Onyshkevych, V. Raskin, E. Viegas, Y. Wilks, and R. Zajac. 1996. Lexicons in the Mikrokosmos project. *Proceedings of the Society for Artificial Intelligence and Simulated Behavior Workshop on Multilinguality in the Lexicon*, Brighton, U.K.

Nirenburg, S., J. Carbonell, M. Tomita, and K. Goodman. 1991. *Machine Translation: A Knowledge-Based Approach*. San Mateo, CA: Morgan Kaufmann.

Nirenburg, S., and C. Defrise. 1991. Practical computational linguistics. In R. Johnson and M. Rosner, eds., *Computational Linguistics and Formal Semantics*. Cambridge, U.K.: Cambridge University Press.

Nirenburg, S., and C. Defrise. 1993. Aspects of text meaning. In J. Pustejovsky, ed., *Semantics and the Lexicon*, 291–323. Dordrecht: Kluwer.

Nirenburg, S., R. Frederking, D. Farwell, and Y. Wilks. 1994. Two types of adaptive MT environments. *Proceedings of COLING-94*, Kyoto, Japan.

Nirenburg, S., and K. Goodman. 1990. Treatment of meaning in MT systems. *Proceedings of TMI-90*. Austin: Linguistic Research Center, University of Texas.

Nirenburg, S., and V. Lesser. 1986. Providing intelligent assistance in distributed office environments. *Proceedings of the Third International ACM Conference on Office Automation Systems*, Providence, RI, November. Reprinted in A. Bond and L. Gasser, eds., *Readings in Distributed Artificial Intelligence*, 590–598. San Mateo, CA: Morgan Kaufmann.

Nirenburg, S., V. Lesser, and E. Nyberg. 1989. Controlling a natural language generation planner. *Proceedings of IJCAI-89*, Detroit, August.

Nirenburg, S., and L. Levin. 1991. Syntax-driven and ontology-driven lexical semantics. *Proceedings of the ACL Workshop on Lexical Semantics*, Berkeley, CA, June.

Nirenburg, S., and L. Levin. 1992. Syntax-driven and ontology-driven lexical semantics. In J. Pustejovsky and S. Bergler, eds., *Lexical Semantics and Knowledge Representation*, 5–20. Berlin: Springer-Verlag.

Nirenburg, S., I. Nirenburg, and J. Reynolds. 1985. The control structure of POPLAR: A personality-oriented planner. *Proceedings of the Third Annual Conference on Intelligent Systems*, Oakland University, Rochester, MI, June.

Nirenburg, S., and E. Nyberg. 1989. Resolution of lexical synonymy at the word level. *Proceedings of the Sixth Annual Israel Conference on Artificial Intelligence and Computer Vision*, Tel Aviv, September.

Nirenburg, S., and V. Raskin. 1986. A metric for computational analysis of meaning: Toward an applied theory of linguistic semantics. *Proceedings of COLING-86*, Bonn, Germany, 338–340.

Nirenburg, S., and V. Raskin. 1987a. The analysis lexicon and the lexicon management system. *Computers and Translation* 2, 177–188.

Nirenburg, S., and V. Raskin. 1987b. Dealing with space in natural language processing. In A. Kak and S. Chen, eds., *Spatial Reasoning and Multi-Sensor Fusion: Proceedings of the 1987 Workshop*, 361–370. Los Altos, CA: Morgan Kaufmann.

Nirenburg, S., and V. Raskin. 1987c. The subworld concept lexicon and the lexicon management system. *Computational Linguistics* 13(3–4), 276–289.

Nirenburg, S., and V. Raskin. 1996. *Ten Choices for Lexical Semantics*. Memoranda in Computer and Cognitive Science MCCS-96-304. Computing Research Laboratory, New Mexico State University, Las Cruces.

Nirenburg, S., and V. Raskin. 1998. Universal grammar and lexis for quick ramp-up of MT systems. *Proceedings of ACL/COLING-98*, Montreal, 975–979.

Nirenburg, S., and V. Raskin. 1999. Supply-side and demand-side lexical semantics. In E. Viegas, ed., 1999. *Breadth and Depth of Semantic Lexicons*, 283–298. Dordrecht: Kluwer.

Nirenburg, S., V. Raskin, and R. McCardell. 1989. Ontology-based lexical acquisition. In U. Zernik, ed., *Proceedings of the First International Lexical Acquisition Workshop (IJCAI-89)*, Detroit, Paper 8.

Nirenburg, S., V. Raskin, and B. Onyshkevych. 1995. *Apologiae ontologiae*. Memoranda in Computer and Cognitive Science MCCS-95-281. Computing Research Laboratory, New Mexico State University, Las Cruces. Reprinted in J. Klavans, B. Boguraev, L. Levin, and J. Pustejovsky, eds., *Symposium: Representation and Acquisition of Lexical Knowledge: Polysemy, Ambiguity, and Generativity*, 95–107. Working Notes, AAAI Spring Symposium Series. Stanford, CA: Stanford University, 1995. Reprinted in a shortened version in *Proceedings of TMI-95*, Centre for Computational Linguistics, Catholic Universities, Leuven, Belgium, 1995, 106–114.

Nirenburg, S., V. Raskin, and A. Tucker. 1986. On knowledge-based machine translation. *Proceedings of COLING-86*, Bonn, Germany, August, 627–632.

Nirenburg, S., V. Raskin, and A. Tucker. 1987. The structure of interlingua in TRANSLATOR. In S. Nirenburg, ed., *Machine Translation: Theoretical and Methodological Issues*, 90–113. Cambridge, U.K.: Cambridge University Press.

Nirenburg, S., and Y. Wilks. 1997. What's in a symbol: Ontology and the surface of language—a dialogue. Invited paper, International Workshop on Linguistic and Ontological Categories, Center for Cognitive and Semiotic Studies, University of San Marino, San Marino, June. Published as Memoranda in Computer and Cognitive Science CS-97-14, Computer

Science Department, University of Sheffield, Sheffield, U.K. Also reprinted in *Journal of Experimental and Theoretical Artificial Intelligence*, 13, 9–23.

Norman, D. A. 1980. Twelve issues for cognitive science. *Cognitive Science* 4, 1–32.

Nunberg, G. 1993. Indexicality and deixis. *Linguistics and Philosophy* 16, 1–43.

Nunberg, G., and A. Zaenen. 1992. Systematic polysemy in lexicology and lexicography. *Proceedings of the EURALEX*, Tampere, Finland.

O'Connell, T., F. O'Mara, and J. White. 1994. The ARPA MT evaluation methodologies: Evolution, lessons, and further approaches. *Proceedings of AMTA-94*, Columbia, MD.

Oflazer, K., M. McShane, and S. Nirenburg. 2001. Bootstrapping morphological analyzers. *Computational Linguistics*, 27(1).

Oflazer, K., and S. Nirenburg. 1999. Practical bootstrapping of morphological analyzers. *Proceedings of the Computational Natural Language Learning (CoNLL-99) Workshop at EACL-99*, Bergen, Norway.

Ogden, C. K., and I. A. Richards. 1923. *Meaning of Meaning*. London: Kegan Paul, Trench, Trubner.

Onyshkevych, B. 1997. An Ontological-Semantic Framework for Text Analysis. Unpublished doctoral dissertation, Center for Machine Translation, Carnegie Mellon University, Pittsburgh.

Onyshkevych, B., and S. Nirenburg. 1991. Lexicon, ontology, and text meaning. *Proceedings of the ACL Workshop on Lexical Semantics*, Berkeley, CA, June. Reprinted in J. Pustejovsky and S. Bergler, eds., *Lexical Semantics and Knowledge Representation*, 289–303. Berlin: Springer-Verlag.

Onyshkevych, B., and S. Nirenburg. 1994. *The Lexicon in the Scheme of KBMT Things*. Memoranda in Computer and Cognitive Science MCCS-94-277. Computing Research Laboratory, New Mexico State University, Las Cruces. Reprinted in B. J. Dorr and J. Klavans, eds., Special Issue: Building Lexicons for Machine Translation II. *Machine Translation* 10(1–2), 1994–1995, 5–57.

Ostler, N., and B. T. S. Atkins. 1991. Predictable meaning shifts: Some linguistic properties of lexical implication rules. *Proceedings of the ACL SIGLEX Workshop on Lexical Semantics and Knowledge Representation*, Berkeley, CA, 76–87. Reprinted in J. Pustejovsky and S. Bergler, eds., *Lexical Semantics and Knowledge Representation*, 87–100. Berlin: Springer-Verlag.

Palmer, F. R. 1986. *Mood and Modality*. Cambridge, U.K.: Cambridge University Press.

Pandit, G. L. 1991. *Methodological Variance: Essays in Epistemological Ontology and the Methodology of Science*. Dordrecht: Kluwer.

Parsons, T. 1972. Some problems concerning the logic of grammatical modifiers. *Synthèse* 21(3–4), 320–334. Reprinted in D. Davidson and G. Harman, eds., *Semantics of Natural Language*, 127–141. Dordrecht: Reidel.

Parsons, T. 1980. Modifiers and quantifiers in natural language. *Canadian Journal of Philosophy* 6, supplement, 29–60.

Parsons, T. 1985. Underlying events in the logical analysis of English. In E. LePore and B. P. McLaughlin, eds., *Actions and Events: Perspectives on the Philosophy of Donald Davidson*, 235–267. Oxford: Blackwell.

Parsons, T. 1990. *Events in the Semantics of English: A Study of Subatomic Semantics*. Cambridge, MA: MIT Press.

Partee, B. 1973a. The semantics of belief sentences. In K. J. J. Hintikka, J. M. E. Moravcsik, and P. Supps, eds., *Approaches to Natural Language*, 309–336. Dordrecht: Reidel.

Partee, B. 1973b. Some transformational extensions of Montague grammar. *Journal of Philosophical Logic* 2, 509–534.

Partee, B., ed. 1976. *Montague Grammar*. New York: Academic Press.

Partee, B. 1984a. Compositionality. In F. Langman and F. Weltman, eds., *Varieties of Formal Semantics: Proceedings of the Fourth Amsterdam Colloquium*, GRASS Series No. 3, 281–311. Dordrecht: Foris.

Partee, B. 1984b. Nominal and temporal anaphora. *Linguistics and Philosophy* 7, 243–286.

Partee, B., A. ter Meulen, and R. E. Wall. 1990. *Mathematical Methods in Linguistics*. Dordrecht: Kluwer.

Pastra, K., D. Maynard, O. Hamza, H. Cunningham, and Y. Wilks. 2002. How feasible is the reuse of grammars for named entity recognition? In *Proceedings of the Third International Conference on Language Resources and Evaluation (LREC 2002)*, Las Palmas, Spain.

Paul, H. 1886. *Prinzipien der Sprachgeschichte*. Halle a.S.: Niemeyer.

Payne, T. E. 1997. *Describing Morphosyntax: A Guide for Field Linguists*. Cambridge, U.K.: Cambridge University Press.

Pearl, J. 1984. *Heuristics: Intelligent Search Strategies for Computer Problem Solving*. Reading, MA: Addison-Wesley.

Peeters, B., ed. 2000. *Lexicon-Encyclopedia Interface*. Amsterdam: Elsevier.

Pericliev, V. 1990. On heuristic procedures in linguistics. *Studia Linguistica* 44(1), 59–69.

Picard, R. W. 2000. *Affective Computing*. Cambridge, MA: MIT Press.

Pinker, S. 1989. *Learnability and Cognition: The Acquisition of Argument Structure*. Cambridge, MA: MIT Press.

Pollack, J. 1990. Recursive distributed representations. *Artificial Intelligence* 46, 77–105.

Pollard, C. 1984. Generalized Phrase Structure Grammars, Head Grammars, and Natural Language. Unpublished doctoral dissertation, Stanford University, Stanford, CA.

Pollard, C., and I. A. Sag. 1994. *Head-Driven Phrase Structure Grammar*. Stanford: CSLI/ Chicago: University of Chicago Press.

Polya, G. 1945. *How to Solve It*. Princeton, NJ: Princeton University Press.

Polya, G. 1954. *Mathematics of Plausible Reasoning, Vol. 1: Induction and Analogy in Mathematics*; *Vol. 2: Patterns of Plausible Inference*. Princeton, NJ: Princeton University Press.

Polya, G. 1962, 1965. *Mathematical Discovery*. 2 vols. New York: Wiley.

Popper, K. R. 1959. *The Logic of Scientific Discovery*. New York: Basic Books.

Popper, K. R. 1972. *Objective Knowledge: An Evolutionary Approach*. Oxford: Clarendon Press.

Post, H. R. 1971. Correspondence, invariance, and heuristics: In praise of conservative induction. Reprinted in S. French and H. Kamminga, eds., *Correspondence, Invariance, and Heuristics: Essays in Honour of Heinz Post*, 1–43. Dordrecht: Kluwer, 1993.

Postal, P. M. 1971. On the surface verb "remind." In C. J. Fillmore and D. T. Langendoen, eds., *Studies in Linguistic Semantics*, 181–270. New York: Holt, Rinehart and Winston.

Prince, E. F. 1979. On the given/new distinction. In D. Farkas, W. Jacobsen, and K. W. Todrys, eds., *Papers from the Fourteenth Regional Meeting of the Chicago Linguistic Society*, 267–278. Chicago: University of Chicago Press.

Prince, E. F. 1981. Toward a taxonomy of given-new information. In P. Cole, ed., *Radical Pragmatics*, 223–255. New York: Academic Press.

Proclus. 1987. *Proclus' Commentary on Plato's Parmenides*. Princeton, NJ: Princeton University Press.

Proclus. 1989. *Lezioni sul "Cratilo" di Platone*. Rome: Universitá di Catania.

Pustejovsky, J. 1991. The generative lexicon. *Computational Linguistics* 17(4), 409–441.

Pustejovsky, J. 1995. *The Generative Lexicon*. Cambridge, MA: MIT Press.

Pustejovsky, J. 1998. Generativity and explanation in semantics: A reply to Fodor and Lepore. *Linguistic Inquiry* 29(2), 289–311.

Pustejovsky, J., ed. 1993. *Semantics and the Lexicon*. Dordrecht: Kluwer.

Pustejovsky, J., and P. Anick. 1988. On the semantic interpretation of nominals. *Proceedings of COLING-88*, Budapest, Hungary.

Pustejovsky, J., and S. Bergler, eds. 1992. *Lexical Semantics and Knowledge Representation*. Berlin: Springer-Verlag.

Pustejovsky, J., S. Bergler, and P. Anick. 1993. Lexical semantic techniques for corpus analysis. *Computational Linguistics* 19(2), 331–358.

Pustejovsky, J., and B. Boguraev. 1993. Lexical knowledge representation and natural language processing. *Artificial Intelligence* 63, 193–223.

Pustejovsky, J., and S. Nirenburg. 1988. Processing aspectual semantics. *Proceedings of the Tenth Annual Meeting of the Cognitive Science Society*, Montreal, August.

Quine, W. V. O. 1953. *From a Logical Point of View*. Cambridge, MA: Harvard University Press.

Quine, W. V. O. 1960. *Word and Object*. Cambridge, MA: MIT Press.

Quine, W. V. O. 1970. On the reasons for the indeterminacy of translation. *Journal of Philosophy* 67(6), 178–183.

Quine, W. V. O. 1994. Promoting extensionality. *Synthèse* 98(1), 143–151.

Rabin, M. 1977. Decidable theories. In J. Barwise, ed., *Handbook of Mathematical Logic*. Studies in Logic and the Foundations of Mathematics, vol. 90, 595–629. Amsterdam: North-Holland.

Raskin, V. 1971. *K teorii yazykovykh podsistem* (Toward a Theory of Language Subsystems). Moscow: Moscow State University Press.

Raskin, V. 1974. A restricted sublanguage approach to high quality translation. *American Journal of Computational Linguistics* 11(3), microfiche 9.

Raskin, V. 1977a. Literal meaning and speech acts. *Theoretical Linguistics* 4(3), 209–225.

Raskin, V. 1977b. Problems of justification in semantic theory. In W. U. Dressler and W. Meid, eds., *Proceedings of the Twelfth International Congress of Linguists*. Innsbruck, Austria: *Innsbrucker Beiträge zur Sprachwissenschaft*, 223–226.

Raskin, V. 1979. Theory and practice of justification in linguistics. In P. L. Clyne et al., eds., *Papers from the Parasession on the Elements*, 152–162. Chicago: Chicago Linguistic Society.

Raskin, V. 1980. Determination with and without articles. In J. Van der Auwera, ed., *The Semantics of Determiners*. London: Croom Helm–University Park.

Raskin, V. 1983. *A Concise History of Linguistic Semantics*. 3rd ed. W. Lafayette, IN: Purdue University.

Raskin, V. 1985a. Linguistic and encyclopedic knowledge in text processing. In M. Alinei, ed., Round Table Discussion on Text/Discourse I, *Quaderni di Semantica* 6(1), 92–102.

Raskin, V. 1985b. Once again on linguistic and encyclopedic knowledge. In M. Alinei, ed., Round Table Discussion on Text/Discourse II, *Quaderni di Semantica* 6(2), 377–383.

Raskin, V. 1985c. *Semantic Mechanisms of Humor*. Dordrecht: Reidel.

Raskin, V. 1986. Script-based semantic theory. In D. G. Ellis and W. A. Donohue, eds., *Contemporary Issues in Language and Discourse Processes*, 23–61. Hillsdale, NJ: Erlbaum.

Raskin, V. 1987a. Linguistics and natural language processing. In S. Nirenburg, ed., *Machine Translation: Theoretical and Methodological Issues*, 42–58. Cambridge, U.K.: Cambridge University Press.

Raskin, V. 1987b. What is there in linguistic semantics for natural language processing? In S. Nirenburg, ed., *Proceedings of the Natural Language Planning Workshop*, 78–96. Blue Mountain Lake, NY: Rome Air Development Center.

Raskin, V. 1990. Ontology, sublanguage, and semantic networks in natural language processing. In M. C. Golumbic, ed., *Advances in Artificial Intelligence: Natural Language and Knowledge-Based Systems*, 114–128. New York: Springer-Verlag.

Raskin, V. 1992. Using the powers of language: Noncasual language in advertising, politics, relationships, humor, and lying. In E. L. Pedersen, ed., *Proceedings of the 1992 Annual Meeting of the Deseret Language and Linguistic Society*, Provo, UT: Brigham Young University, 17–30.

Raskin, V. 1994. Frawley: *Linguistic Semantics*. Review article. *Language* 70(3), 552–556.

Raskin, V. 2000. Afterword to V. Raskin, S. Attardo, and D. H. Attardo, Augmenting linguistic semantic description for NLP: Lexical knowledge, encyclopedic knowledge, event structure. In B. Peeters, ed., *Lexicon-Encyclopedia Interface*, 481–483. Amsterdam: Elsevier.

Raskin, V., D. H. Attardo, and S. Attardo. 1994a. The SMEARR semantic database: An intelligent and versatile resource for the humanities. In D. Ross and D. Brink, eds., *Research in Humanities Computing 3*, 109–124. Oxford: Clarendon Press.

Raskin, V., S. Attardo, and D. H. Attardo. 1994b. Augmenting formal semantic representation for NLP: The story of SMEARR. *Machine Translation* 9(1), 81–98.

Raskin, V., and S. Nirenburg. 1995. *Lexical Semantics of Adjectives: A Microtheory of Adjectival Semantics*. Memoranda in Computer and Cognitive Science MCCS-95-288. Computing Research Laboratory, New Mexico State University, Las Cruces.

Raskin, V., and S. Nirenburg. 1996a. Adjectival modification in text meaning representation. *Proceedings of COLING-96*, Copenhagen, 842–847.

Raskin, V., and S. Nirenburg. 1996b. Lexical rules for deverbal adjectives. In E. Viegas, S. Nirenburg, B. Onyshkevych, N. Ostler, V. Raskin, and A. Sanfilippo, eds., *Breadth and Depth of Semantic Lexicons: Proceedings of a Workshop Sponsored by the Special Interest Group on the Lexicon of the Association for Computational Linguistics, Supplement to the 34th Annual Meeting of the Association for Computational Linguistics, Proceedings of the Conference*, 89–104. University of California, Santa Cruz.

Raskin, V., and S. Nirenburg. 1998. An applied ontological semantic microtheory of adjective meaning for natural language processing. *Machine Translation* 13(2–3), 135–227.

Raskin, V., and S. Nirenburg. 1999. Lexical rules for deverbal adjectives. In E. Viegas, ed. *Breadth and Depth of Semantic Lexicons*, 99–119. Dordrecht: Kluwer.

Rayward-Smith, V. J. 1995. *Applications of Modern Heuristic Methods*. Henley-on-Thames, U.K.: A. Walter.

Read, A. W. 1948. An account of the word "semantics." *Word* 4.

Reeves, C. R., ed. 1993. *Modern Heuristic Techniques for Combinatorial Problems*. New York: Wiley.

Reichenbach, H. 1938. *Experience and Prediction*. Chicago: University of Chicago Press.

Reicher, M. E. 1998. Works and realizations. In Guarino, 1998c, 121–132.

Reifler, E. 1955. The mechanical determination of meaning. In W. H. Locke and A. D. Booth, eds., *Machine Translation of Languages: Fourteen Essays*, 136–164. Cambridge, MA: Technology Press of MIT.

Reinhart, T. 1983. *Anaphora and Semantic Interpretation*. Chicago: University of Chicago Press.

Resnik, P., and D. Yarowsky. 1997. A Perspective on word sense disambiguation methods and their evaluation. *Proceedings of the SIGLEX Workshop Tagging Text with Lexical Semantics: Why, What, and How?*, Washington, DC.

Richmond, S. A. 1996. A simplification of the theory of simplicity. *Synthèse* 107(3), 373–393.

Riesbeck, C. 1975. Conceptual analysis. In R. C. Schank, *Conceptual Information Processing*. Amsterdam: North-Holland.

Roget, P. M. 1852. *Thesaurus of English Words and Phrases, Classified and Arranged so as to Facilitate the Expression of Ideas and Assist in Literary Composition*. London: Longman, Brown, Green, and Longmans.

Rooth, M. 1992. A theory of focus interpretation. *Natural Language Semantics* 1, 75–116.

Rorty, R. 1967. *The Linguistic Turn*. Chicago: University of Chicago Press.

Rorty, R. 1979. *Philosophy and the Mirror of Nature*. Princeton, NJ: Princeton University Press.

Rorty, R. 1991. *Objectivity, Relativism and Truth: Philosophical Papers, 1*. Cambridge, U.K.: Cambridge University Press.

Rosenkrantz, R. D. 1976. *Inference, Method, and Decision*. Dordrecht: Reidel.

Ruch, W., ed. 1998. *The Sense of Humor*. Berlin: Mouton de Gruyter.

Russell, B. 1905. On denoting. *Mind* 14, 479–493.

Russell, S., and P. Norvig. 1995. *Artificial Intelligence: A Modern Approach*. Englewood Cliffs, NJ: Prentice-Hall.

Ryle, G. 1949. *The Concept of Mind*. London: Hutchinson.

Ryle, G. 1953. Ordinary language. *Philosophical Review* 62, 167–186. Reprinted in C. E. Caton, ed., *Philosophy and Ordinary Language*, Urbana: University of Illinois Press, 1963.

Samarin, W. J. 1967. *Field Linguistics*. New York: Holt, Rinehart and Winston.

Sanfilippo, A. 1995. Lexical polymorphism and word disambiguation. In J. Klavans, B. Boguraev, L. Levin, and J. Pustejovsky, eds., *Symposium: Representation and Acquisition of Lexical Knowledge: Polysemy, Ambiguity, and Generativity*, 158–162. Working Notes, AAAI Spring Symposium Series. Stanford, CA: Stanford University, 1995.

Sanfilippo, A., E. J. Briscoe, A. Copestake, M. A. Marti, and A. Alonge. 1992. Translation equivalence and lexicalization in the ACQUILEX LKB. *Proceedings of TMI-92*, Montreal.

Sanfilippo, A., and V. Poznanski. 1992. The acquisition of lexical knowledge from combined machine-readable sources. *Proceedings of ANLP-92*, Trento, Italy, 80–88.

Saussure, F. de. 1916. *Cours de linquistique générale*. Paris: Payot.

Schäfer, B. 1998. Inheritance principles and the community of heirs. In Guarino, 1998c, 108–120.

Schank, R. 1975. *Conceptual Information Processing*. Amsterdam: North-Holland.

Schank, R., and R. Abelson. 1977. *Scripts, Plans, Goals, and Understanding*. Hillsdale, NJ: Erlbaum.

Schank, R., and C. Riesbeck. 1981. *Inside Computer Understanding*. Hillsdale, NJ: Erlbaum.

Schank, R., and R. Wilensky. 1977. Response to Dresher and Hornstein. *Cognition* 5, 133–145.

Schubert, L. K., M. A. Papalaskaris, and J. Taugher. 1983. Determining type, part, color, and time relationships. *IEEE Computer* 16(10), 53–60.

Searle, J. R. 1969. *Speech Acts*. Cambridge, U.K.: Cambridge University Press.

Searle, J. R. 1975. Indirect speech acts. In P. Cole and J. L. Morgan, eds., *Syntax and Semantics, Vol. 3: Speech Acts*, 59–82. New York: Academic Press.

Searle, J. R. 1979. Metaphor. In J. R. Searle, *Expression and Meaning*, 76–116. Cambridge, U.K.: Cambridge University Press. Also in A. Ortony, ed., *Metaphor and Thought*. Cambridge, U.K.: Cambridge University Press, 1979.

Searle, J. R. 1980. Minds, brains, and programs. *Behavioral and Brain Sciences* 3, 417–457. Reprinted in D. R. Hofstadter and D. C. Dennett, eds., *The Mind's I*. New York: Bantam, 1981.

Searle, J. R. 1982a. The myth of the computer. *New York Review of Books*, April 29, 3–6.

Searle, J. R. 1982b. Plenary Paper at the Conference on Contemporary Issues in Language and Discourse Processes, Michigan State University, East Lansing, MI, August.

Searle, J. R. 1986. Introductory essay: Notes on conversation. In D. G. Ellis and W. A. Donohue, eds., *Contemporary Issues in Language and Discourse Processes*, 7–19. Hillsdale, NJ: Erlbaum.

Searle, J. R. 1989. How performatives work. *Linguistics and Philosophy* 12(5), 535–558.

Searle J. R. 1997. *The Mystery of Consciousness: Including Exchanges with Daniel C. Dennett and David J. Chalmers*. New York: A New York Review Book.

Selz, O. 1935. Versuch der Hebung des Intelligenzniveaus: Ein Betrag zur Theorie der Intelligenz und ihrer erziehlichen Beeinflussung. *Zeitschrift für Psychologie* 134, 236–301.

Shannon, C. E., and W. Weaver. 1949. *The Mathematical Theory of Communication*. Urbana: University of Illinois Press.

Shavlik, J. D., and T. G. Dietterich, eds. 1990. *Readings in Machine Learning*. San Mateo, CA: Morgan Kaufmann.

Shelton, S. J. 1997. Coreference: An ontological semantic approach. Unpublished doctoral dissertation, Interdepartmental Program in Linguistics, Purdue University, West Lafayette, IN.

Sheremetyeva, S., and S. Nirenburg. 1996. Interactive knowledge elicitation in a patent expert's workstation. *IEEE Computer*, July, 57–64.

Sheremetyeva, S., W. Jin, and S. Nirenburg. 1998. Rapid deployment morphology. *Machine Translation* 13(4), 239–268.

Sheremetyeva, S., and S. Nirenburg. 2000a. Acquisition of a language computational model for NLP. *Proceedings of COLING-2000*, July 31–August 4, Saarbrücken, Germany.

Sheremetyeva, S., and S. Nirenburg. 2000b. Towards a universal tool for NLP resource acquisition. *Proceedings of the Second International Conference on Language Resources and Evaluation*, Athens, May 31–June 3.

Shieber, S. M. 1986. *An Introduction to Unification-Based Approaches to Grammar*. Lecture Notes 4. Stanford, CA: CSLI.

Shoham, Y. 1987. Temporal logics in AI: Semantic and ontological considerations. *Artificial Intelligence* 33, 89–104.

Simon, H. A. 1968. On judging the plausibility of theories. In B. Van Rootselaar and J. F. Staal, eds., *Logic, Methodology and Philosophy of Science III: Proceedings of the Third International Congress for Logic, Methodology and Philosophy of Science*, Amsterdam 1967, 439–459. Amsterdam: North-Holland.

Simon, H. A. 1977. *Models of Discovery and Other Topics in the Methods of Science*. Dordrecht: Reidel.

Simon, H. A. 1979 (vol. 1), 1989 (vol. 2). *Models of Thought*. 2 vols. New Haven, CT: Yale University Press.

Simon, H. A. 1983. *Reason in Human Affairs*. Stanford, CA: Stanford University Press.

Simons, P. M. 1987. *Parts: A Study in Ontology*. Oxford: Clarendon Press.

Smith, B. 1996. Mereotopology: A theory of parts and boundaries. *Data and Knowledge Engineering* 20(3), 287–303.

Smith, B. 1997. Boundaries: An essay in mereotopology. In L. H. Hahn, ed., *The Philosophy of Roderick Chisholm*, 534–561. Chicago-LaSalle: Open Court.

Smith, B. 1998. Basic concepts of formal ontology. In Guarino, 1998c, 19–28.

Sober, E. 1975. *Simplicity*. Oxford: Clarendon Press.

Somers, H. L. 1986. *Valency and Case in Computational Linguistics.* Edinburgh: Edinburgh University Press.

Somers, H. 1998. Lewis Carroll: Computational stylometrics, imitation, and stylistic schizophrenia. *Proceedings of the Lewis Carroll Phenomenon: An Interdisciplinary Centenary Conference,* Cardiff, Wales, April.

Sowa, J. F. 1984. *Conceptual Structures: Information Processing in Mind and Machine.* Reading, MA: Addison-Wesley.

Sowa, J. F. 2000. *Knowledge Representation: Logical, Philosophical, and Computational Foundations.* Pacific Grove, CA: Brooks/Cole.

Sparck Jones, K. 1991. They say it's a new sort of engine: But the SUMP's still there. In Y. Wilks, ed., *Theoretical Issues in Natural Language Processing,* 136–140. Hillsdale, NJ: Erlbaum.

Sperber, H. 1958. *Geschichte der deutschen Sprachen.* Berlin: Walter de Gruyter.

Sproat, R. W. 1992. *Morphology and Computation.* Cambridge, MA: MIT Press.

Staal, J. F. 1967. Some semantic relations between sentoids. *Foundations of Language* 3, 66–88.

Stalnaker, R., and R. Thomason. 1973. A semantic theory of adverbs. *Linguistic Inquiry* 4, 195–220.

Stefik, M. 1995. *Introduction to Knowledge Systems.* San Francisco: Morgan Kaufmann.

Steinberg, D. D., and L. A. Jakobovits, eds. 1971. *Semantics: An Interdisciplinary Reader in Philosophy, Linguistics and Psychology.* Cambridge, U.K.: Cambridge University Press.

Stern, G. 1931. *Meaning and Change of Meaning.* Göteborg: Göteborgs Högskolas Årsskrift. Reprinted: Bloomington: Indiana University Press, 1964.

Stevenson, M., and R. Gaizauskas. 2000. Using corpus-derived name lists for name entity recognition. *Proceedings of the Sixth Conference on Applied Natural Language Processing and First Conference of the North American Chapter of the Association for Computational Linguistics,* Seattle.

Strawson, P. 1993. Back cover blurb for S. Haack, *Evidence and Inquiry: Towards Reconstruction in Epistemology.* Oxford: Blackwell.

Stumme, G., and A. Madche. 2001. FCA-Merge: Bottom-up merging of ontologies. *Proceedings of IJCAI 2001,* Seattle, 225–230.

Tannen, D. 1980. The parameters of conversational style. *Proceedings of ACL,* Philadelphia, 39–40.

Tarski, A. 1935. Einige Methodologische Untersuchungen über die Definierbarkeit der Begriffe. *Erkenntnis* 5, 80–100. English translation in A. Tarski, *Logic, Semantics, Metamathematics.* Oxford: Clarendon Press, 1956.

Tarski, A. 1941. *Introduction to Logic and to the Methodology of Deductive Sciences.* New York: Oxford University Press.

Tarski, A., in collaboration with A. Mostowski, and R. M. Robinson. 1953. *Undecidable Theories.* Amsterdam: North-Holland.

Tarski, A. 1956. The semantical conception of truth. In L. Linsky, ed., *Semantics and the Philosophy of Language.* Urbana: University of Illinois Press. Reprinted in the 2nd paperback edition, 1972, 13–47.

Thomason, R. H. 1972. A semantic theory of sortal incorrectness. *Journal of Philosophical Logic* 2(2), 209–258.

Thomason, R. H., J. F. Horty, and D. S. Touretzky. 1987. A calculus for inheritance in monotonic semantic nets. *Methodologies for Intelligent Systems: Proceedings of the Sixth International Symposium*, Charlotte, NC, 280–287.

Thomason, R. H., and D. S. Touretzky. 1991. Inheritance theory and networks with roles. In J. F. Sowa, ed., *Principles of Semantic Networks*, 231–266. San Mateo, CA: Morgan Kaufmann.

Touretzky, D. S. 1984. Implicit ordering of defaults in inheritance systems. *Proceedings of AAAI-84, Austin, TX*, 322–325.

Touretzky, D. S. 1986. *The Mathematics of Inheritance Systems*. Los Altos, CA: Morgan Kaufmann.

Touretzky, D. S., J. Horty, and R. Thomason. 1987. A clash of intuitions: The current state of non-monotonic multiple inheritance systems. *Proceedings of IJCAI-87*, Milan, 476–482.

Trier, J. 1931. *Der Deutsche Wortschatz im Sinnbezirk des Verstandes*. Heidelberg: Winter.

Tulving, E. 1985. How many memory systems are there? *American Psychologist* 40, 385–398.

Turing, A. 1950. Computing machinery and intelligence. *Mind* 59, 434–460. Reprinted in A. R. Anderson, ed., *Minds and Machines*, 4–30. Englewood Cliffs, NJ: Prentice-Hall, 1964.

Tversky, A., and D. Kahnemann. 1973. Availability: A heuristic for judging frequency and probability. *Cognitive Psychology* 5, 207–232.

Tversky, A., and D. Kahnemann. 1983. Probability, representativeness, and the conjunction fallacy. *Psychological Review* 90(4), 293–315.

Ullmann, S. 1951. *The Principles of Semantics*. Glasgow: Blackwell.

Uspenskiy, V. A. 1960. *Lektzii o vychislimykh funktziyakh* (Lectures on computable functions). Moscow: Fizmatgiz. French translation: V. A. Ouspenski, *Leçons sur les fonctions calculables*. Paris: Hermann, 1966.

Van Fraassen, B. C. 1980. *The Scientific Image*. Oxford: Clarendon Press.

Van Fraassen, B. C. 1989. *Laws and Symmetry*. Oxford: Clarendon Press.

Varzi, A. C. 1994. On the boundary between mereology and topology. In R. Casati, B. Smith, and G. White, eds., *Philosophy and the Cognitive Sciences*, 423–442. Vienna: Hölder-Pichler-Tempsky.

Varzi, A. C. 1996. Parts, wholes, and part-whole relations: The prospects of mereotopology. *Data and Knowledge Engineering* 20(3), 259–286.

Varzi, A. C. 1998. Basic problems of mereotopology. In Guarino, 1998c, 29–38.

Vendler, Z. 1967. *Linguistics in Philosophy*. Ithaca, NY: Cornell University Press.

Vendler, Z. 1968. *Adjectives and Nominalization*. The Hague: Mouton.

Verkuyl, H. 1972. *On the Compositional Nature of the Aspects*. Dordrecht: Reidel.

Verkuyl, H. 1993. *A Theory of Aspectuality*. Cambridge, U.K.: Cambridge University Press.

Viegas, E. 1997. Mismatches and divergences: The continuum perspective. *Proceedings of TMI-97*, Santa Fe, NM, 216–223.

Viegas, E., ed. 1999. *Breadth and Depth of Semantic Lexicons*. Dordrecht: Kluwer.

Viegas, E., K. Mahesh, S. Nirenburg, and S. Beale. 1999. Semantics in action. In P. Saint-Dizier, ed., *Predicative Forms in Natural Language and in Lexical Knowledge Bases*, 171–203. Dordrecht: Kluwer.

Viegas, E., S. Nirenburg, B. Onyshkevych, N. Ostler, V. Raskin, and A. Sanfilippo, eds. 1996a. *Breadth and Depth of Semantic Lexicons. Proceedings of a Workshop*, Santa Cruz, CA.

Viegas, E., B. Onyshkevych, V. Raskin, and S. Nirenburg. 1996b. From *submit* to *submitted* via *submission*: On lexical rules in large-scale lexicon acquisition. *Proceedings of ACL-96*, University of California, Santa Cruz, 32–39.

Viegas, E., and V. Raskin. 1998. *Computational Semantic Lexicon Acquisition: Methodology and Guidelines*. Memoranda in Computer and Cognitive Science MCCS-98-315. Computing Research Laboratory, New Mexico State University, Las Cruces.

Vinogradova, O. S., and A. R. Luria. 1961. Ob' 'ektivnoe issledovanie smyslovyx otnosenij (An objective investigation of sense relations). In *Tezisy dokladov mezvuzovskoj konferencii po primeneniju strukturnyx i statisticeskix metodov issledovanija slovarnogo sostava jazyka* (Abstracts of Papers of the Inter-University Conference on the Application of Structural and Statistical Methods of Exploration of the Vocabulary of Language) Moscow.

Vossen, P., ed. 1998. *EuroWordNet: A Multilingual Database with Lexical Semantic Networks*. Dordrecht: Kluwer.

Wagner, G. 1998. *Foundations of Knowledge Systems: With Applications to Databases and Agents*. Dordrecht: Kluwer.

Wallas, G. 1926. *The Art of Thought*. New York: Harcourt Brace.

Waltz, D. L. 1982. The state of the art in natural-language understanding. In W. G. Lehnert and M. H. Ringle, eds., *Strategies for Natural Language Processing*, 3–35. Hillsdale, NJ: Erlbaum.

Waltz, D. L., and J. B. Polack. 1985. Massively parallel parsing: A strongly interactive model of natural language interpretation. *Cognitive Science* 9(1), 51–74.

Webber, B. 1991. Structure and ostention in the interpretation of discourse deixis. *Language and Cognitive Processes* 6, 107–135.

Webelhuth, G. 1992. *Principles and Parameters of Syntactic Saturation*. New York: Oxford University Press.

Weinreich, U. 1966. Explorations in semantic theory. In T. A. Sebeok, ed., *Current Trends in Linguistics*, vol. 3, 395–477. The Hague: Mouton.

Weir, D. J., K. Vijay-Shanker, and A. K. Joshi. 1986. The relationship between tree adjoining grammars and head grammars. *Proceedings of ACL-86*, Columbia University, New York, 67–74.

Weisgerber, L. 1951. *Das Gesetz der Sprache als Grundlage des Sprachstudiums*. Heidelberg: Quelle & Meyer.

Wellander, E. L. 1973. *Riktig svenska*. Stockholm: Esselte studium.

Wertheimer, M. 1945. *Productive Thinking*. New York: Harper.

Whorf B. L. 1953. *Language, Thought, and Reality*. New York: Wiley.

Wielinga, B. J., and A. T. Schreiber. 1993. Reusable and shareable knowledge bases: A European perspective. *Proceedings of the First International Conference on Building and Sharing of Very Large-Scaled Knowledge Bases*, Japan Information Processing Development Center, Tokyo.

Wilensky, R. 1983. *Planning and Understanding*. Reading, MA: Addison-Wesley.

Wilensky, R. 1986. *Some Problems and Proposals for Knowledge Representation*. Cognitive Science Report 40. University of California, Berkeley.

Wilensky, R. 1991. *Extending the Lexicon by Exploiting Subregularities*. Report UCB/CSD 91/616. Computer Science Department, University of California, Berkeley.

Wilks, Y. A. 1971. Decidability and natural language. *Mind* 80.

Wilks, Y. A. 1972. *Grammar, Meaning and the Machine Analysis of Language*. London: Routledge and Kegan Paul.

Wilks, Y. A. 1975a. Preference semantics. In E. L. Keenan, ed., *Formal Semantics of Natural Language: Papers from a Colloquium Sponsored by the King's College Research Centre*, 321–348. Cambridge, U.K.: Cambridge University Press.

Wilks, Y. A. 1975b. A preferential pattern-matching semantics for natural language. *Artificial Intelligence* 6, 53–74.

Wilks, Y. A. 1977. Making preferences more active. *Artificial Intelligence* 11, 197–223.

Wilks, Y. A. 1982. Some thoughts on procedural semantics. In W. G. Lehnert and M. H. Ringle, eds., *Strategies for Natural Language Processing*, 495–516. Hillsdale, NJ: Erlbaum.

Wilks, Y. A. 1992. Form and content in semantics. In M. Rosner and R. Johnson, eds., *Computational Linguistics and Formal Semantics*, 257–281. Cambridge, U.K.: Cambridge University Press.

Wilks, Y. A. 1994. Stone soup and the French room. In A. Zampolli, N. Calzolari, and M. Palmer, eds., *Current Issues in Computational Linguistics: In Honor of Don Walker*. Dordrecht: Kluwer.

Wilks, Y. A. 1996. Homography and part-of-speech tagging. Presentation at the Mikro-Kosmos Workshop, Computing Research Laboratory, New Mexico State University, Las Cruces, August 21.

Wilks, Y. A. 1997. Senses and texts. *Computers and the Humanities* 31(1), 77–90.

Wilks, Y. A. 1998. Is word-sense disambiguation just one more NLP task? Memoranda in Computer and Cognitive Science Computer Science Department, University of Sheffield, Sheffield, UK Printed. In *Proceedings of the SENSEVAL Conference*, Herstmonceaux, Sussex.

Wilks, Y. A. 1999. *The "Fodor"-FODOR Fallacy Bites Back*. Technical Report CS-98-13. Department of Computer Science, University of Sheffield, Sheffield, U.K. Reprinted in P. Bouillon and F. Busa, eds., *The Language of Word Meaning*. Cambridge, U.K.: Cambridge University Press, 2001.

Wilks, Y. A., and D. Fass. 1992a. Preference semantics. In S. C. Shapiro, ed., *Encyclopedia of Artificial Intelligence*, 2nd ed., 1182–1194. New York: Wiley.

Wilks, Y. A., and D. Fass. 1992b. Preference semantics: A family history. *Computing and Mathematics with Applications* 23(2).

Wilks, Y. A., D. Fass, C. M. Guo, J. McDonald, T. Plate, and B. Slator. 1990. A tractable machine dictionary as a basis for computational semantics. *Machine Translation* 5, 99–151.

Wilks, Y. A., B. Slator, and L. M. Guthrie. 1996. *Electric Words: Dictionaries, Computers, and Meanings*. Cambridge, MA: MIT Press.

Wilks, Y. A., and M. Stevenson. 1997. Sense tagging: Semantic tagging with a lexicon. *Proceedings of ANLP-97*, Washington, DC.

Wilson, D. 1975. *Presuppositions and Non-Truth-Conditional Semantics*. New York: Academic Press.

Winograd, T. 1972. *Understanding Natural Language*. New York: Academic Press.

Winograd, T. 1977. On some contested suppositions of generative linguistics about the scientific study of language. *Cognition* 5, 151–179.

Winograd, T. 1983. *Language as a Cognitive Process, Vol. 1: Syntax*. Reading, MA: Addison-Wesley.

Wittgenstein, L. 1953. *Philosophical Investigations*. Oxford: Blackwell.

Woods, W. A. 1975. What's in a link: Foundations for semantic networks. In D. G. Bobrow and A. M. Collins, eds., *Representation and Understanding: Studies in Cognitive Science*, 35–82. New York: Academic Press.

Woods, W. A. 1981. *Procedural Semantics as a Theory of Meaning*. Research Report No. 4627. Cambridge, MA: Bolt, Beranek, and Newman.

Woolridge, M. 2002. *An Introduction to Multiagent Systems*. Chichester, England: Wiley.

Wundt, W. M. 1921. *Elements of Folk Psychology: Outlines of a Psychological History of the Development of Mankind*. London: Allen and Unwin–Macmillan.

Yarowsky, D. 1992. Word-sense disambiguation using statistical models of Roget's categories trained on large corpora. *Proceedings of COLING-92*. Nantes, 454–460.

Yarowsky, D. 1995. Unsupervised word sense disambiguation rivaling supervised methods. *Proceedings of ACL-95*, Cambridge, MA.

Yngve, V. H. 1996. *From Grammar to Science*. Amsterdam: Benjamins.

Zajac, R., M. Casper, and N. Sharples. 1997. An open distributed architecture for reuse and integration of heterogeneous NLP components. *Proceedings of ANLP-97*, Washington, DC, 245–256.

Zaliznyak, A. A. 1967. *Russkoe imennoe slovoizmenenie* (The Russian nominal inflection). Moscow: Nauka.

Zanakis, S. H., J. R. Evans, and A. A. Vazacopoulos. 1989. Heuristic methods and applications: A categorized survey. *European Journal of Operations Research* 43, 88–110.

Zangwill, N. 1996. Good old supervenience: Mental causation on the cheap. *Synthèse* 106(1), 67–101.

Zernik, U., ed. 1989. *Proceedings of the First International Lexical Acquisition Workshop (IJCAI-89)*, Detroit, Paper 8.

Zernik, U., ed. 1991. *Lexical Acquisition: Exploiting On-Line Resources to Build a Lexicon*. Hillsdale, NJ: Erlbaum.

Zholkovsky, A., N. N. Leont'eva, and Yu. S. Martem'yanov. 1961. O printsipial'nom ispol'zovanii smysla pri mashinnom perevode (On a principled use of sense in machine translation). In *Mashinnyy perevod* 2. Moscow: USSR Academy of Sciences.

Zvegintzev, V. A. 1957. *Semasiologiya* (Semasiology). Moscow: Moscow State University Press.

Zvegintzev, V. A. 1958. *Isstoriia arabskogo iazykoznaniia* (A history of Arab linguistics). Moscow: Moscow State University Press.

Zvegintzev, V. A. 1960. Teoretiko-lingvisticheskie predposylki gipotezy Sepira-Uorfa (The linguistic theoretical premises of the Sapir-Whorf hypothesis). In V. A. Zvegintzev, ed., *Novoe v lingvistike*, vol. 1, 111–134. Moscow: Isdatel'stvo inostrannoy literatury.

Zvegintsev, V. A. 1964. Ocherk istorii yazykoznaniya do XIX veka (An essay on the history of linguistics before the 19th century). In V. A. Zvegintsev, *Istoriya yazykoznaniya XIX–XX vekov v ocherkakh i izvlecheniyakh* (A history of 19th–20th century linguistics: Essays and excerpts), 7–27. Moscow: Prosveshchenie.

Zvegintzev, V. A. 1968. *Teoreticheskaya i prikladnaya lingvistika* (Theoretical and computational linguistics). Moscow: Prosveshchenie.

Zwicky, A. M., J. Friedman, B. C. Hall, and D. E. Walker. 1965. The MITRE syntactic analysis procedure for transformational grammars. *Proceedings of the Fall Joint Computer Conference*, 317–326. New York: Spartan.

Zwicky, F. 1957. *Morphological Astronomy*. Berlin: Springer.

Zwicky, F. 1966. *Entdecken, Erfinden, Forschen in Morphologischen Weltbild*. Munich: Droemer Knaur. English translation: *Discovery, Invention, Research through the Morphological Approach*. New York: Macmillan, 1969.

Index